Painting at the edge

EDITOR LAURA NEWTON

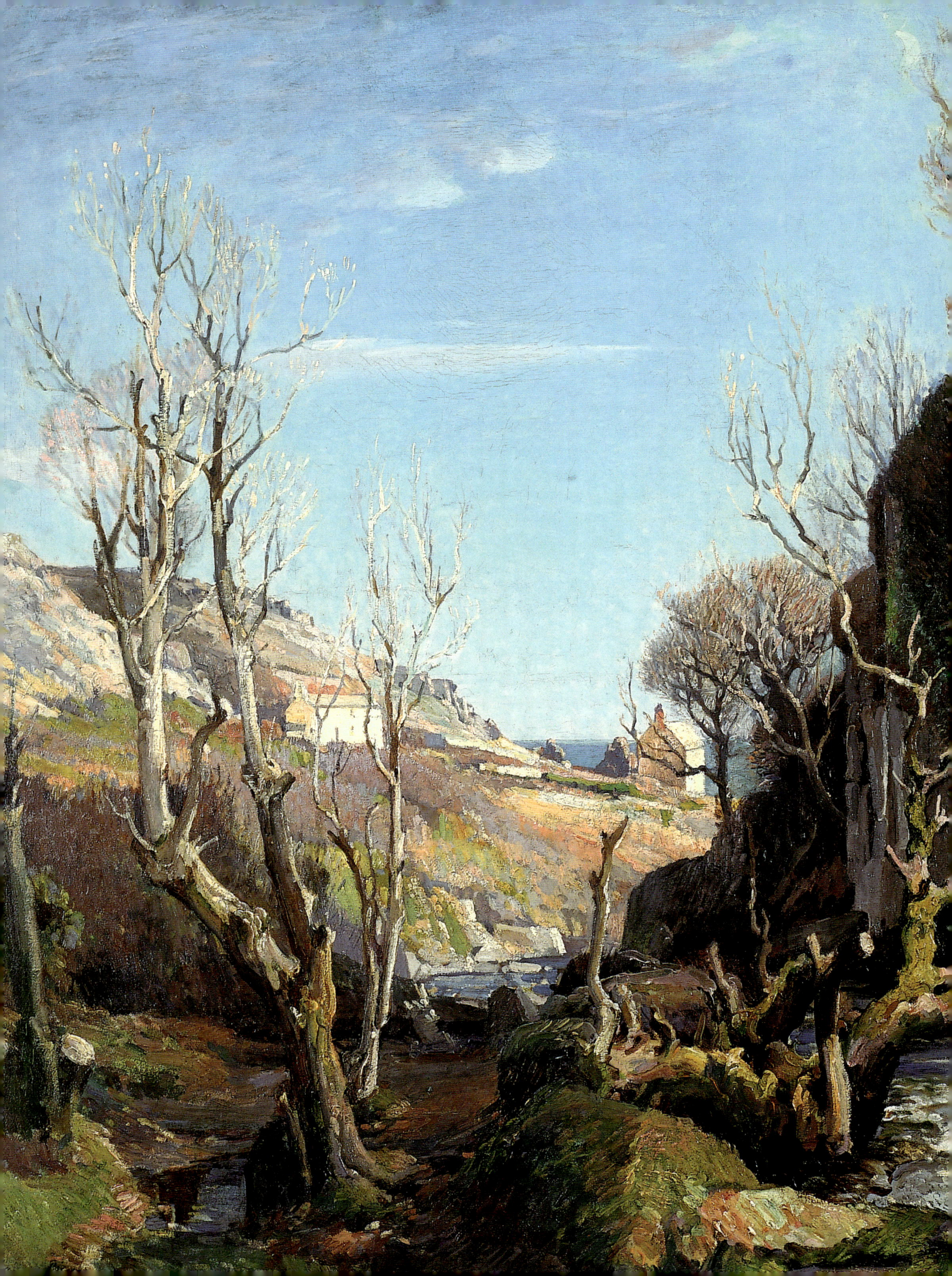

Painting at the edge

BRITISH COASTAL ART COLONIES 1880–1930

ALISON BEVAN • YSANNE HOLT • KENNETH McCONKEY • LAURA NEWTON
RICHARD SCOTT • DAVID WILKINSON • AUSTIN WORMLEIGHTON

Sansom & Company
Penlee House Gallery & Museum

EDITOR LAURA NEWTON

First published in 2005 by Sansom & Company Ltd.,
81g Pembroke Road, Bristol BS8 3EA

ISBN hardback 1 904537 29 4
softback 1 904537 26 X

British Library Cataloguing in Publication Data: A catalogue record for this book is available from the British Library.

Designed and typeset by Gendall Design, Falmouth, Cornwall and printed by HSW Print, Tonypandy, Mid Glamorgan.

Text set in Frutiger and Bembo.

Every effort has been made to trace owners and obtain permissions for illustrations. Any questions should be addressed to the publisher in the first instance.

Exhibition sponsored by WWW.JORDANCHARD.COM JORDAN & CHARD FINE ART NEWLYN, ST IVES & LAMORNA

FRONTISPIECE
S. J. Lamorna Birch, *In Our Old World Valley*, c.1921, oil on canvas
Penlee House Gallery and Museum, Penzance © Artist's Estate

Contents

Preface

No island race can be unaffected by the draw and power of the sea. Britain's culture and history are innately linked with maritime matters, so it is perhaps inevitable that one of the key periods of British art history – 1880 to 1930 – is marked by the flourishing of art colonies dotted around our coastline.

Artists have long taken temporary inspiration from coastal life, and continue to do so; virtually every seaside village in Britain has hosted the occasional visiting artist. What marks out the eight localities featured in this publication is that they were not just transitory holiday locations, they were settled artists' communities.

Although each of these colonies has been celebrated in some way through exhibitions and publications, this is the first time they have all been brought together in one exhibition and book. Fittingly, this is happening in the 'Year of the Sea', marking the 200th anniversary of the Battle of Trafalgar. By combining these concurrent colonies, it is possible not only to see what unites and divides their artistic approaches, but also the personal ties between each, exemplified in the list at the back of the book, where several artists appear in more than one place.

This is the sixth partnership between Penlee House and Sansom & Company, and we are indebted to them for their enthusiasm for the Newlyn colony. Having published books on Walberswick and Cullercoats, they were in a unique position to bring together a pool of knowledge stretching way beyond our usual Cornish sphere.

The book is also a collaboration with the University of Northumbria, with Laura Newton providing not only the Cullercoats and Staithes chapters, but also superb editorship – a challenging task with such disparate information. We are, of course, grateful to Kenneth McConkey for his scholarly introduction and to Ysanne Holt for her chapter on the Scottish colonies. Thanks are due too to Austin Wormleighton, David Wilkinson and Richard Scott, who each provided expertise in their own subject areas, to David Tovey, Katie Herbert, Hanna Oakes and Gendall Design for their invaluable contributions.

We are particularly indebted to those public galleries and private collections who have supplied images and lent paintings, and to the sponsors of the exhibition, Jordan & Chard Fine Art (specialists in the three Cornish colonies). Finally, no such project could happen without the constant support of our parent body, Penzance Town Council, and the hard work and enthusiasm of the entire Penlee House team. On behalf of all those involved, we hope that you enjoy this exploration of 'Painting at the Edge'.

ALISON BEVAN
Director, Penlee House Gallery & Museum, Penzance

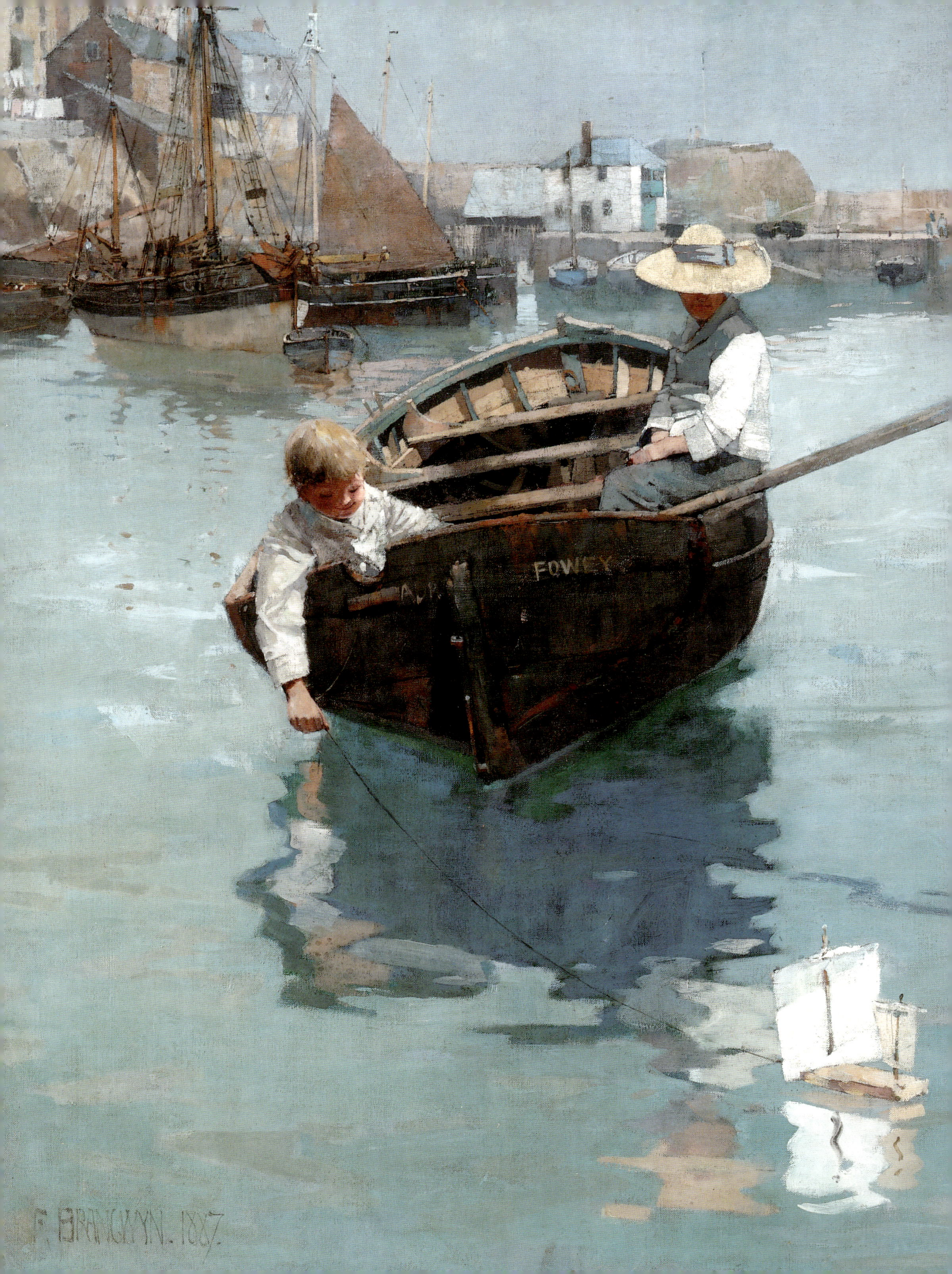
FOWEY
F. BRANGWYN. 1887.

CHAPTER 1

'The Pallid Gleam of the Imagination': Coastal Art Colonies in Britain at the turn of the Twentieth Century

KENNETH McCONKEY

In one of his most memorable passages, D.S. MacColl addressed William Dyce's fearful rendition of *Pegwell Bay, Kent: A Recollection of October 5th 1858* (fig 1). He said,

> One thinks of him dwelling on the shores of chalk that he painted in a desperate pallid gleam of imagination in his *Pegwell Bay* at the Tate. The blue waves, and the goddess bearing dolphins do not come: only nicely dressed ladies pick their insect steps across the seaweed, and the portent of a comet hangs above this truest of Dyce's histories.[1]

There was something scary about the ordinariness of *Pegwell Bay.* The sea that, in the hands of others, would be showing its might, had pulled back; the rugged cliffs, which should speak of the majesty of this 'sceptred isle', had lost out to geological exactness; and middle-class pilgrims for whom Donati's Comet was of no special significance, appear oddly contingent. For MacColl, a man of the *fin-de-siècle* and an advocate of the New English Art Club, Dyce's painting defied expectation. He wondered why, being a painter of history, an exalted muralist for the House of Lords and a friend of Prince Albert,

Fig.1
William Dyce, *Pegwell Bay, Kent – a Recollection of October 5th 1858*
1859–60, © Tate, London 2005

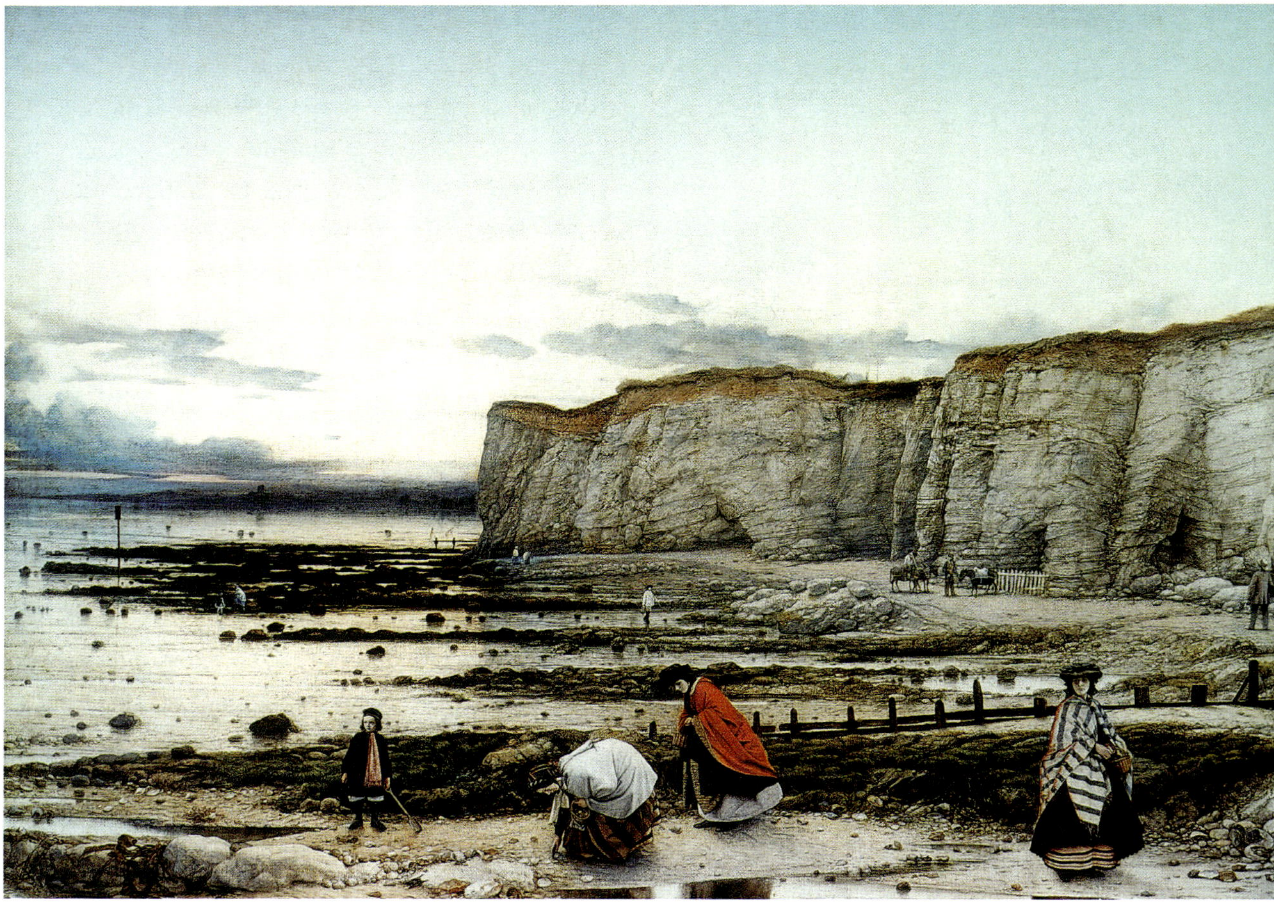

you would go to these gloomy cliffs and paint them with such wearisome precision? Yet by the time he was writing in 1902, there were many answers to this question and MacColl had seen the evidence in the huge popular interest in marine and coastal genre painting. Dyce's portent had not stopped two succeeding generations of painters from going to the English coast to look out into the beyond. The phenomenon became so noteworthy that Lord Leighton, on one memorable occasion, at the selection council of the Royal Academy summer exhibition, faced with yet another rendition of the foreland at Whitby, sank back in his chair and sighed, 'Ah Whitby! What a place that must be. I really must go there some time and see it'.[2] Some stretches of the British coast were evidently so familiar that one did not need to have gone there to be able to recognize them.

Even as Dyce was painting Pegwell Bay, James Clarke Hook was abandoning fashionable scenes of medieval history to re-invent a genre that, in the absence of great heroic sea battles and naval reviews, was no longer prominent in annual exhibitions.[3] Hook, from 1854 onwards, went regularly to Clovelly on the north Devon coast, and within two years was introducing it to Royal Academy visitors. Within a further two years he lured other artists to this huddle of tiny cottages beside a small harbour, cut off from civilization by a range of steep hills. Its fame spread by word-of-mouth during Hook's seven annual visits to Devon, and although it was not large enough to support a substantial colony, Henry Moore went there in 1857, Edwin Edwards in the early 1860s and Charles Napier Hemy by 1864.[4] The titles of Hook's earliest Clovelly canvases speak for themselves.

Fig.2
James Clarke Hook, *Welcome, Bonny Boat!*, 1856
Harris Museum and Art Gallery, Preston

Fig.3
John Brett, *Britannia's Realm*, 1880

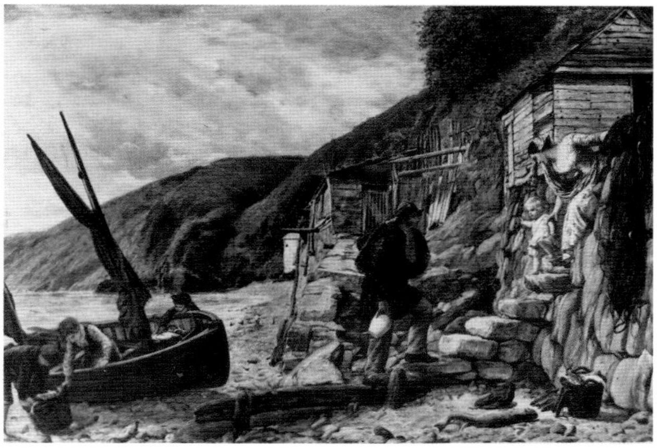

Welcome, Bonny Boat!, (1856, fig.2), for instance, illustrates the return of a lone fisherman to his young family and the familiar wooded hills of north Devon. These comforts are absent from *Luff Boy!* (1859), a scene in which the mariners confront nothing but the elements. Hook, we are told, could 'haul on to a rope, shoot a net, take a turn at the tiller, or pull an oar, much as if his duties in life led him to do these things and nothing else'.[5] The freshness of his experience, rendered 'without any artistic mystery', did not go unnoticed.[6] Yet the claim that his authenticity was somehow free from the materialistic and aesthetic values of his society needs further examination. It was not so simple.

By the 1870s Hook was surrounded by a new school of marine painters who, emerging from the shadows of Turner and the Pre-Raphaelites, were interested in coastal topography and atmospherics. Each painter had particular haunts – Henry Moore and Charles Napier Hemy working the English Channel, while John Brett recorded the Welsh and Cornish coasts, and Colin Hunter kept a sloop on the Clyde at Helensburgh, for forays to the Western Isles.[7] Hook, Brett, Moore, Hemy, Hunter and others took to sea, holding up the discomfort of working in storm-tossed conditions as the measure of their truth to nature.[8] Hook's later success lay more with depictions of life on the shore, than those at sea.[9] Fishing, unloading catches, mending boats, nets and lobster cages became rich sources of subject matter, upon which grander themes, to do with the family, social cohesion in coastal communities, primitive religion and superstition, and the meaning of marriage, maternity and death rituals, could be written. In the wider context of an island race, ruling the waves and commanding an empire, these tropes were highly significant. Nowhere are they more graphically expressed than in the tiny fishing smacks placed on a limitless expanse of sea in Brett's *Britannia's Realm,* (1880, fig.3).[10] Nowhere was *Britannia's Realm* more celebrated than in the national collection, where the 'disconsolate five millions' who were denied beach holidays could, during the summer of 1904, study the waves 'as they roll across canvas' in the 'torrid rooms' of the Tate Gallery.[11] Such pictures found their markets, not just on the walls of the Royal Academy, or in public museums, but through distribution as 'premium' plates in *The Graphic* and other illustrated papers. Hook's opulence – he bought a farm in Surrey based on sales and royalties – stood as an example of success to the students he taught at the Royal Academy Schools. They admired his simple, direct approach to teaching and he was credited as the inventor of the 'square brush' method, later perfected by Henry Herbert La Thangue and the members of the Newlyn School.[12]

However, Hook's principal legacy to the younger generation was that he had been one of the originators of what by the end of the 1870s had become a new industry – the artists' colony. The emergence of this phenomenon was directly dependent upon the

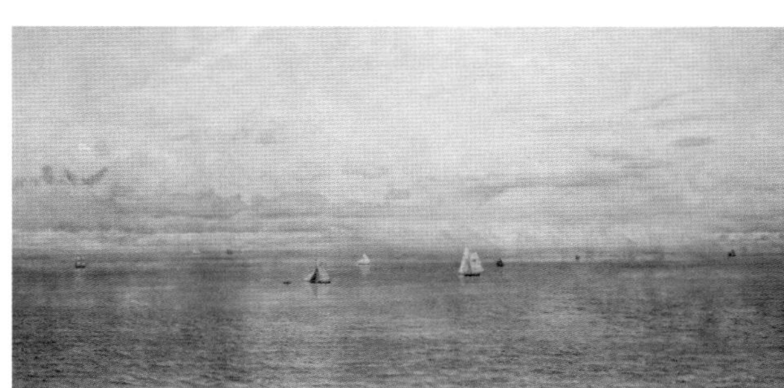

spread of railways, the growth of mass tourism and the popular belief in the health-giving properties of sea-bathing and fresh coastal or country air.[13] By 1880, even the remotest villages were accessible by rail and cart, facilitating a form of 'artistic tourism' – following a trail on which each of the picturesque stations might be illustrated. They were essential to the functioning of the 'colony' – the semi-permanent artist community, located outside centres of training and display. Whilst they brought like-minded painters together in one place, with a concentration of purpose, often in an atmosphere of close competition, colonies were not sustainable without the existence of exhibiting opportunities elsewhere. There had to be an accessible market. Production had to be matched to the aspirations of newly rich collectors, those successful men and women whose art collections embodied mercantile and imperialist attitudes and values.

Although prevalent in Britain, these conditions were by no means unique. The bourgeois consumption of spectacular nature generated similar phenomena elsewhere in Europe. A direct relationship can be struck between the growth of cities, the spread of industrial production, improved rail links and the transformation of channel ports and harbours such as Dover and Dieppe into coastal resorts boasting a full complement of sea-front hotels and casinos.[14] We can view such changes through the work of Eugène Boudin, Johan-Barthold Jongkind and the Impressionists. However, the enlightened opportunism involved in following bourgeois money and power to the coastal resort merged with other myths. Rural artists' colonies in France began with temporary migrants, initially categorized as 'bohemians', who were automatically at odds with the values of metropolitan society.[15] Democrats, republicans and anarchists in France, often considered uncouth, they made their way to the countryside, in some instances, to escape surveillance.[16] Their imagery differed from that of the history painters of the establishment in fairly obvious ways in that it eschewed the conventional procedures of the studio, refused classical erudition and cast a fresh eye on the natural world. In mid-nineteenth-century France, the most obvious place to do this was the village of Barbizon, in the forest of Fontainebleau.[17] Five years before Hook's discovery of Clovelly, Jean-François Millet had gone to Barbizon with his family, refugees from the conflagration of the 1848 revolution. On arrival, he found a party of landscape painters, all of whom, for one reason or another, had fallen out with the establishment.[18] While in the 1860s a few *peintres étrangères* sought out the Barbizon colony, it experienced an enormous surge in popularity in the years immediately following the Franco-Prussian War and the Commune.[19]

Such was the overcrowding by the time of Millet's death in 1875, that a group of British, Irish and American art students from the atelier of Carolus-Duran, finding no rooms available, crossed the forest to the village of Grez-sur-Loing, a few miles from Fontainebleau.[20] It is difficult to overestimate the significance of this act. It was a starting pistol shot for an entire generation. Colonies spilled over and spread. Painters like W.J. Hennessy explored Normandy and Calvados, Phil Morris was at Dieppe in the late 1870s, Percy Macquoid illustrated Breton costumes, at the same time as Henry Blackburn, in the company of the illustrator, Randolph Caldecott, was extolling the virtues of Brittany in the new journal, *The Magazine of Art.*[21] Within a few years, these travellers' tales were entwined with romantic fiction in Blanche Willis Howard's popular novel of artist life, *Guenn.*[22] Concentrations in and around inter-connected towns and villages between Quimper and Lorient – Beg-Meil, Concarneau, Pont-Aven, Quimperlé, and Le Pouldu – were plotted in animated student conversation in smoke-filled Paris cafés.

There were groups within groups, often linked to par-

Fig.4
Stanhope Forbes, *The Old Convent, Quimperlé*, 1882, oil on canvas
Private collection, photograph courtesy Sotheby's, London

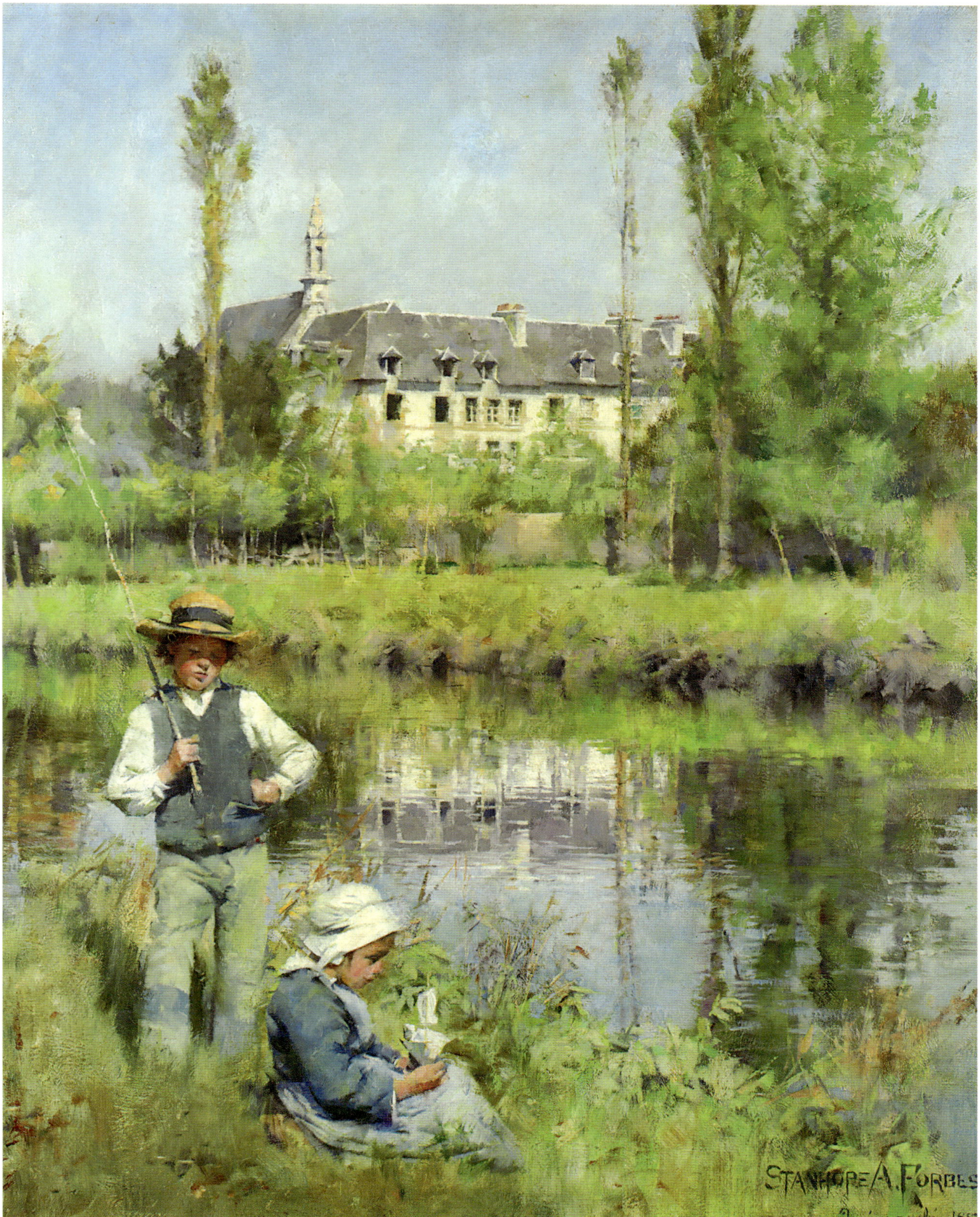

Fig.5
Henry Herbert La Thangue, *A French Boat Building Yard*, 1882
National Maritime Museum, Greenwich

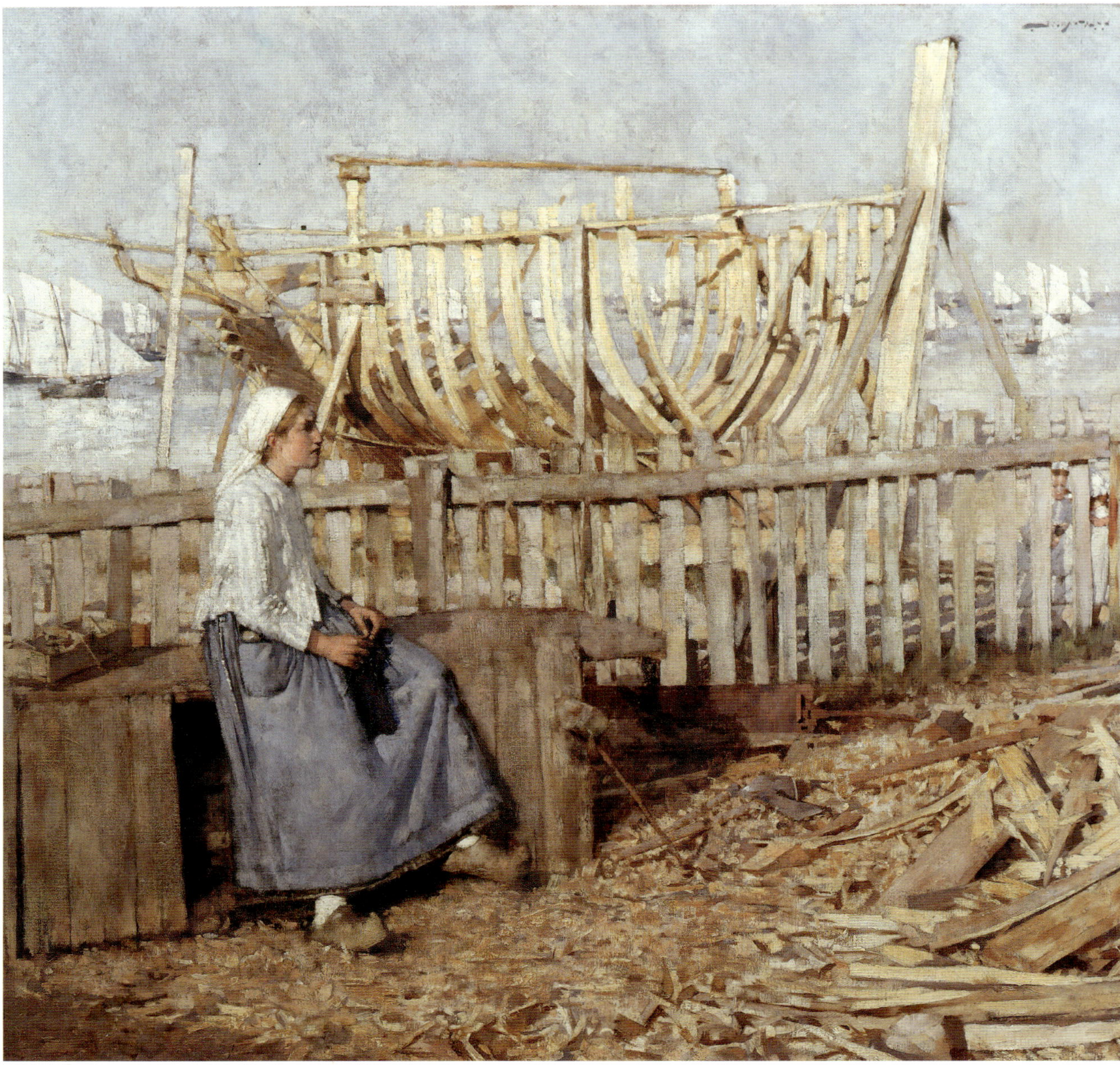

ticular hotels and stylistic sub-sets. What emerged in Brittany was a series of colonies which, like Newlyn, Lamorna and St. Ives in later years, attracted artists who might decamp from one sect to another and from one location to another, as their work progressed. Some moved deliberately to get away from others. Each had its high point and as the prestige of one waxed, another waned. It was often the location itself, recognized instantly by familiar motifs, that drew the new arrivals. The bridge at Grez, the church of Notre-Dame-de-l'Assumption at Quimperlé and the Ville Close at Concarneau took on complex associations. Such landmarks in their natural setting, repositories of history and culture, were reclaimed for a bourgeois city-dwelling public. A new modern language of the picturesque emerged which placed less emphasis upon noble crags, waterfalls and sham classical ruins. Fuelled by positivism, this post-Darwinian generation believed

Fig.6
Walter Osborne, *Apple Gathering, Quimperlé*, 1883
National Gallery of Ireland, Dublin

that vision was the most important of the senses and that the secrets of life lay dormant, unseen, in material objects, in people who had been left out of art and in the humble, remote and neglected towns and villages where they lived. No one looking at Stanhope Forbes' *The Old Convent, Quimperlé* (1882, fig.4), Henry Herbert La Thangue's *A French Boat Building Yard* (1882, fig.5) or Walter Osborne's *Apple Gathering, Quimperlé* (1883, fig.6) could regard the scene as conventionally picturesque.[23] The sunlight that fell on an ancient church tower or piece of medieval carving, also brought a busy market place, a boat yard, or a child in an orchard to life.

Sites and situations were chosen with an eye to what was currently acceptable in Salon terms. Colony production was largely pre-determined by institutional practices and political agendas. The habit of decamping to the coast or the countryside for the summer months, well-established by 1880, was now built into

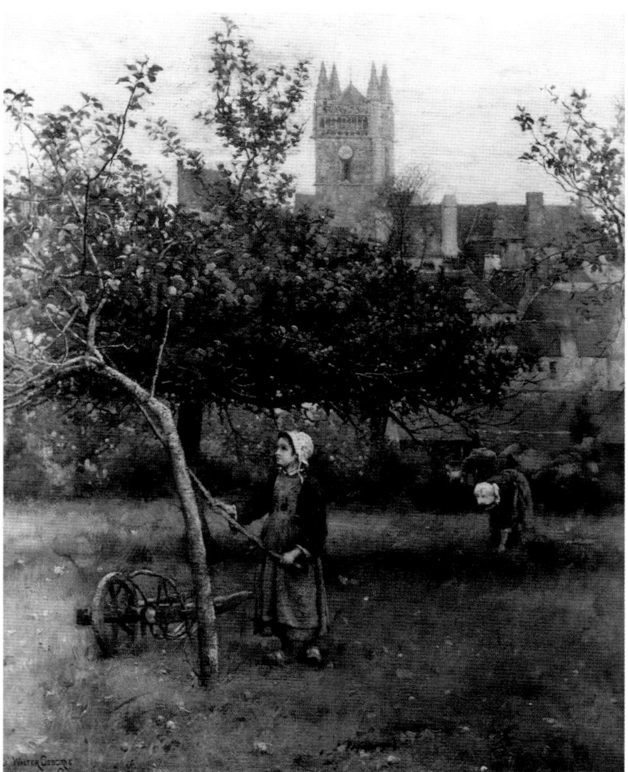

the academic year. Bohemianism, defined in student terms in the final quarter of the nineteenth century, was left for the end of term. The work of the colonists reflected the important changes that were taking place generally in European painting, led by the French. In the early years of the Third Republic, when the threat of insurrection remained strong, rigorous policies of de-centralization were pursued, and, applied to art, this meant state patronage for rural and coastal scenes depicting fishermen as doughty as those in Hook's paintings. The leading exponent of this 'Salon' or *'plein air'* Naturalism was Jules Bastien-Lepage, an artist who, according to Emile Zola, was superior to the Impressionists in that he knew how to realize works which, in their handling and high key, aimed to replicate lived experience.[24] Bastien-Lepage believed fervently in the young painter finding his or her vocation in his own 'corner of the world', in his case his home village of Damvillers. This idea became, if anything, more potent following his early death in December 1884. Forbes, a recent arrival in Newlyn, wrote of him, 'So the greatest artist of our age is dead?' He went on,

> I wish I had met him at Concarneau last year. His reputation, you will see will now increase in a wonderful manner – amongst artists generally there is very little lack of appreciation of his work. But when they … collect his wonderful pictures … in Paris shortly … his influence on the young will become more powerful than ever.[25]

Eighteen months before, in the summer of 1883, Bastien-Lepage had collected his followers around him at Concarneau and explained his method. If A.S. Hartrick is to be believed, this consisted of 'tips' using 'brushes two inches in width' – nicknamed 'the square brush act'.[26] It became what MacColl, looking back in 1894, described as a 'mannerism',

> recognized by a swaggering way of painting across forms, by a choppy rendering of planes, and by an attention to values at the expense of colour. Incidentally associated with this manner in the painting itself is a prosaic and photographic taste in the choice and rendering of subjects … in illustration of which the picture is staged.[27]

Forbes and the Newlyn group, James Guthrie and the 'Glasgow Boys' who visited him at Cockburnspath in East Lothian, and solitary, but inspirational, figures like George Clausen and La Thangue, all emphasized their dedication to working only on the motif. The huge practical difficulties of blocking in large, unwieldy canvases in unstable weather conditions however, called for a series of concealed day-to-day note-taking practices in sketchbooks, in studio studies and small on-the-spot *plein air* oil sketches, supplemented from time to time by photographs. Method became dogma. A regular pattern of paint-marks reduced the presence of the individual maker, and implied systematic, if not 'scientific' observation. Unpredictable 'effects' derived from scumbling, scraping or glazing were regarded as untruthful. A painting should be naturalistic in the sense that it should replicate the everyday appearances, and the exotic or unusual elements permitted in the finished product were only those verifiable on the motif.

There was thus an approved style and subject matter, and a reputation that, if forged in France, might underwrite an artist's standing in his or her home market. These at least were the starting assumptions of the many art students who went to Paris in the early years of the Third Republic. Immediate camaraderie in artist colonies was extended from long-term artist-residents to seasonal visitors. The local inn, of an evening, provided the setting for often informal group criticisms, liberally supported by cheap wine and other recreational pursuits. Colonies were collectives, and rather than mimicking strict master/pupil relationships, they often adopted the conventions of the more informal ateliers. Young painters learned as much from one another as from the senior members. In this regard there was little difference between rural and coastal colonies, save for the obvious fact that unlike Barbizon, the ports of the English Channel and the Bay of Biscay, were places on the edge. While there were way-stages in the Seine valley, at Giverny and Vétheuil for instance, the 'poetry' of the country gave way to the 'prose' of fishing villages, whose hardy inhabitants presented the visitor with a way of life ostensibly untouched by industry. Religious rituals in northern towns of the Belgian and Pas-de-Calais coast, first portrayed by Alphonse Legros, were rediscovered at the turn of the century. Grand hotel and casino resorts were, for the most part, avoided since they attracted a different breed of bourgeois artist/holiday makers who already had celebrity connections, or whose work depended largely upon portrait commissions.

Of the first generation of Francophile colonists, Forbes stands out as the painter who lived out his Breton colony experience. Newlyn was, in his terms, an 'English Concarneau', and while the garb and backdrop of his fishermen was Cornish, his manner of representing them was at first regarded as 'mostly ugly' and 'distinctly French'.[28] His need for authenticity overrode this criticism and it explains the tone of self-justification in his letters and elsewhere, for not attempting to set himself up in Ledbury Road or St John's Wood. A useful distinction can be made here with the Glasgow Boys, whose rural colonies were not badged as schools. Glasgow, like Liverpool and Manchester, was a hub of the Empire with its own vibrant art economy, operating through training establishments and exhibiting opportunities. Forbes' later establishment of an art

Fig.7
Stanhope Forbes, *The Health of the Bride*, 1889, oil on canvas
© Tate, London 2005

Fig.8
Stanhope Forbes, *By Order of the Court*, 1890, oil on canvas
National Museums Liverpool (The Walker)

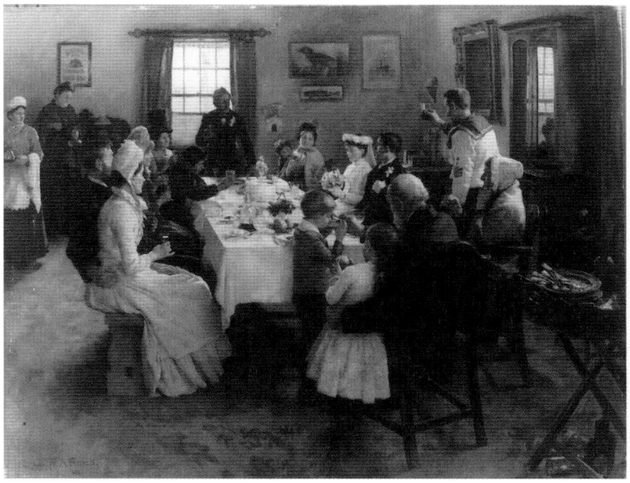

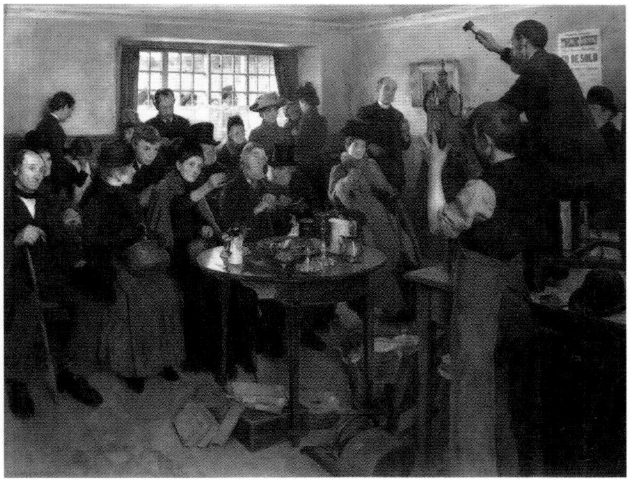

school, his support for a permanent art gallery at Newlyn, and even the friendly rivalry with the neighbouring colony at St. Ives, were attempts to give Cornwall its own functioning network.[29] He was in any case a 'democrat' for whom nationalistic considerations were initially much less important than 'the representation of events in which we ourselves might take part'.[30] Later interpretations of Naturalism, upon which Forbes continued to depend throughout the rest of his career, stressed its public legibility. Working- and lower-middle-class provincials were depicted without caricature, vulgarity or condescending prettiness. Classic Newlyn naturalist paintings, *The Village Philharmonic* (1888), *The Health of the Bride* (1889, fig.7), and *By Order of the Court* (1890, fig.8) for instance, were designed to be consumed in a public space by the very types they represented.[31] They were the by-product of mass visual and verbal literacy. Their author and his school were convinced of the moral rightness of finding beauty in ordinary things and they consistently recreated the congenial conditions in which to pursue their goal.

How important was this phenomenon? The fact that pictures of fisherfolk could ultimately carry messages to do with desirable national characteristics, was ultimately advantageous.[32] Like it or not, the works of coastal genre painters were bound up in national identity and this is clear in the work of John Robertson Reid and those closer to Hook's generation, who took on the Bastien-Lepage mantra. Reid's *The Rival Grandfathers* (1884, Walker Art Gallery, Liverpool), for all its innocence, anecdote, and apparent objectivity, powerfully demonstrates the theme of continuity implicit in representations of youth and age. Focusing a telescope, scanning the horizon, was reading the future – the distant clouds tomorrow's climate. In the case of Frank Brangwyn's *Fowey Harbour, Cornwall* (1887, fig.9), there may be no 'old salts', but the youthful 'water rats' will become the sailors of tomorrow. Based in one of the Wentworth Studios in Chelsea, the home of the 'square brush' school, Brangwyn, a mariner *manqué,* was a member of the Naval Volunteers along with Frank Short, Nelson Dawson and Percy Jacomb Hood.[33] Having made several long sea voyages by 1892, Brangwyn, in his depictions of storm-tossed vessels, celebrated the stoic, weather-beaten mariner as the epitome of national virtue. This theme, written on the anxious faces of wives and mothers was frequently replayed – from the earliest Cullercoats pictures of Henry Hetherington Emmerson such as *Waiting for the Boats* (1870, page 116), through the Newlyn watercolours by Walter Langley, like *Among the Missing, Scene in a Cornish Fishing Village* (1884, page 31), to works

Fig.9
Frank Brangwyn, *Fowey Harbour, Cornwall*, 1887, oil on canvas
Private collection, photograph courtesy Christie's, London

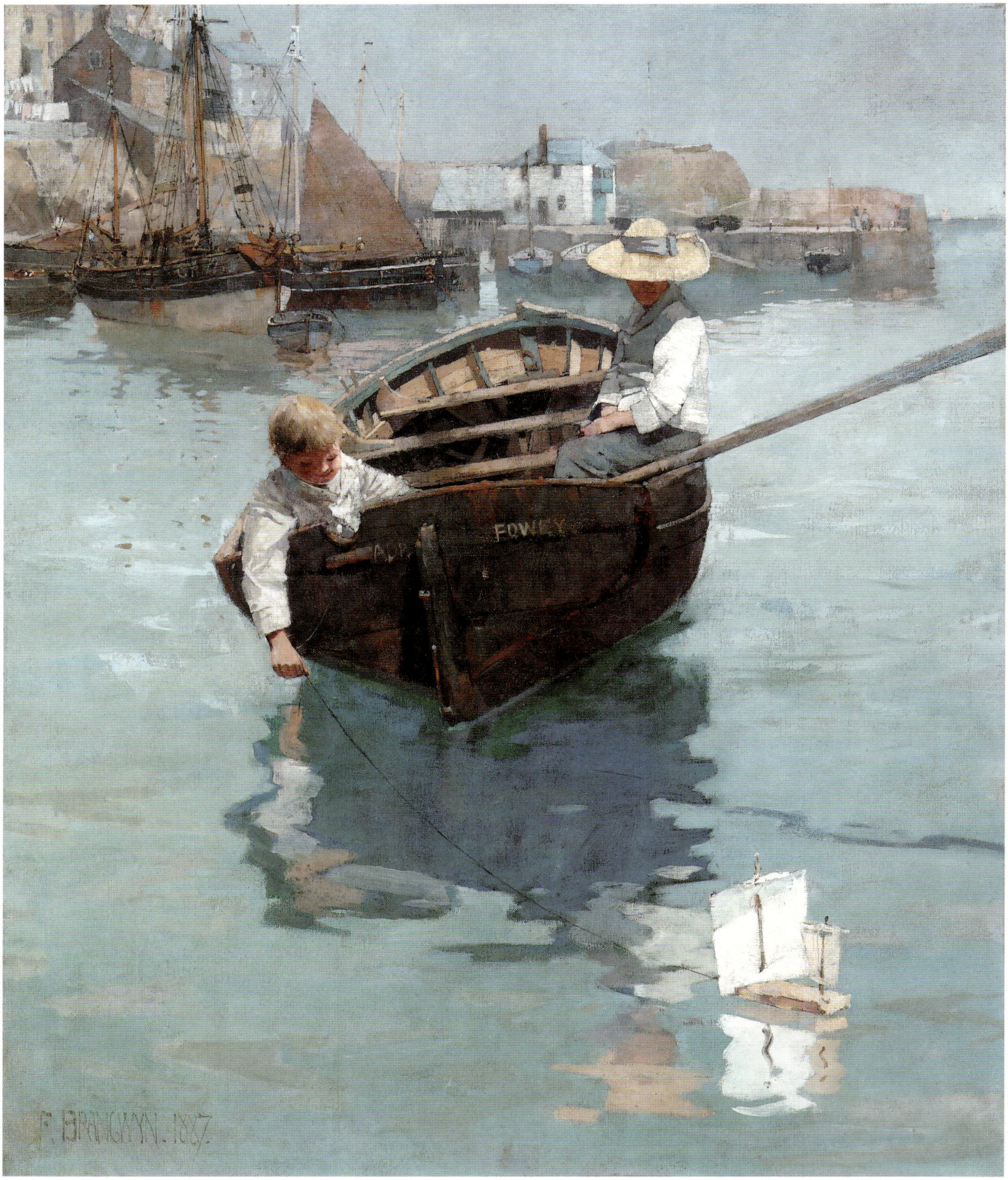

such as Harold Knight's *The Last Coble* (1900, page 102), in which the entire village congregates expectantly on the shore at Staithes.[34]

In France, colonies like Concarneau and Quimperlé, which had mushroomed during the 1870s had, by the mid-1880s, begun to split into factions. These were often based around particular hotels and language groups, and reflected the stylistic continuum between Rustic Naturalism, Impressionism, Divisionism and what, by 1890, had emerged as *Synthètisme.*[35] The Breton colonies were ever-changeable, making for frequent shifts in allegiances. Americans who formed friendships with their English counterparts were, like Arthur Hoeber, Willard Metcalf, Howard Butler, Frank Chadwick and Edward Emerson Simmons, sometimes persuaded to break a return journey to the United States with a trip to Britain. Cross-fertilization was particularly evident in Walberswick and St. Ives, colonies which attracted a varied and international artist clientele.[36] The former had, as Richard Scott has shown, a long and distinguished association with artists, enhanced in the 1880s by the existence of a railway connection to Southwold.[37] It witnessed the rapid development of the work of Philip Wilson Steer, in successive visits between 1884 and 1891.[38] Flat, fluid strokes of paint give way to experiments with 'dots' of pure colour. A sketch of *Walberswick,* for instance, shows a girl overlooking the estuary, while on the reverse, in a very different style, is a partially completed painting of the shoreline with a figure, executed entirely in dots.[39] Steer's Divisionism was never systematically adopted, but was no less transforming for that. Sand spits dissolve in a shimmering haze in *Figures on the Beach, Walberswick* and girls on holiday, in full white skirts with sashes, and military-style tunics, flit past the viewer in a few dry, light-hearted, brushstrokes. There is a new way of looking; a new sense of purpose. Fortified by thoughts of the bracing sea air, the energetic descendants of Dyce's disorientated shell-collectors arrive on the beach at Walberswick, to be part of a new vision.

Just as painters were spreading out from Concarneau to Beg-Meil and beyond in the mid-nineties, the secluded coves and leafy inlets around Newlyn seemed increasingly attractive. The most important of these was discovered, as Austin Wormleighton has shown, by Samuel John 'Lamorna' Birch in 1892 – an artist who painted 'grand manner' landscapes comparable to those of E.A. Waterlow.[40] Around the turn of the century some of those who were taught by Forbes made the short trip to Lamorna where a lively colony was established.[41] However, many others were already disembarking from the Penzance train at St. Erth Junction and taking the branch line to St. Ives, such that by 1890 it was more cosmopolitan than Newlyn.[42] Indeed, within a few years, and before the advent of Lamorna, it had already overtaken Newlyn as the colony of choice.[43] It may have lacked the concerted force of Forbes, Bramley, Gotch and Langley's monumental exhibition-pieces, but there the sea was not grey, but opalescent.[44] Adrian Stokes, Julius Olsson, William Henry Bartlett and others were attracted to the magic effects of sea and cloud they were able to study on the north coast.[45]

All of this, wrapped up in studio talk, in a proliferating art and tourist literature, ensured that prior to the Great War, places like Concarneau and St. Ives retained their importance, even though in later standard accounts they were no longer of interest.[46] For new painters of the nineties like the Scots, Eric Forbes-Robertson and Robert Brough, and the Irish, Roderic O'Conor, Walter Chetwood Aiken and William John Leech, the Breton colony remained a necessity.[47] Such experience was, by definition, collective and, acquired in youth, it contained glimpses of a *beau idéal.* It involved the inevitable transition back to a true, or

Fig.10
George Henry, *Autumn*, 1888
Renfrew Museums and Galleries

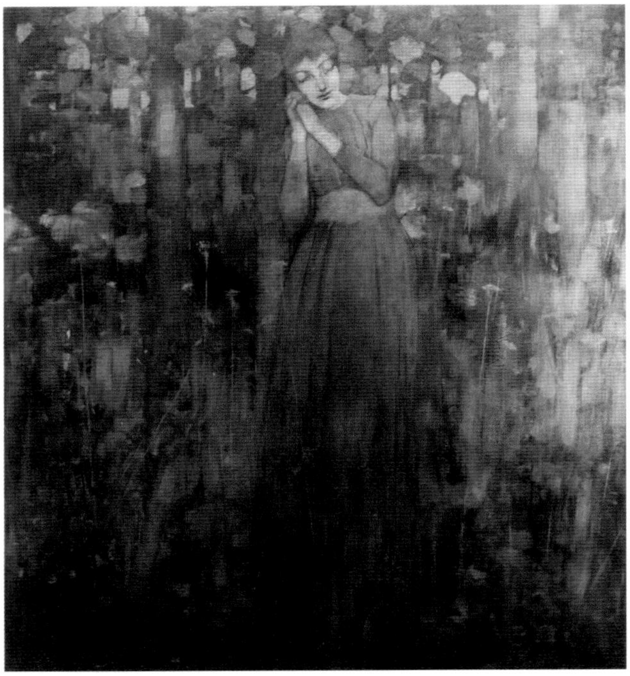

adopted, place of origin. It was intimately tied to separation, loss and rediscovery. The effect in Scotland was reportedly of an immediate and specific kind. Confidently embraced by James Guthrie and Edward Arthur Walton in the early eighties at Cockburnspath, the flat square-brush impasto lasted for no more than five years before it was swiftly adapted, possibly as a result of discussion of Gauguin's methods. Changes are first evident in George Henry's *Autumn* (c.1888, fig.10), whilst in *A Galloway Landscape* (1889), the enfolding hillsides of the Solway shoreline are accentuated with an eye to abstract simplification.[48] His unique collaboration with Edward Atkinson Hornel charged this landscape with magic and miracle equivalent to that of Finistère and Morbihan. The fecundity of their works, like *The Druids Bringing in the Mistletoe* (see page 150) and Hornel's *Summer* (fig.11), was immediately apparent. They provided an escape from the impasse of Naturalism for painters like Arthur Melville and Brangwyn, leading to new definitions of the 'decorative', in which the teasels and tangle-weeds beloved by the Naturalists could be put to other uses.

The route to the Celtic Elysium, to *Tir-nan-Og,* taken by a sturdy Scot had none of the coy and timorous eclecticism of his Cornish counterparts. While Brangwyn went off in search of piratical adventure with *The Buccaneers* (1892, Fine Art Society), Forbes resolutely remained perched on the hillside overlooking Mount's Bay. Important changes in his work, though ostensibly preserving his neutrality, admitted a grander sweep. His fishing community was no longer confined to the quotidian. Newlyn saw the construction of a new stone pier in 1893, strong enough for the iron-clad vessels tactfully omitted from his later, colourful depictions of the harbour scene. The advent of steam trawlers which led to the rapid decline of the fishing fleets all around the British coast went, for the most part, unrecorded. In *The Seine Boat* (1904, fig.12), for instance, the coastal waters become a timeless realm. While the physiognomies of his 'salts' might convey classic Cornish profiles, one would have to look elsewhere within the Cornish School to find a way down into the deep Celtic past of the region. Beach holidays and old fishing boats hastily refitted as pleasure craft were the new subjects for Laura Knight's and Harold Harvey's generation. Whilst there had been an air of desperation in 1897 when the critic of *The Artist* declared that 'the Newlyn fisherman and his fish are still hunted down and bagged', a growing consciousness of change was evident when the 'Cornish School' was displayed in force at the Whitechapel Art Gallery in 1902.[49] Newlyn and St. Ives, along with Lelant, Sennen, Polperro, Fowey and Falmouth were brigaded together. They were, according to Lewis Hind, 'united in their loyalty to truth'.[50] There was to be no equivalent memorial to the Glasgow Boys. The Glasgow International Exhibition of 1901 was not seen as an opportunity for celebration. Raeburn vastly outnumbered Guthrie; Clausen outnumbered Lavery. E.A. Wal-

Fig.11
Edward Atkinson Hornel, *Summer*, 1891
National Museums Liverpool (The Walker)

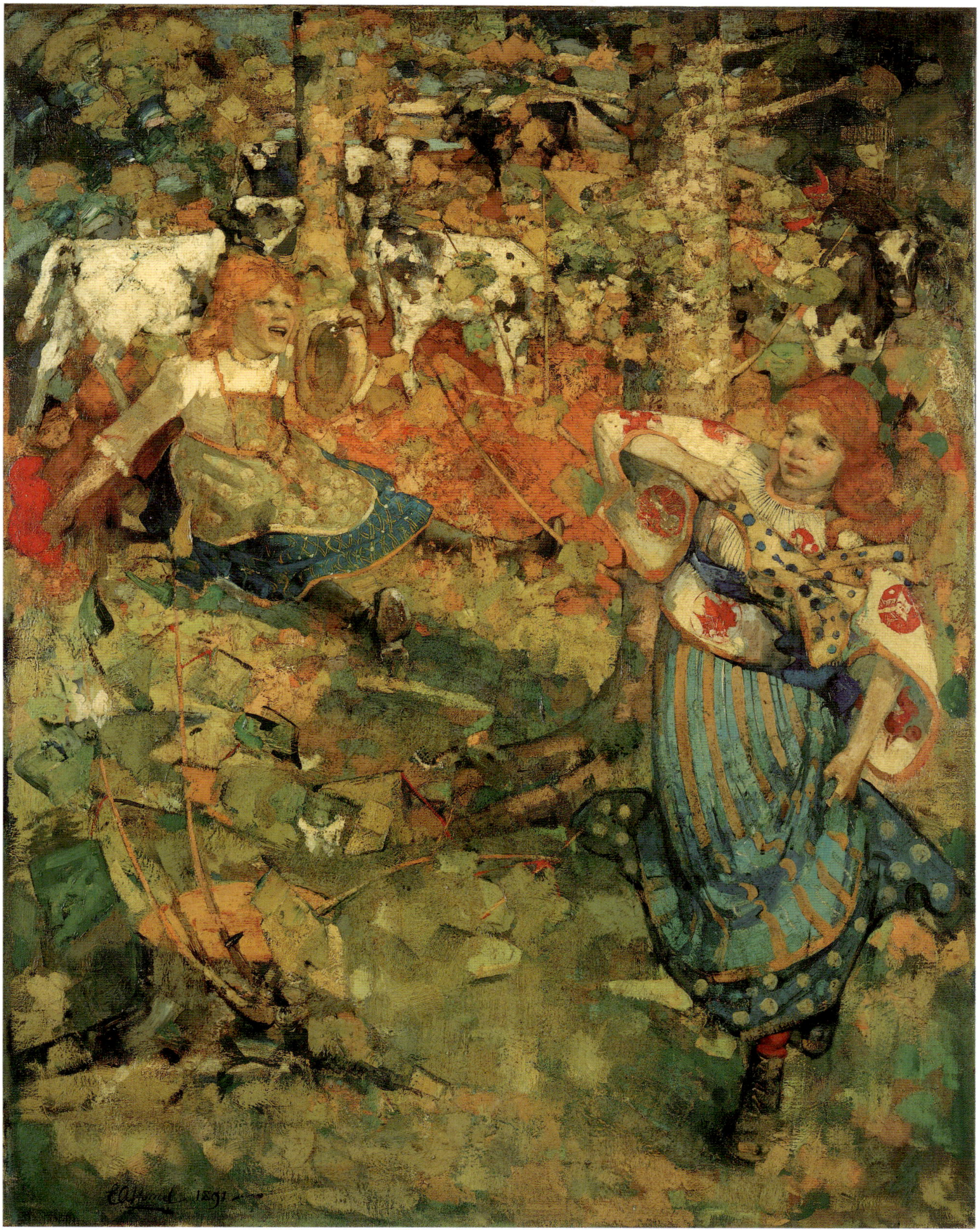

Fig.12
Stanhope Forbes, *The Seine Boat*, 1904, oil on canvas
Private collection, photograph courtesy Pyms Gallery, London

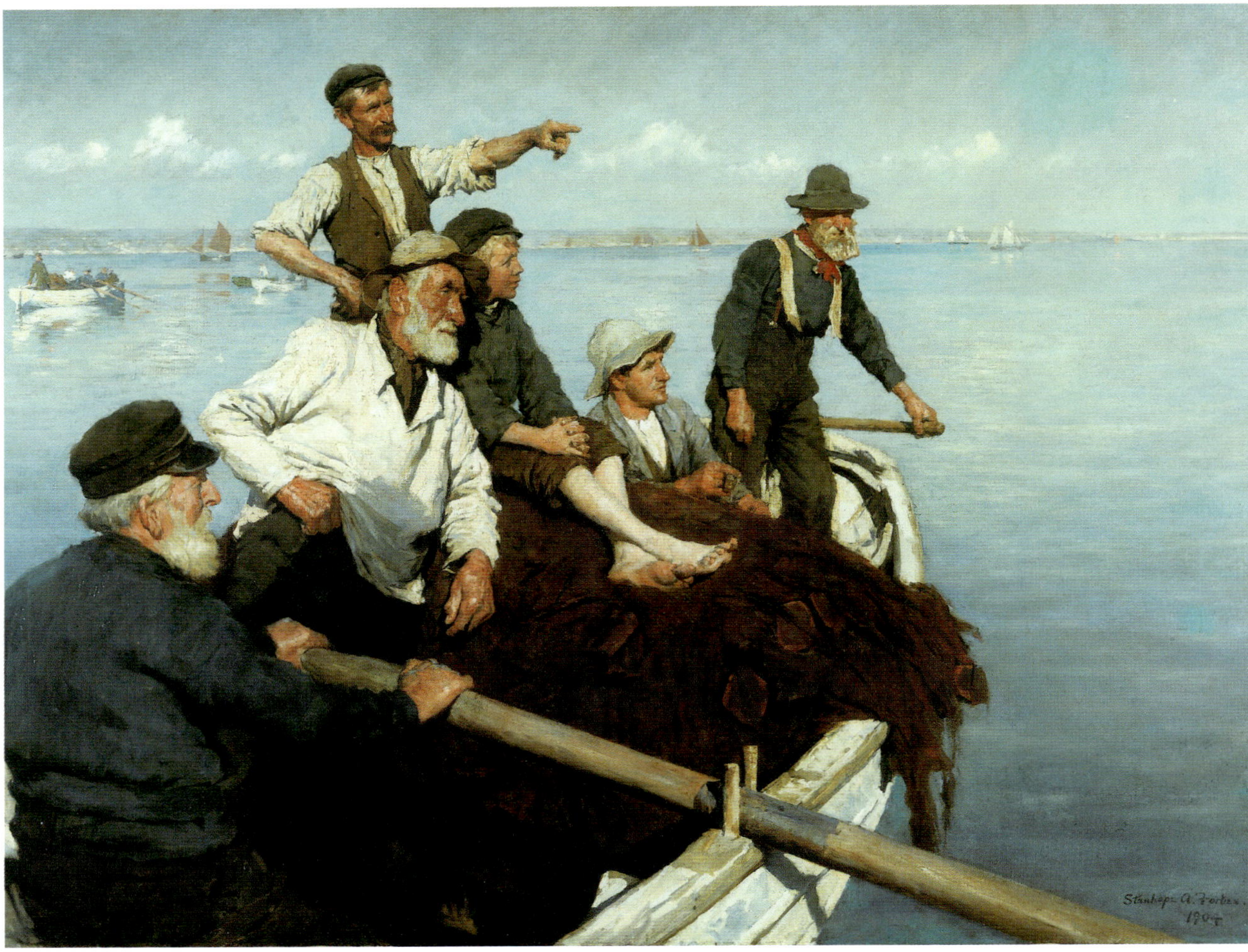

ton and Lavery had already moved to Cheyne Row and Cromwell Place respectively. Henry was soon to follow them to Glebe Place, while Hornel was ensconced in Kirkcudbright. By 1902 only Guthrie and William Kennedy retained Glasgow addresses.

There were those coughing millions for whom the tide only rose and fell in a gold frame in the Tate Gallery. Yet for the Edwardian artist, the more remote and reductive the setting, the greater was the appeal and the purity of perception. D.Y. Cameron at Berwick and Ben Ledi, Paul Henry at Achill, Munnings and John at Lamorna, J.D. Innes at Arenig, Gauld, Hornel and Oppenheimer at Kirkcudbright, have consigned the cups and spoons of Forbes' bridal reception to the country sale, in favour of earth, air and water. When all else was gone these remained in the public domain of the municipal art gallery, products of artists' colonies, providing vicarious experience for the labouring masses. It may seem facile, but the concept, practices and support for the artists' colony – even the term 'colony' itself – were all intimately related to the bigger world of commercial imperialism.

Ultimately the coastal colony parked its painters on the edge, and left them there to contemplate the immensity, along with the bourgeois couples who congregate on sand spits in the paintings of Boudin, and in this, MacColl's meditation on Dyce is understood.

Notes

1. D.S. MacColl, *Nineteenth Century Art,* James Maclehose and Son, 1902, p.115.

2. G.D. Leslie, *The Inner Life of the Royal Academy,* 1914, John Murray, p.135; quoted in Kenneth McConkey, *The Restless Wave,* exhibition catalogue, Newcastle upon Tyne Polytechnic Art Gallery, 1978, p.5.

3. Hook was first recommended to go to Clovelly by C.W. Cope. Articles on his work began to appear in the 1870s and he was fêted with an *Art Annual* in 1888 (F.G. Stephens, *J.C. Hook RA: His Life and Work,* J.S. Virtue, 1888). Hook's work has seldom been surveyed in recent years in its entirety.

4. Henry Moore went to Clovelly in 1857, remarking that there he discovered the 'size and extent [of the sea] as seen from high cliffs'. The village was also made famous by Charles Kingsley in *Westward Ho!* (1855) and Charles Dickens in one of his *All Year Round* Christmas stories. It was described as an 'artist's haunt' in W.W. Fenn, 'Favourite Sketching Grounds: Clovelly', *The Magazine of Art,* vol.3, 1880, pp.87-91; see also Frederick Pollock, 'Clovelly', *The English Illustrated Magazine,* December 1884, pp.153-163. For Henry Moore see Elizabeth Ruhlmann, 'Henry Moore: his Family and his Art' in Julian Hartnoll, *The Moore Family Pictures,* exhibition catalogue, York City Art Gallery, 1980, pp.3-20. For Hemy see Andrew Greg, *Charles Napier Hemy, RA, 1841-1917,* exhibition catalogue, Tyne and Wear Museums, 1984.

5. Wilfrid Meynell ed., 'James Clarke Hook RA', *The Modern School of Art,* vol.1, Cassell & Co, c.1887, p.72.

6. Ibid, p.76. Ruskin for instance greatly praised Hook's work. For further reference see Rosemary Treble, *Great Victorian Pictures,* exhibition catalogue, Arts Council, 1978, p.45.

7. For reference to Brett, see Ann Sumner ed., *John Brett: A Pre-Raphaelite on the Shores of Wales,* exhibition catalogue, National Museum of Wales, 2001. Hunter's work has so far evaded Victorian specialists. For further reference see James L Caw, *Scottish Painting, 1620-1908* [1908], Kingsmead Reprint, 1975, pp.324-6. Moore also worked off the west coast of Scotland.

8. While later painters like Stanhope Forbes and Henry Scott Tuke made a virtue of working in difficult circumstances, a committed Victorian marine painter like Hemy operated from the vantage of a well-appointed sea-going studio. See Arthur Fish, 'The Work of C Napier Hemy ARA', *The Magazine of Art,* 1900, p.3.

9. See Richard Ormond, 'Seascapes of the Imagination', *Antique Collector,* vol.55, no.9, 1984, pp.80-85.

10. Sumner, *Brett,* p.76. On the implicit national rhetorics in marine and coastal genre painting, see Kenneth McConkey, *Memory and Desire, Painting in Britain and Ireland at the turn of the Twentieth Century,* Ashgate, 2002, pp.113-4.

11. Hugh Stokes, 'Sea Pictures', *Ladies Realm,* May-October 1904, p.442.

12. George Thomson, 'H.H. La Thangue and his Work', *The Studio,* vol.9, 1896, p.171, notes that Hook purchased 'an armful of large square brushes which he distributed among the students'.

13. For a discussion of the spread of tourism in the late nineteenth century see Lynne Withey, *Grand Tours and Cook's Tours, A History of Leisure Travel, 1750-1915* [1997], Aurum Press ed., 1998. See also John Urry, *The Tourist Gaze,* Sage, 1990.

14. See John Willett, Anna Gruetzner Robins and Sophie Bowness, *The Dieppe Connection, The Town and its Artists from Turner to Braque,* exhibition catalogue, Herbert Press Ltd, 1992.

15. Malcolm Easton, *Artists and Writers in Paris, The Bohemian Idea, 1803-1867,* Edward Arnold Ltd, 1964. For a seminal survey of key artists' colonies see Michael Jacobs, *The Good and Simple Life, Artist Colonies in Europe and America,* Phaidon Press, 1985. For a wide-ranging discussion of European rural colonies see Nina Lübbren, *Rural artists' colonies in Europe,* Manchester University Press, 2001.

16. Nicholas Green, *The Spectacle of Nature, Landscape and Bourgeois culture in Nineteenth Century France,* Manchester University Press, 1990.

17. R.L. Herbert *Barbizon Revisited,* exhibition catalogue, California Palace of the Legion of Honour, 1962. See also Green, *The Spectacle,* and Steven Adams, *The Barbizon School and the Origins of Impressionism,* Phaidon, 1994.

18. The canonization of Millet occurred within the years immediately after his death with the appearance of Alfred Sensier's *J-F Millet, Peasant and Painter* (MacMillan and Co, 1881), and with the high prices achieved for his works.

19. One of the most interesting cases in this regard is that of the Irish painter Nathaniel Hone who was in Barbizon c.1857. For further reference see Julian Campbell, *Nathaniel Hone the Younger,* exhibition catalogue, National Gallery of Ireland, 1991.

20. The group included both Robert Louis Stevenson and his cousin, R.A.M. Stevenson, along with the Irish painter, Frank O'Meara. Within a few years, the Scots, Arthur Melville and James Campbell Noble, the Irish painter, John Lavery, the English, Louis Welden Hawkins and William Stott of Oldham, and Americans, Alexander Harrison, Will Low, Ruger Donoho,

Willard Metcalf, Robert Vonnoh and many others, had found their way there. For further discussion see Toru Arayashiki ed., *The Painters in Grez-sur-Loing,* exhibition catalogue, Tokyo: Japan Association of Art Museums, 2000.

21. For Hennessy see Mary Mather, 'Calvados', *The English Illustrated Magazine,* 1884-5, pp.201-212, 259-270. See also Henry Blackburn, 'Sketching Grounds, Pont-Aven and Douarnenez, Sketches in Lower Brittany', *The Magazine of Art,* vol.2, 1879, pp.6-9; Blackburn favoured Douarnenez, to the north west of Quimper, over other ports. See also T.M. Macquoid, 'Costumes and characteristics of South Brittany', *The Magazine of Art,* vol.2, 1879, pp.89-93; and Henry Blackburn, *Artistic Travel, A Thousand Miles towards the Sun,* Sampson Low and Co., 1892, pp.61-128.

22. For the influence of Blanche Willis Howard's *Guenn, A Wave on the Breton Coast,* (1884) see David Sellin, *Americans in Brittany and Normandy, 1860-1910,* exhibition catalogue, Phoenix Art Museum, 1982, p.44; see also Jacobs, *Good and Simple Life,* pp.66-73.

23. For Osborne, see Jeanne Sheehy, *Walter Osborne,* exhibition catalogue, National Gallery of Ireland, 1984, p.54. For La Thangue, see Kenneth McConkey, *A Painter's Harvest, H.H. La Thangue, 1859-1929,* exhibition catalogue, Oldham Art Gallery, 1978, pp.8-9.

24. For reference to Bastien-Lepage see Andre Theuriet, *Jules Bastien-Lepage and His Art,* Seeley Service and Co, 1892; and Julia Cartwright, *Jules Bastien-Lepage,* Portfolio Monograph, 1894.

25. Stanhope Forbes letter to his mother, 15 December 1884, Tate Britain Archives.

26. A.S. Hartrick, *A Painter's Pilgrimage through Fifty Years,* Cambridge University Press, 1939, p.28. Although credited to Hook, see note 12 above, this method was closely allied to standard atelier pedagogy. For further reference see Albert Boime, *The Academy and French Painting in the Nineteenth Century,* Phaidon Press, 1971.

27. D.S. MacColl, 'Professor Brown: Teacher and Painter', *The Magazine of Art,* 1894, p.407.

28. *The Athenaeum,* 8 June 1889, reviewing Forbes' *The Health of the Bride,* at the Royal Academy exhibition. At Newlyn the 'backdrop' was, for the most part easterly, giving a grey light, while at Concarneau, it was westerly.

29. See Melissa Hardie ed., *100 Years in Newlyn, Diary of a Gallery,* Patten Press in association with Newlyn Art Gallery, 1995. There were of course the much reported cricket matches which took place between the artists of Newlyn and St. Ives.

30. Stanhope A. Forbes, 'The Treatment of Modern Life in Art', in *Transactions of the National Association for the Advancement of Art and its Application to Industry, Birmingham Meeting, MDCCCXC,* 1891, pp.123-130.

31. A perspicacious contemporary critic, P.G. Hamerton, in *The Present State of the Fine Arts in France,* Seeley and Co, 1892, pp.13-4, makes these points in connection with Albert Fourié's *A Wedding Feast at Yport* (1887, Musée des Beaux Arts, Rouen), an open-air version of *The Health of the Bride.*

32. For a discussion of this see Laura Newton, *Cullercoats: A North-East Colony of Artists,* Sansom & Company, 2003 and 'The Cullercoats Artists' Colony c.1870-1914', unpub. PhD thesis, Northumbria University, 2001, especially Chapter 5 and conclusion.

33. Rodney Brangwyn, *Frank Brangwyn,* William Kimber, 1978, pp.32-46. Brangwyn's studio was shared with Ernest Dade, one of the founders of the Staithes Art Club, a painter who, before going to the Académie Julian in 1884, had worked as a deck-hand.

34. For reference to Langley see Roger Langley, *Walter Langley, Pioneer of the Newlyn Art Colony,* Sansom and Company, 1997.

35. For distinctions between the hotels, see Frank L Emanuel, 'Letters to Artists – Concarneau, Brittany, as a sketching ground', *The Studio,* vol.4, 1895, p.183; see also Sellin, *Americans,* pp.38-42, 43-5; Jacobs, *Good and Simple Life,* pp.61-6.

36. In the 1880s Hoeber and Metcalf visited Walberswick and Butler, Chadwick and Simmons, St. Ives.

37. Richard Scott, *Artists at Walberswick, East Anglian Interludes, 1880-2000,* Art Dictionaries Ltd, 2002.

38. For Steer at Walberswick see Bruce Laughton, *Philip Wilson Steer,* Clarendon Press, 1971, pp.6-31.

39. Derek Hill Collection, The Glebe Gallery, Donegal. See Bruce Laughton, 'Some early panel sketches by Wilson Steer', *Apollo,* January 1966, p.53.

40. Austin Wormleighton, *A Painter Laureate, Lamorna Birch and his Circle,* Sansom and Company, 1995, pp.52-6.

41. Ibid., pp.97-108; see also John Branfield, *Ella and Charles Naper, Art and Life at Lamorna,* Sansom and Company, 2003.

42. Jacobs, *Good and Simple Life,* pp.143-166. See also Tom Cross, *The Shining Sands, Artists in Newlyn and St Ives, 1880-1930,*

West Country Books, The Lutterworth Press, 1994, pp.85-105; and for the period after 1927, David Tovey, *Creating a Splash, The St Ives Society of Artists, The first 25 years (1927-1952),* exhibition catalogue, Wilson Books, 2003.

43. By the end of the nineties, it was noted that while St. Ives 'is the greater innovator, and its range runs the gamut from "impressionistic" to the purely decorative and "primitive" ... Newlyn work is not largely marked by a spirit of progress and innovation'. There were nevertheless concerted efforts to brigade the two colonies together as the 'Cornish' school, although this title did not stick. See H.M.F., 'St. Ives and Newlyn "Academy" shows', *The Artist,* May 1897, pp.223-6.

44. C.L.H., 'From Cornwall to Whitechapel', *The Academy and Literature,* 5 April 1902, p.369.

45. W.H. Bartlett, 'Summer time at St. Ives, Cornwall', *The Art Journal,* 1897, p.294.

46. In addition to popular Muirhead's and Baedeker guides from the 1890s, there was a growing literature on Brittany, following Blackburn's *Artistic Travel,* through to Octave Le Braz, *The Land of Pardons* [1894], Methuen ed., 1906, and the lavishly illustrated Dorothy Menpes, *Brittany,* Adam and Charles Black, illus Mortimer Menpes, 1905.

47. For Brough see Jennifer Melville, *Robert Brough ARSA,* exhibition catalogue, Aberdeen Art Gallery, 1995. For O'Conor, see Jonathon Benington, *Roderic O'Conor,* Irish Academic Press, 1992. For Leech, Denise Ferran, *William John Leech,* exhibition catalogue, National Gallery of Ireland with Merrell Holberton, 1996.

48. For a discussion of these issues see Roger Billcliffe, *The Glasgow Boys,* John Murray, 1985, pp.240-4.

49. HMF, 'St Ives', p.225.

50. CLH, 'From Cornwall', p.369.

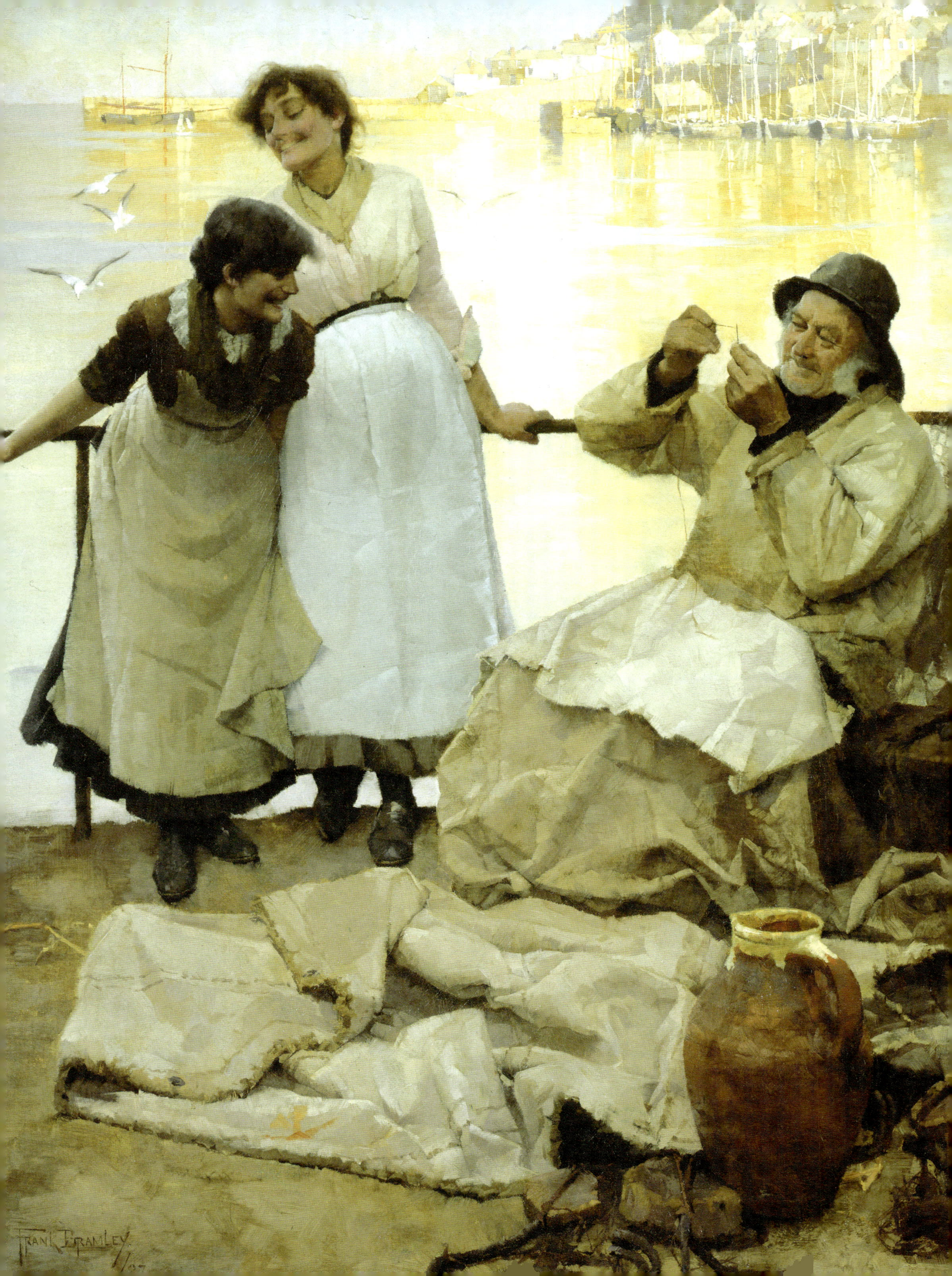
FRANK BRAMLEY

CHAPTER 2

Newlyn
'A Sort of English Concarneau'

ALISON BEVAN

The fishing village of Newlyn lies on the south coast of the Penwith peninsula, in the far south west of Cornwall. Some ten miles further west is Land's End, while less than ten miles north, on the opposite side of the same small peninsula, is St. Ives. Looking east across Mount's Bay, the village overlooks the neighbouring market town and port of Penzance, beyond which lies St. Michael's Mount, with the beaches and cliffs of the Lizard peninsula in the distance.

Today, roadside graffiti greets the visitor to Penwith with the words 'You are not in England', and it could be argued that Stanhope Forbes' description of Newlyn when he arrived in 1884, as 'a sort of English Concarneau', alluded to that sense of 'otherness' which this remote part of Cornwall engenders, as well as to its physical similarities to the Breton landscape and to the burgeoning colony of artists.[1]

Newlyn's fishing industries and rural economy offered a wealth of subjects susceptible to both pathos and idyllic charm. The fishermen's heroic struggle with the elements and the seas – setting out in small boats with only rudimentary navigational aids and no reliable meteoro-

Walter Langley painting on the Cliff at Newlyn, photograph
Newlyn Artists Photograph Album, 1880s, Penlee House Gallery & Museum and Cornwall Studies Centre, Redruth

Page 26
Frank Bramley, *Eyes and no Eyes*, 1887, oil on canvas
Private collection, courtesy of Richard Green Galleries

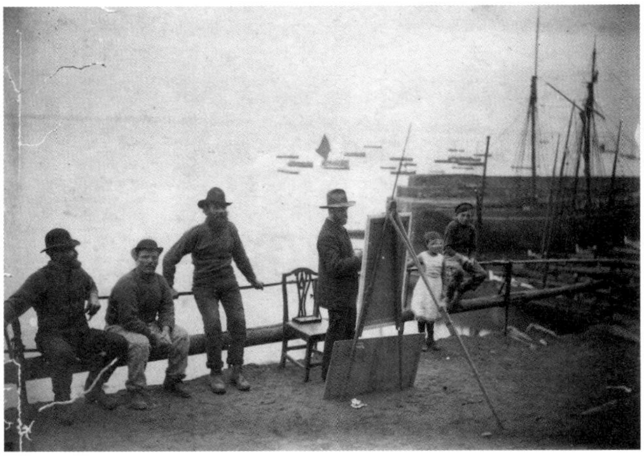

logical equipment to pursue shoals of fish for hundreds of miles – provided real-life tales of loss and communal grief. These intrepid exertions supplemented the villagers' more lucrative, but seasonal, employment in pilchard fishing, which took place close to land and presented an easily accessible spectacle for the artists. Farming, too, was integral to the life of the community and had remained largely unchanged for generations, in field systems dating back hundreds, perhaps thousands, of years which, together with mining and quarrying, provided images of back-breaking labour set amidst the lush fecundity resulting from the mild, damp climate.

By 1880 the neighbouring town of Penzance boasted the West of England's first art school, a museum, a subscription library and an acclaimed learned society, while Newlyn was still unsophisticated.[2] An article in the *Cornishman* that year describes it in detail, acknowledging that the hopelessly irregular construction of its houses, the maze of lanes, crooked streets and blind alleys were what made it picturesque, but adding that it had a forlorn and ragged air.[3]

> Several times, I have been shocked and disgusted with the state of the thoroughfares, mud and filth and rotten fish lying about and trampled underfoot. And then the smells! In certain conditions of the atmosphere the effluvia are something appalling and anyone with a delicate olfactory apparatus would barely survive the stinks and stenches.

It was in this setting that the colony later known as the Newlyn School began to form in the early 1880s. With some notable exceptions, the artists were predominantly male, English and middle-class. Few had sufficient private income not to depend on sales of paintings for much of their livelihood, but many had been to Brittany before coming to Newlyn, and most treated the village as they had Concarneau and Pont-Aven, visiting for a season or less and then moving on. Those who did settle for more than a matter of months still spent time travelling abroad, allowing visiting artists the opportunity to use vacant accommodation and studios while holidaying in the village. At least 120 artists are known to have worked in Newlyn at some point between 1880 and 1900, but of these only around a quarter stayed for a sufficiently significant length of time to be considered true members of the 'School'.[4]

The term 'Newlyn School' began as a definition of the colony in the 1880s and 1890s: artists who shared a degree of unity of vision and a broadly similar approach to painting. The School was unified in striving for a high degree of naturalism, attempting to record, in a meaningful way, the realities of life around them. This was combined with a painterly concern to capture the effects of natural and/or artificial light, inspired by the French *plein-air* painters.

Of twenty of the core Newlyn artists, eleven had studied in Paris, ten had studied as well, or alternatively, at Antwerp, and all but one had spent at least some of their earlier career in continental Europe.[5] They were all, seemingly, united in their admiration for the champion of French *plein-air* Naturalism, Jules Bastien-Lepage, and they self-consciously embraced his influence. Citing the inspiration of the Barbizon School and of the 'genius Jean-Francois Millet', as well as their, then living, hero

Lepage, Stanhope Forbes later recounted that he and his fellow artists had forsaken their studios 'to set up our easels in country districts, where we could pose our models and attack our work, in sunshine or in shadow, under the open sky'.[6]

For a time, the School was also characterized by the use of the 'square brush technique', also derived from Lepage: a method of laying oil paint onto canvas using a flat, square brush, giving the paint surface a subtle vibrancy. Paintings seen today as being almost too 'safe' and overly representational were derided in their day for the 'unfinished' look this technique gave to the paint surface. The novelist Charles Lee, resident in Newlyn in the 1890s, seems to have captured the voices of the local populace in his novel, *Cynthia in the West*, where one character, Sampy, expresses his disgust for such work: 'when they'm done, these pickshers edn' much account, to my mind … Come close and 'tedn' no pickshe 'tall – 'tis nothing but a mask av onreasonable paint'.[7] Descendants of models and local tradesmen relate tales of their forebears being offered gifts of paintings, which were rejected (to the considerable chagrin of the present generation, keenly aware of their current market value) because they were so alien to the tastes of the day.

It was not just unsophisticated Newlyn locals who rejected this style of painting; many contemporary critics also disparaged the work for its 'consistent squareness of touch', which they considered to be a sign of unwelcome French influence.[8] Stanhope Forbes' *Fish Sale on a Cornish Beach*, which was to be a signature painting for the Newlyn School, was considered for acquisition for the nation by the Chantrey Bequest, but rejected as 'too positively the outcome of a foreign school'.[9]

Relations between the artists in Newlyn and those in nearby St. Ives were cordial, united in friendly rivalry through the artists' cricket matches, but each settlement had an ethos all its own. Stanhope Forbes commented that the two colonies, despite being 'so close together, are yet so distinct in character and diverse in their aim. It is curious how a few miles can affect the style of a body of workers.'[10] Alice Meynell wrote in 1889, 'Seeing that some Newlyners abide at St Ives and some at Lelant and that one dwells in a boat off Falmouth, their nickname is assuredly given to them in the acknowledgement of something they have in common'.[11] Elizabeth Armstrong, who, as Elizabeth Forbes, was ultimately hailed as 'the Queen of Newlyn', initially preferred St. Ives,[12] and Percy Craft, very much a Newlyner, also spent time living in the rival town and executed some of his best known works there. Artists such as William Holt Yates Titcomb (St. Ives) and Marianne Stokes (Lelant), generally overlooked as members of the Newlyn School, seem to have shared the Newlyn School rationale and may be among those to whom Meynell referred.[13]

Although the ripples spread to encompass artists elsewhere, Newlyn was the essential hub for the School, and the identity of its founder – manifested as the first to find the village – is still contested. According to an anonymous 'early settler', writing in the *Magazine of Art* in 1898, 'It was Birmingham that first discovered Newlyn', meaning that Edwin Harris and Walter Langley – both former students of Birmingham School of Art – were first to arrive. Following Harris and Langley, the writer asserts that 'Todd, Suthers, Hall, Bramley, Gotch, Craft and Forbes arrived next, followed by Detmold and Tayler, then Elizabeth Armstrong, Bourdillon, and finally Fortescue and Garstin'.[14]

This chronology is somewhat misleading: many other artists had 'discovered' Newlyn long before this generation arrived. Even within the accepted boundaries of the Newlyn School, it is questionable whether Birmingham can truly be credited with providing the colony's pioneers. Slade student Caroline Burland Yates was certainly one of the earliest

Fig.13
Walter Langley, *Disaster – Scene in a Cornish Fishing Village*, 1889, watercolour, Birmingham Museums and Art Gallery

arrivals. She wrote enthusiastically to her future husband, Thomas Cooper Gotch, in August 1879:

> I never was anywhere I liked so much as here and there is no end of work to be done … If I ask the men or women to stand for a minute they are always quite willing to do so, and afterwards will tell you what they think of your work. But I could not possibly give you an adequate idea of all the delights of Newlyn, so you must judge when you come.[15]

Hence, both Gotch and his close friend Henry Scott Tuke visited Caroline Yates in Newlyn that year, the year before Walter Langley's first chronicled visit,[16] and although the couple did not settle in the village for another three years, Thomas and Caroline married at St. Peter's Church, Newlyn, in 1881.

Regardless of who first 'discovered' it, to any artist striving for rural realism and enchanted by the small fishing villages of Brittany, Newlyn must have seemed almost too good to be true. Here was a village relatively untouched by the Industrial Revolution and 'reeking with subjects',[17] with cheaply available accommodation and willing models. Both geographically and in ambience, this part of Cornwall is closer to Brittany than to London yet, thanks to the introduction of the railway to Penzance in the 1850s, it offered direct and easy access to the capital.

Langley was certainly the first member of what is recognized as the Newlyn School to take up permanent residence in the village, in 1882. Ironically, he took over Pembroke Lodge from another painter, Charles Durdin, who had even built a studio there, but Durdin's links with the School stop with this accident of shared location.[18] Walter Langley differed from most of his fellow Newlyners in two key respects: his background was significantly poorer than theirs, and for much of his career his chosen medium was watercolour, not oil paint. Having grown up with poverty and, by 1880, with a wife and growing family of his own, Langley's chief motivation for settling in Newlyn was money.[19] On the strength of work produced on visits to Cornwall in 1880 and 1881, he had received a commission to paint similar pictures from a Birmingham dealer who offered him £500 for a year's work.

Economics may also have been a factor in his choice of watercolour, as there was an available market for work in this medium. But it was far from being an obvious choice at a time when being shown at the Royal Academy was the zenith of most artists' ambition, and when that institution treated watercolours with little short of disdain. Clearly, he also felt that

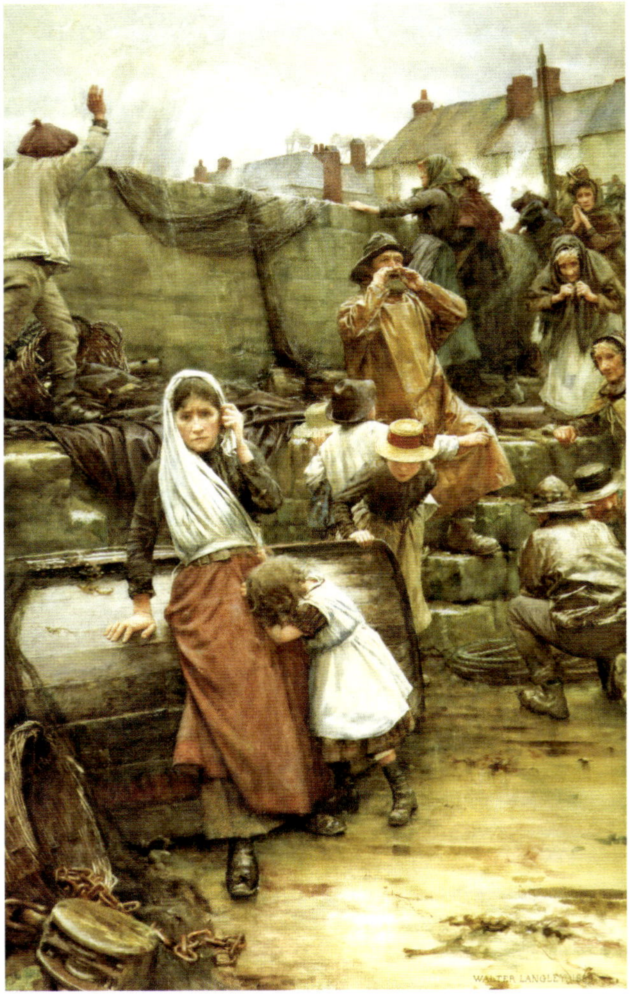

Fig.14
Walter Langley, *Among the Missing – Scene in a Cornish Fishing Village*, 1884, watercolour, Penlee House Gallery and Museum, Penzance

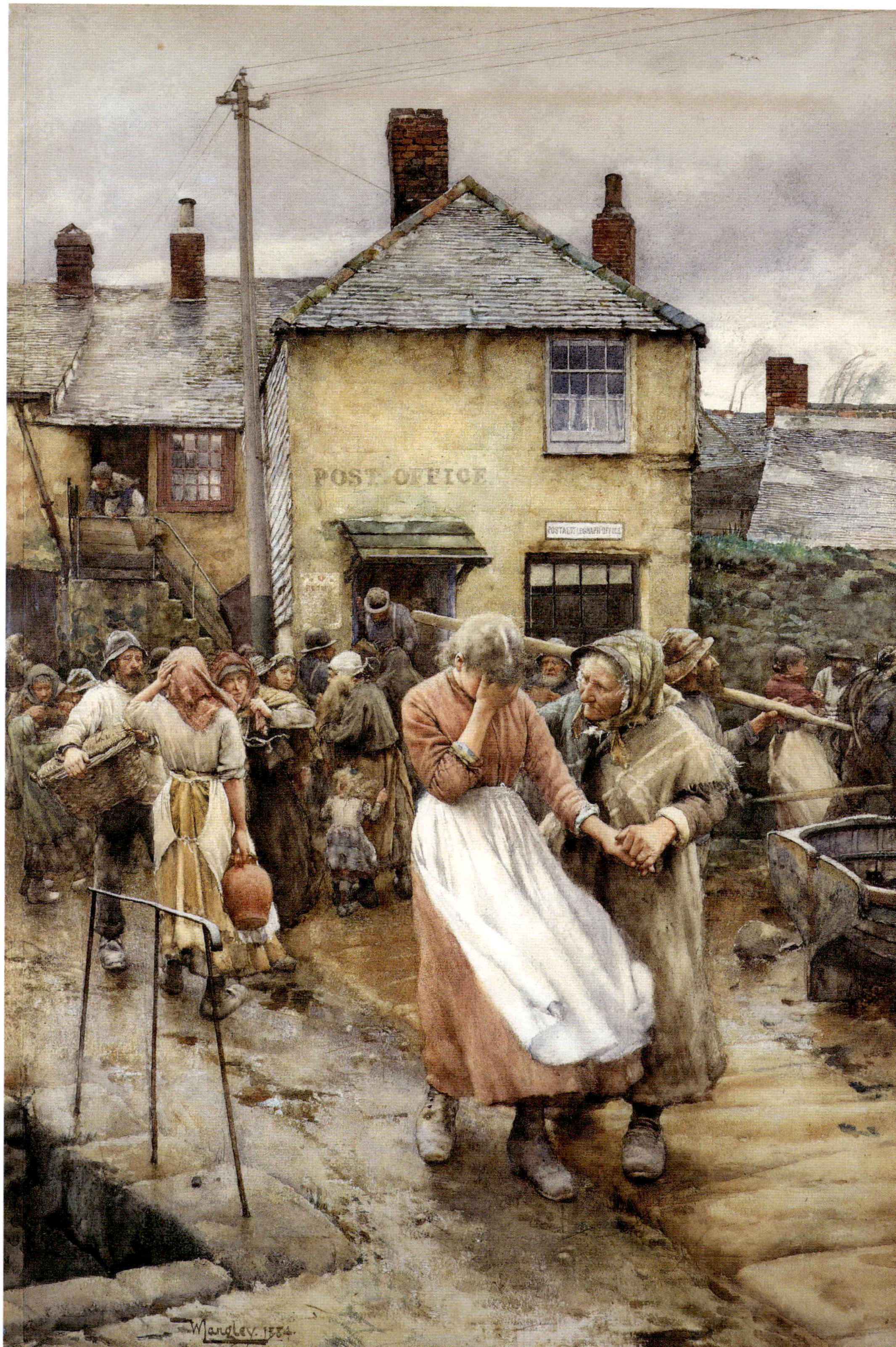

Fig.15
Frank Bramley, *A Hopeless Dawn*, 1888, oil on canvas
© Tate, London 2005

watercolour was his forte: fellow Birmingham Newlyner, William Wainwright, explained it was 'a distinct choice formed by personal preference and artistic conviction that for him it was the medium in which he could reach his highest expression'.[20]

Certainly watercolour brought both artistic and financial success to Langley. His mastery of the medium enabled him to capture the expressions and emotions of his subjects. A *Birmingham Post* art critic, writing in 1886, summed up the quality of his work as showing 'marvellous execution, admirable drawing, fine colour and powerful yet tenderly felt sentiment.' Even today, Langley's work has the power to move the viewer to tears, still 'awakening in the hearts of all who view his pictures, responsive echoes to the calls and needs of brothers and sisters in the humbler walks of life'.[21] Langley's technical skill is matched by his obvious empathy with his subjects: he was moved by the plight of the fishermen and their families and sought to tell their stories (see fig.13). Even in good times, fishermen would only earn around £1 a week to support their families; when times were bad, there was nothing but charity to fall back on, and the loss of a family's breadwinner was, simply, disaster.[22]

Langley's paintings of 1882 and 1883, most notably *But men must work and women must weep*, had earned him the respect of his peers, but the first individual work to bring tangible success was *Among the Missing* (fig.14), painted in 1884. Loosely based on the post office in the Fradgan area of Newlyn, this shows villagers' reactions

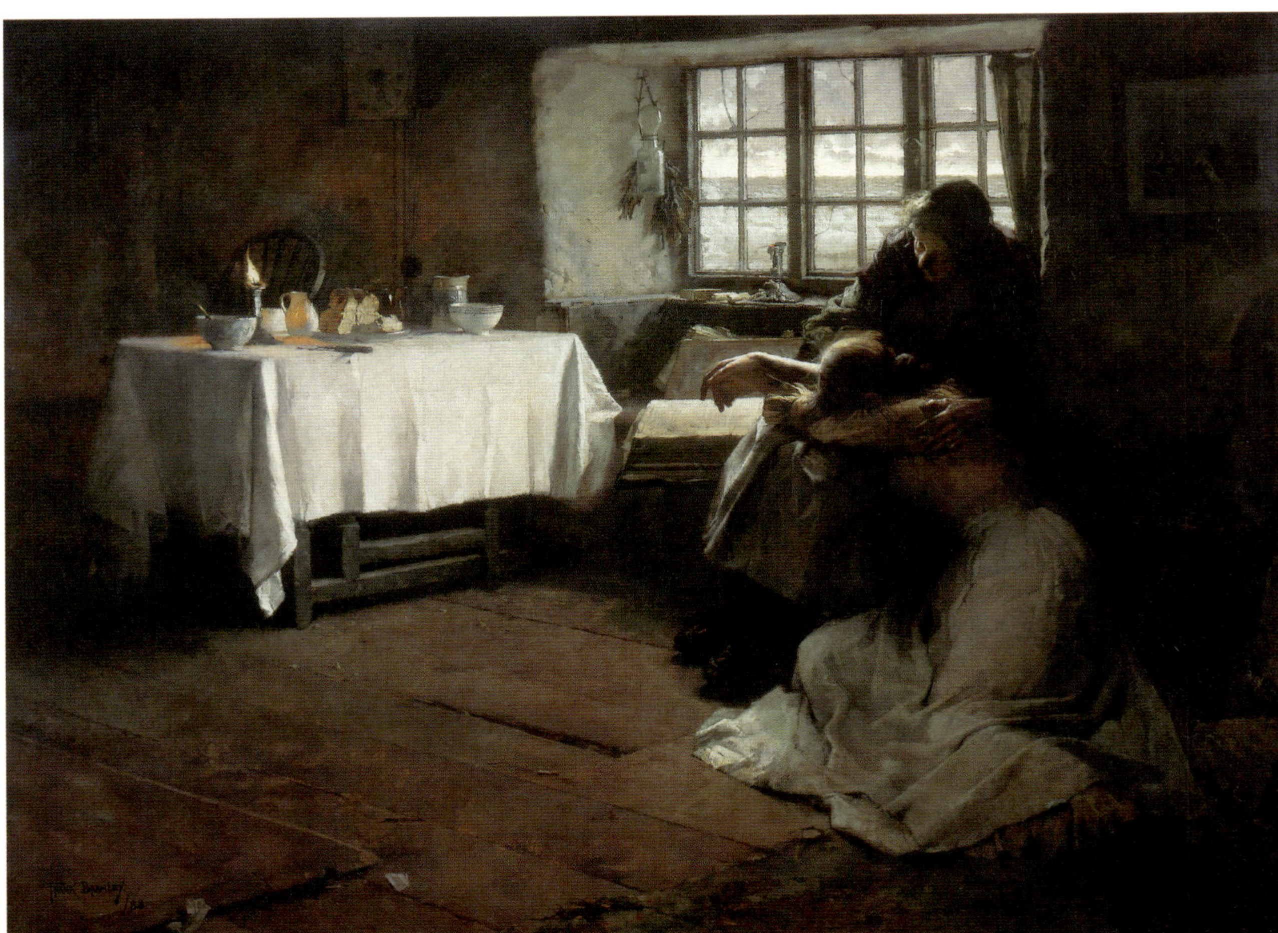

'A Hopeless Drunk and a Hopeful Dawn', menu card from a meal celebrating the sale of Bramley's painting to the Chantrey Bequest. Newlyn Artists Photograph Album, 1880s, Penlee House Gallery and Museum and Cornwall Studies Centre, Redruth

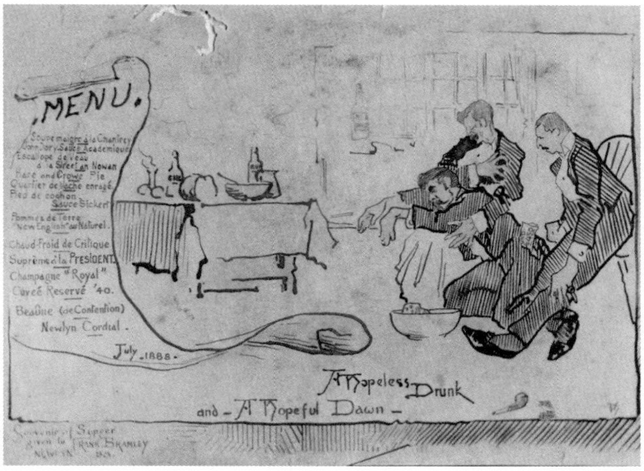

to a telegram, posted to the wall, informing them of the loss of one of the fishing fleet, naming the boat and listing the fishermen who were missing. Shown at the Royal Institute of Painters in Watercolour, it received fulsome praise in the *Magazine of Art*, which heralded it as his most important work to date.[23] Certainly it was the most lucrative, selling to a Manchester businessman for £420, four times Langley's previous highest price.

The same year, the colony gained some of its most important residents, including Fred Hall, Frank Bramley (see fig.15), Leghe Suthers, Albert Chevallier Tayler and Stanhope Forbes. As has often been recounted, Forbes considered other Cornish villages before discovering that Newlyn offered everything he had been searching for. In 1913, he recalled, 'Here every corner was a picture and more important from the view of the figure painter, the people seemed to fall naturally into their places and to harmonise with the surroundings.'[24]

Forbes and Langley came from radically different backgrounds, and it is hardly surprising that they did not immediately take to one another. Stanhope Forbes, the son of railway manager William Forbes and his French wife Juliette (née de Guise), had enjoyed a privileged art education from an early age, completed with private tuition on the continent.[25] It was understandable if Langley was 'coldly friendly' to this potential competitor on his arrival.

Instead of detracting from Langley's standing, however, Stanhope Forbes was to prove a vital addition to the colony. Forbes had already received some acclaim for *A Street in Brittany* when it was shown at the Royal Academy in 1882, but it was his 1885 exhibit, *Fish Sale on a Cornish Beach*, one of his earliest paintings in the village, that proved to be a landmark for him and the colony (fig.16). Looking back some sixteen years later, Norman Garstin wrote that 'The fresh vitality of it seemed like a wholesome breeze from the sea breathed in a studio reeking with oil and turpentine while its brilliant new technique fell upon the younger painters as a revelation. Then the Newlyn artists came to be a name'. Even in 1901, Garstin felt that *Fish Sale*'s 'sterling qualities' were still key to Forbes' work and influence: his 'keen observation, and vehement concentration, an artistic conscience always making for truth, an unerring eye, and a powerful grasp of the essentials; these remain, and leave their mark year by year on the art of England and the world.'[26]

Fish Sale on a Cornish Beach epitomizes Forbes' determination to achieve *plein-air* realism, whatever the circumstances. The idea for the painting came to him almost as soon as he arrived in Newlyn, but it took nearly six months to complete. Looking back, Forbes said he shuddered 'at the recollection of what I endured fighting with the east wind before a large canvas on the sloppy beach between Newlyn and Penzance'.[27] Right at the start, in June 1884, he foresaw the difficulties, writing to his mother that 'painting out of doors in England is no joke and this picture will be a long, weary job'. By December, the problems were all too obvious: 'I sallied forth to have another go at the large picture. I got blown about and rained upon, my model fainted etc.' Only a fanatical advocate of *plein-air* painting would have stuck so fast to his principles.

While Forbes was battling the elements on Newlyn beach, the artists' colony was growing around him. In

Fig.16
Stanhope Forbes, *Fish Sale on a Cornish Beach*, 1885
oil on canvas, Plymouth City Museum and Art Gallery

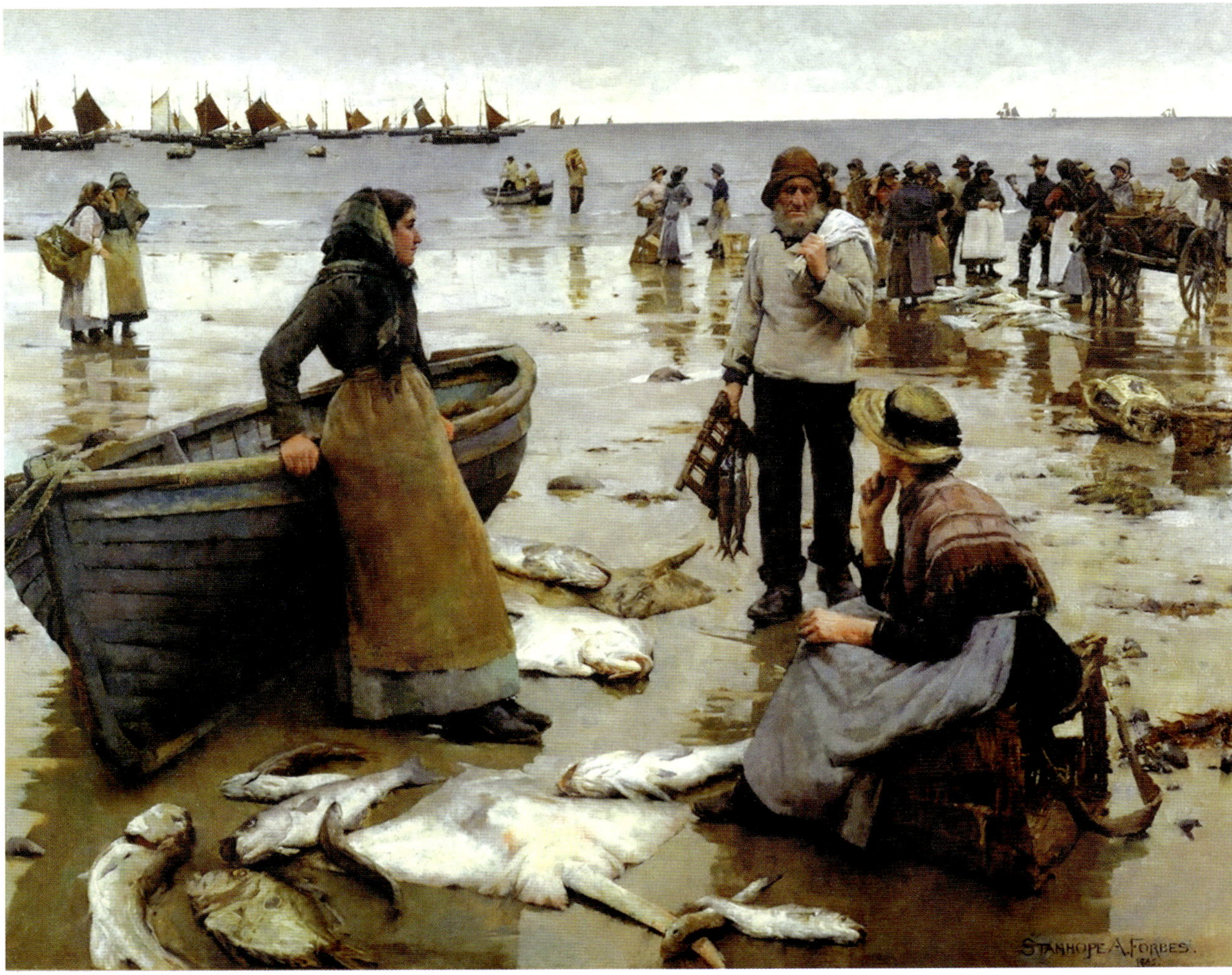

September 1884, the *Cornishman* reported that there were twenty-seven artists residing in Newlyn and the critical acclaim of *Fish Sale* added to the momentum. Existing friendships, built at shared training or sketching grounds, were cemented and new ones formed: the colony Forbes had described on his arrival as 'unsympathetic' had developed a real sense of camaraderie. The frosty start to Forbes' relationship with Langley had begun to thaw, and although some artists kept themselves aloof, social gatherings became part of life in the village, with theatrical performances and concerts.

It was at one such social event, hosted by Edwin Harris and his wife in November 1885, that Forbes met his future wife.[28] Elizabeth Adela Armstrong was a Canadian artist a couple of years younger than Forbes, who, having started her art education in London in her early teens, had a wealth of training and continental travel behind her. She had been in Brittany, but although she met Edwin Harris, she heard about, but did not meet, Forbes, who was only about ten miles away in Quimperlé while she was in Pont-Aven. By the time she arrived in Newlyn she had exhibited and sold works in London (including at the Royal Academy), and paintings like *Boy with a Hoe* (1883) and *Zandvoort Fishergirl* (1884) attest to her mastery of naturalist painting at that stage.

Elizabeth's training and artistic friendships were more

Unknown event: left to right Craft, Millard, Forbes, unknown, Tayler, Garstin; Elizabeth Forbes and her mother in front.
Newlyn Artists Photograph Album, 1880s, Penlee House Gallery and Museum and Cornwall Studies Centre, Redruth

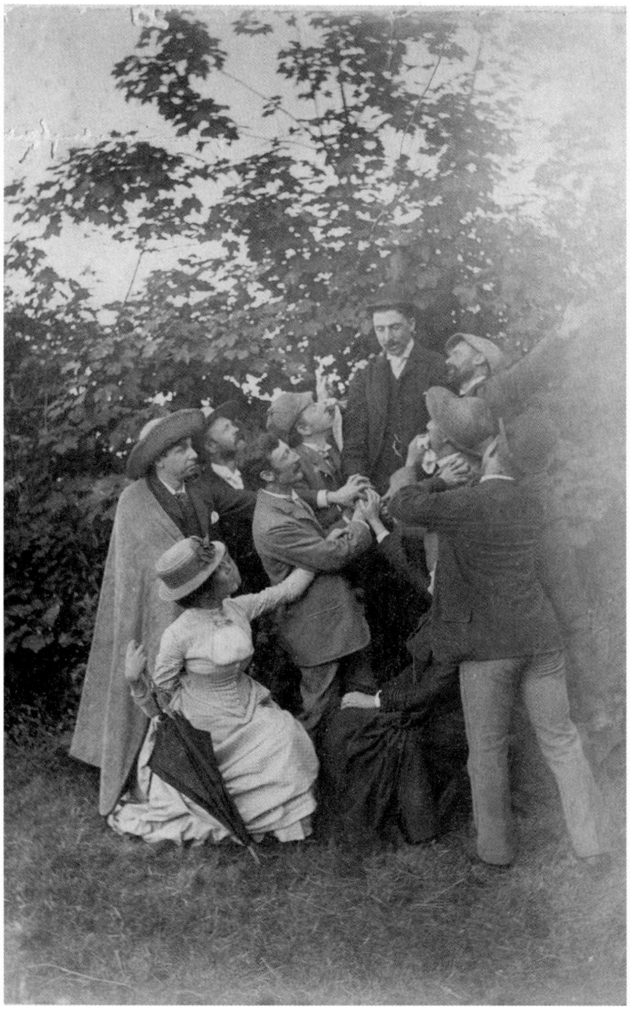

eclectic than Stanhope's. While she admired and emulated the French Rural Naturalists, she also admired and had been befriended by James McNeill Whistler, an artist and, by reputation, a man Stanhope loathed. One of Whistler's protégés, Mortimer Menpes, had taught her etching in Pont-Aven in 1882. Although she loved and excelled in the medium, she gave up etching after her marriage. It has always been assumed that this was because her husband disapproved; she cited practical difficulties, which is plausible, but certainly Stanhope strongly discouraged her from keeping up with Whistler himself.[29] During their long engagement, she largely split her time between London and St. Ives which, with its more cosmopolitan mix of artists, she originally preferred to Newlyn. When they finally married in 1889 she seems to have fast adapted to Newlyn society and became a central figure.

Elizabeth's work had to be sufficiently in keeping with the Newlyn principles not to upset Stanhope, now hailed as 'the father of the Newlyn School', while being different enough from his work not to be in direct competition. Fortunately, she had already found her niche, painting young people and, especially, children. *School is Out*, exhibited at the Royal Academy the year of their marriage, demonstrates her mastery of the square brush technique, capturing light and atmosphere, while choosing a subject unique to herself. During their marriage, Elizabeth's style changed often as she continued to be influenced by what was happening in London and in Europe as much as by her husband, but although she

Fig.17
William Banks Fortescue, *The Fish Fag*
Atkinson Art Gallery, Southport, Sefton MBC
Leisure Services Department

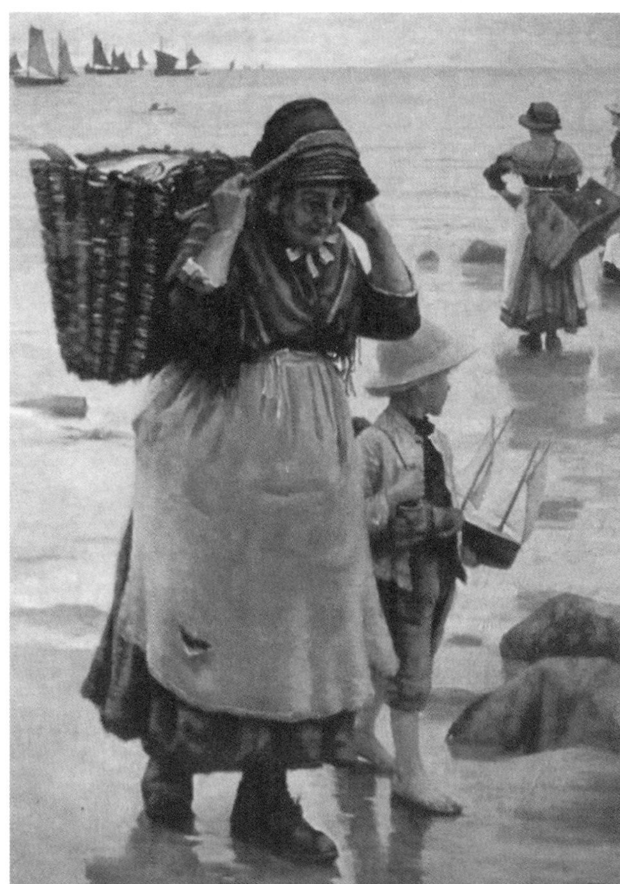

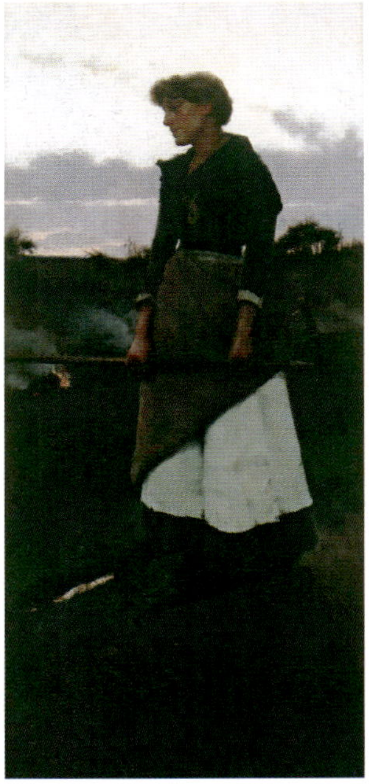

Fig.18
Fred Hall, *In the Fields*, 1886, oil on canvas (related to the artist's *Home from the Fields*), Penlee House Gallery and Museum, Penzance © Artist's Estate / Bridgeman Art Library

sometimes employed medieval-style costume (in the illustrations for her children's book, *King Arthur's Wood*, and paintings like *A Dream Princess*, for example), her subjects remain largely unchanged: children and young women, usually outdoors, but with trees and fields, not the sea, as a backdrop.

While Elizabeth was painting the children and their teacher at Paul School, Stanhope was also working on interior group paintings; *The Village Philharmonic* (1888) and then *The Health of the Bride* of 1889 (see page 17). The sale of the latter painting to Sir Henry Tate for £600 seems to have enabled the couple to marry, perhaps because of the financial independence it brought, or possibly because it proved to Stanhope's mother that, despite her qualms, Elizabeth was not having a detrimental effect on her son's work.

During the couple's three-year engagement, the Newlyn colony had grown in strength and enjoyed the most artistically unified period of its history. Many more artists had come to the village, including Thomas Cooper Gotch, William Banks Fortescue (see fig.17), Norman Garstin, Frank Wright Bourdillon, Frank Bodilly, Percy Craft, Henry Detmold and Frederick McNamara Evans. Taking 1886 as a sample year, the strength and breadth of works is telling. Albert Chevallier Tayler painted his superb *Not Lost but Gone Before*, depicting a widower and his daughter in a churchyard, whilst Fred Hall painted one of his best known Newlyn works, *Home from the Fields* which, like Tayler's picture, depicts the rural rather than seagoing community (fig.18).

Forbes stuck to his fishing theme with the magnificent *Off to the Fishing Ground* of 1885, but also turned inland with *Their Ever Shifting Home*, showing a gypsy family and their vardo. Henry Scott Tuke, based in Falmouth but still – then and now – counted as a Newlyner,

Fig.19
Walter Langley, *Departure of the Fleet for the North*, 1886 watercolour, Penlee House Gallery and Museum, Penzance

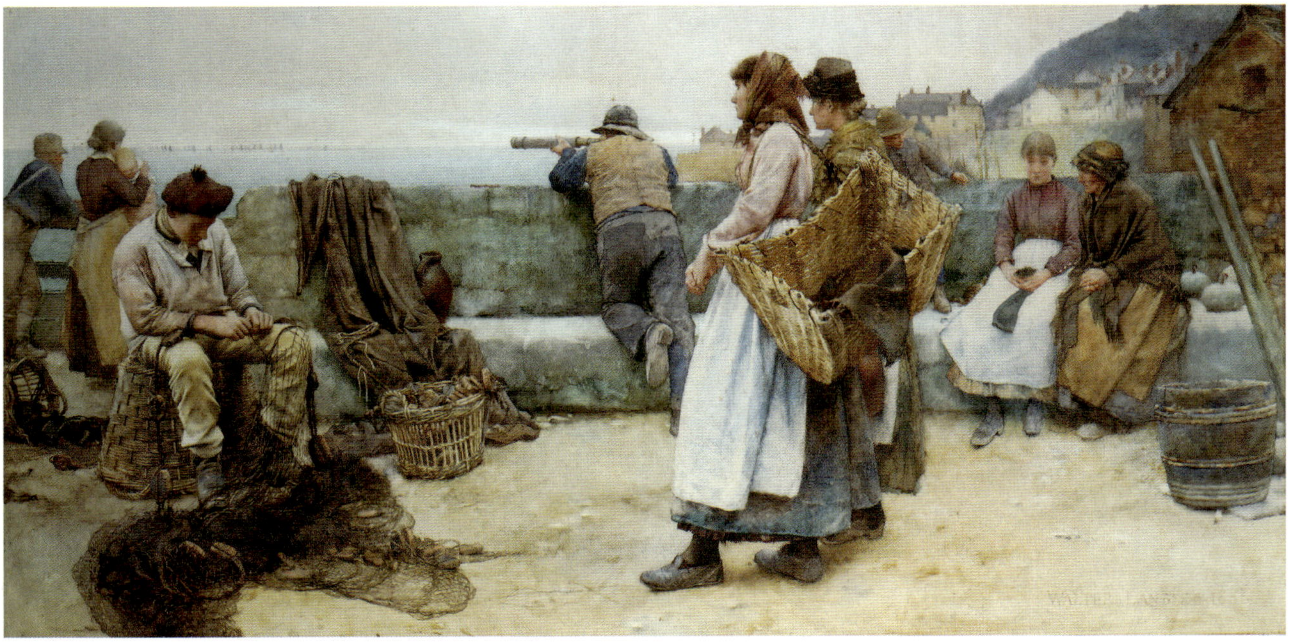

Fig.20
Walter Langley, *The Sunny South*, 1885, oil on canvas
Penlee House Gallery and Museum, Penzance

Stanhope Forbes painting *Their Ever Shifting Home*, 1887
Newlyn Artists Photograph Album, 1880s, Penlee House Gallery & Museum and Cornwall Studies Centre, Redruth

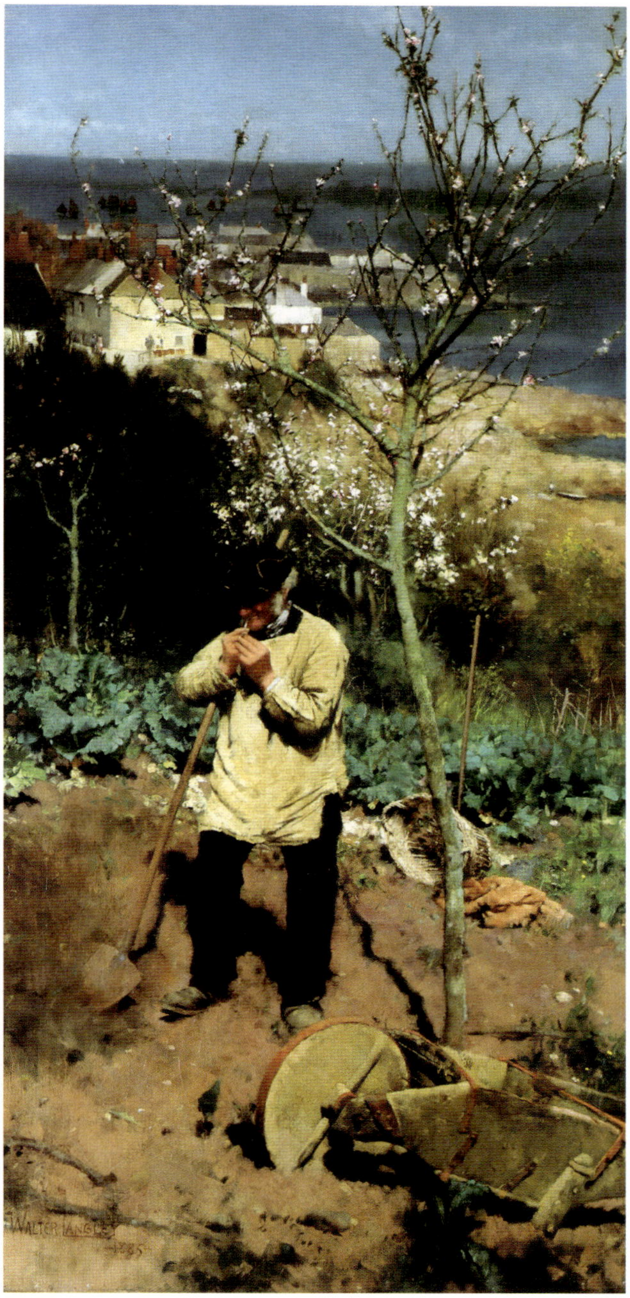

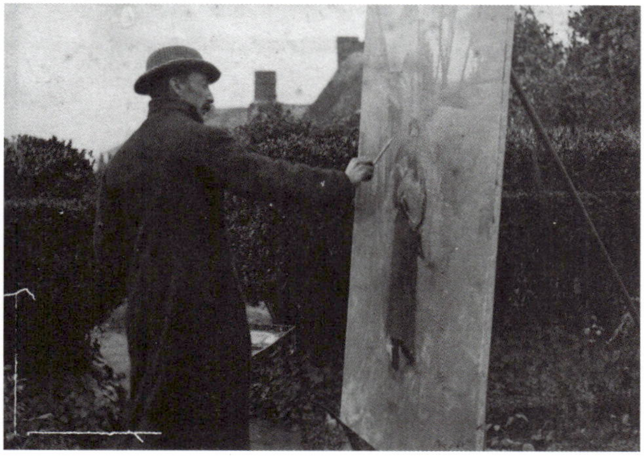

painted *Our Jack*, a lively, square-brush portrait of a young lad set against the backdrop of Falmouth harbour. Leghe Suthers, who is something of a mystery figure (and whose real name, according to George Bednar, was John Lees Suthers) produced the light-hearted *Dame Trimmer*, which may or may not be a Newlyn picture, but is painted very much in the Newlyn style.[30] Langley, who left the village that year (returning in 1887), exhibited his large watercolour, *Departure of the Fleet for the North*, at the Royal Institute of Painters in Water Colours (fig.19). The previous year he had exhibited a major oil painting (his second significant work in that medium, which he later worked in occasionally), *The Sunny South*, a bright, lively picture of his Newlyn neighbour working in the garden (fig.20).

Meanwhile, also in 1886, Forbes, Gotch, Tuke and two Newlyn visitors, Fred Brown and William Blandford Fletcher, were among the fifteen artists who, feeling that the Royal Academy was unreceptive to their style of work, met in London to discuss setting up an alternative venue in which to exhibit.[31] This was the initial meeting of what was to become the New English Art Club, which several Newlyn artists were to join, albeit briefly, as the club went through its turbulent formative years. The NEAC seems to have helped to gain increased acceptance for the Newlyners' work among the art establishment.

The Newlyn School was gaining in critical acclaim and its reputation was reinforced by one key picture, Frank Bramley's *A Hopeless Dawn* of 1888 (page 32). As Alice Meynell wrote in the *Art Journal* of 1889, it is 'a perfect blend of simple but profound human drama and of beautifully executed and very carefully observed effects of light and of colour and tone.'[32] Like Langley's

Left to right standing: Garstin, unknown, Millard, Elizabeth and Stanhope Forbes. Seated: Unknown, Craft, Tayler, Bourdillon. Newlyn Artists Photograph Album, 1880s, Penlee House Gallery & Museum and Cornwall Studies Centre, Redruth

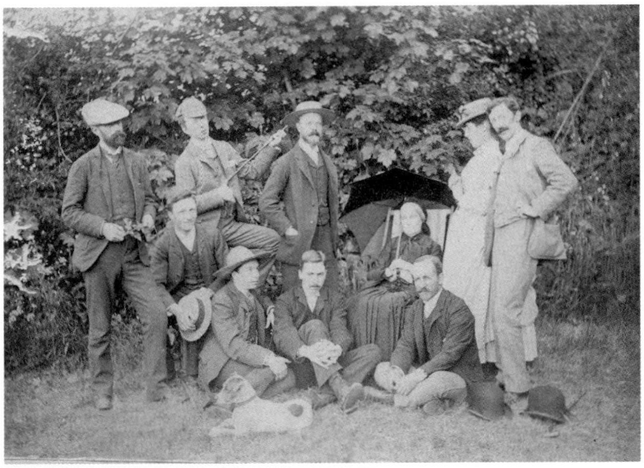

A cricket match: the Newlyn artists played an annual match against St. Ives. Newlyn Artists Photograph Album, 1880s, Penlee House Gallery and Museum and Cornwall Studies Centre, Redruth

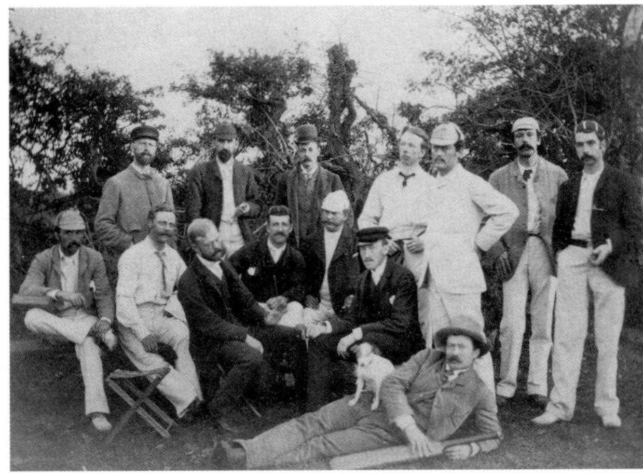

Among the Missing, the power of Bramley's painting lies in its combination of consummate painterly technique and heartrendingly empathetic depiction of its subject. It is clear from the seaweed and glass jar hanging at the window, both rudimentary barometers, that this is a fisherman's home, and the guttering candles and creeping dawn light, illuminating a stormy sea, hint at a night of anguish.

While Bramley records such details with meticulous accuracy, he also employs conscious religious symbolism, giving the lie to the notion that Newlyn School works adhered to strict Naturalism alone. Studies for this painting show that he began by making the fisherman's table, laid out with his uneaten supper, a more obvious echo of an altar table, and the young wife (or widow) originally had her hands raised in supplication. For the fishing community of Newlyn, Christian faith was a key part of their lives; most were Methodists and strict sabbatarians, refusing to fish and barring visiting artists from painting on a Sunday. In the final version, Bramley still alludes to the comfort they sustained from this faith in the form of the open bible and the religious print, but the young woman's slumped posture is much more poignant.[33] *A Hopeless Dawn* met with overwhelming acclaim when it was shown at the Royal Academy and it was purchased there and then by the Chantrey Bequest. The purchase of a Newlyn picture for the nation, as well as the success of a friend and colleague, was cause for celebration and a party was held in Bramley's honour at the Gotches' home.[34]

By 1889 the Newlyn School was at its peak: Alice Meynell's *Art Journal* article that year was the first of many extensive accounts of the colony and the term Newlyn School was thereafter in regular use among artists and critics. The article included fourteen illustrations, eleven by artists named in the article's list of arrivals: Stanhope and Elizabeth Forbes, Bramley, Tayler, Gotch, Hall, Langley, Detmold, Garstin, Craft and Bourdillon, and three by other artists, Benjamin Arthur Bateman (who had arrived in 1885), Frederick Millard (who is featured in a group photograph of 1884) and Henry Scott Tuke, to whom Meynell was referring when she said that 'one [of the Newlyners] dwells in a boat off Falmouth'. Her account was intelligent and enthusiastic, giving an overview of the colony's development and bringing it into popular consciousness.

But just as it was being defined and lauded, the colony was changing. Bateman, who although a more than competent painter made little mark on the colony as an artist, was to make a huge impact by purchasing an area of meadowland in the village, on which he built artists' studios. These consisted of large areas

Fig.21
Norman Garstin, *The Rain it Raineth Every Day*, 1889, oil on canvas
Penlee House Gallery and Museum, Penzance

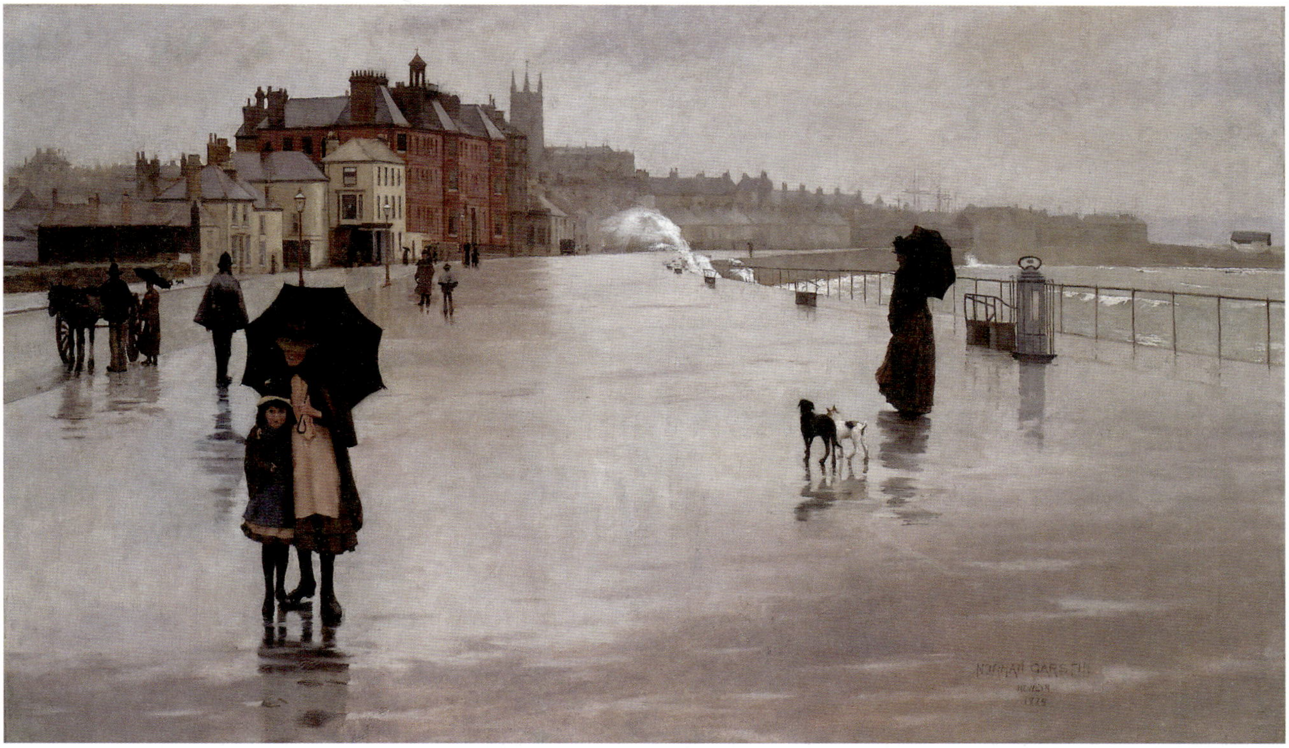

of glass, since the artists wanted to retain the *plein-air* principle of painting in direct natural light, but west Cornwall's damp and windy climate had driven them to take shelter. It was in this meadow, jokingly known as 'California', that the artists began to hold preview exhibitions of work they were sending to the Royal Academy. Forbes and Craft had habitually offered friends, colleagues and models the chance to see their Academy-bound paintings in the studio, but the meadow turned this into a huge social event, where crowds of locals would view paintings by many of the artists.

The meadow proved a huge boon to some painters, enabling them to escape from the confined spaces of disused net lofts with their 'odours of the promiscuous pilchard' and to work in comfort.[35] At least one (possibly Langley) was less impressed, however, describing Bateman as a 'speculative builder' and complaining that development of the meadow attracted the wrong types of people: 'Swells came down for a holiday and called themselves 'Artists', took all the available lodgings and almost crowded the workers out'.[36]

Around this time, the focus of many of the artists began to change. Although Forbes and Langley stuck fast to their rural naturalist vision throughout their careers, others began to take different directions. Feeling he could add nothing to a genre others were covering so well, Frank Wright Bourdillon turned to historic costume painting, commencing with the impressive *On Bideford Sands* of 1889. Fred Hall, an accomplished cartoonist who famously captured most of his fellow painters in witty caricatures, began to introduce humour into his oil paintings, producing works such as *The Result of High Living* (1892). Norman Garstin embraced the *plein-air* principles, but while aspects of *The Rain it Raineth Every Day* (1889, fig.21) recall the gleaming wet sands of Forbes' *Fish Sale*, his work also has something of a Whistlerian influence and reflects his interest in Japanese prints.

A painting class in The Meadow; a group of students with 'The Professor', Stanhope Forbes. Cicely Jesse's Photograph Album, Penlee House Gallery and Museum

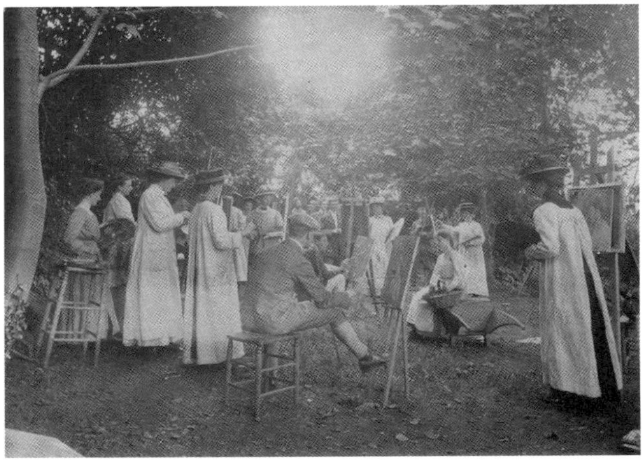

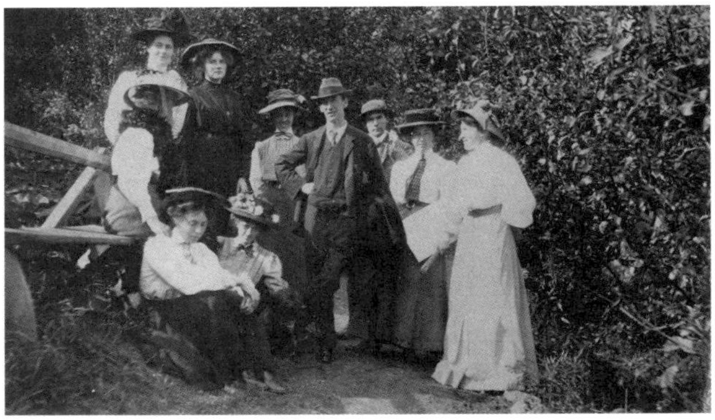

Meanwhile, also in 1889, Gotch and his painter wife, Carrie, were finding yet another source of inspiration by visiting the artists' colony at Skagen, at the northern tip of Denmark, where Gotch painted *The Story of the Money Pig*, more 'Skagen' than 'Newlyn' in style.

This pattern continued throughout the 1890s. Stanhope Forbes stuck resolutely to his principles and continued to paint *en plein-air*, gaining increasing establishment respect (marked by his being elected as a Royal Academician in 1892), but others wavered. The artistic divisions were heightened by another development, which should have been a unifying force. Forbes, Bramley, Langley and Gotch had persuaded the Cornish businessman and philanthropist John Passmore Edwards to fund the building of a gallery in which to exhibit their works. He agreed, and in 1895 the gallery opened its doors. Just as the building of studios had subtly changed the dynamic of the colony, the opening of the gallery seemed to have an equally detrimental effect. Many of the core artists drifted away and those who stayed were by no means unified in their artistic vision, as exemplified by Gotch, by now much more of a Symbolist than a Naturalist, as works such as *The Child in the World* (1895) demonstrate.

The village too had changed. The 1880s had seen the building of two new piers: the South Pier, with its lighthouse, was completed in 1886 and the North Pier, commenced in 1888, was finally 'opened' amid much celebration in 1894. The new piers may have made life significantly safer and easier for the fishermen, but they were less picturesque than the single, tiny, ancient harbour wall that predated them. Some artists continued to depict the harbour as it had been. Attitudes among the local population may have been changing too; no longer were the artists a novelty and in the 1891 census, 84-year-old widow, Elizabeth (Betsy) Lanyon gave her occupation not as 'fishwife' but as 'artist's model'. That census records that there were sixteen artists and two art students in Newlyn, a significant down-turn from the twenty-seven the *Cornishman* had reported seven years earlier.[37]

By the early 1890s Stanhope Forbes had somehow assumed the title – reluctantly at first – of 'father' of the Newlyn School, and in that role it was natural that he should worry over the decline of the colony. Towards the end of the decade, he and Elizabeth returned from a holiday in the Low Pyrenees fired up with a plan to set up a School of Painting, to bring new blood into the community and to continue the ethos of *plein-air* painting.[38] They were not the first to turn to teaching, as Norman Garstin was already supplementing his meagre income from picture sales by taking pupils, most notably the young Penzance-born painter, Harold Harvey. Once again, Forbes was doing for the sake of art what a fellow artist was doing to survive.

Fig.22
Doris 'Dod' Procter (née Shaw), *Early Morning, Newlyn*
oil on canvas, Glynn Vivian Art Gallery © Artist's Estate / Bridgeman Art Library

Their 'Newlyn School of Painting' opened in October 1899 in the studios in the meadow. Although some contemporary records call it the 'Stanhope Forbes School of Painting', it was from the outset very much a partnership. Stanhope soon earned the epithet 'Professor', but Elizabeth's role was just as important. It was she who posed the model at the start of the week and took part in 'crits' – giving feedback and guidance on work, and as many of the students were young women travelling away from home for the first time, she vetted accommodation and saw to the practicalities of their stay. When Elizabeth died prematurely at 52 in 1912, the School continued, with a former pupil, Maud Palmer, taking over the role of helpmate to Stanhope, first in the School and then by becoming his second wife.

The School ran for just over forty years, attracting some important artists to the village. No register of students has been traced, and although nearly two hundred students have been documented,[39] this may be as little as a quarter of the total.[40] One of the earliest arrivals was Frank Gascoigne Heath, 'the sunshine painter', who went on to settle in Lamorna; his future wife, Jessica Doherty,

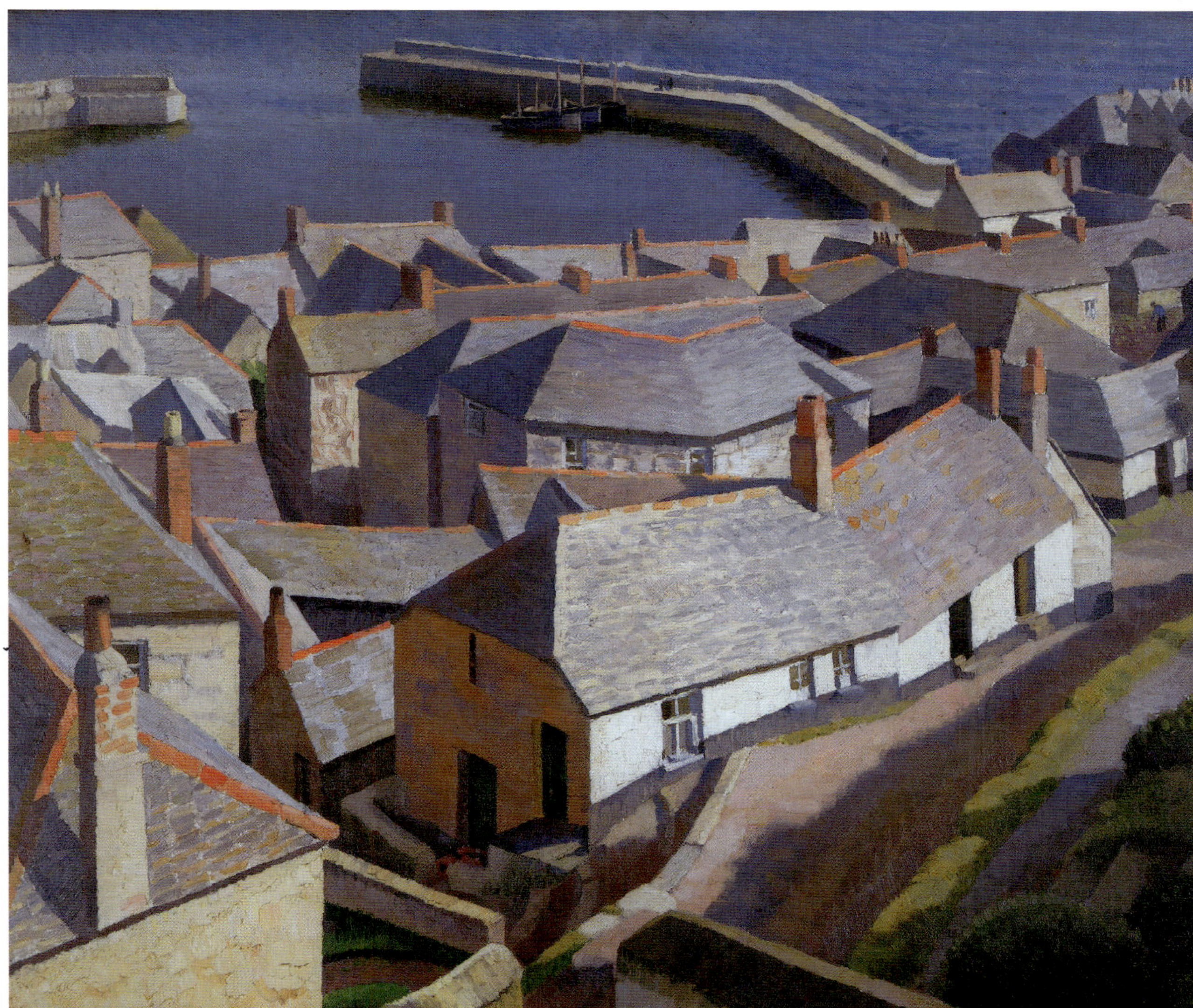

was a fellow pupil. Several students stayed in the area, some remaining in Penzance and others, like Heath, joining the growing colony a few miles along the coast at Lamorna. Those who remained in Cornwall included Robert Morson Hughes and Eleanor Hughes (née Waymouth), Geoffrey and Jill Garnier (née Blyth), Ruth Alison, Edith Florence Munnings (née Carter-Wood), Dorcie Sykes and Marjorie 'Midge' Bruford.

The most celebrated pupils of the Forbes school were Ernest Procter and his future wife, Doris 'Dod' Shaw. Ernest arrived in 1906 and Dod, along with her mother and brother who also attended the School, arrived in 1907 (when she was only 15). Best known for her figure paintings, especially *Morning* (1926) – purchased for the nation by the *Daily Mail*, Dod showed her love for the village by depicting it in a rare landscape, *Early Morning Newlyn* (fig.22), the same year; she remained in the village most of her life, dying there in 1972. Surprising other inclusions are Arthur Lett Haines, partner of the painter Cedric Morris, who must have attended the School while they were both staying in the area in 1918, and the St. Ives Modernist John Wells, who studied with Forbes for a month in 1928 and returned to spend most of his painting career (which did not begin until 1945) in Forbes' old studio.

Forbes was loved and respected by his students, and despite holding fast to his original principles in his own work, he seems to have been open to innovation in the work of his pupils. An article about the School appeared in the Christmas 1911 edition of the *Art Journal*, which records his enthusiasm:

> Many painters loathe teaching: Mr Forbes enjoys it. He finds stimulation in the contact with young minds; he likes to watch immature work growing mature; he is sympathetic, and I am sure that ... he approaches his teaching work as a joy ... not a duty. He warms, he does not numb effort; he lingers in the class-rooms as if he were a paternal older student, but the days that this apostle of plein-air painting (who has never gone back on his conviction that plein-air painting is the right way of painting) likes best are the fine days when the students pitch their easels in a glade of the Meadow, shaded and sheltered by overhanging trees.[41]

Forbes' vibrant art school re-energized the colony. Artists already established in their careers were attracted by the artistic and intellectual camaraderie it offered as much as by the light and landscape. One such was Samuel John Birch, who was to settle a few miles away in the Lamorna valley (a place which became so synonymous with his life and art that he adopted it as his moniker), but who was also a central figure in the Newlyn colony, playing a lead role in supporting other artists and sustaining the Art Gallery.[42] Others were Harold and Laura Knight, who had previously spent time in Staithes and who would go on to be key members of the Lamorna colony, but who first settled in Newlyn. In her own way Laura Knight continued the *plein-air* tradition, and Harold's first painting in Newlyn, *A Village Wedding*, captures village life in a way that echoes the earlier painters. The Knights, Procters and Harveys – Harold and his wife Gertrude – were to strike up a close friendship which had a profound influence on Harvey's work in particular.

Having begun his career influenced by his tutor, Norman Garstin, and been through phases where his paintings emulate those of both Stanhope and Elizabeth Forbes, Harold Harvey now absorbed the influence – both in composition and in handling of paint – of all four of his new artist friends. Although he also developed his own vocabulary, individual works show clear echoes of Laura Knight and Dod Procter, and especially of the Dutch-interior inspired works of Harold Knight, to which can be attributed a whole series of 1920s works, such as *The Critics* of 1922. Ernest Procter was to effect a less discernible influence on Harvey's work, but these two struck up a particularly close bond, venturing into business together in 1920 to run an art school of their own. The school ran until at least 1928, but neither artist was a natural teacher and students recalled them spending very little time in the studio; it is perhaps telling that Harvey's own depiction of the school, *The Critics*, shows Gertrude Harvey and her friend Ella Naper, rather than either of the Principals of the school, assessing a student's work.

Meanwhile, the ripples of influence from the Forbes school continued to shape the artistic community of Newlyn. In 1912, one student, Kay Earle, travelled to London for an interview for a job as a designer with a Yorkshire textile manufacturer Alec Walker, and her enthusiastic account of life in the fishing village (as well as her own personal charms, one suspects) led him to follow her back to Cornwall that day. Both the village and the girl clearly lived up to expectations, for six years later he married Kay and in 1920 he set up the Cryséde factory in Newlyn. Neither the marriage nor the business were to last more than a decade (though Cryséde continued in St. Ives, where production had been transferred in 1926), but for a while Walker's stunning designs for silks and linens were skilfully block-printed in Newlyn and were exported from the village to Paris, America and Australia.

Cryséde was one of several tangible examples of how the artists created employment for locals. From the outset, the secondary income provided by artists to their sitters, and also to landladies and other suppliers, would have been a welcome boost – although fees for modelling were not high, and there are many local stories of artists 'forgetting' to pay promised pennies to child models. Another form of support had come in the 1890s, when a group of artists including Gotch, Bramley and Craft, with financial support from local benefactor T.B. Bolitho, set up the Newlyn Industrial Class, training young fishermen to produce repoussé copperware. The classes were led by J.D. MacKenzie, a painter who had arrived in the village in 1888, who provided the designs for the Industrial Class to execute. Expert assistance with the technicalities of metal-beating was provided by John Pearson, an established craftsman and a founder member of the Guild of Handicraft, who trained the artisan workers to produce their wares. The Industrial Class provided occupation and income to support fishermen in lean times and the chance for less able-bodied individuals to earn their keep.[43]

The legacy of the Newlyners continued throughout the twentieth century and into the twenty-first. Just as core Newlyn School painters were not confined to the village, artists from the later generation of 'St. Ives School' Modernists, Terry Frost, John Wells and Denis Mitchell settled in Newlyn, as have many others. Economic impact studies have shown that the area's artists are among the main contributors to the local economy.

There is, of course, no single shared vision or common style today, but the magical quality of light still inspires both amateur and professional artists to visit or stay. There are still painters painting *en plein-air* and there are resident artists of national and international repute, whose work is often showcased at Newlyn Art Gallery, although most of these use media undreamed of when the gallery opened.

Work by the Newlyn School can be seen at Penlee House Gallery & Museum in Penzance. In recent years a growing number of publications have celebrated different aspects of the artists' lives and work in fact and fiction. Although much has changed, the remaining elements and ambience of Newlyn still allow visitors to experience echoes of the heyday of Newlyn, the village itself and the artists who came to paint.

Notes

1. Stanhope Forbes, letter to his mother, 1884, quoted in Caroline Fox and Francis Greenacre, *Painting in Newlyn, 1880-1930*, exhibition catalogue, Barbican Art Gallery, London, 1985, p.54.
2. The Royal Cornwall Geological Society, founded in 1814, was the second oldest geological society in the country.
3. 'A Perambulating Contributor', *The Cornishman*, quoted in Roger Langley, *Walter Langley: Pioneer of the Newlyn Art Colony*, Sansom & Company, 1997.
4. George Bednar, *Every Corner was a Picture*, Truran Books, 2nd ed. 2004.
5. David Tovey, *W.H.Y. Titcomb: A Newlyner from St. Ives*, Wilson Books, 2003 and Bednar, *Every Corner was a Picture*.
6. Stanhope Forbes, transcript of lecture entitled 'Cornwall from a Painter's Point of View', given at the Royal Cornwall Polytechnic Society in 21 August 1900, quoted in Fox and Greenacre, *Painting in Newlyn*, p.13.
7. Charles Lee, *Cynthia in the West*, (1900) quoted in Simon Parker ed., *Chasing Tales: The Lost Stories of Charles Lee*, Gis 'On Books, 2002.
8. 'Current Art IV', *Magazine of Art*, vol.VIII, p.464, quoted in Fox and Greenacre, *Painting in Newlyn*, p.16.
9. 'Art in June', *Magazine of Art*, vol.VII, 1885, quoted in ibid., p.9.
10. Stanhope Forbes quoted in Fox and Greenacre, *Painting in Newlyn*.
11. Alice Meynell, 'Newlyn', *Art Journal* 1889, quoted in Tovey, *W.H.Y. Titcomb*.
12. Obituary in *The Pall Mall Gazette*, 28 March 1912, and Judith Cook, Melissa Hardie & Christiana Payne, *Singing from the Walls: The Life and Art of Elizabeth Forbes*, Sansom & Company, 2000.
13. Tovey, *W.H.Y. Titcomb*.
14. *Magazine of Art*, 1898, quoted in ibid.
15. Letter from Caroline Burland Yates to Thomas Cooper Gotch, sent from Gwavas Terrace, Newlyn on 26 August 1879: collection of Pamela Lomax.
16. Roger Langley, *Walter Langley: Pioneer of the Newlyn Art Colony*, Sansom & Company, 1997.
17. Tuke writing in 1884, quoted in Fox and Greenacre, *Painting in Newlyn*.
18. Langley, *Walter Langley*. Durdin was born Charles Durdin Kelly in Plymouth in 1850, but his date of death is unknown: Bednar, *Every Corner was a Picture*.
19. As Roger Langley's biography records, Walter was the eighth child (of an eventual eleven) of William Langley, who had married Walter's mother when she was sixteen and already pregnant with their first child, while he was an eighteen-year-old tailor's apprentice.
20. Clarendon Art Fellowship lecture on Langley, given by Wainwright in 1923, quoted in Langley, *Walter Langley*.
21. Langley, *Walter Langley*.
22. In 1880, the fragility of such an existence was brought home to the whole country when the Newlyn lugger, *The Jane* (PZ26) was lost with all hands just yards from the shore, in view of the townspeople; happening the same year as Langley's first visit, it must have affected him greatly.
23. *Magazine of Art* quoted in Langley, *Walter Langley*.
24. Stanhope Forbes, 'Cornwall from a Painter's Point of View'.
25. Langley had spent his evenings studying at Birmingham School of Art and had been able to study at the South Kensington Schools only through winning a scholarship. Forbes, meanwhile, had been schooled at Dulwich College, followed by private art tuition in Brussels, formal training at Lambeth and then the Royal Academy schools, finally enrolling at the studio of Leon Bonnat in Paris. His uncle, James Staats Forbes, was an avid collector of naturalist paintings, including works by painters of the French Barbizon and Dutch Hague Schools. Caroline Fox, *Stanhope Forbes and the Newlyn School*, David and Charles, 1993.
26. Norman Garstin, 'The Works of Stanhope Forbes RA', *The Studio*, vol.23, 1901, quoted in Fox and Greenacre, *Painting in Newlyn*, p.59.
27. P.G. Hamerton, 'The Lighthouse', *Scribners Magazine*, vol.XV, June 1894, p.690, quoted in Fox and Greenacre, *Painting in Newlyn*, p.16.
28. Fox and Greenacre, *Painting in Newlyn*, although George Bednar (*Every Corner was a Picture*), gives the date of their first meeting as Friday 5 February 1886.
29. Mrs Lionel Birch, *Stanhope A. Forbes, A.R.A., and Elizabeth Stanhope Forbes, A.R.W.S.*, Cassell, 1906.
30. Bednar, *Every Corner was a Picture*.
31. Pamela Lomax, *A Golden Dream: Thomas Cooper Gotch*, Sansom & Company, 2004.
32. Fox, *Stanhope Forbes and the Newlyn School*.
33. The print depicts Raphael's *Christ giving the keys to St. Peter*.

34. The Malt House, where the Gotches lived from 1887 until about 1900.
35. Bourdillon quoted in Fox and Greenacre, *Painting in Newlyn*, p.21.
36. *Magazine of Art*, 1898, quoted in Fox and Greenacre, *Painting in Newlyn*, p.19.
37. Veronica Chesher ed., *Newlyn Life 1870-1914*, Penwith History Group, 2003.
38. Cook, Hardie & Payne, *Singing from the Walls.*
39. Iris M. Green, *Posing the Model*, Iris Green, 2002.
40. Based on an estimate of 20 pupils per year over 40 years.
41. C. Lewis Hind, 'Stanhope A Forbes RA', *Art Journal*, 1911.
42. Melissa Hardie, *100 Years in Newlyn: Diary of a Gallery*, Patten Press and Newlyn Art Gallery, 1995.
43. One such was polio victim Obed Nicholls.

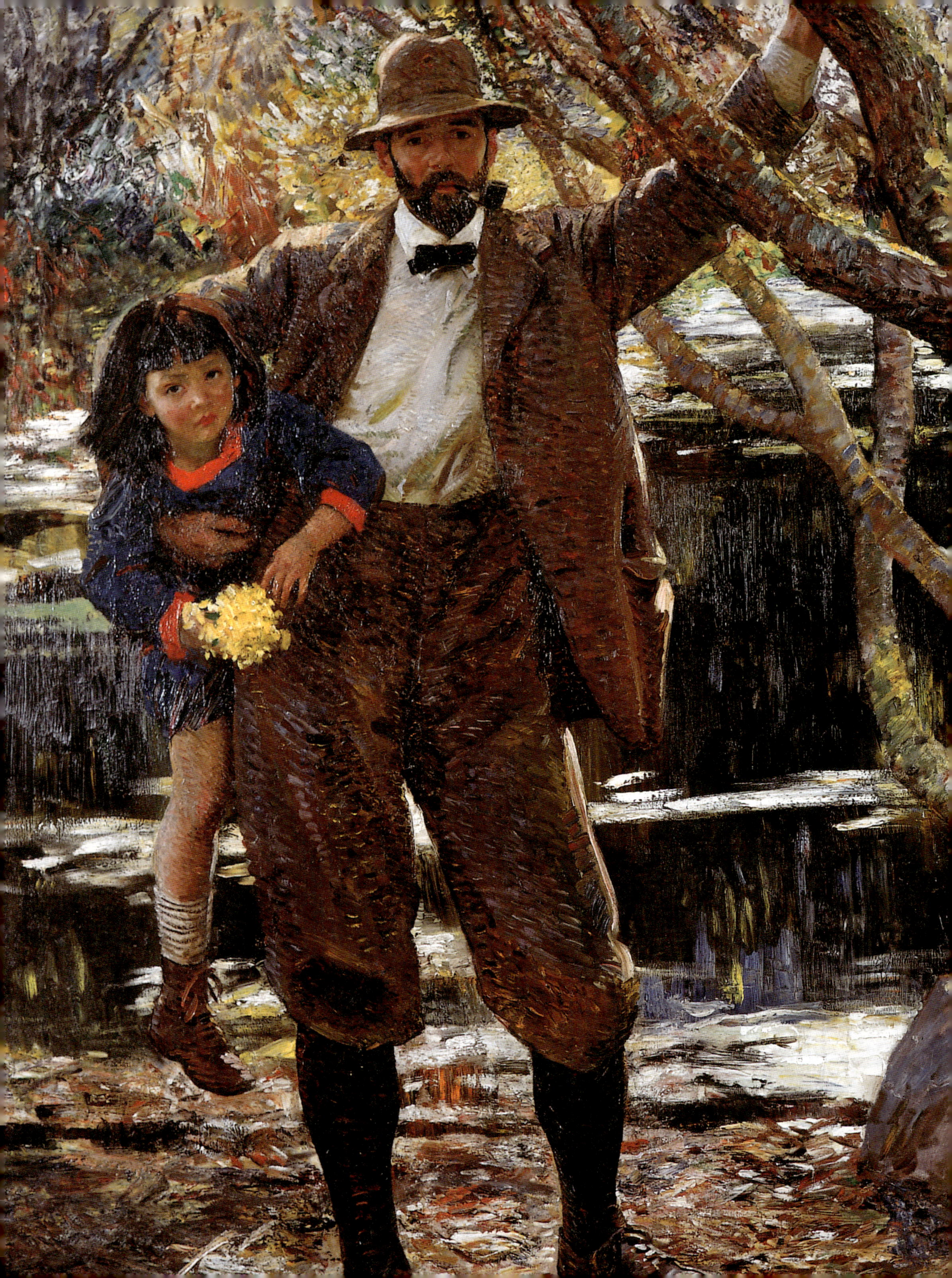

CHAPTER 3

Lamorna
A Place Apart

AUSTIN WORMLEIGHTON

In the 1890s the London author Arthur Norway picked his way along the tracks and rutted roads between Lands End and Penzance gathering material for a book. At Lamorna he paused at the cove, looked up the valley with its tumbling trout stream and ancient mills and wondered what might persuade anyone to live in a place 'so wild and lonely and difficult of access.' He went on to answer his own question. 'I conclude,' he wrote, 'that it was its very loneliness that fitted it for occupations which thrive best when seen by fewest eyes.'[1] What Norway did not reveal was that apart from the clear evidence of the occupations of quarrying and fishing, the valley then already had its first resident artist, Samuel John Birch – or Lamorna Birch as he was later to style himself. Neither could he have foreseen that within a decade the incoming artists who gathered around Birch as members of his circle would be engaged in an occupation seen by a great many eyes.

Throughout the nineteenth century a gentle stream of painters and sketchers, writers, fern collectors and ornithologists had visited Lamorna – some hoping for sightings of the elusive golden oriole and the purple

Lamorna Birch, 1926, photograph

heron – but until Birch's arrival no artist had established a permanent home there. Lamorna, five miles beyond the railway terminus at Penzance, was always a place apart. It is at the heart of what purists insist is the 'real' Cornwall, a timeless countryside of literature, superstition and legend that tapers towards the first and last valleys of England and the great granite headlands of Lands End. This patchwork peninsular of small dairy farms, hamlets and moorland is bound at its edges by rocky coves, desolate beaches and massive cliff formations, its character shaped definitively and forbiddingly by the moods of sun, rain, mist and wind. The poet John Heath-Stubbs found it a 'hideous and wicked country, sloping to hateful sunsets and the end of time', while the artist and sculptor Sven Berlin said it opened up the deeper rooms of experience in man 'awakening powers of perception which search beyond the frontiers of normal events.'[2]

Lamorna was the smallest and last of the Cornish colonies. For 30 years from the first decade of the twentieth century, more than 100 professional painters, sculptors, etchers, writers, poets and potters lived or worked from the valley. In addition, an incalculable number of part-time or leisure painters visited the colony. The artists' homes and studios were strung out along the northern rim of the valley and down its western flank where a single-track road followed a trout stream all the way to the sea, a distance of little more than a mile. Some painters visited Lamorna out of curiosity and remained there for the rest of their lives. Others were 'bed and breakfast' members of the colony, staying for a season or two or longer. Few of those artists failed to return and so the population of the colony constantly shifted around a small but permanently settled core of artists and writers. Without a church, the spiritual heart of the community lay somewhere between the temperance hotel and the public house. But a seamless kind of hospitality offered by artists in

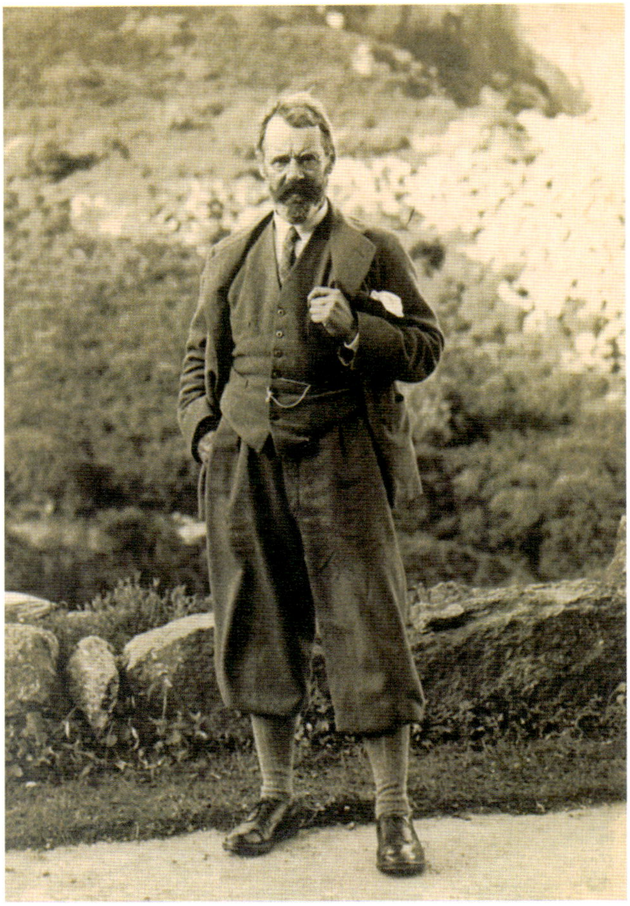

their homes and their eagerness to throw open their studios for parties helped to make up for any shortcomings and also for the lack of an artists' club.

The name Samuel John Lamorna Birch is synonymous with the art of Lamorna. A painter of pure landscape he was among the most prolific painters of his day, producing more than 20,000 pictures of all kinds in a working life of some seventy years. He was part of a small brotherhood of fishermen-artists who flourished in Victorian and Edwardian England. An angler of the first rank, his undisguised fortune was working at Lamorna from a studio beside the stream where he could paint or fish according to whim. It was a world away from his impoverished upbringing in Manchester, that 'wretched, sordid place' of his recollection, where the smoke from mill chimneys was so dense that people

Fig.23
S. J. Lamorna Birch, *Penzance Fair.* oil on canvas
Private collection © Artist's Estate

Frank Gascoigne Heath painting at Lamorna, 1910, photograph
Lamorna Birch Estate

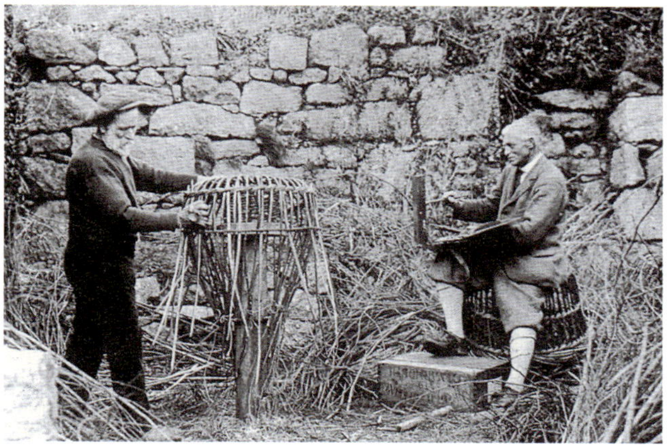

saw clearly out of doors only on Sundays.[3] His distinctive appearance made him one of the most recognizable figures in any of the Cornish colonies; so well known that in the 1920s and 1930s newspaper photographers would quip that a photograph of Birch was one that needed no identifying caption. He was a slight, upright man with a pointed beard and small round spectacles, usually seen in heavy brown tweeds with knickerbocker trousers and an old felt hat covered in fishing flies.

The son of a house painter, Birch had been working in a mill warehouse near Lancaster and painting only at weekends when he decided to make the break to become a full-time painter. He visited Newlyn for the first time in 1889 to witness life in the colony under Stanhope Forbes, and after establishing a friendship with Forbes, returned three years later with £25 savings in his pocket and his world possessions packed into a tin trunk. He took lodgings at Boleigh Farm, at the head of the Lamorna Valley, where his first studio in a barn was shared with rats and mice. From there he struck out independently, drawing inspiration from the Barbizon painters of France, particularly Corot, and eager to observe the tenets of Rural Naturalism.

Birch is credited as the founder of the colony but he did not actively set out to establish a colony at all; the colony simply sprang up around him, helped by his gregarious nature and the Arcadian life he encouraged others to share. Sir Alfred Munnings said Lamorna saw little of the painters of Newlyn, 'the hills and distance between them were too much'.[4] But in practice there were no barriers of any kind and so much movement between the colonies that Lamorna soon came to be seen as an offshoot of Newlyn. To this day artists who lived and worked in Lamorna are often described as Newlyners or members of the Newlyn School. This is partly because many of them had passed through Newlyn on their way to a more settled base at Lamorna.

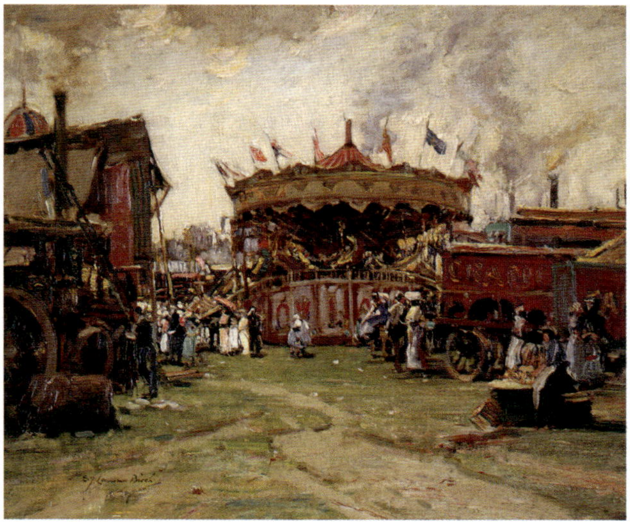

Those working around Birch were landscape, animal, bird and portrait painters, members of a group now regarded as amongst the British Impressionists. They included Munnings, Harold and Laura Knight, Charles Walter Simpson and Algernon Newton, who all arrived in the first decade of the twentieth century. The work of these painters was driven in the main by the landscape, and their experiments in light and colour were to enrich the imagination of every artist following in their stead. Within this group were other artists, strongly influenced by Birch's painting of water – particularly rivers and woodland streams – and reflected light, and his idiosyncratic use of colour. These painters included Garstin Cox, Herbert George, John Gutteridge Sykes, Charles Joshua Kelsey, Frank Gascoigne Heath and Stanley Horace Gardiner

Fig.24
S. J. Lamorna Birch, *In Our Old World Valley*, c.1921, oil on canvas
Penlee House Gallery and Museum, Penzance © Artist's Estate

who studied under Birch or took advice from him. Their work gave rise to a particular style of Lamorna art and their unmistakable imprint is sometimes referred to as the work of the 'sunshine painters'.[5]

Birch's chief interest was in the organic and architectural elements of the landscape and it was this concentration on natural sculptural forms and the juxtaposition of trees, rock and water that marked the greatest initial difference between the colony at Lamorna and the painters of Newlyn and St. Ives (fig.24). These compositional devices were used graphically in large river paintings for which Birch is now best remembered, but more particularly in his pencil sketches and watercolours which were spontaneous reactions to light and atmosphere. It was a style borrowed from the late eighteenth and early nineteenth centuries and the work of artists such as Thomas Girtin and Cornelius Varley.

The development of the colony was helped significantly by Birch's high public profile, both as a painter and fisherman. He exhibited throughout the United Kingdom and his work was purchased for permanent collections across the world.[6] It was thanks largely to his prominence at the Royal Academy, where he exhibited 237 pictures, that Birch came to enjoy the friendship of practically every leading British painter of

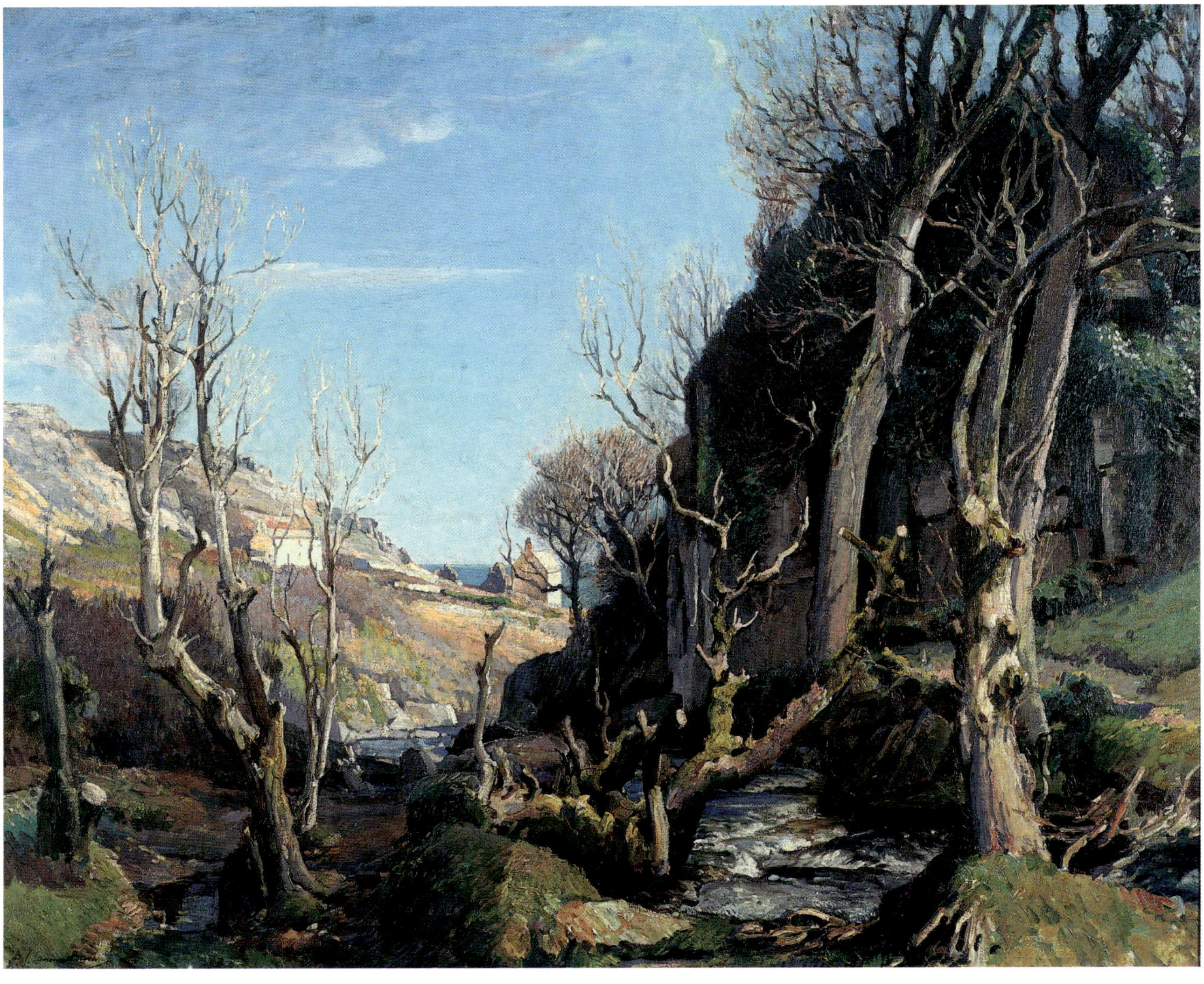

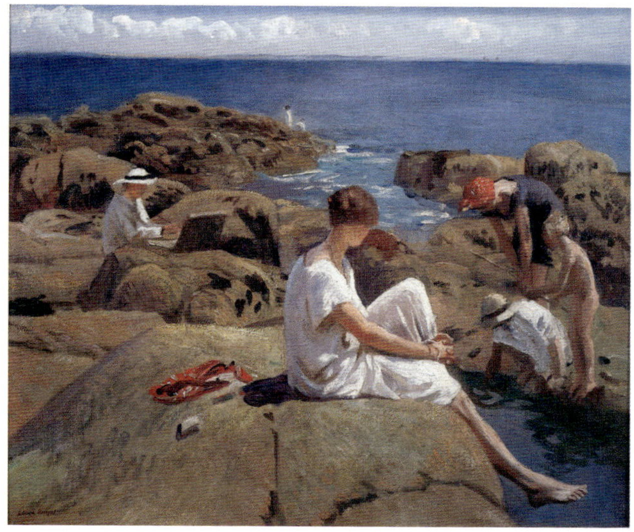

Fig.25
Dame Laura Knight, *A Summer's Day by the Rock Pool*
oil on canvas, Private collection © Artist's Estate

his day. Sir George Clausen, Augustus John and Frederick Cayley Robinson, though never part of the colony, were among artists who spent time in Lamorna, intent on tasting life in this sublimely beautiful valley. It had appeared to them then, and remains today, like one vast outdoor studio with sufficient subjects to last a life-time. Thomas Cooper Gotch, the Knights and Augustus John were among those who painted portraits of Birch's daughters, Elizabeth Lamorna ('Mornie') and Joan, during visits to Birch's home at Flagstaff Cottage before the First World War. The girls were beautifully observed as children of Arcady growing up in a kind of fairyland. Ernest Gillick also sculpted them in their woodland environment.[7]

This was a landscape idealized in the poetry of W.H. Davies and Arthur Wimperis, and by the artist and writer Charles Walter Simpson. East and west from the headlands overlooking Lamorna cove were the subjects of great canvases with monolithic cliffs and gilded clouds, while on the floor of the valley, among trees hung with beards of lichen and beside the purling waters of the trout steam, a more intimate kind of art was practised. It is here that the stream runs into the sea and where daffodils and rushes grow right up to the salt-water line. When springtime arrived, Laura Knight remembered that it seemed that the trees were rootless and weightless 'suspended in a pulsating atmosphere, pregnant with moisture of the Atlantic mist'.[8] Munnings thought that there was nothing, anywhere, quite like this coast, where he remembered lying on sweet-smelling turf and watching sea pinks trembling in the wind. 'There were spots where I could laze and be idle and drowsy enough in Norfolk,' he wrote, 'but of all places on the right day, I find myself more and more longing to be back on those Cornish cliffs, lying in the sun, listening to the incessant sound of the surf.'[9]

As soon as Birch realized that a colony was forming he encouraged artists of all disciplines and persuasions to join him, particularly if they were technically sound or innovative.[10] Birch believed the stimulation of new faces and new ideas benefited everyone and it was only in advanced old age and the start of the revolution in St. Ives that he was heard to rail against Modernism and Abstraction. 'Why should I tear out my hair when I can't finish a picture properly?' he had asked his wife in a letter to her in 1939. 'Why not send it to the Academy covered in yellow and blue and call it "Spring"?' But by this time he had become accustomed to changing public taste in art and the moods and swings of the market. Some artists arriving in Lamorna were unconventional by the standards of their day, while others introduced the seed of rebellion. None of this seemed to surprise Birch, who enjoyed the gypsy-type freedoms. His colony was characterized by an unusually fine brand of friendship and mutual help, largely unspoilt by petty squabbles and acrimony. To outsiders it seemed that Lamorna painters toiled hard – though often in different artistic directions – but still found the time for everyday pleasantries such as afternoon tea and an ever-tempting picnic.

It is a moot point whether the surrealist painter and writer Ithell Colquhoun could have worked anywhere other than Lamorna. She was drawn there by its supernatural elements, 'nature-spirits weeping, imprisoned and misused by Druidism in decay.' Her studio home at the mouth of the valley had no piped water or electricity and she liked to sunbathe in the nude beside the stream in her garden. 'Lamorna can do anything to me,' she wrote memorably.[11] A short way down the valley at that time the abstract painter and sculptor Marlow Moss, who had been a friend of Mondrian in Paris, was living and working reclusively, far removed from any shared tradition.[12]

Some years earlier the landscape and figure painter Hannah Gluckstein, heiress to the J. Lyons food and catering empire who chose to be known simply as Gluck, arrived in the valley having shaken off all trappings of wealth and status. She surprised villagers by cropping her hair like a man, smoking a pipe and strolling through the village wearing red jockey breeches, a cloak and a black homburg hat. She had paired off with a fellow London art student Effie Craig. They lived together in London during the winter but spent long, lazy summers from 1915 onwards in Lamorna, exploring their art and extending their intimate relationship. It was probably newcomers like Gluck and Craig whom Munnings had in mind when he observed that Cornish people soon got to know the artists and 'everybody understood their ways'.[13]

The same judgement applied to more than twenty writers who arrived as residents or visitors. Among them was the poet W.H. Davies, who lived rough in the gardens of studios, sleeping out of doors and encouraging a camp-fire culture among the artists, based largely it would seem on the consumption of bottled beer and sausages. Davies' portrait was painted several times by the Knights. One portrait by Laura was bought for the collection at Merthyr Tydfil; another by Harold is in the Welsh national collection in Cardiff.[14] Arnold Bennett became friendly with the Birch family after renting a cottage in the cove in the 1930s and was remembered strolling through the village hands thrust deep into the pockets of an old tweed jacket, a cigarette dangling from his mouth. Dylan Thomas stayed with friends in a cottage near The Wink public house just before the Second World War. Although dismissing Lamorna lightly as a place where one could buy a Surrealist 'for a couple of whiting', he married in Penzance and is thought to have caught the germ of his idea for *Under Milk Wood* at the nearby fishing village of Mousehole. For many years a thorn bush outside Oriental Cottage, where Thomas stayed, was known as 'Dylan's' because of the number of times he had fallen into it on his way home from the public house. Birch's son-in-law James Lennox Kerr, who had a writing hut on the cliff above Flagstaff Cottage, wrote more than 30 books, mostly for children.

Artists and writers were able to see how their presence changed the character, even destroyed the innocence, of this small fishing community, and a few could reflect on how different things had been at the start of the twentieth century. The countryside around Lamorna then had much in common with the landscape of northern France and with the painting communities at Pont-Aven, Grez-sur-Loing and Concarneau. It was insular, primitive and slow to change, ingredients that made it an attractive sketching ground to those British artists who had worked in France in the 1890s. Even the farm buildings in Cornwall looked as if they had been plucked straight out of a Breton landscape. As in Brittany, the Lamorna countryside supported a genuine peasantry with arcane customs and superstitions, a people caricatured by C.E. Vulliamy as late as 1925 as possessing a restful depth of ignorance and a 'presence that helps you to realise that you have travelled far into an unfamiliar land.'[15] It is easy to imagine how in this backward environment artists enjoyed practising the *plein-air* code of the Barbizon painters of France.

In the 1890s there was still an excess of Victorian

Fig.26
S. J. Lamorna Birch, *Old Quay Lamorna from my Garden*
oil on canvas, Private collection © Artist's Estate

taste for the English pastoral idyll and for a time this was the market Lamorna painters pursued with zeal, though not in the controlled conditions of a studio like most other British painters of the day. In spring and summer they set off at sunrise, cycling around the countryside in search of subjects, often translating them on to large canvases, perhaps 7ft x 5ft, which were carried over fields like huge kites to be anchored to the ground with ropes and stones. At night any unfinished work was stored in the barns of local farms. 'It was our creed that beautiful things should be painted on the spot,' Birch said. In old age he had looked back on those days, remembering that his 'greatest thrill' was painting in a high wind and an ever-changing light.[16]

During his studies in Paris in 1895-96, Birch adopted the additional name of 'Lamorna' to avoid being confused with the Newlyn painter Lionel Birch. On his marriage in 1902 he moved to Flagstaff Cottage at the bottom of the Lamorna valley, taking over the tenancy of a former harbour master's cottage from the author Charles Marriott and converting a stable beside the stream into a studio.[17] Marriott was then already a published novelist but his future lay as a critic and writer on art.[18] His acerbic criticism of painting and painters introduced Birch and his friends to a

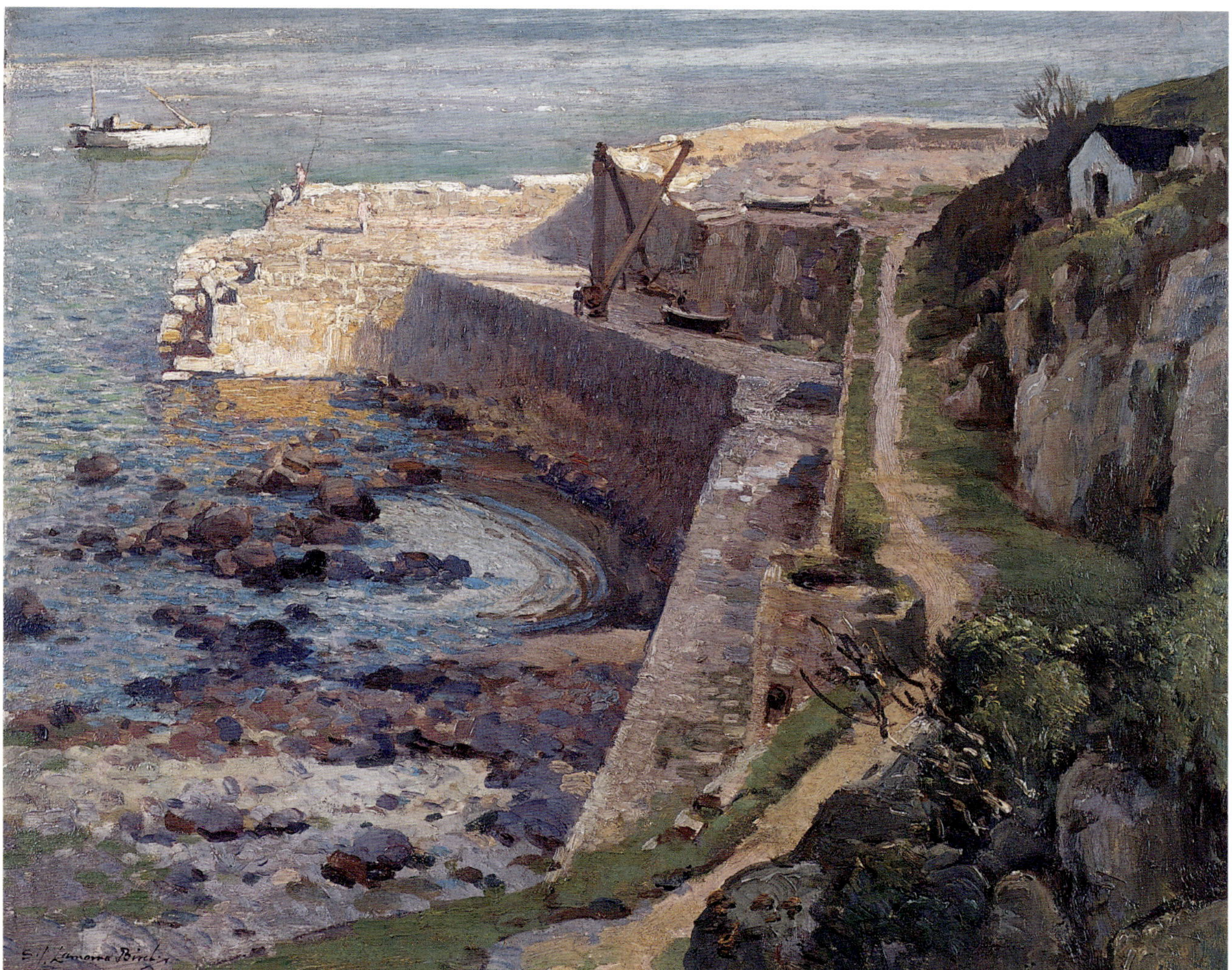

Lamorna Birch's studio beside the Lamorna stream, 2003, photograph

side of art they had not previously addressed too seriously: that their work had not only to face the critical judgement of buyers and galleries, but the attention of Fleet Street and the academic art journals. Before leaving Flagstaff Cottage to join the literary circle of Havelock Ellis in St. Ives, Marriott fired several parting shots towards Newlyn and in later years, writing with the assurance of the future art critic of *The Times*, he said anything resembling a school at Newlyn had ceased to exist by 1901. 'The so-called Newlyn School was a gathering of artists for company and the advantage of light, rather than a definite movement with a permanent influence on British art.'[19]

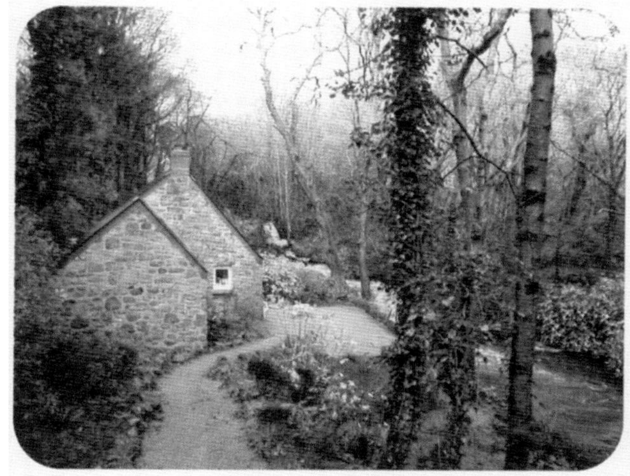

Birch's arrival at the cottage came at a time when there was already a recognizable circle of painters at Lamorna. By the turn of the century artists had begun to settle into properties around the northern rim of the valley at Trewoofe (pronounced Trove) and farther east towards the Clapper Mill, helping to establish this first generation of painters. They included the landscape and sea painter Charles H. Thompson and his wife Heather, a painter of portraits and miniatures, and the Manchester-born James Noble Barlow, who had been taking pupils to Lamorna for landscape tuition since the 1890s. Henry Scott Tuke, the marine and portrait painter, was then cycling to Lamorna from Falmouth to meet Birch and an old Quaker school friend, the landscape painter Arthur Tanner who rented Cappy Cottage in the village. They enjoyed a boisterous friendship, taking off for long walks along the cliffs sketching and painting, and in the evenings playing billiards and pingpong and the cut-throat card game of euchre, a form of seamen's poker. All three were innovative. Tuke adopted a method of sketching on an oil panel prepared with a scumbled surface, an idea perfected by Birch and Tanner which became known as the 'Tanner-Birch System'.[20]

This early influx of painters was helped by letters written by Marriott. On leaving Lamorna he spread the word freely of the delights of the Lamorna valley, registering it as a place where creative people might gather in a spirit of brotherhood. This clear endorsement brought to Lamorna the writer and critic Charles Lewis Hind, a founding editor of *The Studio*, and his friends among the London literati, all of whom were welcomed by the artists, joining them on painting and fishing excursions. But there was one other important influence at that time, without which the colony would not have developed as strongly or as quickly as it did.

Colonel Camborne Paynter, who owned Lamorna cove and the land and property to the west of the valley, including Flagstaff Cottage, was forward-looking and imaginative. At the age of 37 he epitomized the new spirit of the Edwardian age. His vision widened while serving as an army officer, he set about managing and modernizing the estate which had been in his family since 1326. He welcomed the artists, saying that they brought colour, intellect and style to this backward-looking community. Paynter built, adapted and rented properties for their use and in this way had a strong bearing on the development of the colony. For Harold and Laura Knight, Paynter offered the first substantial form of patronage they had known, renting them a house, Oakhill, building studios for both of

Fig.27
Sir Alfred J Munnings, *Laura Knight Painting*, c.1911
oil on canvas, Norwich Castle Museum and Art Gallery
© Sir Alfred Munnings Museum

them in the valley and providing Laura with a painting hut on the cliff just to the west of Flagstaff Cottage.

The arrival of the Knights in Lamorna was probably the defining moment in the establishment of a colony. In November 1907 they were walking in Morrab Road, Penzance with the Newlyn painter Norman Garstin when they met Birch. The Knights had recently arrived from Staithes, on the Yorkshire coast, and were still feeling their way in an adopted home. Garstin introduced Birch who asked them, 'Are you doing anything next Sunday? Come over and have lunch with me.' Laura remembered setting off in heavy boots and splashing through mud and puddles on their way to Lamorna. Passing through a gate at the top of a narrow lane they discovered a densely wooded valley 'already speckled with the yellow of early primroses and white anemone' of springtime. 'It was well-worth getting wet feet, for it would seem that we had suddenly entered Paradise,' she recalled.[21]

On Sundays before the First World War, Birch and his wife Houghton, also a painter, entertained artists at Flagstaff Cottage. They came from far and wide

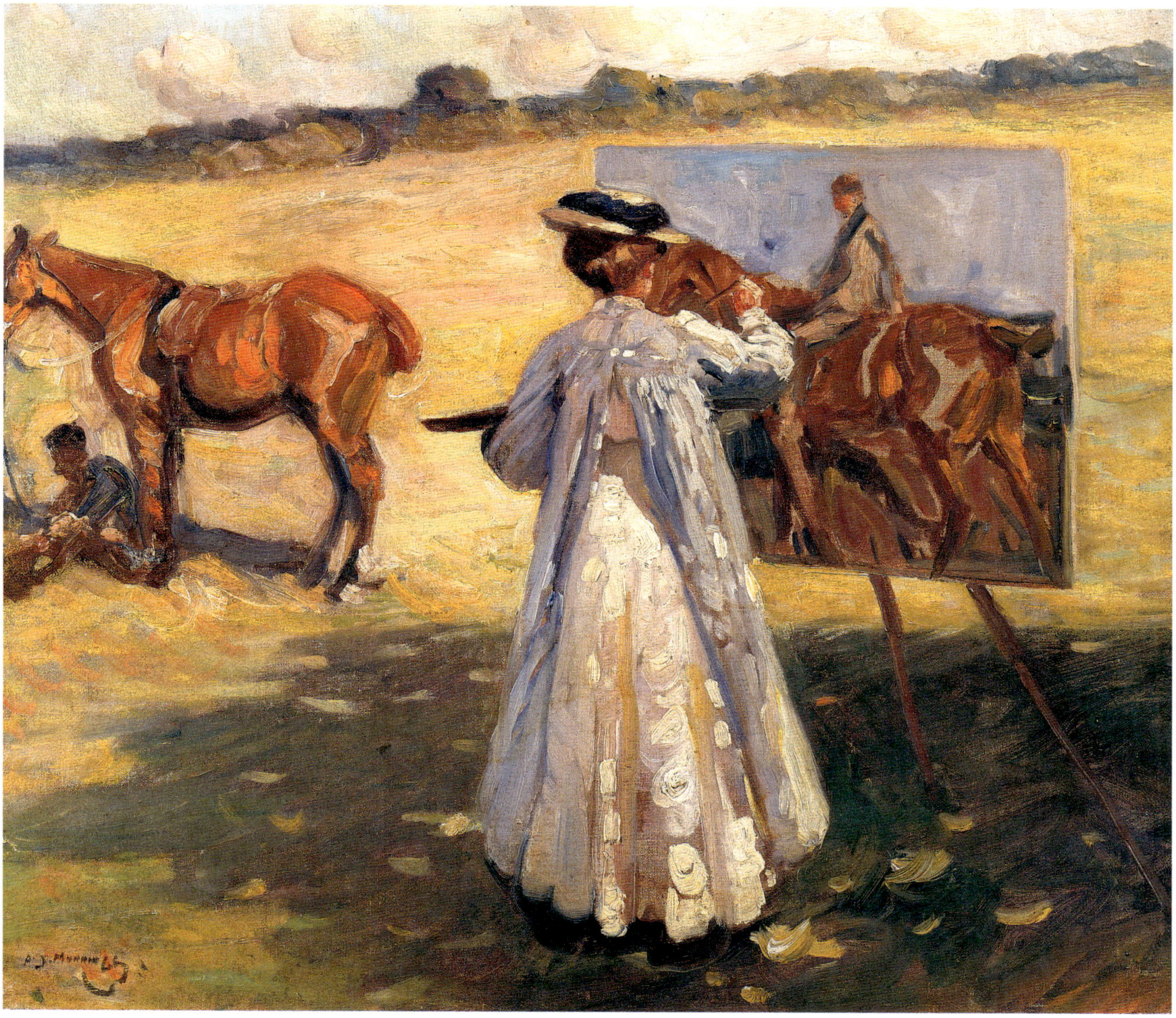

Fig.28
Sir Alfred J Munnings, *The Lamorna Inn*, 1915, oil on canvas
Courtesy of the Sir Alfred Munnings Museum

but mostly from Newlyn, welcoming the opportunity to relax, gossip and talk about studio problems. Birch liked to sing and tap dance and tell risqué stories while Houghton, known to everyone as 'Mouse', prepared Cornish fish pies topped with cream, and pasties 'the like of which I never tasted,' Laura recalled. Often there were trout which Birch had caught in the stream and which he lightly fried in oatmeal, or pies and casseroles made with game he had shot in the woods. It was on social occasions such as these that Laura found that she could feel 'drunk' on lemonade. The Knights were now friends of Stanhope and Elizabeth Forbes and of students of their painting school, who also joined the Birches for the Sunday parties.

In 1907 there was a particularly talented group at the school. They included Eleanor Waymouth – a 25-year-old New Zealander and the future wife of the Lamorna painter Robert Morson Hughes, 17-year-old Dod Shaw – the future Dod Procter, and Fryniwyd ('Fryn') Tennyson Jesse – a great-niece of the poet Alfred Lord Tennyson and herself a novelist, painter, poet and short-story writer of local distinction. Fryn was one of the most beautiful women many had met. Her head of rich golden curls was so much her crowning glory that friends vied for the privilege of washing and combing it. Munnings, resplendent in horse-fair suit and red cravat, then visited Cornwall only for holidays and was overwhelmed by the company of so many young ladies from the Forbes' school. Fryn caught his eye, in particular, and it was remembered that he once sat beside her on the Lamorna cliffs combing her beautiful auburn tresses.

By the time Munnings settled at Lamorna in 1911 he had already established his name in Norfolk as a painter of horses and gipsy life. His studio in Lamorna was above a stable at the village mill, where he kept his horses and from where he rode out each day with his paints, keeping in touch with horse and hound

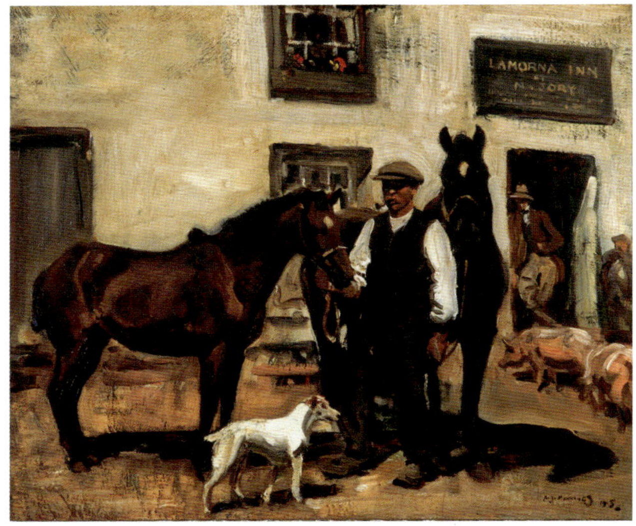

and country pursuits much as he had done in Norfolk. Whenever there was a party or 'open house' at a painter's home it was Munnings, with his rude charm and recitations of ballads and poems, who kept the parties going long after dark. He lived at Cliff House, the temperance hotel, but found more congenial company at The Wink, the public house where, like most other painters, he preferred to pay for food and drink with paintings (see fig.28). Before long, the landlord Nick Jory had built up a most impressive collection of art.

At about this time Birch made his first recorded reference to Lamorna as a colony. It was a casual remark in a letter to his wife but it expressed what everyone could then see for themselves. The valley was home to an increasing number of painters and new houses were springing up at a rate that made Laura Knight think Lamorna was becoming suburban. Benjamin Eastlake Leader, son of the Victorian landscape painter B.W. Leader, was now in the valley with his artist wife Belle; Frank Gascoigne Heath and Algernon Newton were both building new houses; while the landscape painter Charles Naper and his jeweller and potter wife Ella moved into a new property at Trewoofe. All had arrived in Lamorna from other parts of England. Munnings was now joined in Cornwall by a young animal

Fig.29
Frank Gascoigne Heath, *Gulls in Newlyn Harbour*, 1909
oil on canvas, Royal Institute of Cornwall /
Royal Cornwall Museum © Artist's Estate

Fig.30
Harold Knight, *The Maiden*, c.1916, oil on canvas
Private collection © The Estate of Harold Knight 2005
All Rights Reserved DACS

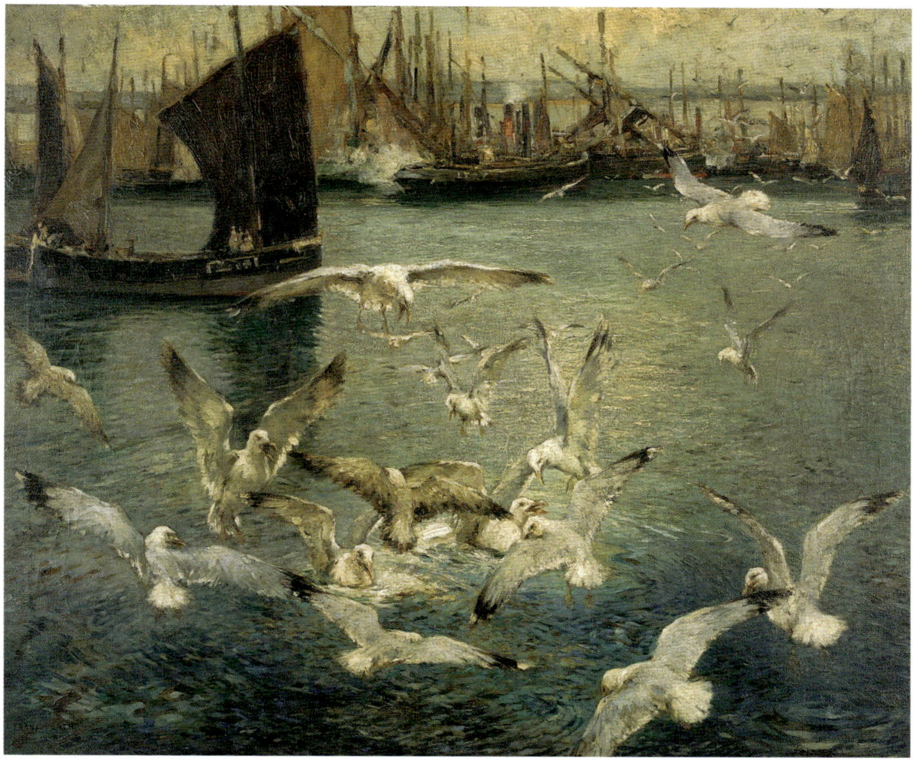

mate studies of home life, and he now also painted occasional landscapes in the company of Birch and Gotch (see fig.30). Laura found that she was now aware that eye and hand could work together 'without conscious intervention of thought'.[24] Faced with a blank canvas she was able to work straight from the subconscious. With this gift, freshly discovered, she tackled the painting of the nude female figure in direct sunlight. Villagers were wide-eyed, a mixture of curiosity

and bird painter, Charles Walter Simpson, who had studied under him in Norfolk. Villagers were tightly bound into the life of the colony. Munnings always had a coin for any village lad prepared to hold a horse to a tether while he painted it and Henry Tippett, who farmed at Boleigh, provided a carrier service for paintings. He would arrive at the studios with his horse and cart and stack the pictures under potato sacks for the onward journey to Penzance railway station and thence to the Royal Academy.

For the Knights it was a period that defined their future as painters. Laura remembered it as a time of 'tremendous output' for them both.[22] Harold had now established his name as a painter of portraits and interiors, which provided their basic income. 'Fryn' Tennyson Jesse remembered that 'their brilliant painting stunned the whole colony.'[23] Harold used Laura's imported models, often Italian waitresses from Soho, 'resting' actresses or even prostitutes, for more inti-

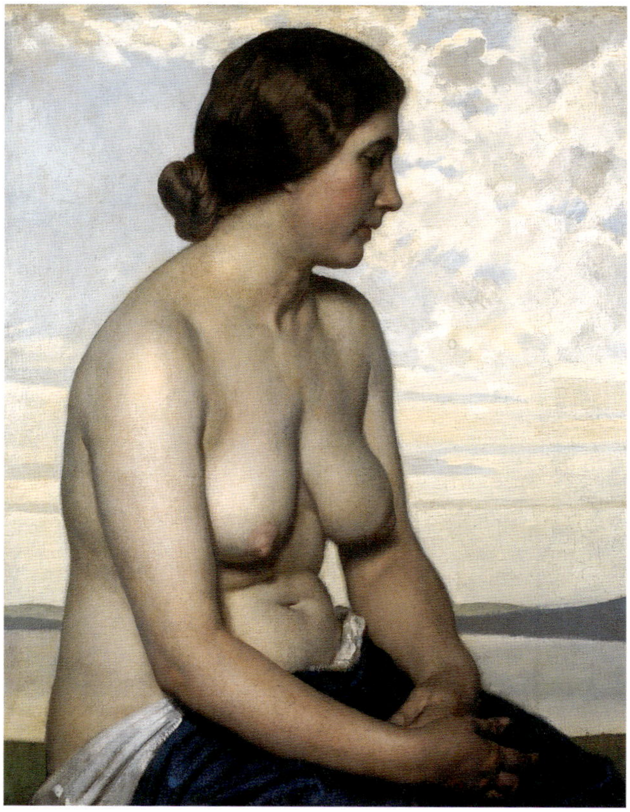

Fig.31
Dame Laura Knight, *At the Edge of the Cliff*, oil on canvas
Illustration courtesy of David Messum, The Studio, Lords Wood, Marlow © Artist's Estate

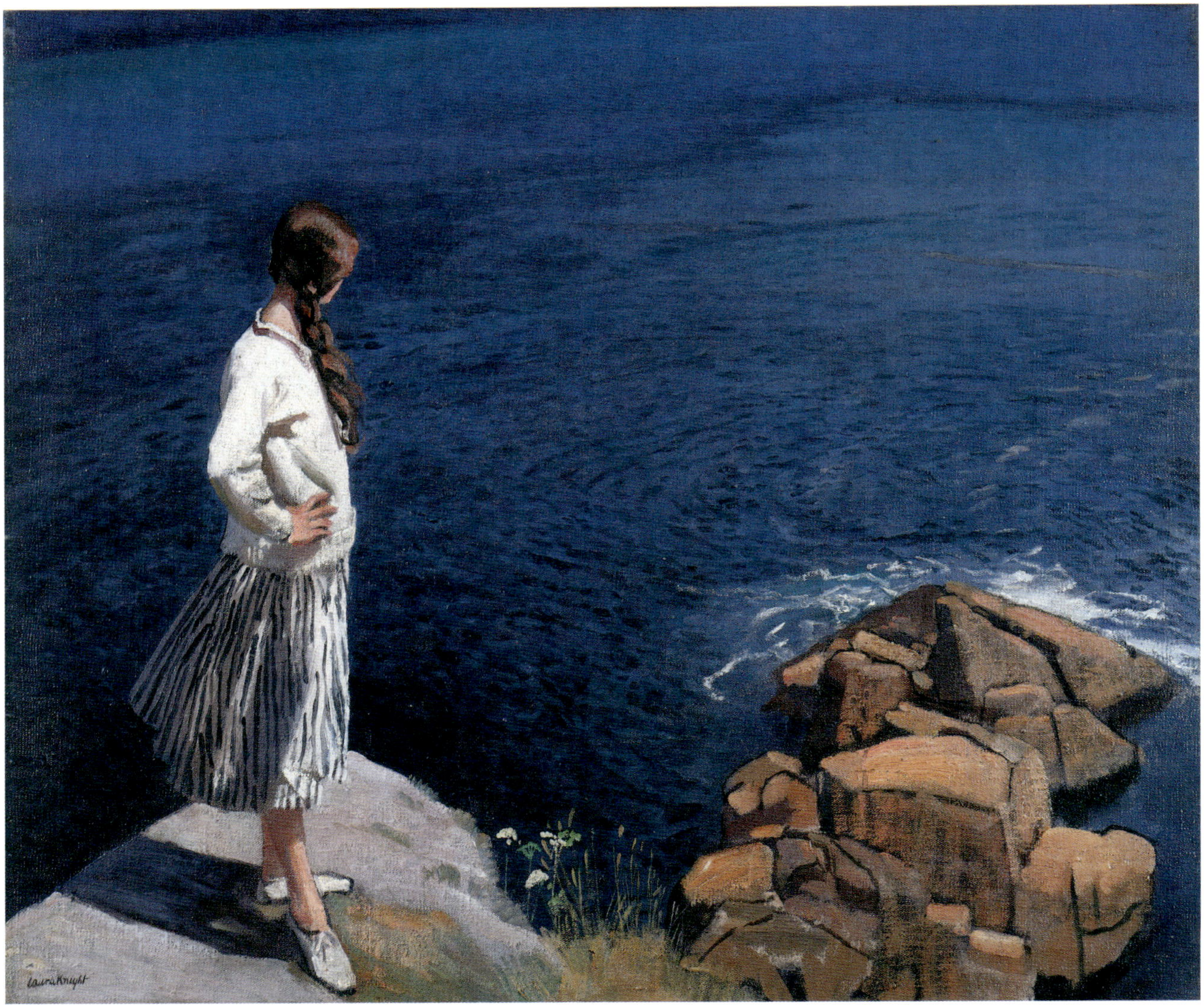

and disapproval, but they were told that Laura Knight could paint in any manner she chose because Colonel Paynter said she could.

Laura worked from Carn Barges, close to the spot where artists bathed in rock pools and gathered for picnics, and it was there that her early bravura figure painting reached a peak of expression (see fig.31). From the cove she struggled over rocks to reach the cliff path to her hut, holding aloft huge canvases. The hut was flanked by small patches of higher ground cultivated for daffodils and spring flowers. From there she studied the effects of light on flesh, drawing hundreds of quick studies in pencil and thinned oil pigment, emphasizing amber, purple and pink revealed against dark shadow.

The hut, long since gone, was made of timber with a tin roof and measured about nine feet by six feet. The locations of many ravishing studies of women painted against a sea of Caribbean blue may now be identified by the rocks painted from the doorway of that hut.[25] *Daughters of the Sun*, one of the largest canvases Laura had attempted up to then, was painted from Carn Barges. She posed her models in the nude in golden sunlight, painting with broad, liquid strokes and thick impasto. The picture was exhibited at the

Fig.32
Dame Laura Knight, *Lamorna Birch and his Daughters*, 1913–1934, oil on canvas, courtesy of University of Nottingham © Artist's Estate

Laura Knight shows Academicians her picture of the artist and his daughters, photograph

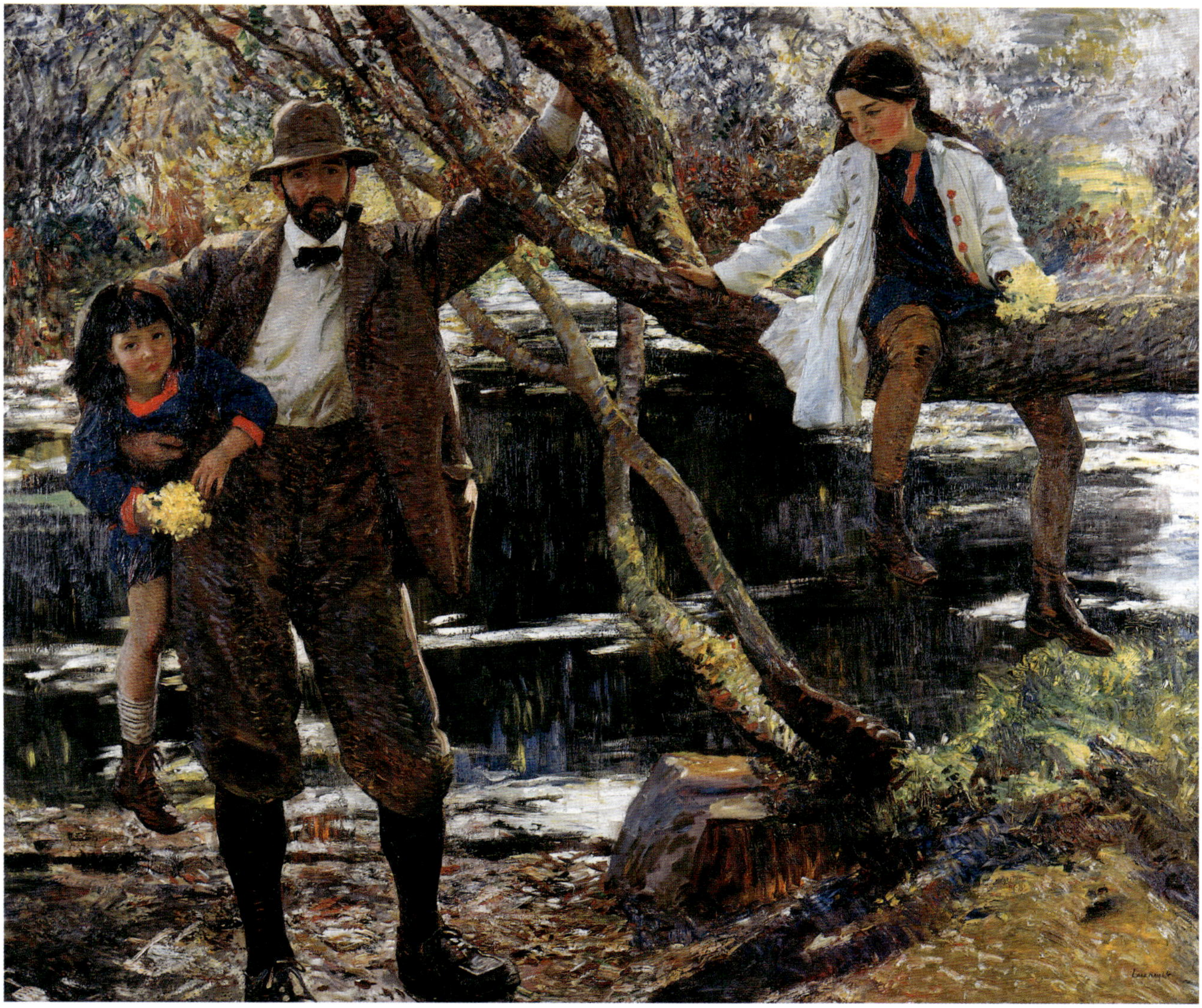

1911 Royal Academy summer exhibition but failed to sell at £600. It was later damaged in store, cut up by Laura and destroyed. An even larger canvas destined for greater critical acclaim was started two years later from the Letter Studio in woodland close to the stream.[26] *Lamorna Birch and his Daughters*, a canvas measuring 90in x 107in, showed Birch in unfamiliar white shirt and bow tie with his two daughters, four-year-old Joan dangling under his right arm like a rag doll and nine-year-old Mornie sitting astride the bough of a tree (fig.32). The painting was voted Picture of the Year

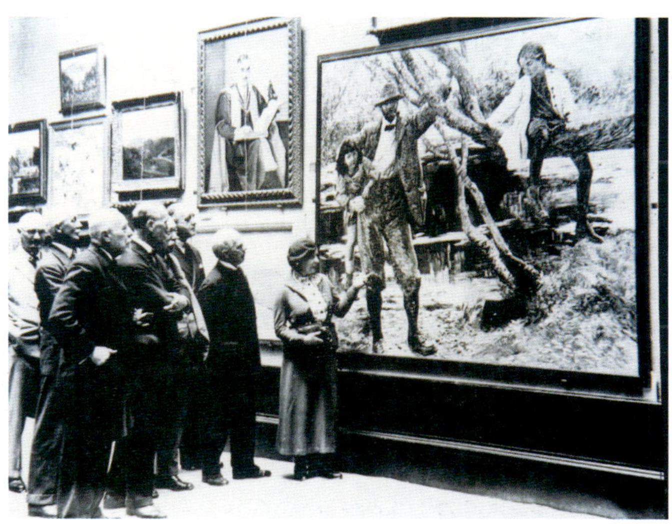

Fig.33
Charles Naper, *Nanjizal Towards Lands End*,
oil on canvas, Private collection © Artist's Estate

Fig.34
Sir Alfred J Munnings, *Going to the Meet of the Western Foxhounds*, c.1913, oil on canvas, Laing Art Gallery, Newcastle upon Tyne © Sir Alfred Munnings Museum

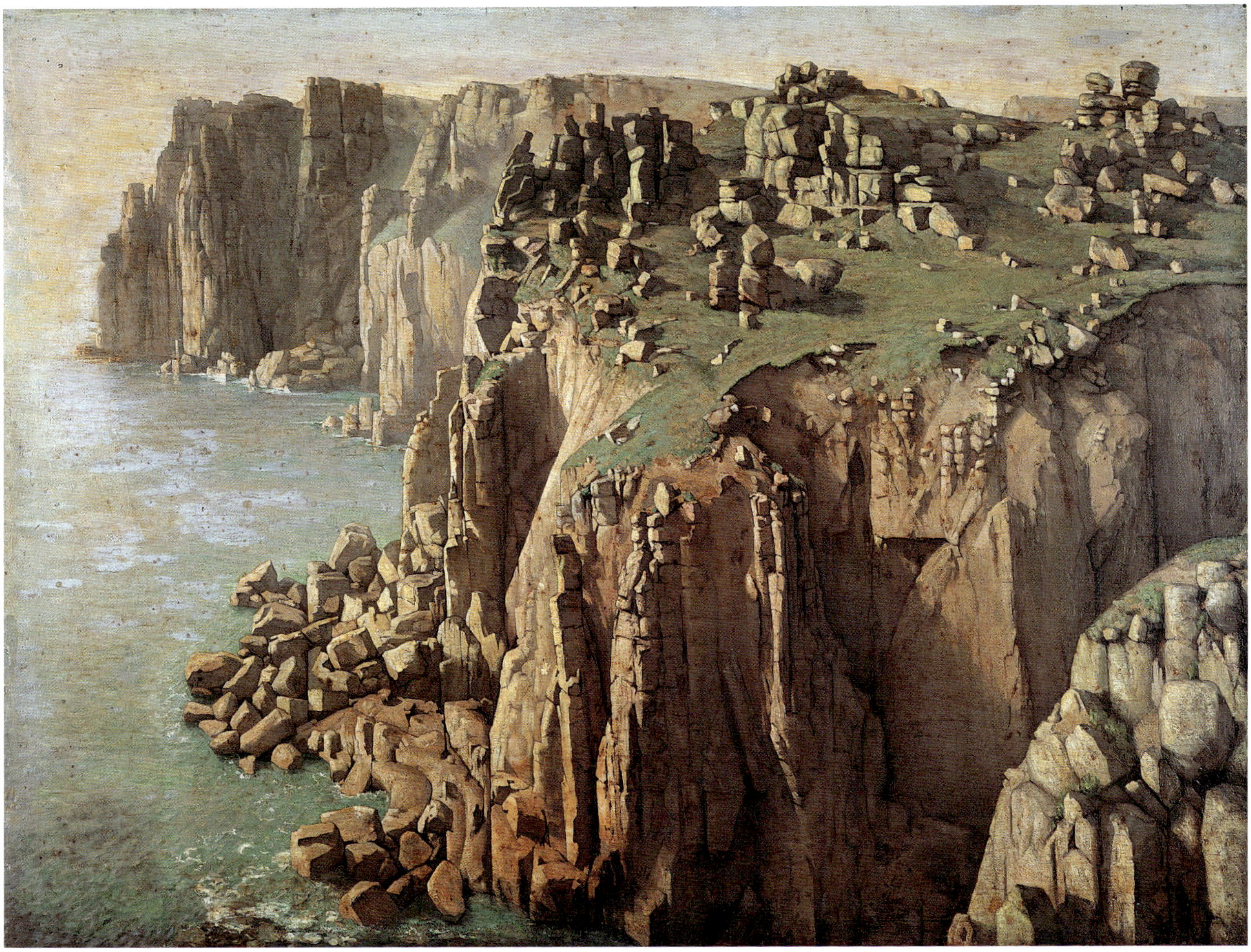

at the 1934 Royal Academy summer exhibition. Although started in 1913 the canvas lay unfinished in Laura's studio until January 1934, by which time both Birch daughters had married and were on their way to becoming Royal Academy exhibitors.

All artists were drawn towards the wild western-most edge of the peninsular. Charles Naper and Robert Morson Hughes painted memorable work among the granite outcrops of Treen and Porthgwarra near Lands End (see fig.33), while the sands of Sennen Cove – a coastal wilderness tucked around the corner from Lands End, was a favoured painting location for Laura Knight

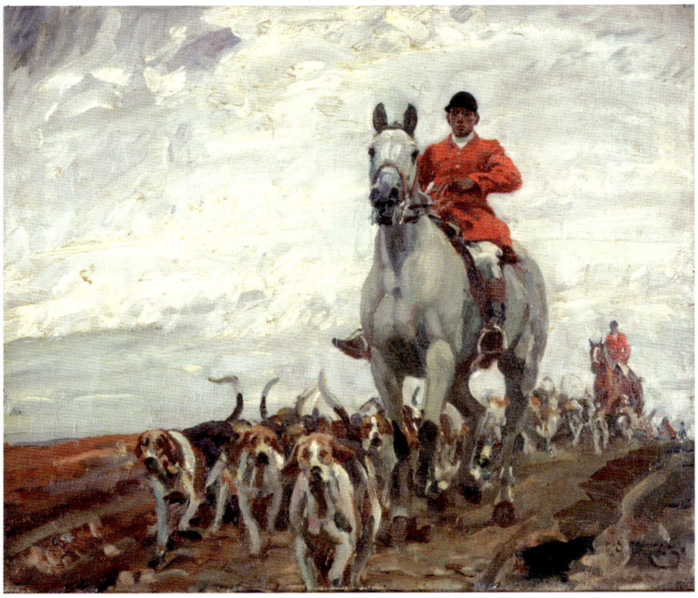

as well as being a tuition ground for students at the Forbes' school. Elizabeth Forbes complained every year about the dreariness of winter, a time when 'we poor painters cower over studio fires, the rain streams on the skylights and the sodden mists blow up from the sea.' She yearned for springtime when the students' baggage wagon could again trundle out of Newlyn piled high with easels, paint boxes and canvases and head for Sennen.[27] Munnings produced some outstanding work on Zennor moor, south of St. Ives, a place he found even more primitive than Lamorna. He lodged in the village of Zennor, painting animal studies and following the Western Foxhounds with his paints, often in the company of another Lamorna horse painter and huntsman Richard Copeland Weatherby (see fig.34). But this early phase of the Lamorna colony was soon scarred by tragedy.

Munnings' first romantic attachment in Cornwall had been to the shy and nervous Florence Carter Wood, known as 'Bloat', daughter of a wealthy London brewer, who studied at the Forbes school with her brother Joey. So different were they in make-up and personality that their marriage was thought by friends to have been ill-judged at best, but none was able to foretell its tragic end. In July 1914 Bloat killed herself by taking cyanide in her room at the Lamorna hotel where she had begun married life. Her death sent a wave of shock throughout the valley, and in the words of Laura Knight 'put an end to all joy'.[28] With war only weeks away, the first golden phase of the colony came to an abrupt end. In 1918, the Knights left Cornwall for St. John's Wood, London, where Harold, after a difficult time in Cornwall defending his pacifism, took lucrative commissions for portraiture, and Laura turned to painting the ballet, circus and Romany life. But for the next 30 years they retained their love for Lamorna, maintaining a studio in the valley and never losing their friendship with Birch and his family.

Munnings also left Lamorna, suppressing any feeling over Bloat's death and not mentioning her in any of his autobiographical writing. He trained army horses for the war and worked as an official artist for the Canadian government, painting a remarkable series of pictures of life behind the Front in France. After the Armistice he settled at Castle House at Dedham, Essex, where he built his reputation as a sporting artist and painter of horse portraits.

Many artists who had been in the vanguard of pre-war experimentation returned to more conventional forms of expression in the 1920s. The trauma for Birch was that he had been too old to fight and suffered the guilt of being a painter in time of war. He purged a troubled conscience by painting large canvases with cliffs standing fortress-like against invading seas; and landscapes with deep vistas, wide river valleys and sunburst skies, alluding to the strength and unconquerable spirit of the nation (see fig.35). These sent a subliminal message across the world that although bruised and bloodied by war the mother nation was still in good heart.

By the 1930s, a second generation of painters was already established in the valley and Birch was a household name throughout the English-speaking world. He had more pictures in public exhibitions overseas than any other British painter and his colony was recognized throughout the old Dominions. He carried this torch for Lamorna throughout the turbulent 1930s when fashion and taste in art swung erratically, refusing to accept that there was a method of working other than 'the good old way'. This view found little opposition in the studios of Lamorna, where Stanley Horace Gardiner and later Denys Law were among those who continued to craft their landscapes in the same unhurried manner. When Birch died on 7 January 1955 the 'good old way' of painting was in decline, reflected in the number of unsold pictures found among his studio collection.

Fig.35
S. J. Lamorna Birch, *Tregiffian Cliff near Lamorna*, c.1922, oil on canvas, Bristol City Art Gallery © Artist's Estate

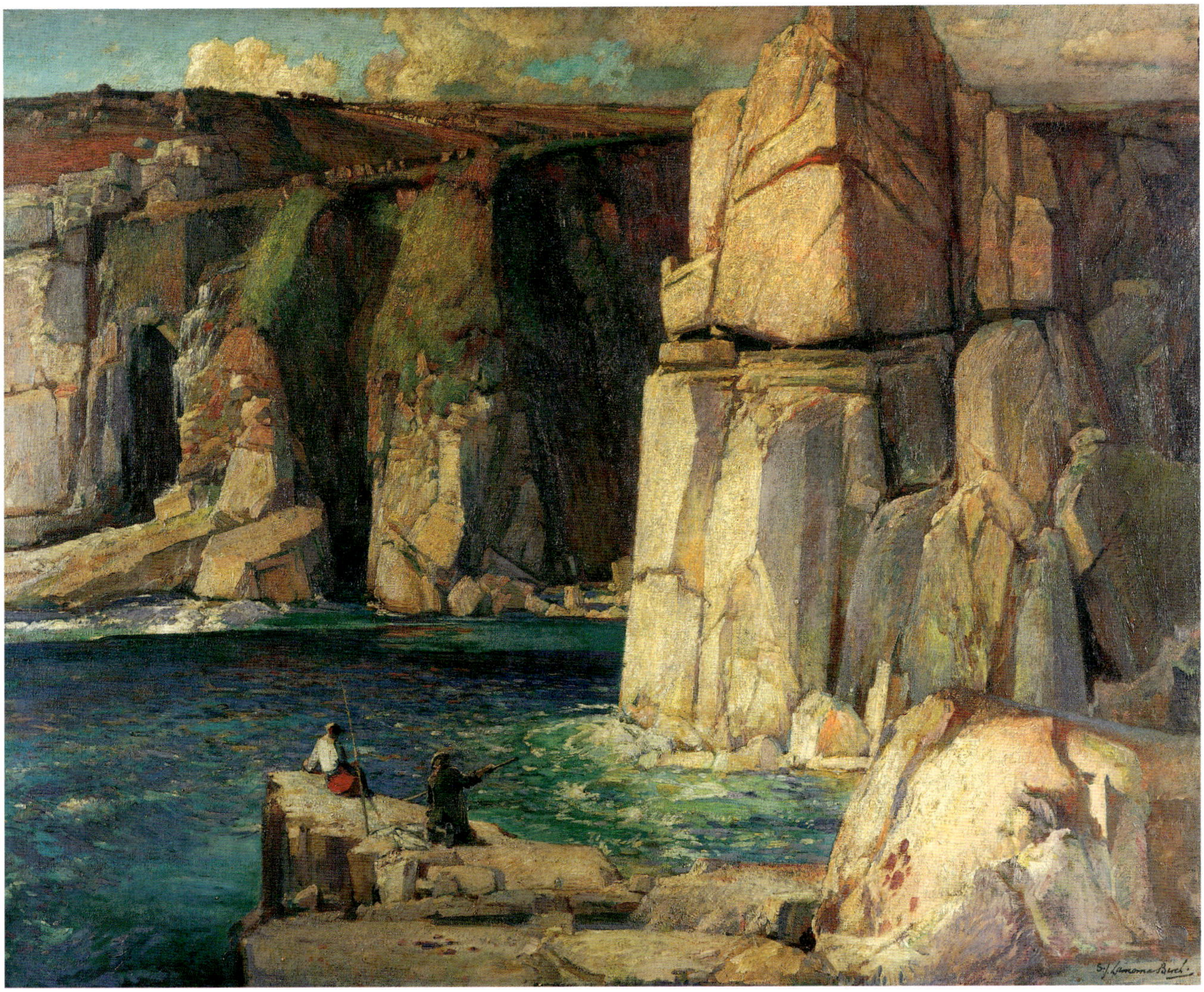

Lamorna Birch painting in Lamorna Cove in 1926 accompanied by his daughter *Mornie*, photograph

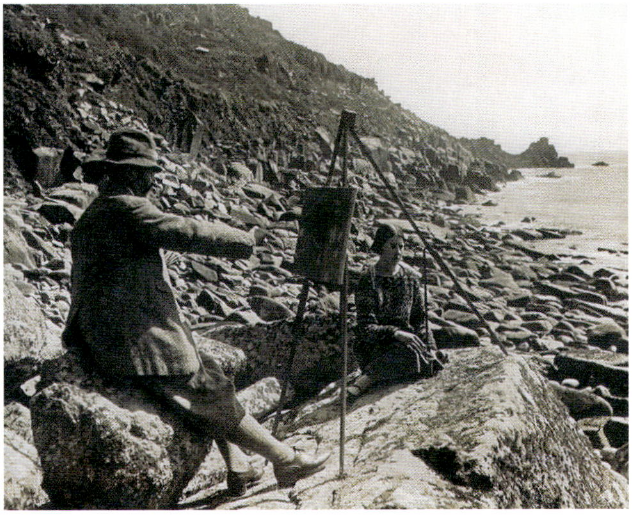

Artists still live and work in the Lamorna valley. Some are the children, grandchildren and even great-grandchildren of earlier generations of painters, but few of them rely on art for their livelihood. However, the colony spirit survives through a painting group established by Birch's elder daughter Mornie who died in 1990, though this is essentially a grouping of amateur artists working for pleasure rather than profit. A Lamorna Society, formed after the publication of the biography of Lamorna Birch in 1995, is building an important archive on all Lamorna painters and the creative life of the valley.[29]

Notes

1. Arthur Hamilton Norway, *Highways and Byways in Devon and Cornwall*, Macmillan, 1897, p.298.
2. Sven Berlin archive, Private collection; and Berlin's correspondence with Austin Wormleighton.
3. Sentiment expressed in Birch's unpublished diary written during a visit to New Zealand in 1936; Private collection.
4. Sir Alfred Munnings, *An Artist's Life*, Museum Press, 1950, p.296.
5. An observation often made informally by auctioneers dealers and collectors.
6. Birch visited more than six countries with his paints. At the age of nearly 70 he embarked on a world tour, ending in New Zealand and Australia where he remained for a year.
7. Both daughters took up art and exhibited at the Royal Academy.
8. Dame Laura Knight, *Oil Paint and Grease Paint*, Ivor Nicholson and Watson, 1936, p.205.
9. Munnings, *An Artist's Life*, p.271.
10. The etcher and Rome scholar Job Nixon was urged to settle at Lamorna in 1930 after a heavily persuasive lunch with Birch in London.
11. Ithell Colquhoun, *The Living Stones*, Peter Owen, 1957, p.42.
12. Marlow Moss (1890-1958) worked in Cornwall intermittently between 1919 and 1958, settling in the Lamorna valley after 1939.
13. Munnings, *An Artist's Life*, p.276.
14. Davies' 'Leisure' has the celebrated opening lines: 'What is this life if, full of care,/ We have no time to stand and stare'. His Lamorna poetry is included in *The Poems of W.H. Davies*, Jonathan Cape, 1934 and 1940.
15. C.E. Vulliamy, *Unknown Cornwall*, John Lane, 1925, p.6.
16. Birch's New Zealand diary.
17. Flagstaff Cottage sits sentinel-like on a ledge half way up Tregurnow Cliff, looking out across the cove to the eastern headland. The old quarry workings seen from the cottage appear in many paintings.
18. Marriott's novel, *House on the Sands* (John Lane, 1903) was written at Flagstaff Cottage.
19. *The Morning Post*, 14 November 1923.
20. Tuke painted Birch's head into a picture called *The Stowaway* on 17 March 1903 and painted his portrait in watercolour in the Lamorna studio on 10 November 1905.
21. Dame Laura Knight, 'Lamorna Birch as I knew him', Memorial Essay 1957, published in the 32nd annual volume of The Old Water-Colour Society's Club.
22. Dame Laura Knight, *The Magic of a Line*, William Kimber, 1965, p.139.
23. Joanna Colenbrander, *A Portrait of Fryn*, Andre Deutsch, 1984, p.44.
24. Knight, *Oil Paint*, p.196.
25. Keith Gardiner, son of the painter Stanley Gardiner, recently discovered the site of the hut. Taking bearings from it he has pinpointed the locations of several pre-1914 pictures.
26. The Letter Studio was built for Laura Knight by Colonel Paynter. It was later owned by the artist and designer John Tunnard (1900-1971).
27. E. Stanhope Forbes, 'An Easter Holiday', *The Studio*, vo.43, 1908, pp.191-99.
28. Knight, *Oil Paint*, p.200.
29. Austin Wormleighton, *A Painter Laureate. Lamorna Birch and his Circle*, Sansom & Company, 1995.

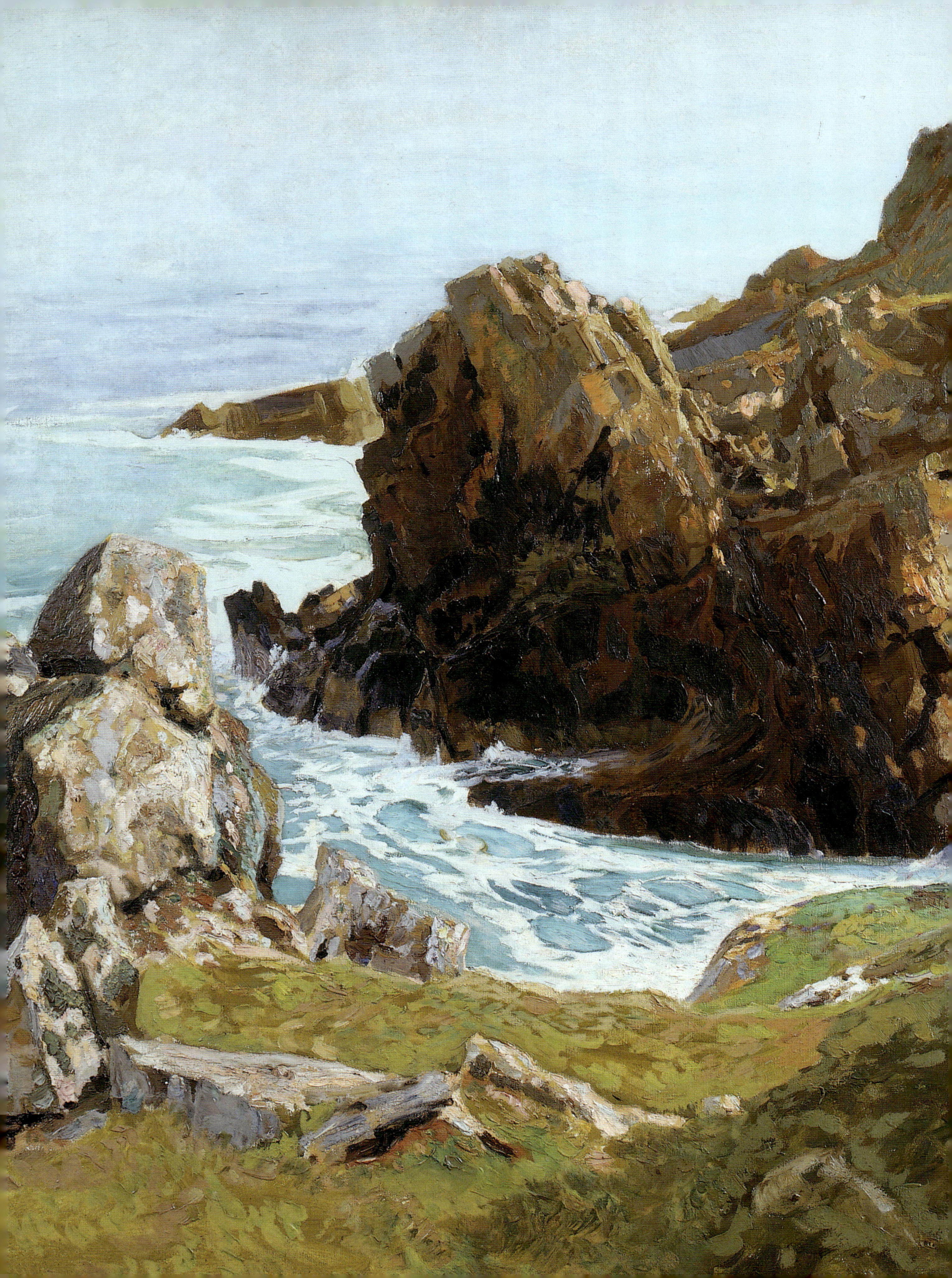

CHAPTER 4

St Ives
The Legendary Quality of Light?

DAVID WILKINSON

The clarity of the reflected light from the Atlantic has long been given as the reason why so many artists flocked to St. Ives in the 1890s. But the truth might be that for the newcomers the attraction of this then rancid little fishing port was that word was out: any number of artists – Royal Academicians and students – were heading down to Cornwall. News of the evolving art colony in St. Ives featured strongly in the literary and art journals of the late nineteenth century.

The light may well have been a bonus to Whistler, Sickert and Mortimer Menpes in 1884, but they were not the first to venture so far west and neither did they stay. But Louis Grier, who arrived around the same time, did, and Henry Harewood Robinson came hot on his heels. By the late 1880s there were more than eighty painters in town, including Americans, Australians and Scandinavians, and when Robinson left, five years later, the great art-rush of the 1890s had thrown up a thriving art club of one hundred members.

It is continuity that distinguishes St. Ives from other art colonies. Like a security blanket, there is an all-encompassing, historical palimpsest about the place.

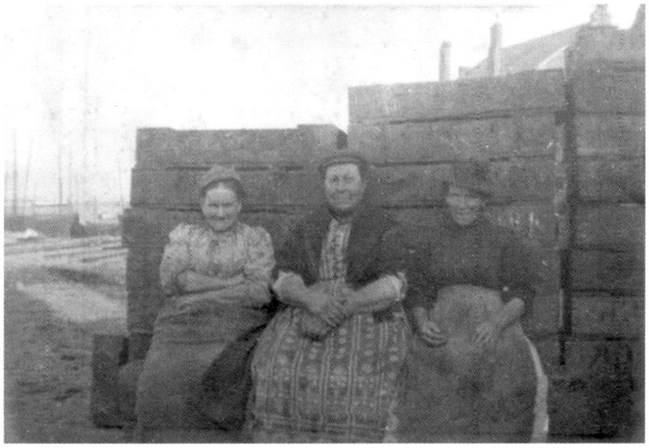

Fisherwomen, St Ives, photograph

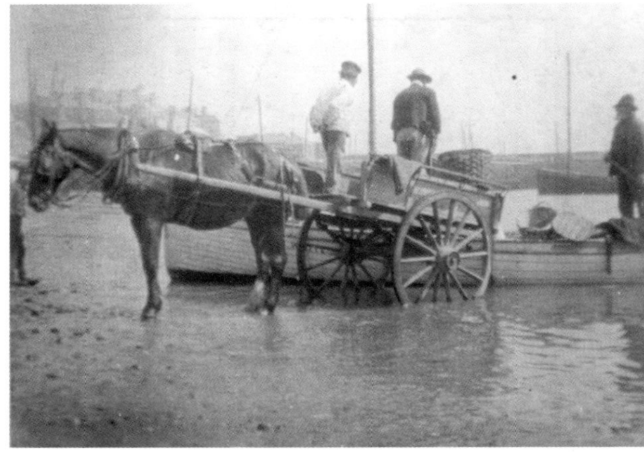

Horse and cart at St Ives Quay, photograph

A plethora of blue plaques would come to celebrate any number of like minds who followed one another into almost any given house in town. From the earliest days of the colony, there has been a cosmopolitan community in St. Ives: 'ex-patriots' from England and beyond. With the decline in mining and fishing, art became the new industry. Even the Cornish townsfolk talk art. In St. Ives, 'town and gown' have at times been as one, with the likes of Julius Olsson a town councillor and justice of the peace. The St. Ives Arts Club still meets in the building in which it was founded one hundred and fifteen years ago. And, despite the occasional acrimonious dispute, artists have huddled together in groups and societies for the mutual benefits they afford: the St. Ives Society of Artists, the Crypt Group, the Penwith Society of Artists and those that even now struggle for exhibition space. The foundation of Tate St. Ives stands as a tribute to an almost endless number of private galleries that preceded it. There are studios all over the town, some of which have been in existence for over a hundred years. The local planners have a stated policy to support the creation and retention of studios and charitable trusts have long been set up with the same aim. St. Ives-based painters have influenced the turn of significant, international movements in art. In the 1950s, with the direct links to New York and Abstract Expressionism, and with Patrick Heron an influential critic, the term 'St. Ives' came to denote style as well as habitat. St. Ives-based painters have been members of every national art association and their work hangs in municipal collections throughout the country and abroad. And critical interest in St. Ives has yielded a niche publishing phenomenon which threatens to rival 'Bloomsbury'.[1]

Yet 'St. Ives' is by no means just about painters and sculptors, and it is interesting to consider the influence that others have had on the evolution of the colony. The significance of the Leach Pottery, in continuous use for over eighty years now, is beyond measure. The students of Bernard Leach have spread his influence worldwide.[2] And this community would be incomplete without its critics, writers, editors and photographers: the media by which a painter's reputation is made or broken. A long line of idiosyncratic scribes has alerted the art world to St. Ives and brought their influence to bear: Charles Marriott and C. Lewis Hind, who both also enjoyed sojourns across the peninsula at Lamorna, the Czech art historian Professor Josef Paul Hodin, Sir Herbert Read (poet, critic, first President of the Penwith Society in 1949 and Trustee of the Tate Gallery in 1965), the American critic Clement Greenberg and the London critics who still make the long journey to St. Ives when a new exhibition opens at the Tate Gallery.

Since 1889, the local newspaper in its varying forms – *St. Ives Weekly Summary*, *The St. Ives Times* and now

Fig.36
Robert Borlase Smart, *Morning Light, St Ives*, oil on canvas
Royal Institute of Cornwall / Royal Cornwall Museum

St. Ives Times and Echo – has kept a dedicated record of the comings and goings among the creative community. Harold Sawkins and Leonard Richmond, both with strong St. Ives connections, were editors of *The Artist* magazine that kept the amateur painter in touch. The freemasonry of art and even the art history of the colony have all contributed towards the spirit that binds the creative population to this day. In one family alone, three generations have had a lasting impact on St. Ives. For over a hundred and twenty years there has been a succession of influential role models living in and around St. Ives: from the early days of Julius Olsson and Louis Grier, through the quietly influential early-twentieth-century years of Robert Borlase Smart (see fig.36), to the reign of the modernists Ben Nicholson and Dame Barbara Hepworth and finally to the recently deceased Patrick Heron and Sir Terry Frost.

In the early years alone, Bellair Terrace – comprising no more than twenty-odd houses – was home to almost forty painters and writers including Walter Sickert's brother Bernard, a competent landscape, portrait and figure painter, and their father, the landscape and figure painter, Oswald Sickert; the landscape painter, John Mallard Bromley; Allan Deacon, a portrait painter; the landscape and decorative painter, Guy Kortright; the landscape, figure and marine painter, Henry E. Detmold; the painter and etcher Alfred Hartley and his wife, the flower painter, Nora Hartley; Helene Schjerfbeck, the landscape painter who ranks high among the Scandinavians to have visited St. Ives, along with her Finnish travelling companion, Maria Wilk; the landscape painter, John Henry Titcomb; the Argentine-born naturalist and writer, W. H. Hudson and the coastal and landscape painter, Charles Mottram.

One of the earliest writer-critics to have sharpened his pencil on St. Ives was Charles Marriott. The son of a Bris-

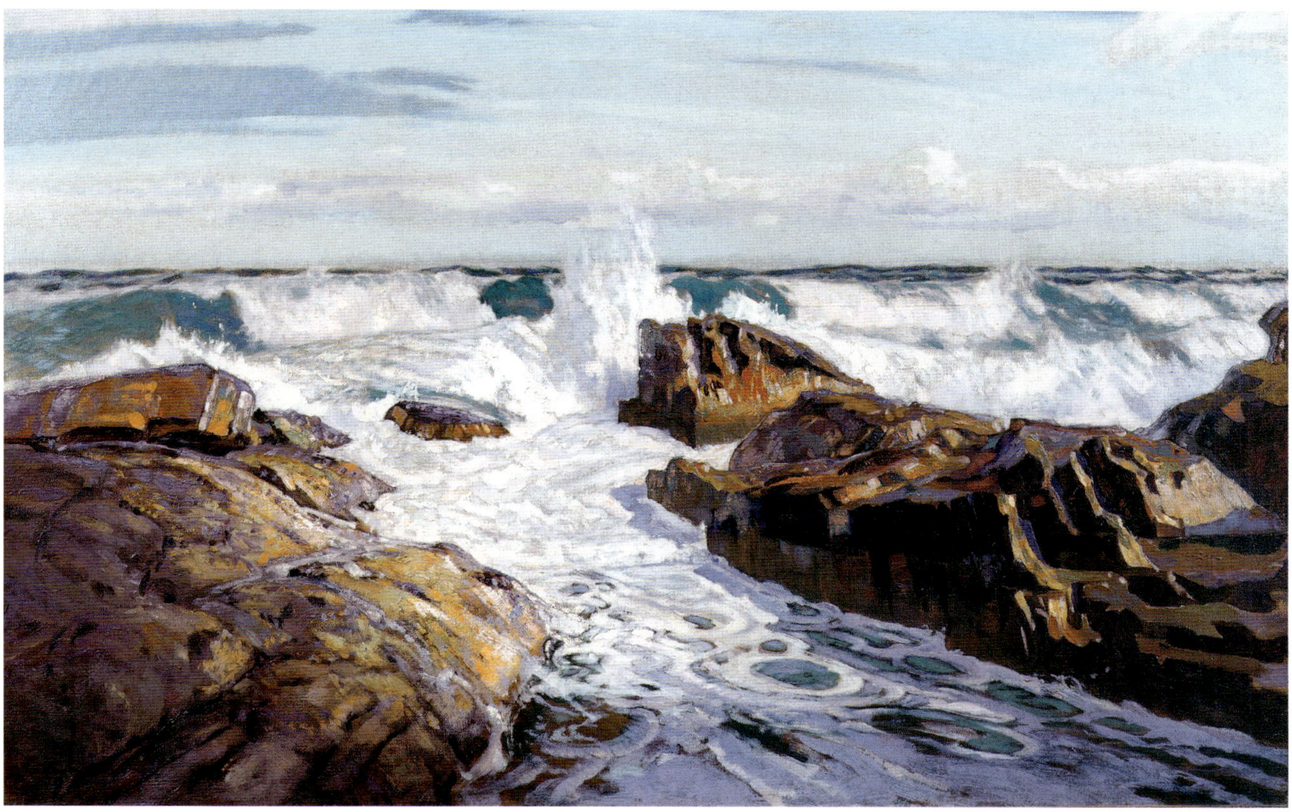

tol brewer, Marriott first came to Cornwall in 1889. After an absence of twelve years, he and his first wife, Dora, returned to Cornwall in 1901 after the publication of his first novel. They took up residence at Flagstaff Cottage, Lamorna, but within a year they were in St. Ives, living in The Terrace where the views matched those from Talland House where, as children, Virginia Woolf and her sister Vanessa Bell spent their summers with their parents, Leslie and Julia Stephen, just a few hundred yards away.

Marriott's drawing room was his *salon*. His taste was discriminating, his perception impeccable and, initially, his view of the painters of St. Ives, favourable; indeed, in 1908, he was appointed President of St. Ives Arts Club. On his arrival he believed that St. Ives housed the only significant group of painters to be found in Cornwall. It was a view that would later change. He published around twenty novels before turning to art, and went on to lecture in art at Liverpool University. But his most influential posting was as art critic to *The Times* between 1924 and 1940. Marriott was a great stylist of whom his friend, the drama and music critic, Gerald Cumberland had once said that he would rather go without dinner than split an infinitive. Now, Cumberland added: 'his art criticism is wonderfully fine but a life standing on the polished floors of galleries between Bond Street and Leicester Square is soul-corroding and heart-breaking. Marriott's mind no longer darts and leaps. It moves gently, very gently.'[3] The esteem in which Marriott held St. Ives art diminished as his influence expanded. It wasn't only the St. Ives artists who suffered. Lamorna Birch, who was towards the forefront of Marriott's friends in West Penwith and who had taken on Flagstaff Cottage when Marriott moved to St. Ives, was deeply hurt when his friend began to ignore his work.

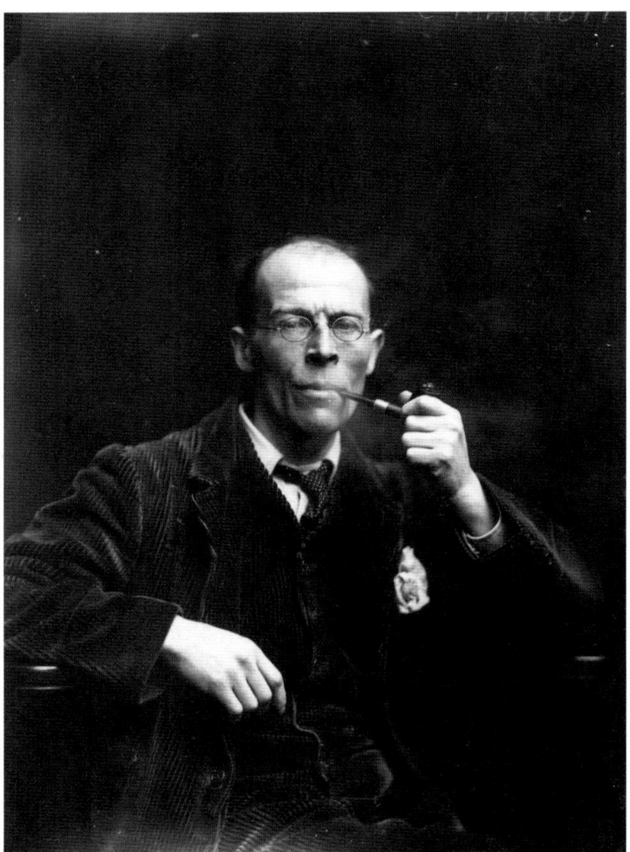

Charles Marriott, an influential writer on the local art scene, photograph by W H Lanyon, courtesy of Andrew Lanyon

There were great friendships and comings-and-goings between the artists then living in Cornwall. Marriott recalled that the marine painters, Henry S. Tuke and Napier Hemy would turn up from Falmouth. Tuke and Hemy were among the elder statesmen of painters working in Cornwall and also the best of raconteurs, sharing an immense store of reminiscences. Another natural wit was the American, Lowell Dyer. As did so many others, Dyer came to Cornwall fresh from the Académie Julian in Paris. He never achieved more than a footnote in the history of art but his sense of humour was a passport to practically everyone of interest both in Paris and St. Ives, where he chose to spend the remainder of his days. By 1899 he was renting a studio from the landscape artist, Thomas Millie Dow who had taken on Talland House after Leslie Stephen left following the death of his wife, Julia, in 1895. It was while he was in Paris, in 1890, that Dyer had met the poet Arthur Symons and Dr. Havelock Ellis, both of whom had strong connections with St. Ives. Between 1868 and 1873, Symons spent three childhood years in St. Ives and, as his *Notes on my Poems,*

Fig.37
Adrian Stokes, *Upland and Sky*, 1886–88, oil on canvas

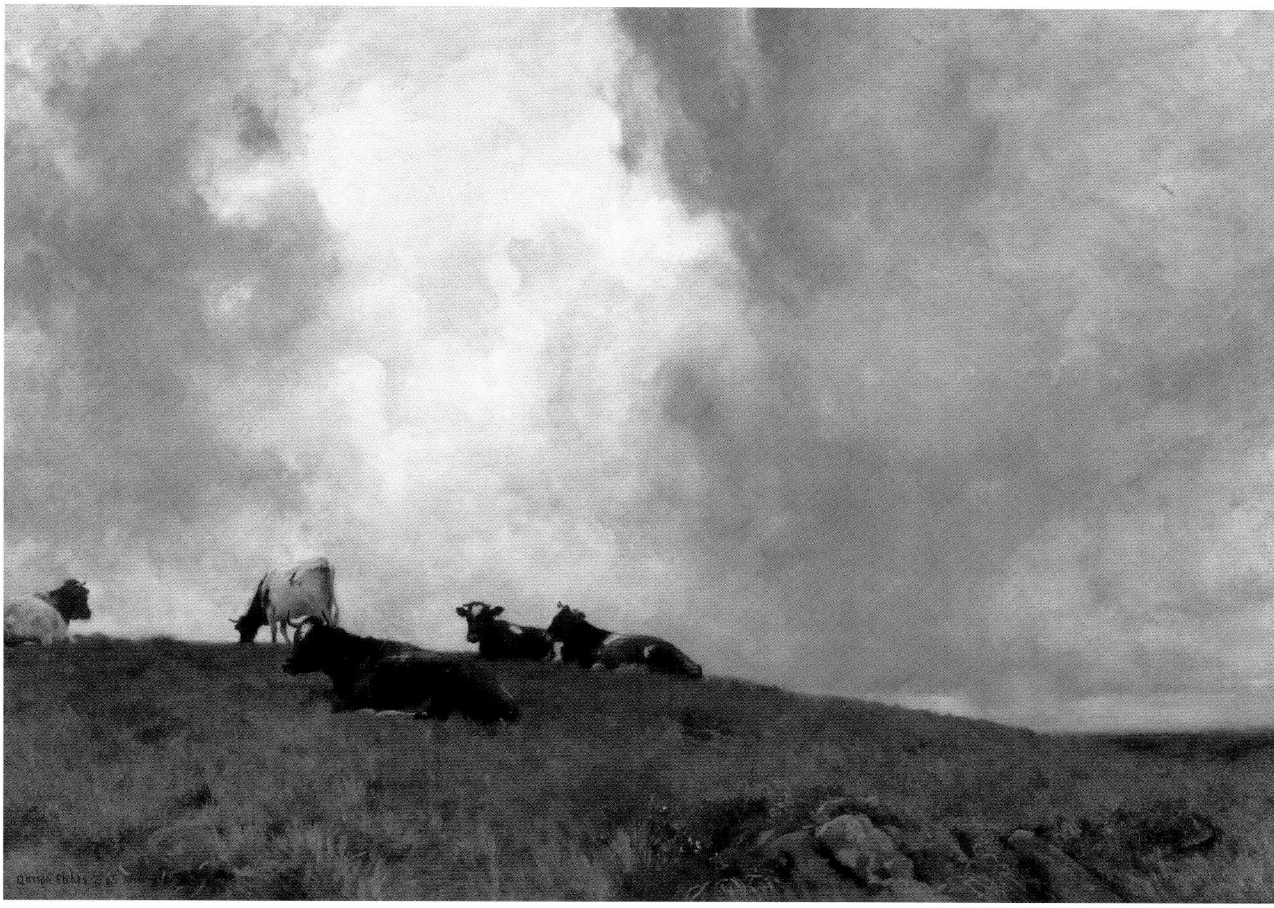

published in 1916, suggest, his muse remained rooted in the 'the iron-bound coast of Cornwall'. Havelock Ellis had courted Edith Lees in the streets of St. Ives in 1890. This sexually ambivalent couple married in 1891 and by 1894 had returned to Carbis Bay where they remained for the next ten years.

Another literary figure, C. Lewis Hind, editor of the influential art journal *Academy*, first visited St. Ives in May 1895, when he stayed for a year, taking a studio and becoming a student of Julius Olsson. But he would return to St. Ives on and off for the next ten years. He also stayed at Lamorna with Marriott in the early 1900s. Of the St. Ives painters, Moffat Lindner, Louis Grier, Adrian Stokes (see fig.37) and John Alfred Arnesby Brown were among his closest companions.

Ranger Gull's novel, *Portalone* (1903) was the first fictional account of the art colony in St. Ives dedicated, not to Charles Marriott, whom he had known for some time, but to his new-found comrade-in-arms, Alan Gardner Folliott Stokes, whose photograph – looking more like a rough-and-ready gamekeeper than a painter – still hangs on the walls of St. Ives Arts Club. Gull's pen portraits are as telling as any brushmark on canvas, offering clues to the social standing of the painters and to their attitude towards their work.[4] But they caused nothing like the furore which greeted publication of painter and sculptor Sven Berlin's *Dark Monarch* which had to be withdrawn in the face of a hail of writs nearly sixty years later.

In May 1889, the *Daily Telegraph* noted that Louis Grier and Julius Olsson were building up what, one day, might be recognized as the St. Ives School of painting. As a

Fig.38
Julius Olsson, *Moonlit Shore*, 1911, oil on canvas

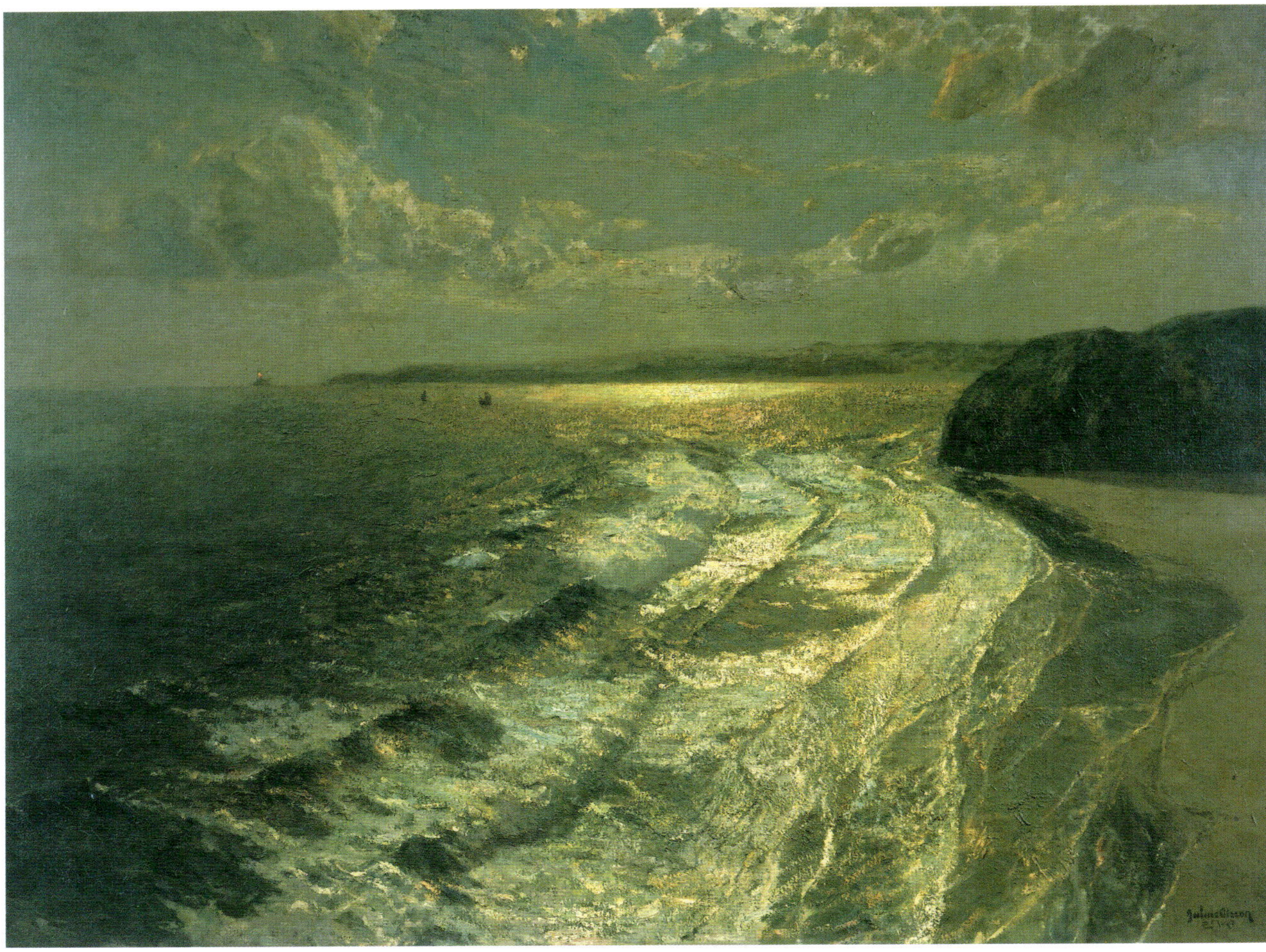

landscape and seascape painter, Grier had long since distanced himself from the narrative paintings coming from nearby Newlyn. He and Olsson had begun to take on students around 1895. Olsson was the driving power (see fig.38), described by Folliott Stokes as 'a big man with a big heart, who paints big pictures with big brushes in a big studio.' He proved to be a hard taskmaster, sending his students out in all weathers to paint around the harbour before returning to his minimalist studio for a final life class in the evening. 'Jo', as his students referred to him, would chastise those who, like the now celebrated Canadian painter, Emily Carr, would run for cover when the wind or rain proved troublesome.

Grier's studio was perfectly placed to host a meeting that led, two years later, to the formation of the St. Ives Arts Club. The first President, in 1890, was Adrian Stokes followed by Henry Harewood Robinson, one of the first to settle in St. Ives. Lowell Dyer took office in 1893, 1894 and again in 1918. Olsson's first election was in 1895, and Millie Dow took on the role in 1898. Marriott took the honours in 1908, a short while before he left St. Ives, but Louis Grier seems never to have allowed his name to be put forward. His amiable presence nevertheless remained the bedrock of the social side of the club. While some painters still drew on the Victorian tradition of literary quotations for titles to their works, Grier remained doggedly attached to the state of the weather for his seascapes. The sea was a common theme for both St. Ives and Newlyn-based painters, but whereas St. Ives seascapes can be tumultuous,

Fig.39
Marianne Stokes, *Polishing Pans*
National Museums Liverpool (The Walker)

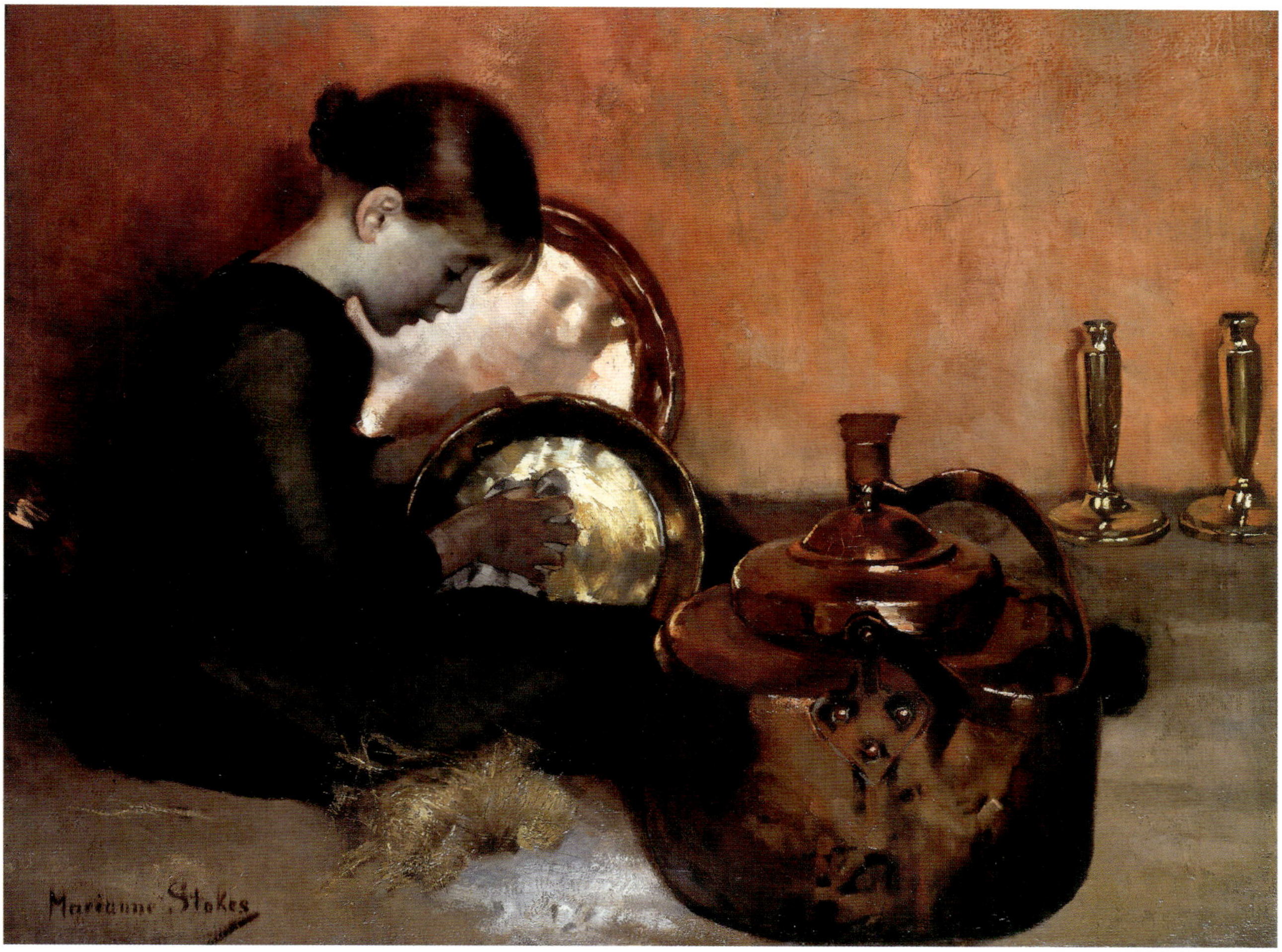

in Newlyn the sea was usually only present as a horizontal backdrop to the human figure.

Overriding the value of membership of their individual art societies, for many in St. Ives the acceptance of work by the Royal Academy Summer Exhibition remained the annual challenge. Each would devote his attention to one significant piece and then invite visitors to see the completed work before submission. 'Show Day' became an event and special railway carriages would be laid on not only to take the crated pieces to London, but to bring in the visitors to the open studios. Writing her 1972 memoir, *The Faulls of St. Ives*, Lillian M. Faull remembers the excitement as 'ladies of grace and position' made their way down'long from the station to the studios. For, as Miss Faull intimates, with only the rare exception, the numerous artists' studios were 'Downalong' in the converted sail lofts around the harbour whereas the artists lived 'Up'long' where the air was a little more savoury.

There has never been a shortage of painting tutors in St. Ives. From the earliest days, any number of lesser-known but competent painters were taking students on painting forays abroad. Marriott's friend, the flower and landscape painter A. Moulton Foweraker, for instance, came to St. Ives from Exeter in 1902 and in 1904 was advertising in *The Studio* a prolonged painting expedition to Spain – 'mainly out of doors' – that was to include two months in Malaga, a month at Cordoba and a month at Granada. The husband and wife team of Gertrude and Algernon Talmage took on students. In the 1920s, Charles

Fig.40
William H Y Titcomb, *Primitive Methodists at Prayer St. Ives*
oil on canvas, Dudley Museum and Art Gallery

Fig.41
Alfred Wallis, *Steamship in Harbour*, oil on card
Private collection

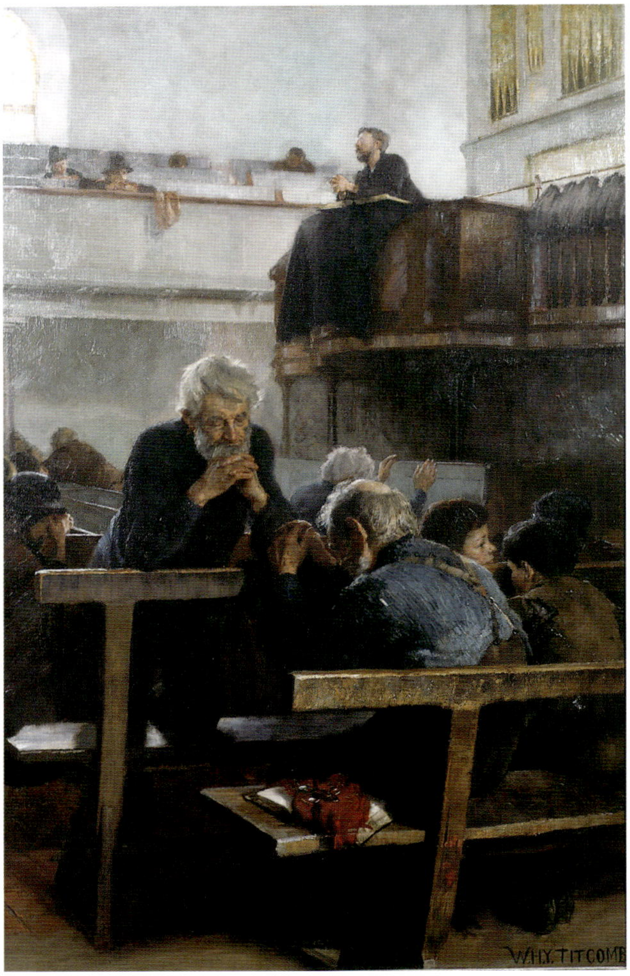

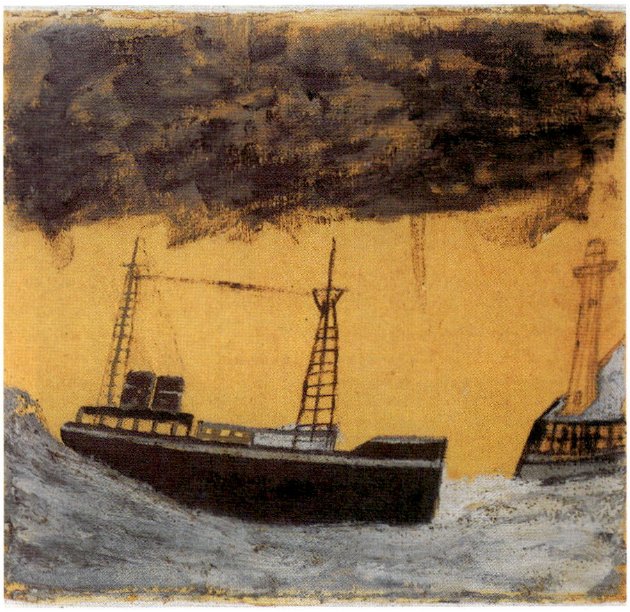

Simpson and his wife, Ruth advertised a 'St. Ives School of Painting' alternating between their Porthmeor Studio and The Shore Studio of Commander George Fagan Bradshaw, who shared duties with them. The landscape and figure painter, Arthur Hayward, took over the Simpsons' studio and he, too, began teaching, as did the portrait and landscape painter Beatrice Pauline Hewett. In the 1950s, with William Redgrave, Peter Lanyon ran a school from his aptly named studio, St. Peter's Loft, which now houses the Penwith Printmakers' workshop. But it was in 1938 that the more formal St. Ives School of Painting, as it is known today, was founded by Leonard Fuller in the Porthmeor Studio complex. Marjorie Mostyn continued running 'The School' for a while after her husband's death, before passing control to Roy Ray.

In 1927 a new and important grouping, the St. Ives Society of Artists, was formed, whose gallery doors remain open today in the Mariners' Chapel. Once through the economic turmoil of the late 1920s, and under the constant wisdom of Borlase Smart, the Society put together a series of supremely successful, national touring exhibitions of work by members. As a result, painters such as Stanley Spencer, Alfred Munnings and Frank Brangwyn were drawn to become members. As the Second World War approached, works by eighty members were hung by the Royal Academy. Never since has any one society similarly dominated those hallowed walls.

To be hung in the Royal Academy remained an aspiration for the many, but the desire for progress led to membership of the New English Art Club for a number of St. Ives painters including Millie Dow, Arthur George Bell, Henry Detmold, Emanuel Phillips Fox, Alfred Hartley, Adrian and Marianne Stokes (see fig.39), Alfred East, Olsson, W.H.Y. Titcomb (see fig.40) and Moffatt Lindner. Despite its cosmopolitan make-up, St. Ives never produced any Fauves, Vorticists, Futurists or Cubists and, curiously, the few who leaned towards Surrealism in Cornwall worked out of Newlyn and the Lamorna valley. But

Fig.42
John Anthony Park, *The Morning Ride, St Ives*, c.1930
oil on board, Private collection

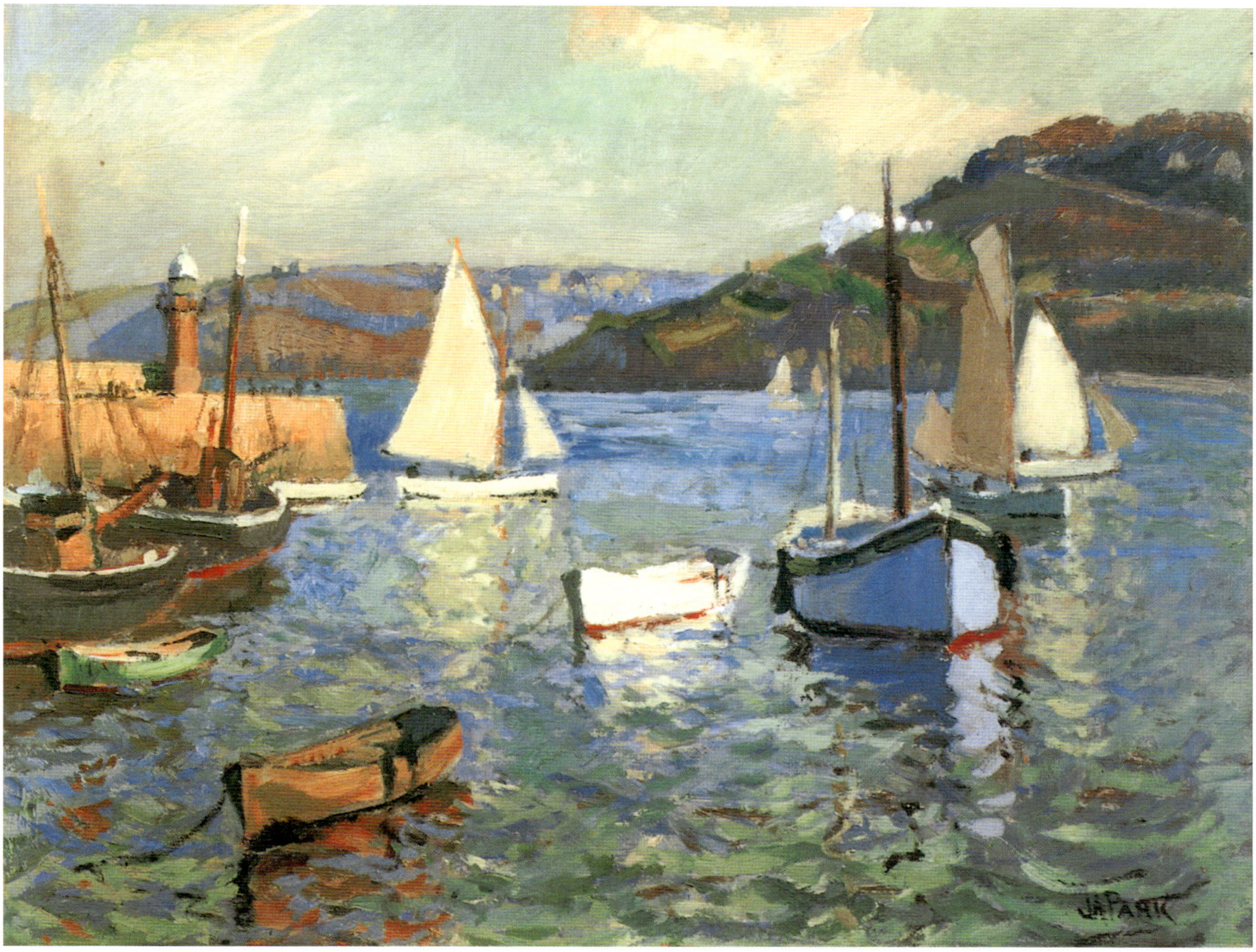

there were one or two Impressionists worthy of note, as Austin Wormleighton's book on John Park makes clear.[5] Park, perhaps akin to the naïve Alfred Wallis, painted for the sheer joy of the experience rather than the financial rewards that never came his way (see fig.42).

Not obviously part of the 'colony', the reclusive, semi-literate Alfred Wallis is an iconic figure from the inter-war years in St. Ives. Anything but 'clubbable', he was, apparently, barely aware of other artists and only started painting at the age of 70, after his wife's death. His well documented 'discovery' by Ben Nicholson and Christopher Wood in the late 1920s led to a wider appreciation, by the cognoscenti, of his primitive paintings: primitive both in technique and materials – he often used scraps of cardboard for his canvases (see fig.41). Paradoxically his work has both an innocence and a sophistication which profoundly influenced younger, avant-garde artists, and his elegantly

Alfred Wallis – the house in Back Road West, St. Ives, where Alfred (pictured c.1938) started painting after his wife's death, photograph

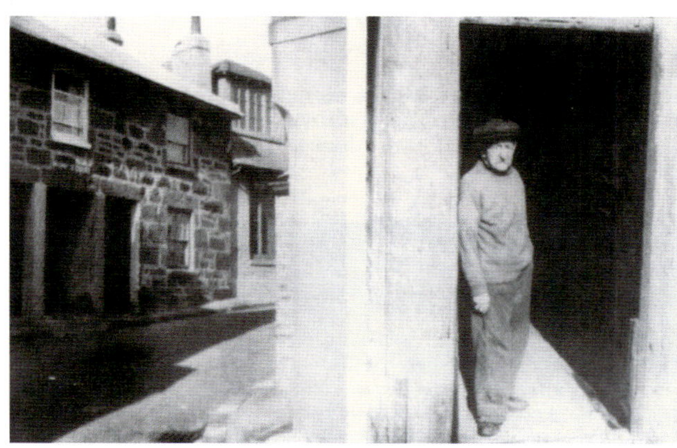

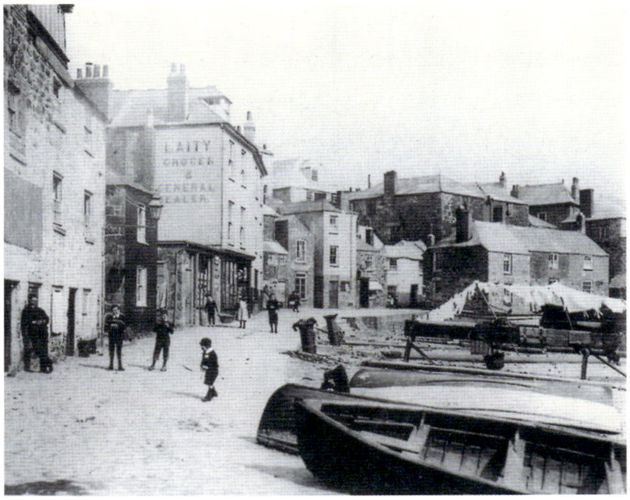

The St. Ives that Wallis knew: Wharf Road viewed from Quick's sail loft, c. 1900, photograph

simple depictions of the Cornish fishing industry are now recognized as some of the most interesting and original of the time.

On his arrival in St. Ives John Park shared the Attic Studio with the portrait photographer W. Herbert Lanyon.[6] In January 1903 Lanyon was offering lessons in 'Pianoforte Playing, Voice Culture and Singing to a strictly limited number of pupils'.[7] Lanyon's Sunday evenings 'at home' became a regular institution and he continued to compose music, a short piece of which was broadcast in the late 1940s. It is through the eye of Herbert Lanyon's lens that we have portraits of his contemporaries. He was

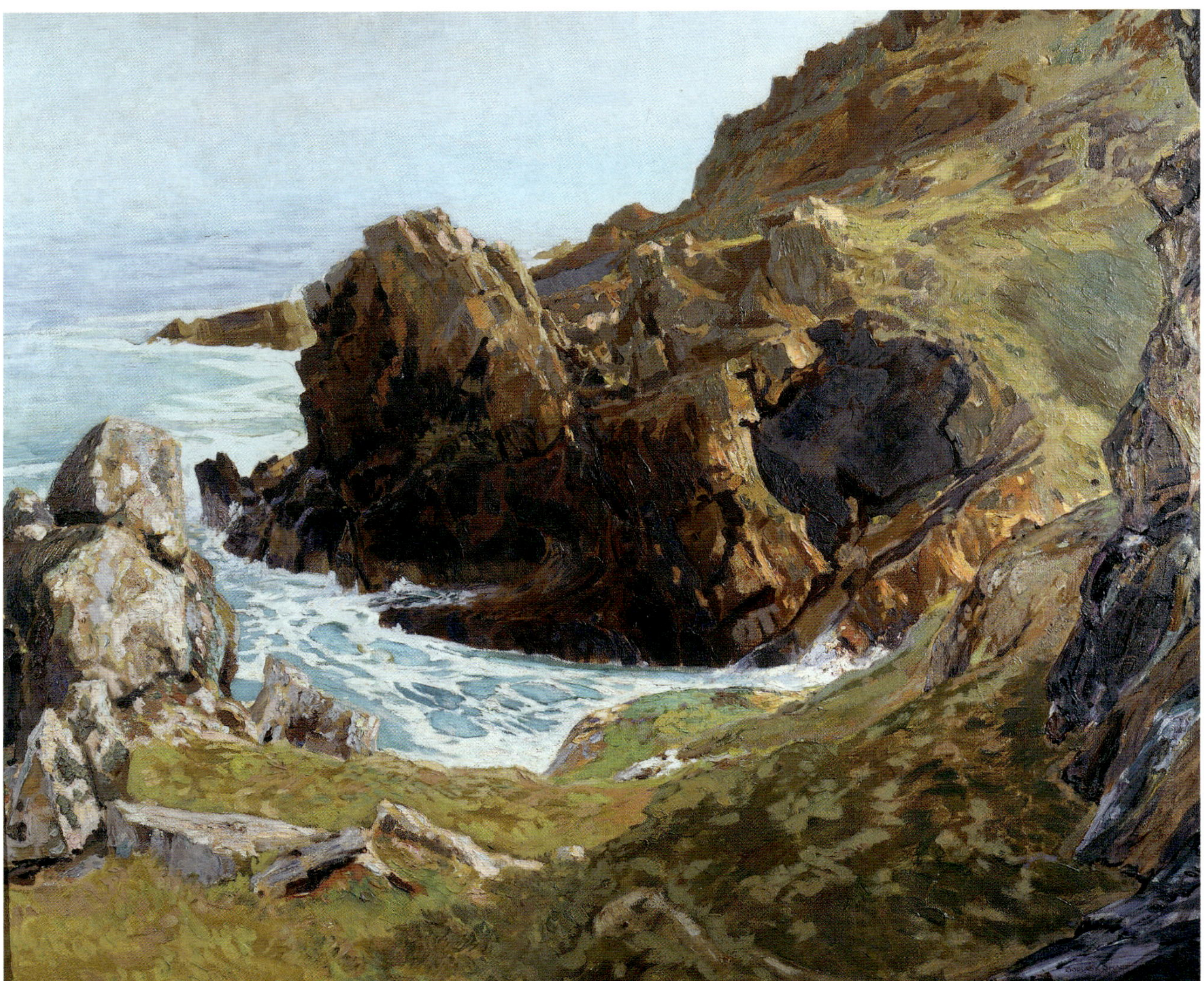

Fig.43
Robert Borlase Smart, *Zennor*, oil on canvas
Royal Institute of Cornwall / Royal Cornwall Museum

Fig.44
Charles W Simpson, *The Line Fishing Season*, oil on canvas
Plymouth City Museum and Art Gallery © Artist's Estate

one of few creative Cornishmen of his time, a fact that became a matter of family pride: Peter Lanyon remains the only native Cornish abstract painter to have achieved international acclaim in the post-Second World War period. To this day Herbert Lanyon's grandchildren remain rooted in the creative arts of West Cornwall and beyond.

For around one hundred years, the Sloop Inn on the harbour front has been one of the most consistent exhibition venues in St. Ives. At times its value has been almost as a *salon des refusés* where practically anyone could get hung. From the beginning of the last century when Louis Grier and his coterie were regulars, to the present time – when alongside portraits of the local fishermen by the recently deceased Hyman Segal, hang the quarterly exhibitions by students at St. Ives School of Painting – the Sloop has been the base for social life and the occasional exhibition. For a period in the late 1940s, the Castle Inn in Fore Street rivalled the Sloop and Downing's Bookshop, run by Councillor George Downing in the 1940s and 1950s, became the important exhibition space for significant moderns.

In the 1880s James Lanham began as a picture framer, colour man and as a studio-letting and packing agent for the national and international transport of

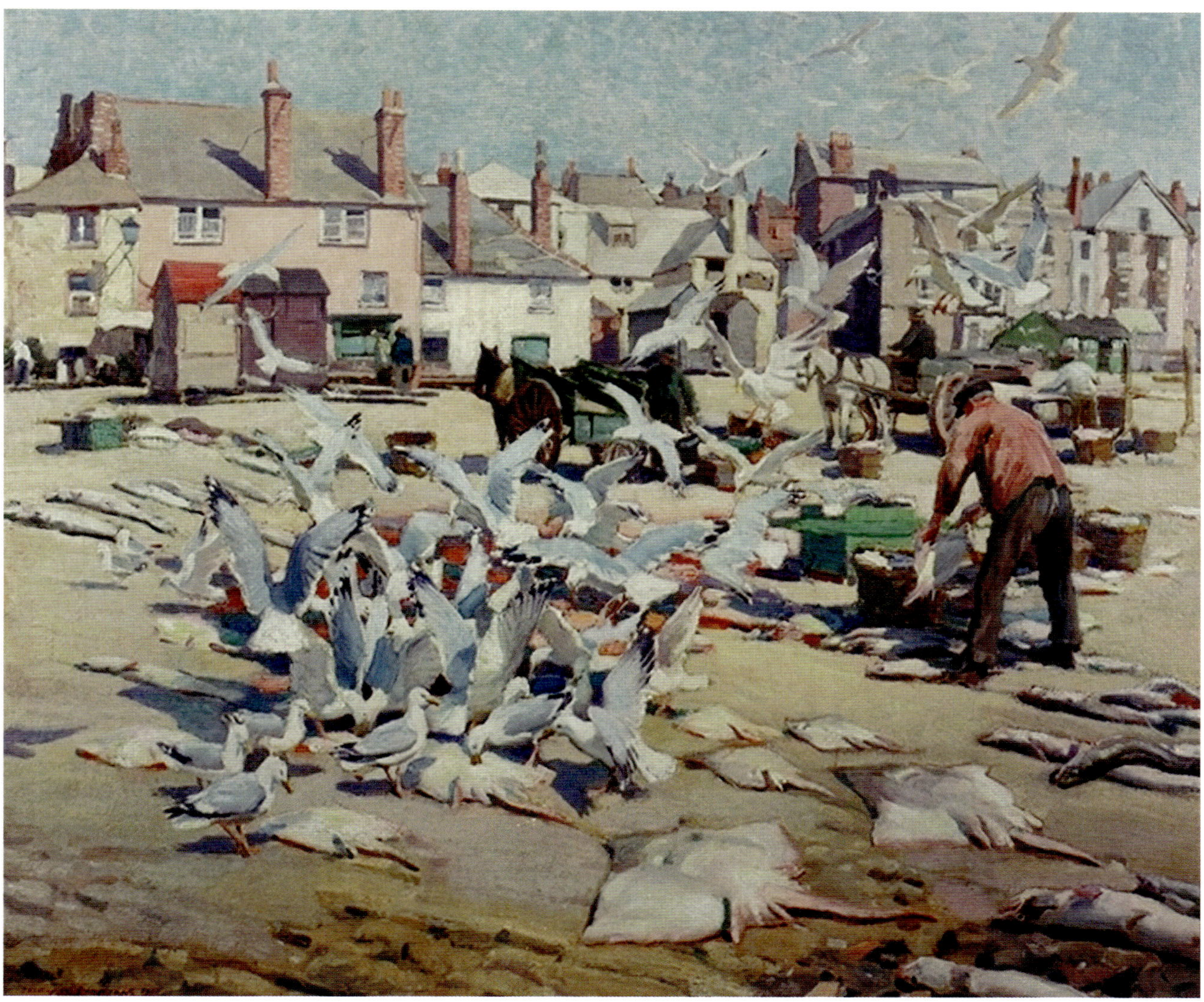

Artist showing painting outside Lanhams, photograph

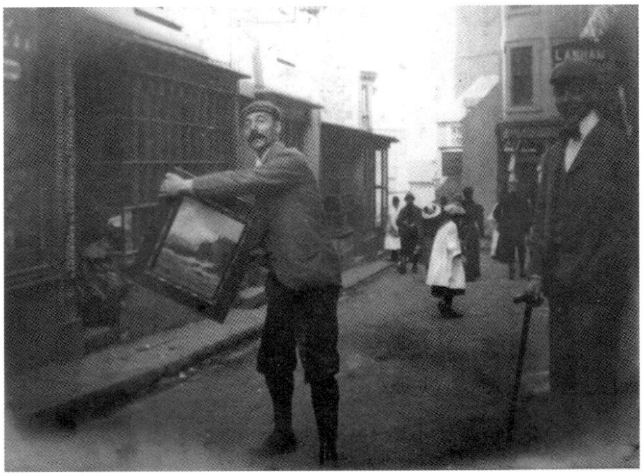

paintings. With an astute business head, he also opened a gallery at his premises with his own stable of painters.[8] But in 1905 a minor mutiny erupted when a deputation that included Grier and Dyer felt it beneath them to have paintings shown in his window. On its formation in 1927, the St. Ives Society of Artists set up its first gallery in number 4 Porthmeor Studios. It moved to number 5 in 1933 and relocated to its current premises, the Mariners' Chapel, in 1945. Below the Mariners' lies the Crypt that, in the form of a rebel exhibition in 1946, witnessed gunpowder plottings that led in 1949 to the formation of the Penwith Society and the onset of the era dominated by Ben Nicholson, Barbara Hepworth and Bernard Leach. The first Penwith Gallery was set up in the old auctioneering premises at 16 Fore Street before finding its permanent home in 1961.

Porthmeor Studios – historically the most important studios in St. Ives – stand right on the beach overlooking the sunset. Before the easels were moved in at the beginning of the last century, they were used as sail and net lofts for the fishing community. A list of tenants of any one of these vast studios underlines the continuity that pervades the town. Number 3, to take one example, has witnessed work by Marcella Smith, Margery Balance, Francis Algernon Spenlove (also known as Francis Raymond), Commander Bradshaw, Francis Bacon, Breon O'Casey, Patrick Hughes and Mollie Parkin, Peter Blake, Roy Walker and Wilhemina Barns-Graham – as eclectic a succession of artists as one could wish for. Number 5, as well as serving as a temporary gallery for the St. Ives Society of Artists, has housed George A. Boyle, Julius Olsson, Robert Borlase Smart and, from the heroic post-war abstract school, Ben Nicholson, Patrick Heron and Terry Frost.

Today, the Porthmeor Studio properties remain under the management of the Borlase Smart John Wells Memorial Trust, standing as testimonials to Smart – one of the most undervalued personalities in the art history of St. Ives and to the recently deceased abstract painter, John Wells. The central courtyard of the Porthmeor Studios still shares access with the fishermen to the net and boat stores below, and retains an innately nineteenth-century feel, although there are controversial plans to bring these studios into the twenty-first century. In recent years, the privately owned Sail Loft and Rope Walk studios in Porthmeor Road have been rebuilt with integral studio accommodation, but the similarly idealistic principles under which the beachside Piazza and Barnaloft complexes were created in the 1960s have since bowed under the pressure for holiday homes.

The arrival of abstract art in the late 1940s brought about the first private, commercial galleries, many of which have come and gone, but seen as an entity they too have provided a certain stability to the sense of art-in-its-place that St. Ives has come to embody. Local fears about the opening of the Tate Gallery in 1993 have been largely offset by the other facilities that have been enabled in the wake of its popularity. Nowadays there is an enviable permanence to art in St. Ives that has little to do with the legendary light. However, there are many who would concede that if one were to lie back on the rocky peninsula known as 'The Island', one could observe the progress of the sun from dawn to sunset, without lifting a brush.

Notes

1. See for example, Marion Whybrow, *St. Ives 1883-1993: Portrait of an Art Colony*, Antique Collectors' Club, 1994; and David Tovey, *Creating a Splash: The St. Ives Society of Artists: The First 25 Years (1927-1952)*, Wilson Books, 2003.

2. See Marion Whybrow, *The Leach Legacy: the St. Ives Pottery and its Legacy*, Sansom & Company, 1996.

3. Gerald Cumberland, *Set Down in Malice*, Grant Richards, 1919.

4. C. Ranger Gull, *Portalone*, Greening & Co., 1903.

5. Austin Wormleighton, *Morning Tide: John Anthony Park and the Painters of Light: St. Ives 1900-1950*, Stockbridge Books, 1998.

6. One of Lanyon's musical manuscripts is on display in St. Ives Museum. Two pieces for piano were published as *Impressions* in 1908 by the Vincent Music Company, London and Thomas J Donlan, Boston. The first, 'Mexican Dance', is dedicated to Charles Marriott. Whilst it cut short a professional career in music, an injury to one of his hands in a train accident did not stop Lanyon from playing.

7. *St. Ives Times*, January 1903.

8. The name of Lanhams survives as a holiday letting agent in its original premises.

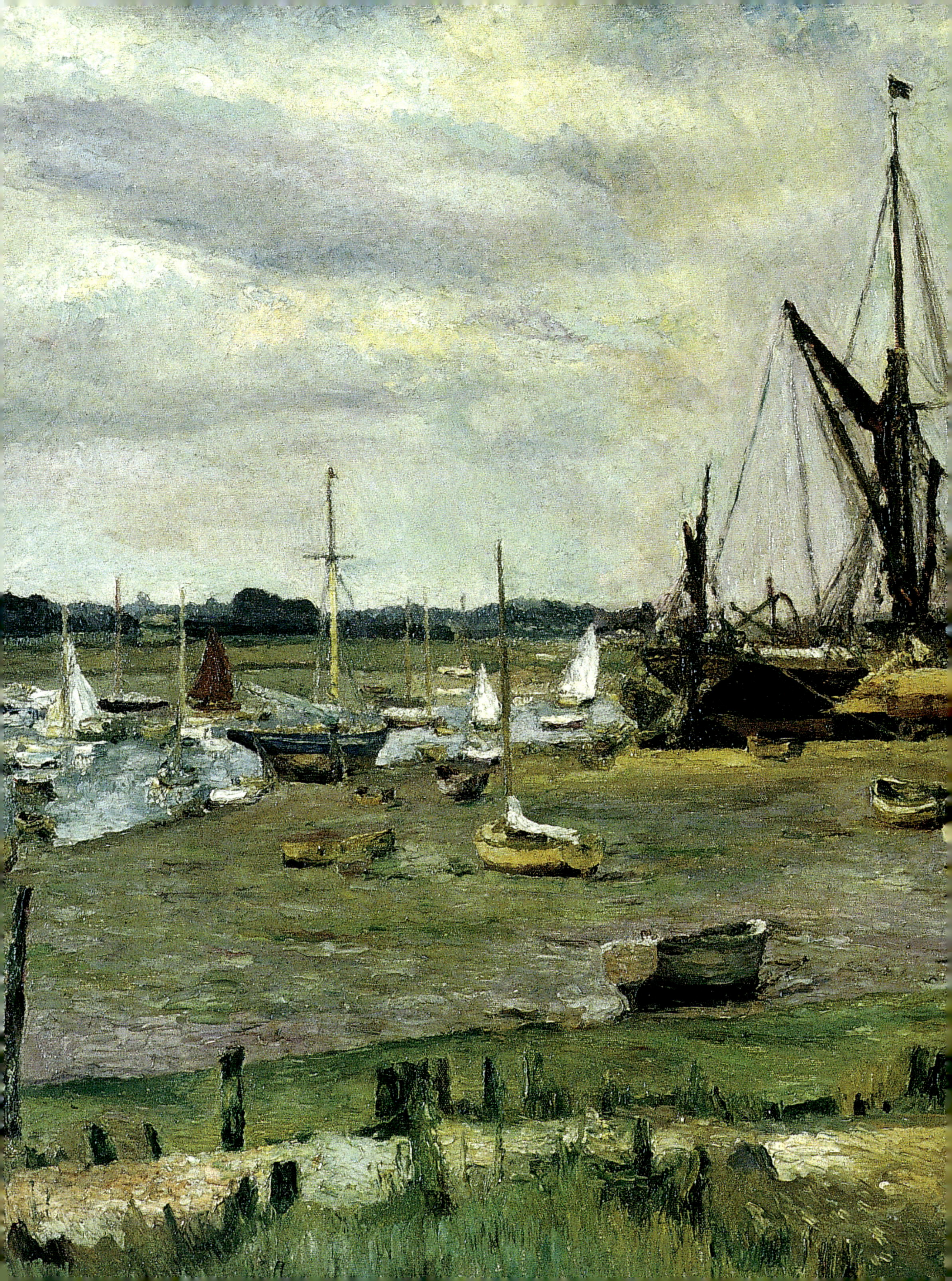

CHAPTER 5

Walberswick
'An Eye for the Quiet Beauties of Nature'

RICHARD SCOTT

The Suffolk village of Walberswick lies midway between Aldeburgh and Lowestoft, on the south bank of the Blyth estuary.[1] Southwold occupies rising ground a mile to the north, while a small village across reedbed marshes to the south is all that remains of the ancient city port of Dunwich, lost to the sea through centuries of coastal erosion.

Visitors to Walberswick in 1880 would have found a hauntingly bleak place, largely devoid of mature trees and dominated visually by the large ruined church at the western extremity and a windmill near the centre.[2] There were two working farms and two inns, The Bell and The Blue Anchor. A scatter of cottages and small houses lined the main street, clustering more densely around the village green with its washing lines and roaming geese. Along the river bank irregular groups of wooden buildings and landing stages served a modest sail-powered fishing fleet, while nearby there were mud flats covered with samphire and mauve sea lavender, and intersected with tidal rivulets. There was no vehicular access to Southwold, but pedestrians could cross by rowing boat ferry, replaced in 1885 by a

Fig.45
Edwin Edwards, *Old Wharves, Walberswick*, 1876, etching
Ipswich Borough Council Museums and Galleries

hand-cranked pontoon version which could accommodate cattle, or a horse and cart.

A substantial surge of young visiting artists in the 1880s cemented Walberswick's already established reputation as an artists' Mecca. Despite the volume of new visitors some historians have been hesitant to describe the village as a colony, on the grounds that very few artist visitors adopted it as their permanent home. While this is also true of some of the more readily accepted colonies, a more compelling reason may be that owing to Walberswick's relative proximity to London, there was neither a 'school' as at Newlyn, nor an established artists' club, as at St. Ives and Staithes. Ian Collins' succinct reference to it as a 'shifting colony' seems an accurate description; whatever its definition, within the span of two centuries the village has been a working destination for a very substantial number of artists with some claim to professional standing.[3]

In the opening years of the nineteenth century Walberswick's artist visitors were drawn to the church ruin, reflecting the prevailing enthusiasm for mysterious antiquity. Cornelius Varley and Peter de Wint both made studies of it, as did Suffolk's most prolific topographical artist of the period, Henry Davy. Even their illustrious contemporary J.M.W. Turner made sketchbook reference to the church tower while on a coastal sea voyage from Harwich to Lowestoft and beyond in the early 1830s.[4]

By the 1870s the activities of the river had attracted the eccentric but highly regarded etcher Charles Keene, better known as a humorous illustrator for *Punch*. Keene was usually accompanied by fellow-etcher Edwin Edwards who had a house in Dunwich (see fig.45), and on occasion by Henry Stacy Marks. Elected Royal Academician in 1878, Marks shared Keene's sense of humour

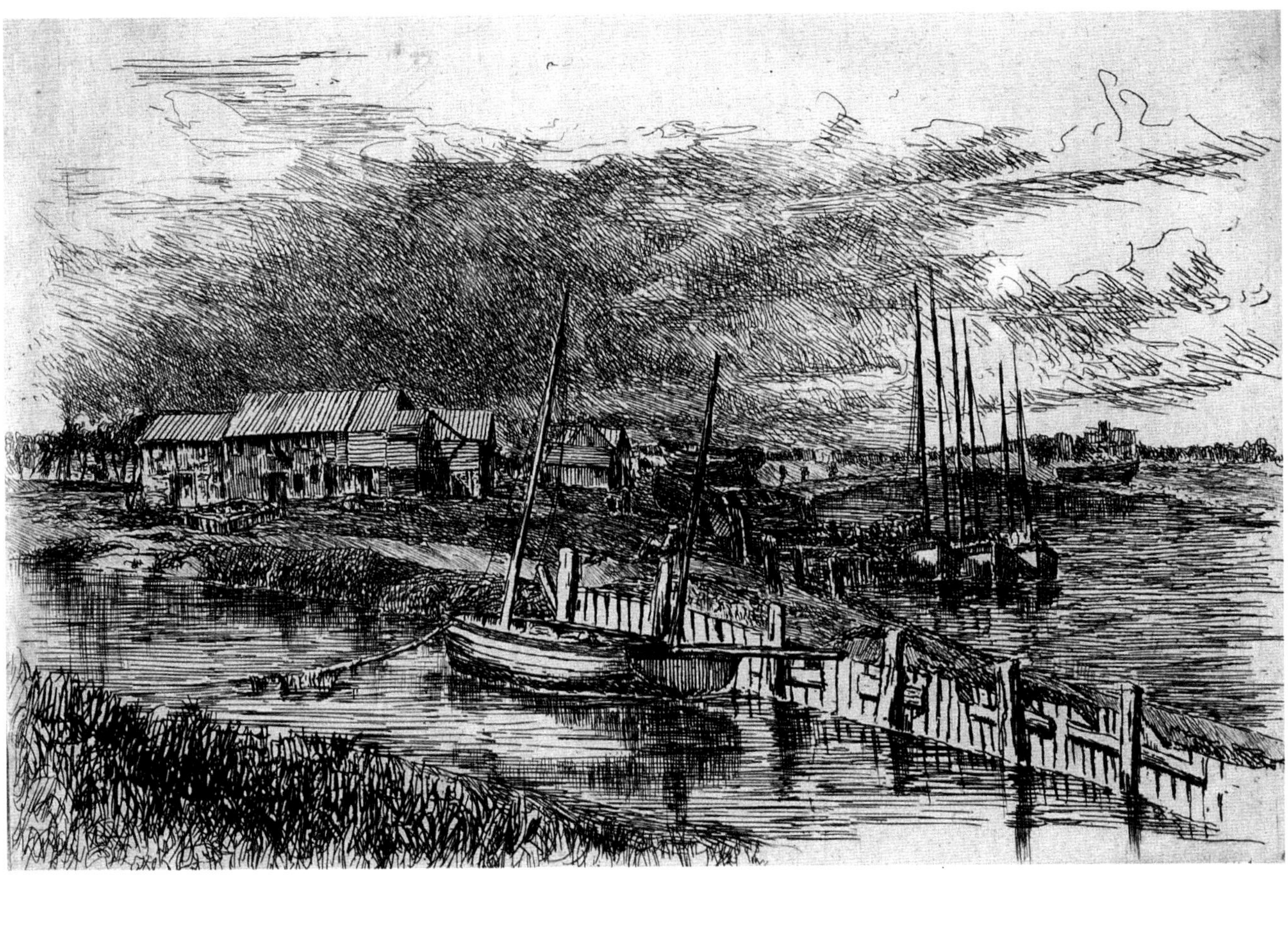

and was frequently unable to keep an element of comedy out of his essentially Victorian paintings.[5]

Around 1880 the Blyth and its riverside clutter found particular favour with etchers. Theodore Dalgliesh had recently studied at The Slade under Poynter and Legros, and while in Walberswick expressed surprise that the river should be so attractive to painters, as it seemed to him to lack colour. Arthur Evershed, also principally an etcher, had taken an unusual route into his artistic career. After seven years' study under Alfred Clint, one of the most prolific and successful Victorian marine painters and etchers, he changed direction and embarked on a medical training. After ten years in practice as a doctor he yielded to an inner imperative and returned to an artistic life. His etchings of the river and of Southwold seafront reflect clearly the rigour of his early training.

Access to Walberswick suddenly became much easier at this time following the opening, on 24 September 1879, of the three-foot gauge Southwold Railway linking Halesworth, nine miles inland on the main Great Eastern Railway, with the coast. By the end of that year there were stations at Wenhaston and Blythburgh, and a rudimentary station at Walberswick was added in September 1881. Suddenly it was possible to travel by rail from London to Walberswick with just one change of train at Halesworth, a facility not available today.[6]

In an article in *The Etcher* in 1881 the view was expressed that the rail link had 'sounded the death-knell of Walberswick as a sketching ground for artists'. In fact the opposite was true; the influx of artists increased sharply, becoming almost a deluge by the middle of the decade. The first of a new surge of young artist visitors arrived in 1884, but in the preceding years some of the more 'establishment' painters of the time made working visits. Arthur Hopkins, brother of the poet Gerard Manley Hopkins, was known as a 'rustic' watercolourist whose work has been compared with that of his contemporary Helen Allingham. He was also a staff artist for *Punch*, where links with Keene may well have precipitated his exploration of Walberswick. Both artists demonstrated searching observation and a certain meaty incisiveness in their riverside drawings. Others active in the village at this time included two prolific exponents of the Victorian watercolour landscape tradition – James Aumonier and James Grace. Both concentrated principally on riverside subjects, and both had been making working visits since the mid-1870s.

The two 'marine Moores' were not related, but they shared an enthusiasm for turbulent seas and a prodigious output of work. After his studies at the Royal Academy Schools, Henry Moore RA had been influenced by the Pre-Raphaelites but later adopted a much more boisterous style.[7] He made two visits to Walberswick, in 1881 and 1884. Woodbridge-born John Moore, one of the most 'collectable' Victorian painters, found a flood of patrons in his native region and seldom felt the need to exhibit outside it. Both artists painted the activities of the Blyth in the early 1880s.

The young artists converging on Walberswick in 1884 came in fairly equal numbers from backgrounds of study in either Paris or Antwerp, but it would be misleading to suggest that there was any sense of tribal competition. Both groups were united in the ideals of the *plein air* painting of everyday life, ideals which led to the formation of the New English Art Club in January 1886. Furthermore, there had already been some intermingling in the artist colonies of Brittany in the preceding years. Additionally, several of this quite tightly-knit community had found studio space in Chelsea, then a very affordable area, making Walberswick seem for a short time like 'Chelsea-on-Sea'. These youthful artists were almost all male and unattached, and the common practice at this time was to travel and work in groups of two or three.

In Walberswick the most prominent figure during these years was Philip Wilson Steer, who arrived in the summer of 1884 with Edward Stott, both having

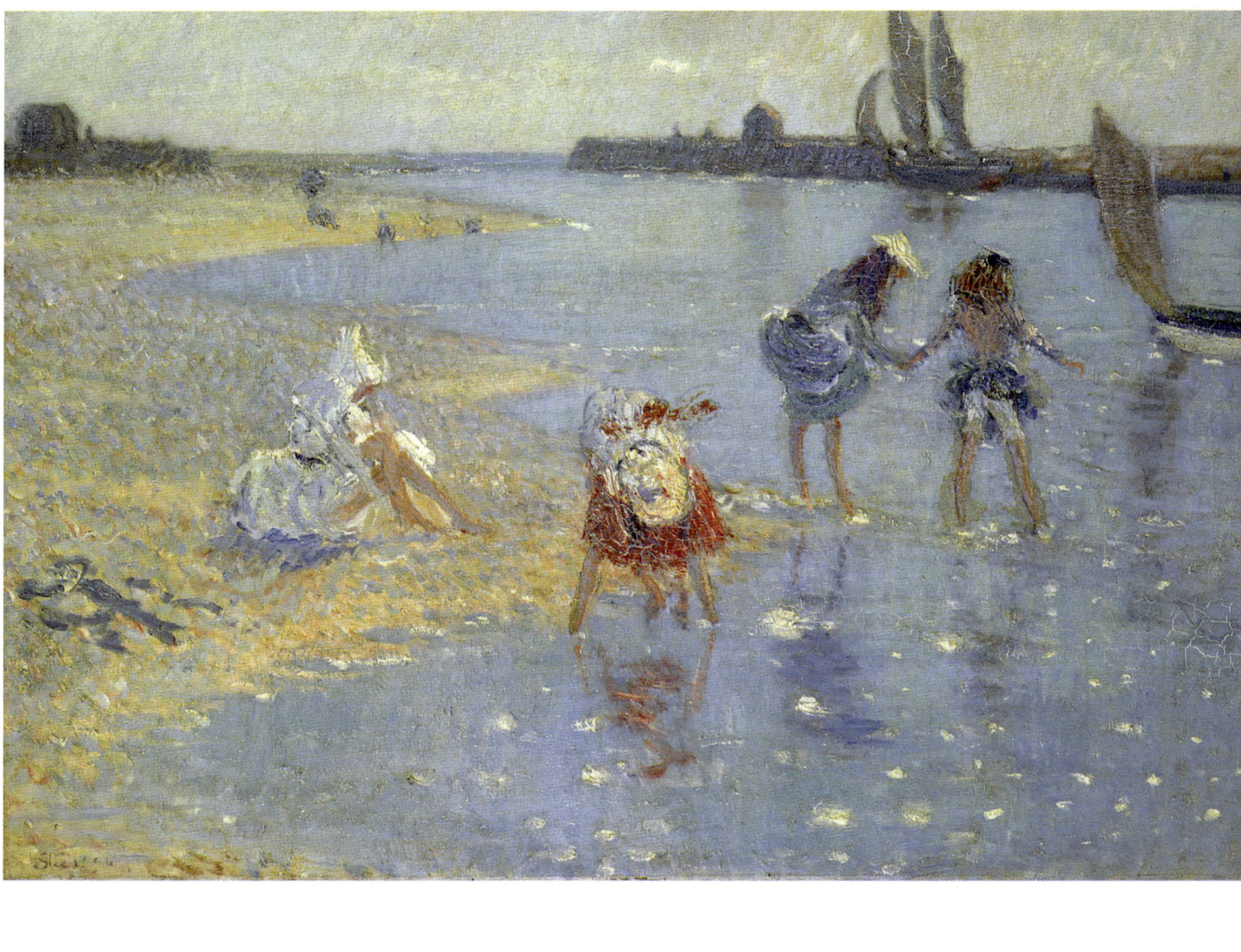

Fig.46
Philip Wilson Steer, *Walberswick, Children Paddling*, 1889–1894
Fitzwilliam Museum, Cambridge © Artist's Estate

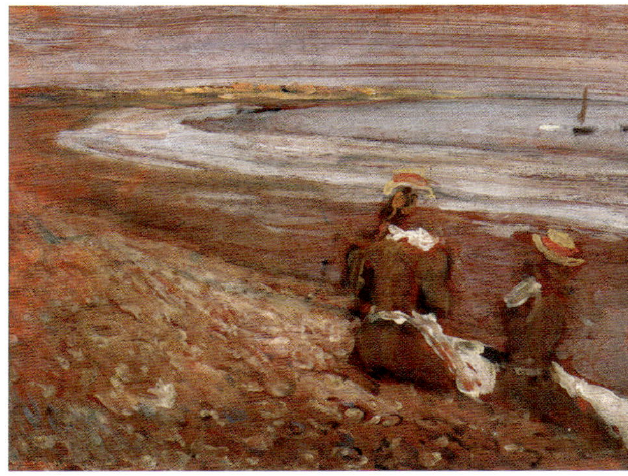

Fig.47
Philip Wilson Steer, *Girls on Walberswick Beach*, oil on panel
Plymouth City Museum and Art Gallery © Artist's Estate

just completed two years' study under Cabanel at the Ecole des Beaux-Arts in Paris. Steer, particularly, infused his painting with something of the colour and exuberance of the Impressionists to which he had recently been exposed, his rich interplay of warm and cool colour applied with what Augustus John described in his autobiography as 'that flickering and voluptuous touch'.[8] These qualities are particularly evident in *Walberswick: Children Paddling*, dated 1894, which despite its appearance of direct spontaneity, with sun-dappled water and mobile figures, was actually completed in the studio using sketches and notations compiled c.1889 (fig.46). Two of the children featured have been identified as Dolly and Emma Brown, daughters of a local fisherman, Jonah Brown.[9] In *Knucklebones* (fig.48), shown at the 'London Impressionists' exhibition at the Goupil Gallery in December 1889, Steer has handled the paint in a different manner, using a bold pointillist approach in the rendering of the shingle on the beach. Again, some of the children have been identified, the girls in brown dresses being

Fig.48
Philip Wilson Steer, *Knucklebones*, 1889
Ipswich Borough Council Museums and Galleries

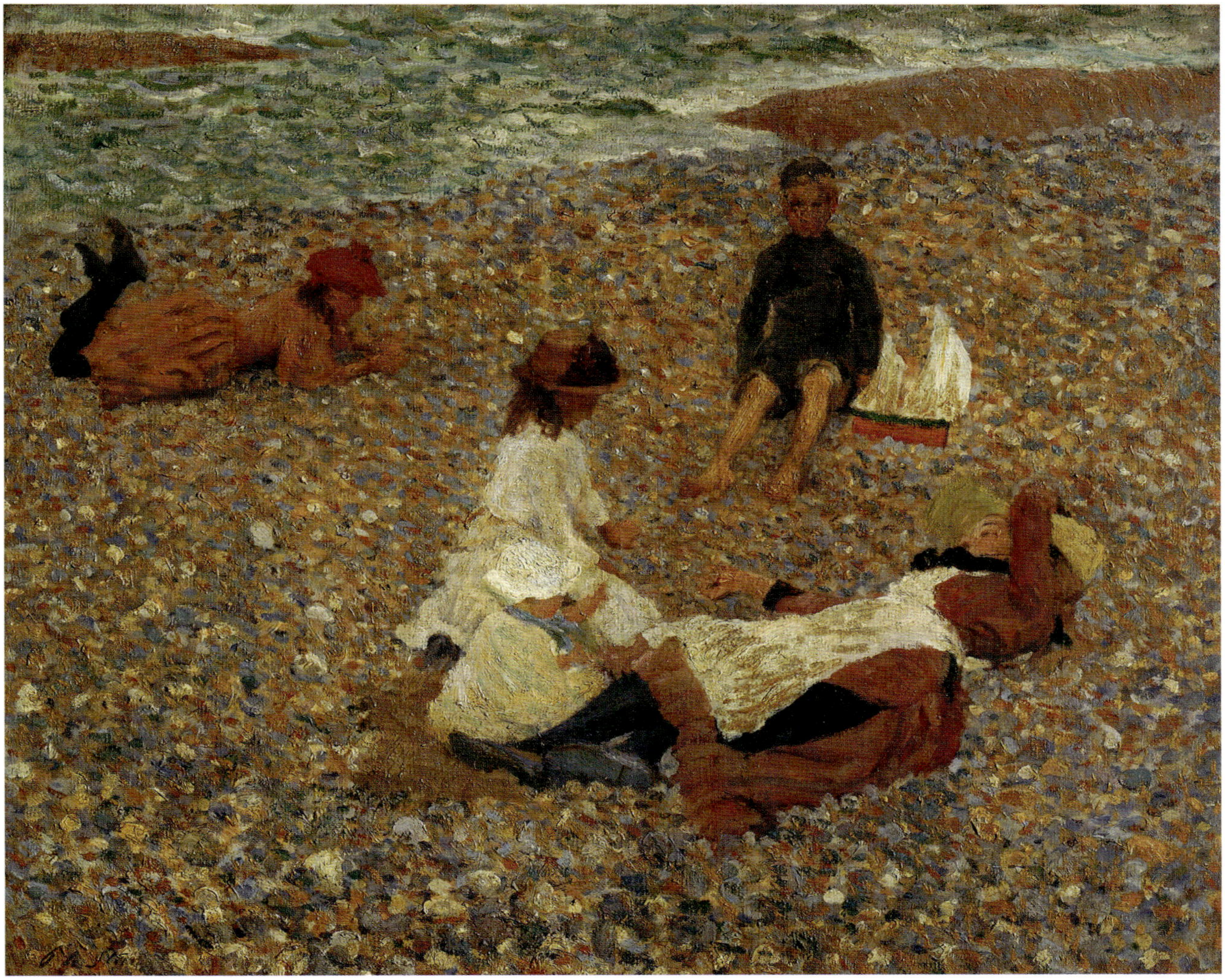

the daughters of the painter James Grace, who was still working in the village.

Steer's name does not appear in accounts of life in the Brittany colonies, but he seems to have compensated by forming a particularly enduring attachment to Walberswick. From 1884 until the end of the decade he returned almost every summer, generating in the process what appears to have been a sense of presidential status among his peers. He made a further visit in 1906 with Georg Sauter and Mark Senior, reinforcing an already traceable link with the artists of Staithes and Runswick Bay.

Other members of Steer's immediate circle who made working visits to Walberswick in the mid-1880s included Frederick Brown and Tom Trythall Rowe. Brown had been at the Académie Julian in Paris during Steer's time there with Cabanel, and was teaching at Westminster School of Art at the time of his fairly brief connection with Walberswick.[10] In 1892 he succeeded Alphonse Legros as Slade Professor. Rowe was a close and enthusiastic member of the group, having already experienced colony life at Quimperlé and Pont-Aven in 1883. He mysteriously stopped exhibiting in London c.1909, the time at which his home in Spring Gardens may have been demolished to make way for Admiralty Arch. He moved to Nottingham, where his death

Fig.49
Sir William Llewellyn, *Summer Time, Walberswick*, 1886
watercolour, Park Walk Gallery, London

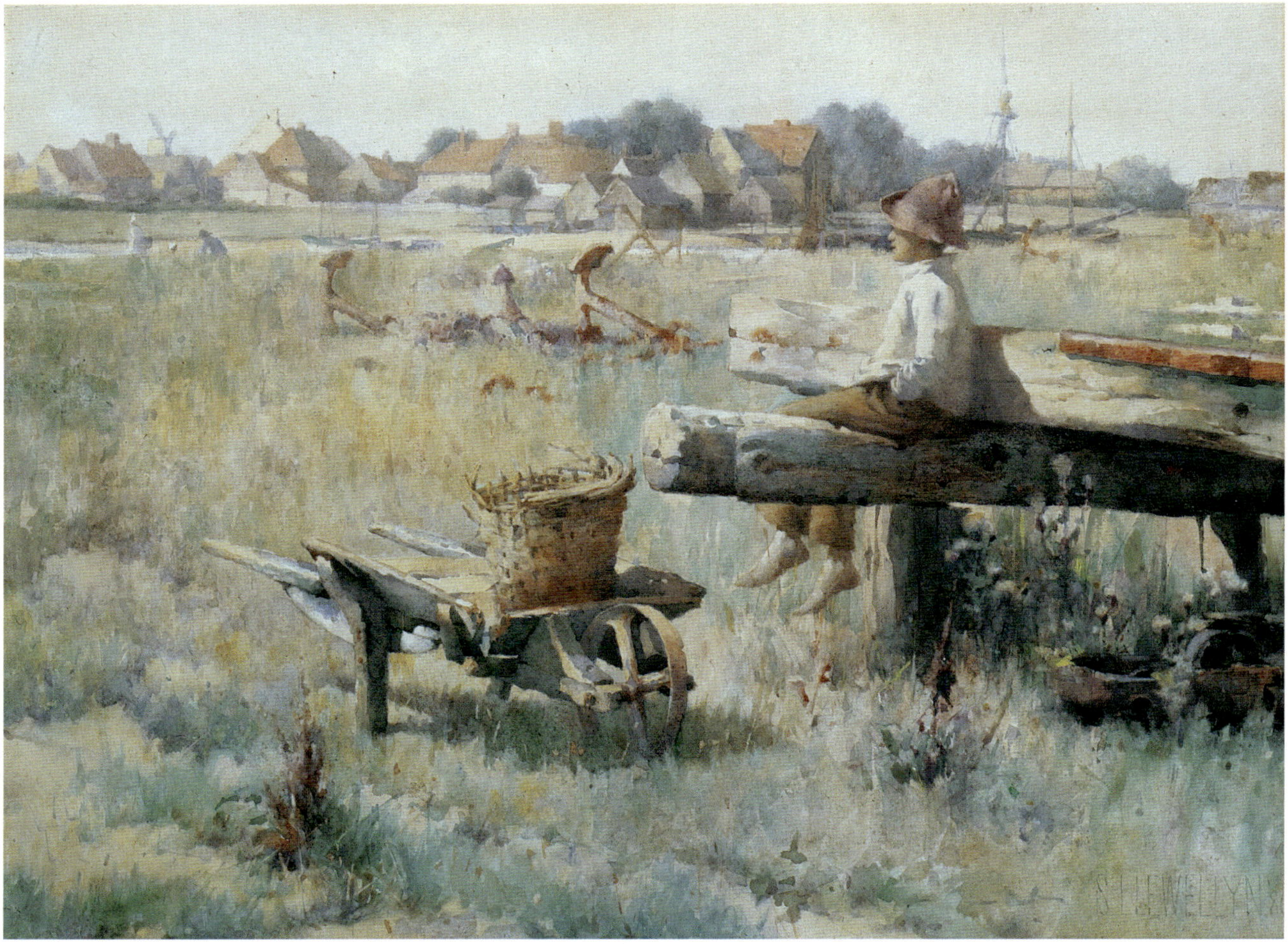

was recorded three decades later. He and Brown were founder members of the New English Art Club, and by 1888 many of the young artists visiting Walberswick had become members.[11]

Nearly all went on to achieve some distinction in their chosen career, none more than William Llewellyn who was elected to the NEAC in 1887 after the almost obligatory final studies in Paris. He painted in Walberswick in 1886 and probably at least once later, interspersed with visits to Staithes and Runswick Bay, before becoming established as an extremely successful portrait painter. He prudently avoided abandoning his Royal Academy ambitions as some of his NEAC contemporaries had done, in pursuit of their ideals. Highlights of a distinguished career included elected membership of most of the national artist bodies, a State portrait of Queen Mary in 1910, a knighthood, and ten years as a particularly enterprising President of the Royal Academy.[12] For his 1886 painting *Summer Time, Walberswick* (fig.49) he chose a scene with a mudflat foreground strewn with riverside paraphernalia, with the village – remarkably unchanged since – in the background.

Sidney Starr was unusual among Steer's acquaintances in making what appears to have been his only Walberswick visit in 1890, a summer when Steer was working in Swanage. By this time Starr, who had been a scholarship-winning student at the Slade as early as 1874, had become a close friend of Whistler and had, a few months previously, been one of ten painters rep-

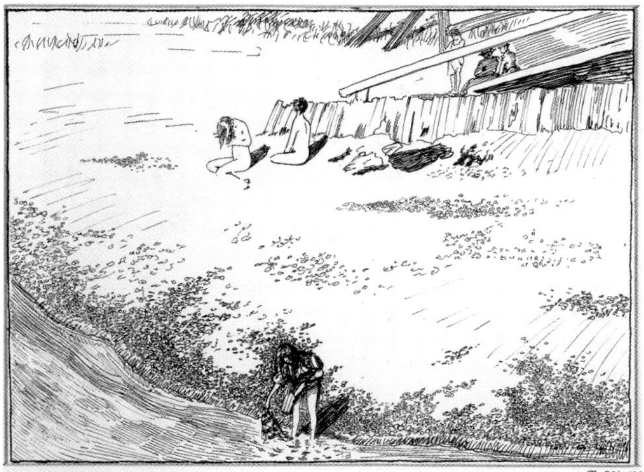

Fig.50
Sidney Starr, *Walberswick Children Bathing*, 1890, ink drawing
Victoria & Albert Museum Picture Library

resented at the 'London Impressionists' exhibition at the Goupil Gallery. Some ink drawings, notable for their simple economy of line, survive at the Victoria & Albert Museum (fig.50). Their theme – children paddling and bathing – recall Steer's enthusiasms, but any thoughts Starr might have had about a return visit to the village were thwarted by his involvement in a scandal which triggered a permanent move to New York, where he enjoyed some success as a muralist.

Paris-based Americans were a powerful presence in the Brittany colonies in the early 1880s, most of them embracing the lifestyle with exuberance. Two such devotees, Arthur Hoeber and Willard Metcalf, made visits to Walberswick in the mid-1880s, almost certainly as a result of friendships formed with British artists while in France. Hoeber reversed the usual procedure of the time by fitting Paris studies into a five-year stay in Concarneau, while Metcalf's enthusiasm for colony life manifested itself in a restless movement from one to another. Starting in Grez-sur-Loing, he fitted his Walberswick visit between spells at Pont-Aven and Giverny. Returning home at the end of the 1880s he was instrumental in establishing two colonies on the Connecticut coast, at Cos Cob and Old Lyme.[13]

The Canadian painter and etcher Elizabeth Armstrong made a fleeting visit to Walberswick, probably with her mother, at some point before her marriage to Stanhope Forbes in 1889. She had studied in Munich, and her visit may have been the result of contacts made on a visit to Pont-Aven in 1882. While in Walberswick she generated material for two etchings.

During the same years there was a modest but important influx of Irish painters. Walter Osborne and Nathaniel Hill had both been pupils of Augustus Burke RHA at the Royal Hibernian Academy Schools in Dublin, but had more recently (1881-83) studied at Verlat's Antwerp Academy. Burke had settled in London in 1882 following the murder of his brother Thomas, Under-Secretary for Ireland, in Dublin's Phoenix Park. Paintings of Walberswick by Burke were shown at the RA in 1884, suggesting a visit in 1883 and the probability that he was the catalyst for the younger artists who had been his pupils, making their visits in 1884 and 1885. Osborne and Hill both produced evocative paintings near the river and among the dunes, incorporating local children who were happy to earn pocket money as models. The children in Osborne's *An October Morning* (fig.51) seem slightly posed, but this deeply atmospheric painting of the north side of the river mouth reveals a considered combination of structure allied to the juxtaposition of warm and cool colours in the foreground shingle bank. Antwerp Academy contemporaries arriving in Walberswick and Southwold during 1884 and 1885 included William Blandford Fletcher, Fred Hall and Max Ludby. During these years Fletcher and Hall were much linked with Newlyn, the remarkable mobility of young artists of the time underlined by Fletcher's additional link with Staithes. During this period Osborne and Fletcher were also spending working time at North Littleton, near Evesham, where they were accompanied by Edward Stott, who may well have been the link that triggered Steer's first visit to Walberswick.

Ludby is altogether more mysterious. He had been at Antwerp Academy from 1882 until 1884, thus overlap-

Fig.51
Walter Frederick Osborne, *An October Morning*, 1885, oil on canvas
Guildhall Art Gallery, London

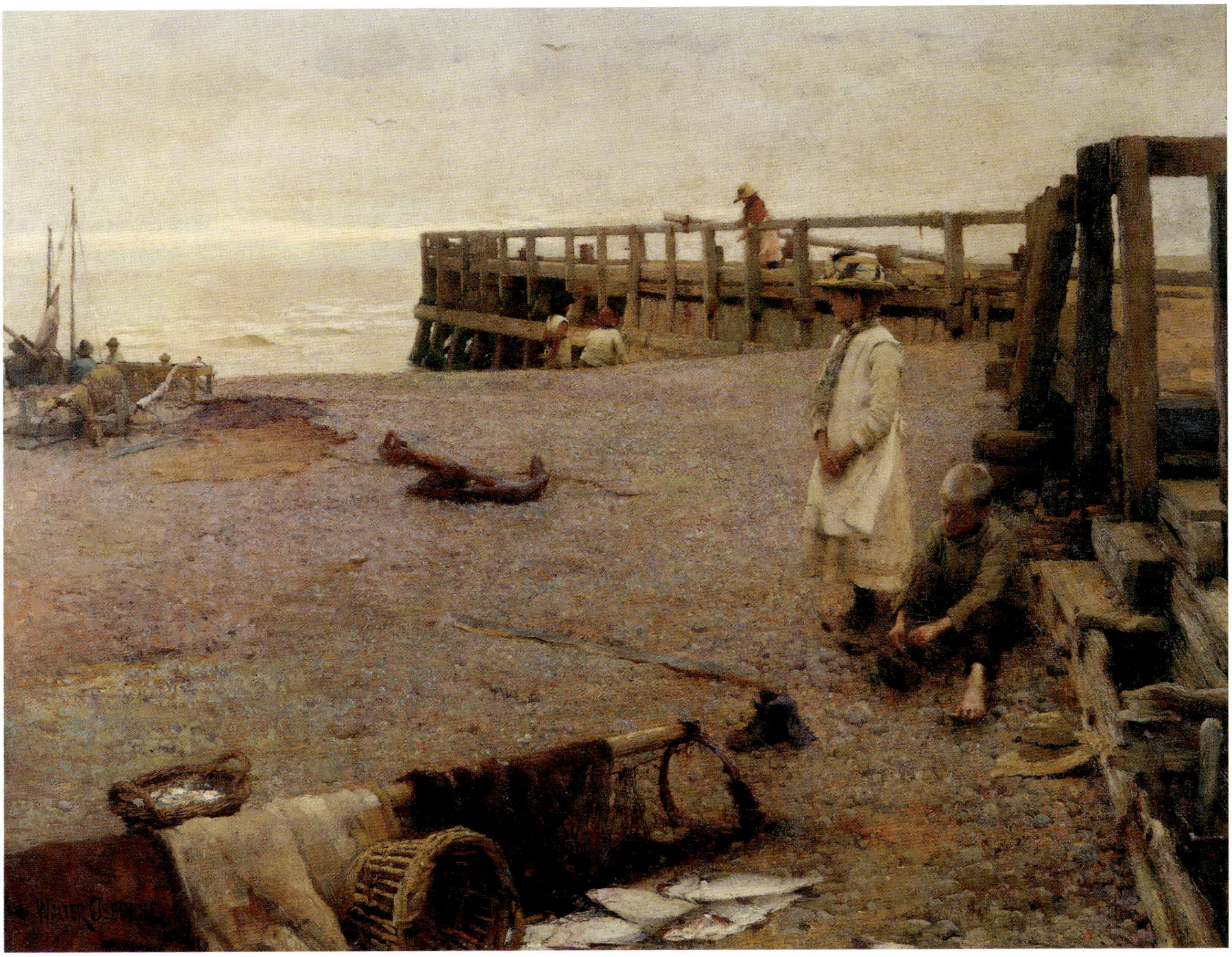

ping only briefly with Osborne and Hill. He was principally a watercolourist who pioneered a popular trend by exhibiting regularly at the RBA, to which he was elected in 1886. Three paintings with Walberswick titles were shown at their exhibition that year.[14]

Other artists of note working in Walberswick in the late 1880s included the watercolourist, illustrator and designer Walter Crane and the prolific St. John's Wood-based Vincent Yglesias. Crane was particularly known as a designer of fabrics and wallpapers, his versatility no doubt adding weight in his appointment as principal of the Royal College of Art in 1898. Like Ludby, Yglesias exhibited substantially with the RBA, to which he was elected in 1888, his Walberswick titles at their exhibitions spanning thirteen years. Notable for an even longer association with the village was Thomas Benham. Works shown at the RA in the late 1880s included a very large Walberswick 'salon piece' in 1889, while he also showed at the ROI, RI and at Tooth's Gallery.[15] Benham became a permanent resident of the village c.1903.

The local community somehow managed to absorb its extra flood of visitors in the 1880s. Both inns offered limited accommodation, but a network of local families accepted the overflow, enhancing meagre incomes and promoting a healthy symbiosis. Village elders in the 1950s and 60s remembered spending summer months as children sleeping in makeshift 'nests' in outbuildings

Fig.52
Sir Frank Short, *The Kissing Bridge*, 1890
Ipswich Borough Council Museums and Galleries

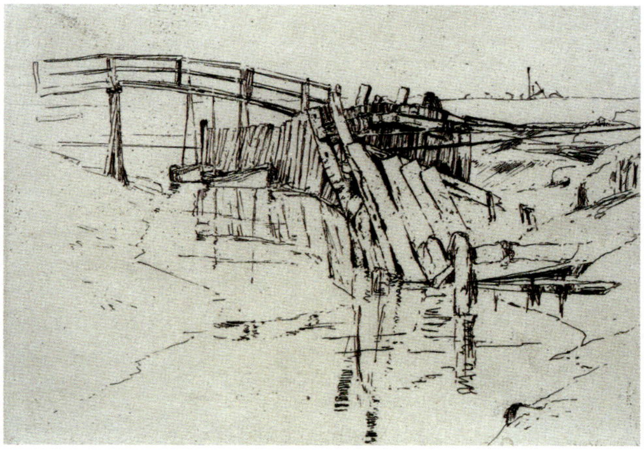

Walberswick ferry at the turn of the century, photograph

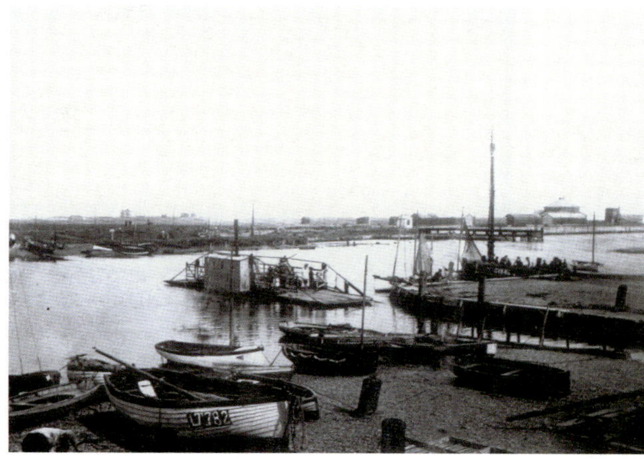

and lofts so that their rooms could be let to artist visitors. Few records were kept, so the 'who stayed where' debate remains largely obscure.

The vision and spirit of the 1880s continued into the 1890s, but with the significant difference that most of the visiting artists were older. This was particularly true in the summer of 1890, when an interesting quartet arrived in the village – Frank Brangwyn, Frank Short, Alexander Mann and Arthur Melville. Although linked by ties of friendship there is no evidence that they arrived together.[16] All were heading for distinguished careers, and all except Brangwyn were in their thirties. Taught by his father and briefly, while in his teens, by William Morris, Brangwyn produced etchings and vigorous pen drawings in Walberswick, later travelling widely to become one of the most respected and successful artists of his time. His career culminated in a knighthood in 1919, an honour also bestowed upon Short in 1911, the year of his RA election. Regarded as the supreme etcher of his day, Short was elected president of the RE in 1910. Mann and Melville both travelled widely as painters after studying in Paris – Mann to Morocco and Latin America, and Melville to Egypt. Both had tasted artist colony life, Mann at Grez-sur-Loing and Melville at Cockburnspath on the Scottish border, much frequented by the 'Glasgow Boys'.

One of the few members of Steer's immediate circle to establish a permanent base in Walberswick was the painter and plantsman Arthur Rendall, who bought Coral Cottage in 1891.[17] Rendall still maintained a studio in Philbeach Gardens, Earls Court, and was remembered as secretary to the Imperial Arts League, formed to help artists in distress. His fine tombstone in Walberswick churchyard, designed by his friend Eric Kennington, incorporates the legend *His Work for Art Endures.*[18]

A fleeting visitor in the early 1890s was one of Newlyn's leading figures, Walter Langley, who was working towards a major London exhibition in 1893. In the words of the artist's grandson Roger Langley, he was seeking to 'leaven the Newlyn bread' with some work generated elsewhere. A small colour sketch of Ferry Knoll, an area of rising ground near the river, survives in private ownership (see fig.53).

Walter Sickert is known to have made visits to the area, but they were fleeting and appear to have been made with a principally social agenda. On an invited visit in 1927 to St Felix School in Southwold, as part of

Fig.53
Walter Langley, *Ferry Road, Walberswick*, c.1891–2, watercolour
Private collection

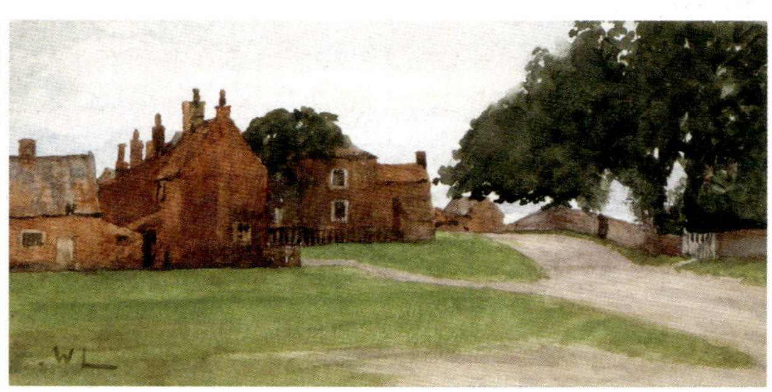

a scheme to expose the 'young ladies' to contemporary art, Sickert recalled that he and Whistler had visited the town in the 1890s, but Whistler had not been particularly smitten with it. Another tantalizing reference to Sickert's presence occurs in a letter written c.1959 to NEAC archivist Margaret Thomas by the painter and former Slade student Clare Atwood. Atwood recalled being informally taught in Walberswick by 'Mr Steer and Mr Sickert'. The former, she wrote, was 'particularly kind' while the latter was 'most inspiring and rather wonderful in an odd way'. Atwood mentions no date, but it is likely to have been during her time as a student at the Slade in the late 1880s.

Other female artists appeared in the village in the 1890s. The Kirkpatrick sisters Ida and Ethel, mentioned in an article on Walberswick in *The Artist* in 1897, made regular visits to the village for nearly two decades. Ida was particularly prolific, known for her atmospheric nocturnes. Florence Cockburn, like many female artists of her generation, studied at Heatherley's School of Art before eventually settling in Walberswick. She had painted in the area in the 1880s, signing Bonneau (her maiden name) and in the 1920s taught art at the village school, where she was remembered as a sound teacher but a fierce disciplinarian.

The years between 1890 and the onset of the First World War marked a time of radical change for Walberswick visually, socially and culturally. Visiting artists continued to pour into the village, a noticeable trend being the high incidence of RBA membership. Notable among them were the coastal and marine painters Alfred Kinsley and George Hillyard Swinstead, who were both extremely prolific, while after the turn of the century a substantial list included Charles Horsley, Frank Spenlove Spenlove and Henry J Sylvester Stannard.

Horsley was born in Manchester and studied at the School of Art before settling in Beckenham, Kent. Walberswick featured prominently in his exhibition titles at the RBA between 1908 and 1916. Spenlove was also very prolific in Walberswick. He, too, had Beckenham connections, opening his private art school – The Yellow Door – there, but when the Spenloves moved to Tite Street, Chelsea, the school was relocated to Victoria Street. The artist's grandson Peter Hopkins remembers Spenlove as a man of theatrical appearance, with curvaceous moustache and monocle, and an enthusiasm for minor practical jokes. Hopkins noted that these had worn thin with Mrs Spenlove, who had another cross to bear: the upper reaches of their house constantly reeked of turpentine.

Sylvester Stannard was the most prolific and successful member of a large painting family. He travelled extensively across Britain, often accompanied by his sister Lilian Stannard who exhibited mainly at the RA. They both reached a wide public through the medium of picture postcards, as did Ida Kirkpatrick. These cards remained in circulation for many years, with postmarks in a local collection ranging from 1907 until 1924. All produced several which depicted Walberswick subjects. Another major pioneer of the picture postcard cult was the versatile etcher, painter, illustrator and teacher Frank Emanuel, who had studied at the Slade and at the Académie Julian in Paris. Topographical details in his paintings around the Blyth suggest that they were produced around 1890.

Visual changes around Walberswick between 1890 and 1914 were mainly concerned with the river and the Southwold skyline, the backdrop to many paintings. The latter started with the building of the cylindrical brick water tower on Southwold common in 1886, dwarfed 51 years later by the giant concrete version erected beside it. In 1889 work commenced on Southwold's most iconic landmark, the lighthouse, slightly eroding the dominance of St Edmund's church. Then, between 1894 and 1898, the two windmills on the common

Fig.54
Francis Newbery, *A Regatta*, oil on canvas
Peter Nahum at the Leicester Galleries

edge were demolished, a third mill near the church having burnt down in 1876.

On the river, the pontoon ferry, which had excited little interest as a subject for artists, suddenly became the focal point in many paintings and etchings when it was endowed with steam power, and the visual romance of smoke, in 1899. Soon afterwards a steam paddle tug, the *Pendennis*, arrived, its purpose being to tow the sail-powered fishing fleet out of the harbour and back when winds were unfavourable. The tug appears in several paintings of the period, an early example being a watercolour, dated 1911, by John Doman Turner.[19] In 1907, further visual change came with the walling of the harbour's north bank.

Arguably the most influential artist visitor to Walberswick at the end of the nineteenth century was Francis Newbery, a distinguished portrait painter and Director of Glasgow School of Art. With his wife Jessie, a watercolourist and embroidery designer, he spent summer vacations for almost twenty years at Rooftree, a semi-detached villa in the main street. His daughter Mary Newbery Sturrock – also a successful artist – recalled in 1981 that her father had been in Walberswick with Steer on at least one occasion in the mid-1880s. While at Rooftree, the Newberys were frequent hosts to the Waltons. Edward Arthur Walton, elected to the Royal Scottish Academy in 1905, was one of the original 'Glasgow Boys' but shared Newbery's enthusiasm for Suffolk. The

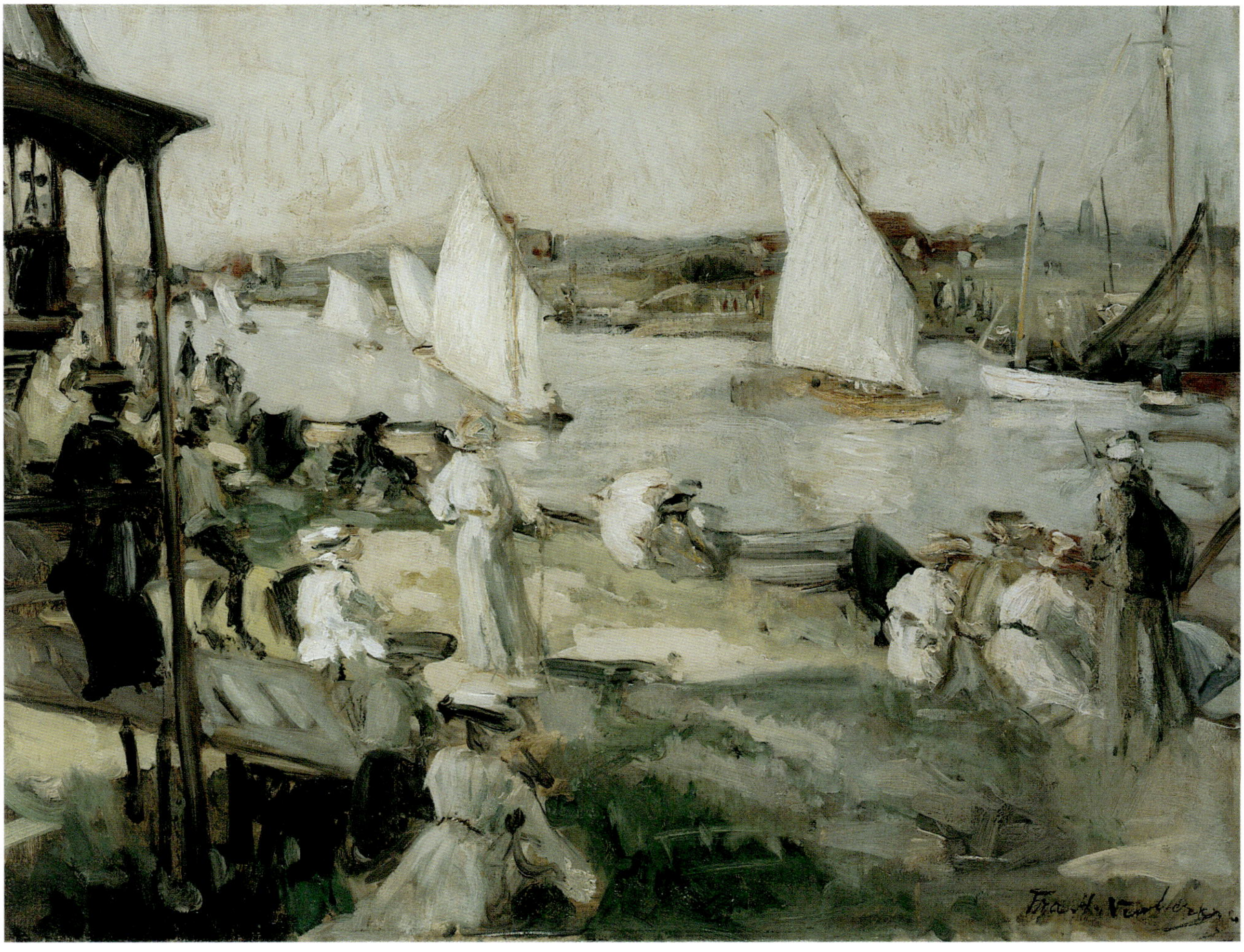

Walton family spent several summers at The Old Vicarage at nearby Wenhaston, where 'EA' completed one of his most acclaimed works, *The Briony Wreath,* employing a local gamekeeper's daughter as his model. Another notable guest of the Newberys was the prolific and successful painter and illustrator Maurice Greiffenhagen. During his visit c.1905 he produced a large and unusual on-board painting of the steam ferry.

The Newberys had a riverside studio, one of a line of converted net sheds which accommodated an artists' colony-within-a-colony from the 1890s until the onset of the Second World War. The buildings differed in shape and size, but shared one vital feature: areas of glass let into north-facing walls. During the Edwardian years an influx of prosperous intelligentsia, mostly from London, began to build the larger houses which are now an established village feature, giving rise to later references to Walberswick as 'NW3-by-the-Sea'. One of the first was Seahome, built for the painter and etcher Thomas Davidson by his architect son Thomas Davidson Jnr.

Davidson Snr. was essentially a Victorian painter whose work was often based on literature and mythology. He had been sufficiently prolific and successful to have had a studio built in Hampstead in 1882 but by the turn of the century he was largely established in Walberswick. The family connection with the village continued into the 1930s: Thomas Davidson had another son, Allan, widely seen as one of the under-rated painters of his generation. As a student the young Davidson won silver and bronze medals at the RA Schools before enrolling at the Académie Julian in Paris. Later he mixed his practice as a portrait and landscape painter with teaching at the Central School of Arts and Crafts, finally settling in Walberswick in the mid-1920s (see fig.55).

Many of the large houses built in Walberswick during the decade before the First World War were designed in the prevailing Arts and Crafts spirit by an extremely unusual architect, Frank Jennings. The Jennings houses differed in size, layout and detail, but most incorporated materials and components salvaged from demolished buildings of much earlier date. The most extreme example was Mercers' Hall, built for his sister, which was a creative fusion of two dismantled buildings transported to the village from Lavenham. Remarkably, many of these Walberswick houses were completed by the time the architect had reached his mid-thirties.

With his artist wife Mildred Hall the enterprising Jennings set up The Walberswick Peasant Pottery Company. This unusual business reached its zenith in the 1920s when it sold pots imported from Quimper in Brittany, painted furniture and a variety of smaller hand-crafted merchandise. Their son, Humphrey Jennings was born at the family home in Walberswick. By the time of his tragically early death he had become particularly known for wartime documentary film, but was also passionately interested in Surrealist painting during the 1930s. He had a solo exhibition of his own work at the London Gallery in 1938.

Charles Rennie Mackintosh and his wife Margaret Macdonald Mackintosh arrived in Walberswick in July 1914 for what was intended to be a recuperative break from an architectural career in Glasgow that had gone badly wrong after well-documented early success.[20] The Newberys had found them accommodation at Millside, next door to Rooftree, as well as arranging for some studio space beside the river. The intention at this stage appears to have been to return to Glasgow in the autumn, but within a month of their arrival war broke out and they decided to let their Glasgow house for a full year, which was at this time the expected duration of hostilities.

Mackintosh was soon at work on topographical drawings and watercolours as well as some of the now-familiar flower studies (see fig.56), while Margaret worked on her gesso panels based on biblical and mythological subjects.[21] At the end of the summer the

Fig.55
Allan Davidson, *Valley Farm, Walberswick*
Ipswich Borough Council Museums and Galleries

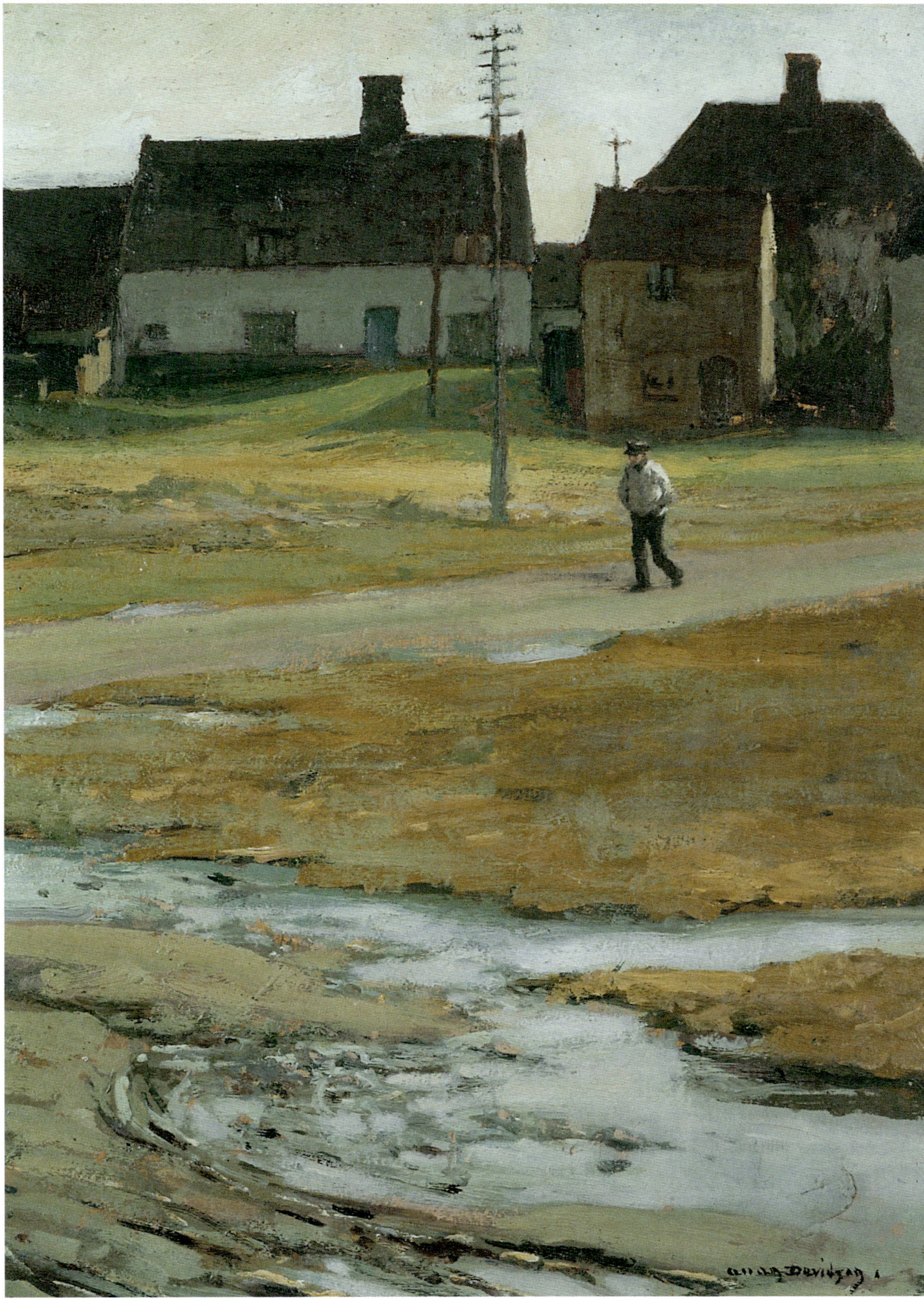

Fig.56
Charles Rennie Mackintosh, *Cactus Flower*, 1915
watercolour on paper, Sheffield Galleries and Museums Trust

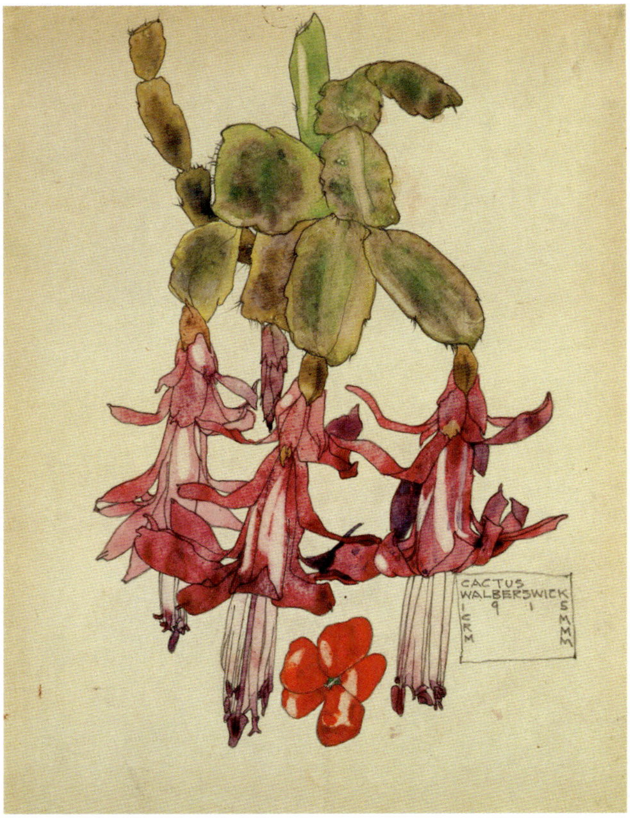

Newberys returned to Glasgow, and ensuing events demonstrated unpleasantly the propensity for war to breed paranoia. As months passed, concerns grew about the solitary and rather uncommunicative Scotsman and his habit of taking nocturnal walks, illuminating his progress with a lantern. With fears of invasion running high, rumours quickly spread that this man might be a spy. Mackintosh had seen no reason, before the war, to be secretive about his links with members of the Viennese Secession and with the German architect Hermann Muthesius and now, tightly wrapped in his own thoughts and worries, he appears have had no sense of the rising ferment of suspicion around him, thus feeling no need to make any attempt to pour oil on troubled waters. When the arrest was finally made, the Mackintoshes were devastated. The wartime powers granted to the police and local authorities were wide-ranging, and they found themselves abruptly banished from three East Anglian counties. When they left for London a chapter closed: they never returned to Suffolk.

The visits of the Newberys petered out from this time, too. Fra Newbery had produced a number of paintings and drawings in the village, including some little-seen work in which biblical scenes were set in Walberswick surroundings, much as Stanley Spencer did at Cookham, but on a more modest scale. For many years Newbery had suffered from a depressive illness, and in 1917 he retired early from Glasgow School of Art, settling the following year in Corfe Castle, Dorset, for nearly three decades of productive retirement.

Bertram Priestman bought a Jennings house, Windy Haugh, in Walberswick in 1914, but spent the war years at Skipton in Yorkshire before returning to the village in 1919. He was probably introduced to Walberswick by William Llewellyn, for whom he worked as a studio assistant after his studies at the Slade. At Windy Haugh he built a garden studio, produced a collection of paintings, became a Royal Academician (in 1923) and tutored private pupils, including Edward Seago, who received particular help with the observation and painting of skies. In *Walberswick Marshes* (fig.57) Priestman painted a view across the Dunwich bay, remarkably little changed in the ensuing eighty years except for the distant horizon, which is now adorned with the Sizewell A and B nuclear power stations. In the 1921 painting a small upward-pointing finger on the distant horizon is the last vestige of All Saints church, Dunwich, still clinging to the crumbling cliff-top.

William Kay Blacklock was a seasonal but very active presence in the village, using a Walberswick address – The Barn – for his exhibition entries between 1908 and 1917. The Birmingham artist Joseph Southall, a devoted enthusiast for the medium of tempera, was also a regular visitor, frequenting the Blyth and Southwold beach for at least twenty years from c.1907.

A number of visual changes occurred around the village during the late 1920s. A new and larger Anchor

Fig.57
Bertram Priestman, *Walberswick Marshes*, 1921
Ipswich Borough Council Museums and Galleries © Artist's Estate

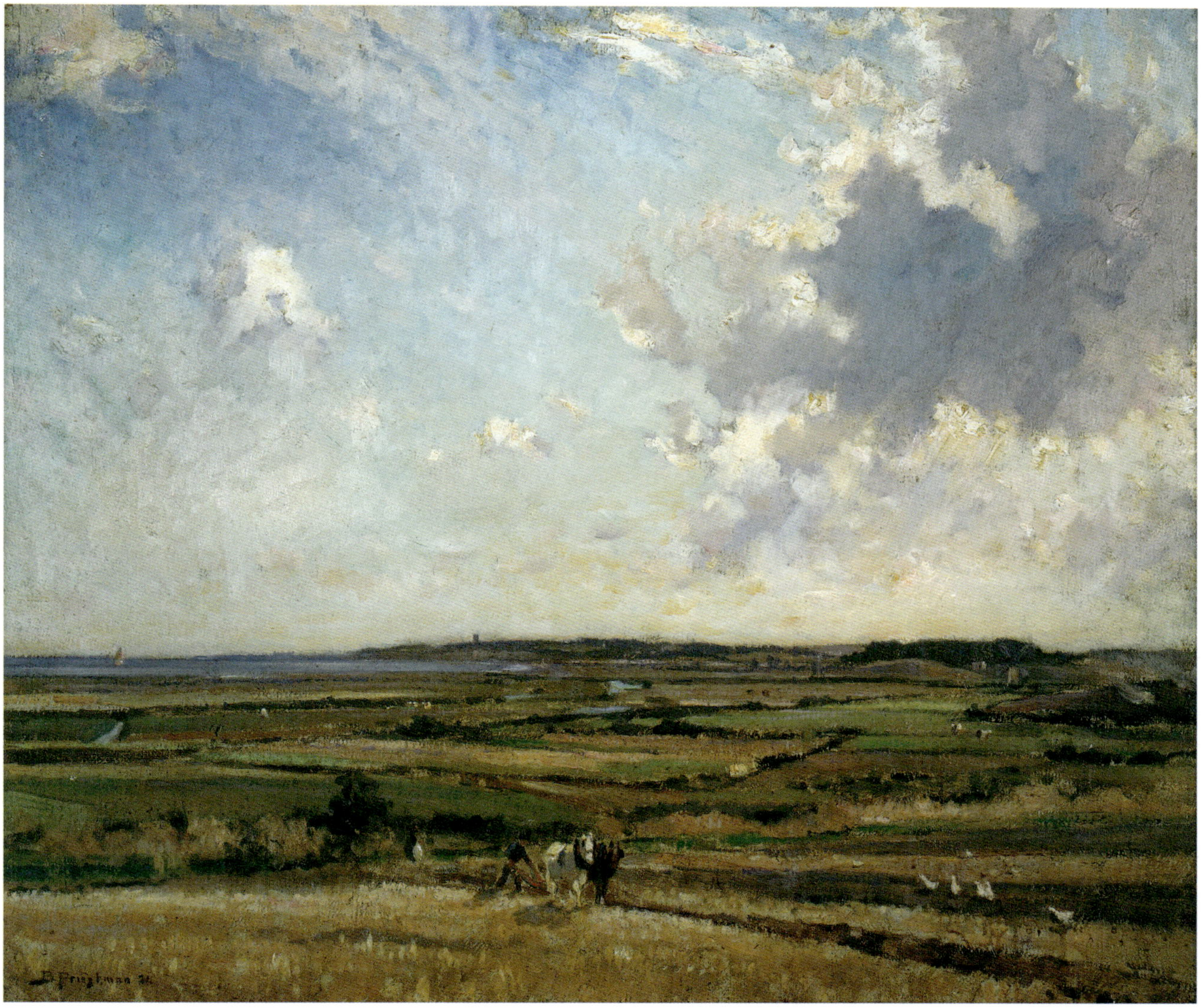

Hotel was built in 1927, replacing the timber-framed inn which for more than half a century had been the temporary home of many visiting artists.[22] The following year the nearby windmill, featured in many Walberswick paintings and etchings, came to grief in a violent storm. Then, in April 1929, the Southwold Railway closed after several years of unequal struggle against growing competition from road transport.[23]

Walberswick's appeal to artists continued seamlessly through the 1930s, and gradually resumed in the 1950s as the scars of wartime military occupation began to heal. Two artistic phenomena of the early 1930s should not escape mention, as both had roots traceable to the late 1920s: the Walberswick Scroll, painted mostly in 1931 but completed in 1932, and The Sole Bay Group, formed in 1933.

'A Dioramic Pictorial Record of a Suffolk Village' was John Doman Turner's description of his extraordinary 123-foot paper scroll, mostly completed in the summer of 1931 and depicting in obsessive detail every house, barn and hut in Walberswick at the time. The execution of the watercolour Scroll is sophisticated in parts and clumsy in others, but is imbued throughout with the haunting sense of time and place which had evolved in the course

Fig.58
Ronald Ossory Dunlop, *The Anchorage, Walberswick*, late 1930s
oil, The Fine Art Society PLC

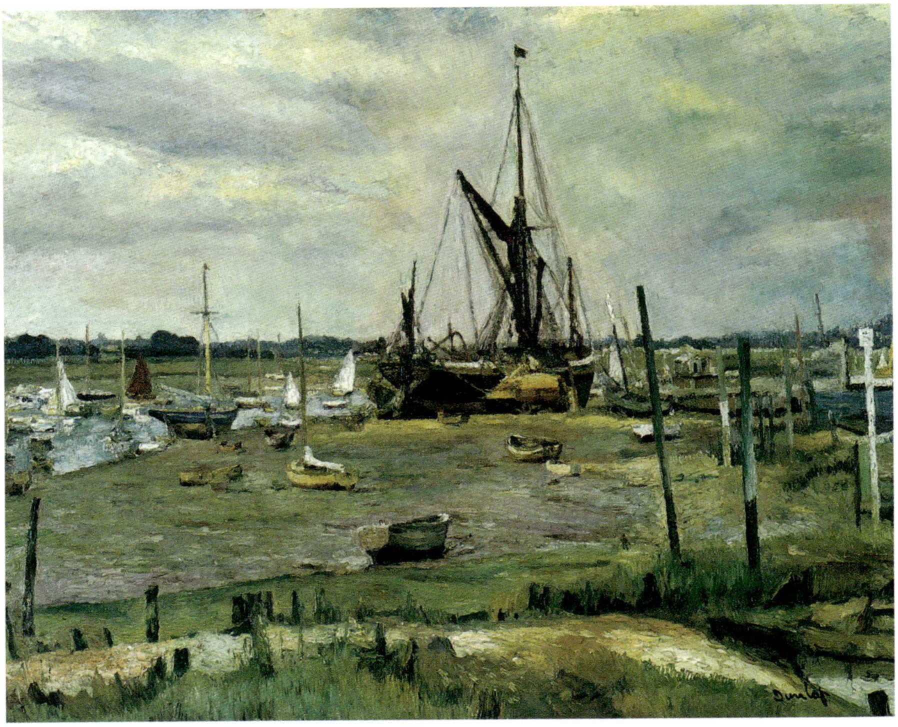

of more than twenty years of working visits. Essentially an amateur watercolourist, Turner was one of the sixteen members of the prestigious but short-lived Camden Town Group, formed in 1911. His seemingly incongruous inclusion arose from his devoted attendance at Sickert's life classes and long-term tutorial help from Spencer Gore, conducted by post on account of Turner's profound deafness.

The Scroll, now sensitively restored and backed on linen, is regularly shown as well as reaching a wider public in video form. Turner produced at least two other scrolls; one of these, completed in 1930, depicts the extended clutter of buildings on the north side of the Blyth. Featured on the Scroll is the front elevation of the c.1700 timber-framed Old Farm, freshly but rather startlingly fitted with state-of-the-art, landscape-format metal-framed windows. This was the home of W.F. Crittall, whose family windows firm was energetically promoting this radical new trend. Crittall was an extremely able artist, having studied at the once-prestigious St John's Wood School of Art before joining the family firm. His enthusiasm to promote the work of others drove him, in 1933, to form The Sole Bay Group, an exhibiting body of professional artists. He adopted the position of chairman, while the 'hands-on' roles of secretary and treasurer were undertaken by one of the rising stars in the local painting firmament, Allan Davidson's nephew Tom van Oss. The inaugural exhibition took place at the Stella Peskett Memorial Hall in Southwold in June 1933 before going 'on tour' to the Jubilee Hall in Aldeburgh. Of the thirty artists featured, nine were – or soon would be – Royal Academicians. The promising career of Van Oss came to a tragic and premature end in 1941: drafted into a coastal camouflage unit at the outbreak of war, he was making an offshore survey when his boat struck a mine.

This short survey has attempted to identify the major events of an important half-century span, with emphasis on individuals judged to have had a particular influence on subsequent events, but a great many with a strong claim for inclusion have had to be omitted. Thanks in part to media exposure, Walberswick is now a very popular holiday destination for those seeking traditional seaside pursuits, yet it retains its magnetism and at the time of writing nine professional artists have a permanent base in the village. At quiet times, particularly at dawn and dusk, to walk along the river banks and adjacent mudflats is to experience the powerful and haunting atmospheric resonance which has affected and inspired many generations of artists.

Notes

1. Title quotation taken from 'Walberswick', *Art Journal,* 1880, p.346.

2. Following the Reformation the church fell into disrepair through loss of tithes and a sharp decline in the town's fortunes, exacerbated by major fires during the seventeenth century.

3. Richard Scott, *Artists at Walberswick: East Anglian Interludes 1880–2000,* Art Dictionaries Ltd., 2002, describes 415 artists with a claim to professional standing who worked in the village.

4. Manchester City Art Gallery hold a painting by Turner showing All Saints' church and the Greyfriars monastery ruin on the cliff-top of Dunwich.

5. Marks' exhibition titles at the RA convey the spirit: *Experimental Gunnery in the Middle Ages* is fairly typical.

6. A bigger station was built in 1902, incorporating a booking office, waiting room and primitive toilet facilities.

7. Henry Moore came from a family of artists. His father William M. and four brothers were all painters. The most notable brother was Albert M. (1841-1893).

8. Augustus John, *Chiarascuro – Fragments of Autobiography,* Jonathan Cape, 1952.

9. Emma (in red) and Dolly (in blue) were both eventually married to painters – Emma to Walter Cadby, and Dolly to Frank Morley Fletcher.

10. Brown's *Walberswick Church: A Hazy Afternoon* was shown at the 'London Impressionists' exhibition at the Goupil Gallery in December 1889.

11. Membership in 1887 rose to 106, of whom 23 can be identified as having made visits to Walberswick.

12. Llewellyn's year of birth was discovered after his death to have been 1858, not 1863 as previously thought.

13. See S.G. Larkin, *The Cos Cob Colony: Impressionists on the Connecticut Shore,* National Academy of Design & Yale University Press, 2001.

14. Ludby's showings at the RI were to be very numerous; he was elected in 1891.

15. *Stranded* was for some years erroneously, but quite credibly, attributed to Charles Rowbotham as a result of a damaged signature.

16. Ties of friendship extended to Brangwyn and Short sharing a Chelsea studio with Llewellyn at this time.

17. Coral Cottage (soon to be renamed Eastwood Cottage) stood in an acre of garden in the form of an arrowhead between two converging roads. Gertrude Jekyll, *Gardens for Small Country Houses,* Country Life, 1912, describes in detail this multi-faceted garden, designed by A Winter Rose.

18. Kennington was a sculptor, painter and draughtsman much influenced by his experience as a war artist in the First World War, and known for work in the field of public memorials.

19. A 1911 painting of *The Pendennis* was shown in the 'John Doman Turner' exhibition at the Michael Parkin Gallery in Motcomb Street, London, in September and October 1997.

20. Dated sketchbook drawings show that Mackintosh had been in nearby Southwold and Blythburgh in 1897.

21. Mackintosh's flower studies produced in Walberswick are believed to be his best. Others were produced around the Kent-Sussex border in 1910 and, briefly, 1918. Some earlier flower studies were made on Holy Island in 1901.

22. The Anchor Inn was dismantled and re-erected further up the main street. It became a private house, Anchorlea.

23. A. Barrett Jenkins, *Memories of the Southwold Railway,* L & S Rexon, 1987.

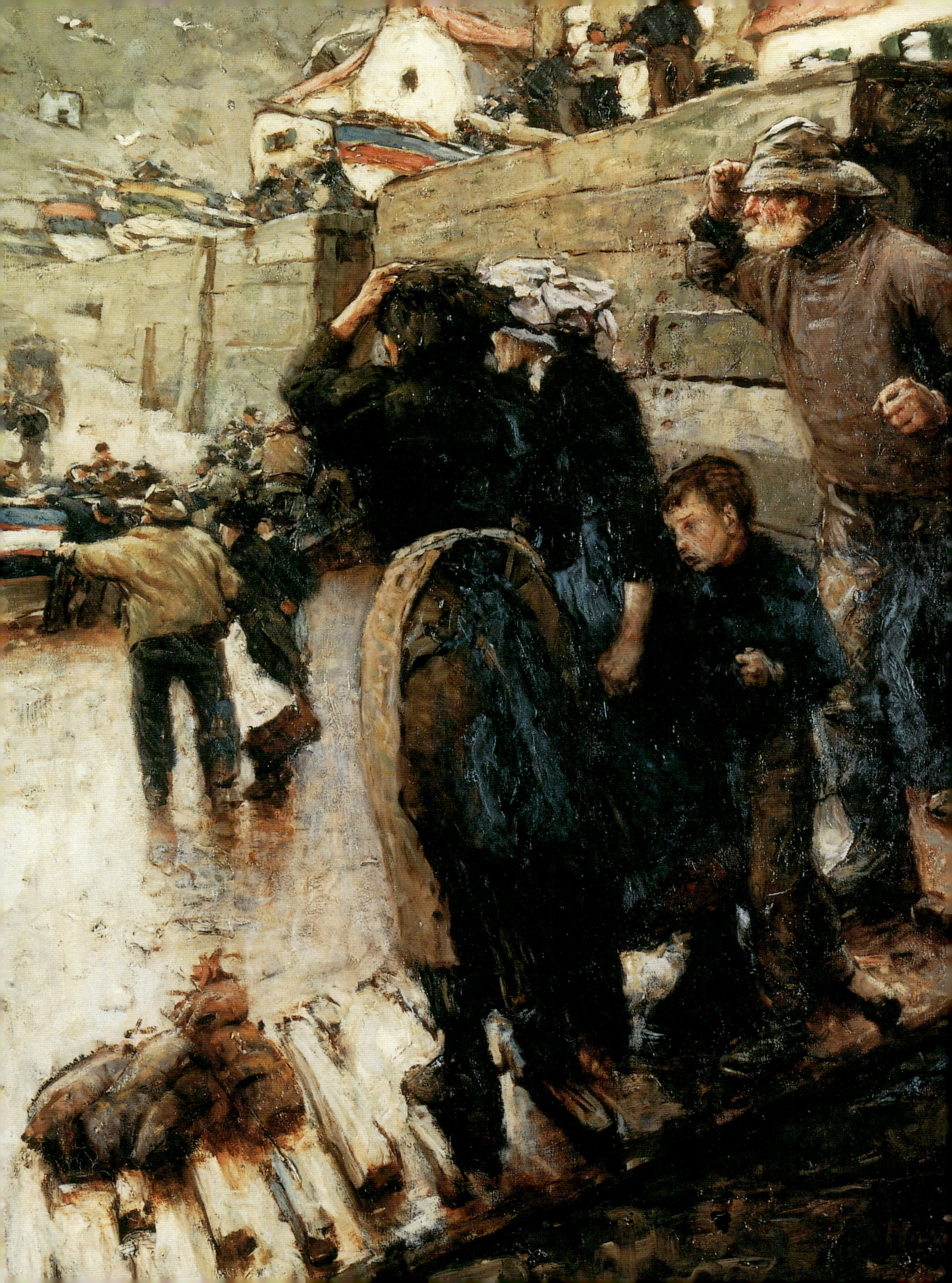

CHAPTER 6

Staithes
'Outside of the World'

LAURA NEWTON

> I have repeatedly said during the last 15 years that I think the time is coming … when Staithes and Runswick – especially Staithes – will be very formidable rivals as painting grounds to Newlyn and Clovelly, not alone because of their rival picturesqueness, and the archaic 'ways' of some of their people – but because they are so situated that it is next to impossible to modernise or over-build them.[1]

Throughout the nineteenth century Staithes was a thriving fishing and boat-building port, the centre of the herring market, where buyers from around Britain, France and Holland flocked during the season, from June to September. However, the yawls and cobles of Staithes found it increasingly difficult to compete with the steam trawlers working out of the larger ports of Hull and Grimsby, leading to a steady and drastic decline in fishing from the village before the First World War.[2] Jet mining, begun in 1840, provided employment during Victoria's reign, but by 1920 the mines were exhausted. Alternative employment at the ironstone mines at Skinningrove, opened in 1874,

Frank M Sutcliffe, *Staithes, circa 1875*, photograph

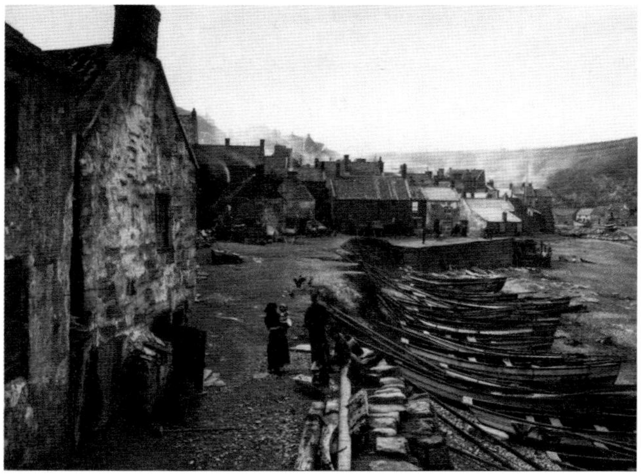

became an increasingly attractive proposition to the young men of Staithes as the fishing fleet declined.

But with the arrival of the railway in 1883, other sources of income became available to the inhabitants of Staithes – tourists and artists. From the early 1880s a number of guidebooks were published aimed at attracting walkers and fossil hunters to the area.[3] The proximity of Whitby as a cultural centre was also important, especially for encouraging writers such as Henry James, J Russell Lowell and George du Maurier.[4] Contemporary newspapers advertised the visual appeal of Staithes and its neighbour Runswick Bay, 'where the houses are studded all over the cliff-side, looking, in fact, as if they had slipped from the cliff above them, and stuck in every possible place.'[5] By 1900 the success of the area as an artists' haven was clear:

> Runswick Bay has long been a resort for the knights of the easel and camera … the higgledy-piggledy arrangement results in the village presenting a very picturesque appearance from points a short distance away, and artists fully appreciate the combination of boats and fishermen on the shore with red-tiled dwellings ornamented with quaint gardens and the frowning cliffs above.[6]

However, the article also suggested that the influx of 'trippers' and the newly-built houses were less welcome, presumably seen as elements which threatened the picturesqueness of the area, which could, in turn, discourage artists. Other reports demonstrate that the local economy was keen to capitalize on the importance of the artists' colony and to make it seem as attractive as possible: 'its people are simple and kindly, admirable as models, and unspoilt as yet by contact with the fashionable people who run down from Whitby, or Saltburn, or Scarborough to inspect and exclaim over its quaintness.'[7]

As with other artists' colonies, Staithes had been used as a sketching ground from the mid-nineteenth century, by artists such as J.B. Pyne, H.B. Carter and J.W. Carmichael. During the 1870s and 80s the popular landscapists James Aumonier and J.W.B. Knight included Runswick in their sketching tours, the results of their trips regularly seen on the walls of London exhibitions.[8] By around 1880 William Gilbert Foster, Frederick Jackson and Mark Senior, artists who would form the nucleus of the colony, were already working in the area. During the 1880s the fledgling colony was characterized by a number of artists visiting during summer months but not settling permanently, including Ralph Hedley and T.M. Hemy from Tyneside, J.V. Jelley, Duff Tollemache, the Canadian artist William Brymner, William Llewellyn, Frank Short and 'Glasgow Boy' Harrington Mann. By around 1890 Spence Ingall, Ernest Dade, Hannah Hoyland, Fred Mayor and Isa Thompson were all working in the area, joined by Robert Jobling, Joseph R. Bagshawe, James Booth, Arthur Friedenson, Roland Henry Hill, Henry Silkstone Hopwood, and Ernest Rigg during the early 1890s. Laura Johnson and Harold Knight first visited Staithes in 1897, and the Edinburgh artist Charles Mackie was already visiting before 1900. It could be argued that Staithes and Runswick represented two distinct colonies, as did Newlyn and Lamorna, because certain artists tended to work mostly at one site rather than the other.[9] Yet the close friendships and mutual co-operation between the two groups seen, for example, in the organization of the Staithes Art Club exhibitions, argues for an inclusive approach here.

Like the colony at Cullercoats, Staithes was characterized by the large proportion of 'northern' artists from the surrounding industrial towns of Yorkshire and Lancashire, who tended to become the more permanent members of the colony. However, Staithes attracted a larger number of important 'outside' artists throughout its lifetime, brought to Staithes by a series of interlinking friendships and shared artistic concerns. These links were forged in the ateliers of Paris, Antwerp, Bruges and London, and in the artists' colonies around Britain and Europe, where chance meetings and mutual friendships spread the word of Staithes' possibilities. During the late 1880s and early 1890s Dade, Friedenson, Hopwood, Ingall, Jackson, Knight, Mayor, Rigg, Harrington Mann, P.M. Teasdale, and J.A. Terry all studied at the Académie Julian in Paris. Lionel Crawshaw also studied in Paris in 1891 after a period in Dusseldorf, whilst Bagshawe trained at Bruges. Friedenson and Hopwood also studied together at Antwerp. Meanwhile, Senior studied under Legros at the Slade in 1881, becoming friends with Fred Brown, Henry Tonks and Philip Wilson Steer.

However, it was possibly the artists' trips to other colonies that were more important for the dissemination of new ideas and techniques, ensuring that this northern colony kept up-to-date with all the latest developments. Mackie played a crucial role in this process. Having studied at the Royal Scottish Academy until 1884, he spent time at Kirkcudbright before meeting Serusier at Huelgoat near the colony in Pont-Aven in 1892 and, through this friendship, meeting Gauguin and other members of the Nabis group in Paris in 1894. His subsequent importance as a teacher of colour theory to the young Laura Johnson is well documented.[10] It is possible that Hopwood and Jackson's visit to Pont-Aven in 1896-7 was inspired by Mackie, although they would no doubt have been aware of the colony during their time at the Académie Julian.[11] Harrington Mann painted regularly at Staithes from the mid-1880s, perhaps prompting Hopwood's visit to Fifeshire in 1887. Blandford Fletcher, who painted at Newlyn and Walberswick in the mid-1880s, was working at Staithes in 1894-5. In 1906 Senior spent the summer at the Walberswick colony with his old friend Steer, before spending subsequent summers until 1910 with Frank Brangwyn in Bruges.[12]

Meanwhile, the network with Scottish artists continued to develop. In 1906 Ernest Archibald Taylor moved to nearby Hinderwell and was a close friend of Hopwood's before his move to Kirkcudbright in 1916. The Leeds artist and Staithes visitor, Owen Bowen, was a friend of the Kirkcudbright-based Glasgow Boy Edward Atkinson Hornel, whilst Charles Oppenheimer worked at Runswick before moving to the Scottish colony in 1909.[13] Evidence from Jackson's 1918 exhibition suggests that he too worked at both Kirkcudbright and St. Ives, with fellow-Mancunian Oppenheimer perhaps providing Jackson's link to the Scottish colony.

However, another important influence must be considered in the work of the Staithes artists, that of Holland. Like the Cullercoats artist George Horton, Frederic S. Richardson visited Holland over a number of years from 1894 until the First World War, his pictures of boats and fishermen on the shoreline, such as *In for the Morning Market* (RA 1899), displaying a debt to the Hague School artist Mesdag.[14] Inspired by an exhibition of Dutch pictures at the Guildhall in London, seen during their honeymoon in 1903, the Knights went to Holland with Hopwood the following year. The influence of Dutch art on their work was clear, as will be discussed later. Harold exhibited some of his Dutch scenes at the

Laura Knight and Fred Jackson painting at Runswick, photograph courtesy of Rochdale Art Gallery

1904 Staithes Art Club exhibition, which also contained Dutch pictures by Robert Jobling (from his 1903 trip), Frank Mason, J Wright and Richardson.[15] Fred Mayor and Jackson also showed Dutch subjects at the Staithes Art Club in certain years. The attraction is not difficult to understand; the Dutch colonies such as Laren would have provided the artists with a 'home from home' – very similar surroundings bordering the North Sea, whose rural inhabitants were well-used to the requirements of artists.

In 1903 a critic of the third Staithes Art Club exhibition commented on 'the Staithes "School" – we use the term not in the meaning of a distinct style of painting, but as a colony of artists who "Bohemianise" annually amid this ideal combination of sea, civilisation, and heather'.[16] Whilst overlooking the permanent nature of the colony, the critic makes clear that, in common with most other colonies, there was no single style of painting at Staithes. So whilst the Bastien-Lepage-inspired square-brush technique held sway over the Newlyn artists throughout the 1880s, in Staithes it was dabbled with but never dominated. This may be partly explained by the fact that, unlike other colonies, there was no patriarchal figure or obvious leader around whom other artists gathered, although some of the older colonists did offer advice or pass on commissions to the younger ones. Instead, the artists were drawn together by unity of purpose, as one critic pointed out: 'Their aims are similar, but their methods are very dissimilar. They each try to give the broad truths of nature, ignoring almost entirely anything which would detract from the first impression.'[17] Fred Jackson concurred, explaining that their work tried to 'represent their honest interpretation of nature'.[18] To these ends, the artists worked largely *en plein air* in all weathers, almost as if the greater the hardship endured, the greater the veracity of their impressions of nature.[19]

Later reminiscences seem to suggest that, in the minds of the artists, there was a link between the characteristics of the Staithes folks' lives – their archaic customs, ascetic piety and heroic labours – and that of the artistic community. Roland Henry Hill talks in terms of a mutual respect between fisherfolk and artists, which allowed the artists to be accepted into this usually closed community, although he glosses over the fact that visitors were becoming an economic necessity for the villagers. Both he and Laura Knight used the example of working with the villagers to help land the cobles in stormy weather as evidence of 'that feeling of mutual help and camaraderie which fostered such a good feeling with the fisher folk'.[20] Knight went even further, linking Harold's achievements directly to the nature of the subjects offered by Staithes: 'the power latent in Harold's brush found food for expression in the wealth of material obtained by living in close com-

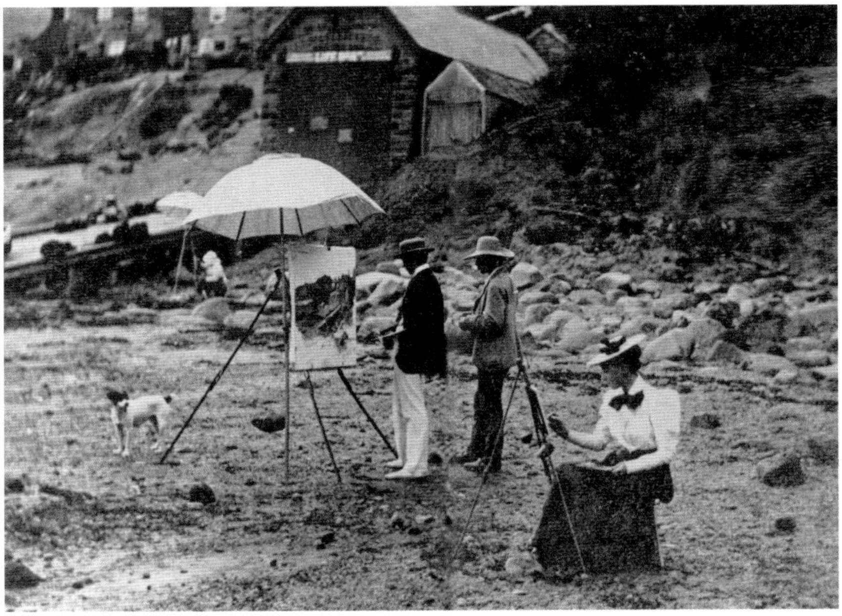

panionship with those salt-water folk, whose toil is great, and whose recompense is small'.[21] Of course these retrospective accounts must be treated with a certain degree of caution; they have become part of the 'mythology' surrounding the colony phenomenon, but collectively they give some indication of how the artists thought of themselves and of why they were attracted to these 'outside of the world' places.

Fred Jackson has been regarded as the lynchpin of the Staithes colony, primarily because of his long association with it, stretching from his first visit c.1883 to his death in 1918. Having attended Oldham School of Art with William Stott, Jackson became involved with the Betws-y-Coed colony through members of the Manchester School, exhibiting his first Royal Academy picture in 1880. In 1883 he went to Italy with Charles Mackie and the following year had pictures accepted by the Paris Salon.[22] He enrolled at the Académie Julian under Lefebvre and Boulanger in 1885 and, probably through his friendship with Stott, became involved in the establishment of the New English Art Club with Steer and Brown. As well as showing at the usual London, Manchester and Glasgow exhibitions, Jackson was a regular exhibitor at the Yorkshire Union of Artists from 1888 and a founder member of the Staithes Art Club in 1901.[23] In 1907 he settled at Ivy Cottage, Hinderwell, having married a local woman, Anne Hodgson. But he continued to travel widely, including France, North Africa and Russia.[24]

Jackson seems to have had a moderately successful career, with a number of regular patrons, one of whom was Samuel Barlow, a Lancashire industrialist and one of the earliest collectors of Impressionist paintings in Britain. In a letter to his father, William Brymner maintained that Jackson knew 'a great many rich cotton spinners and such like hereabouts who are going in for pictures ... Mr Barlow, a rich dye works man has given Jackson about £200 a year for the last five years for all his work.'[25]

Fig.59
Frederick William Jackson, *Coast Scene with Fishermen*
Leeds City Art Gallery

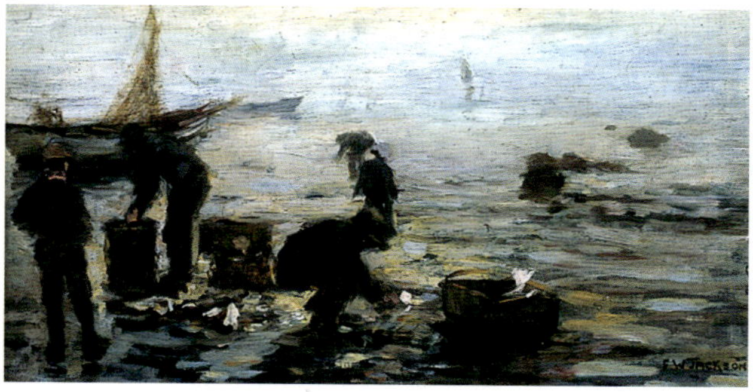

Jackson's style followed the trend fairly typical for coastal colonists, moving from a naturalist treatment of fisherfolk subjects during the 1880s and 1890s, to more impressionistic pictures with more diverse subjects – landscapes, farmyard scenes, cottage gardens and interiors. His smaller paintings, as *The Studio* noted in 1909, displayed an increasingly 'decorative treatment', as in his *Runswick Bay*, 'with its alluring colour of red roof-tops, silvery-green and dove-grey shadows, crowned by a faint violet sky.' However, his larger pictures still 'arrested one's gaze' by 'capable painting and atmospheric quality'.[26]

The undated *Coast Scene with Fishermen* (fig.59) suggests an earlier date in terms of subject and palette, yet its loose handling and exquisite light effects point to a later period. The dramatic contrast between the shadowy foreground figures and the ethereal merging of sea and sky, give this painting a strange, otherworldly quality, very different from the stable earthiness usually engendered by the 'working fishermen' subject. Harold Knight's *The Last Coble* (1900, fig.60), for example, is a more typical treatment of the theme, with its almost monochrome palette and dramatic composition reinforcing the gravitas of the narrative. This is one of Knight's first successful Staithes pictures, bought from the Royal Academy in 1900 by the Holbrook Bequest and presented to Nottingham Castle Museum in 1902.

Henry S. Hopwood's early Staithes work is very similar to that of Knight's in terms of subject and treatment.

Fig.60
Harold Knight, *The Last Coble*, 1900
Courtesy of Nottingham Castle Museums and Art Gallery

Fig.61
Henry Silkstone Hopwood, *Industry*, 1894

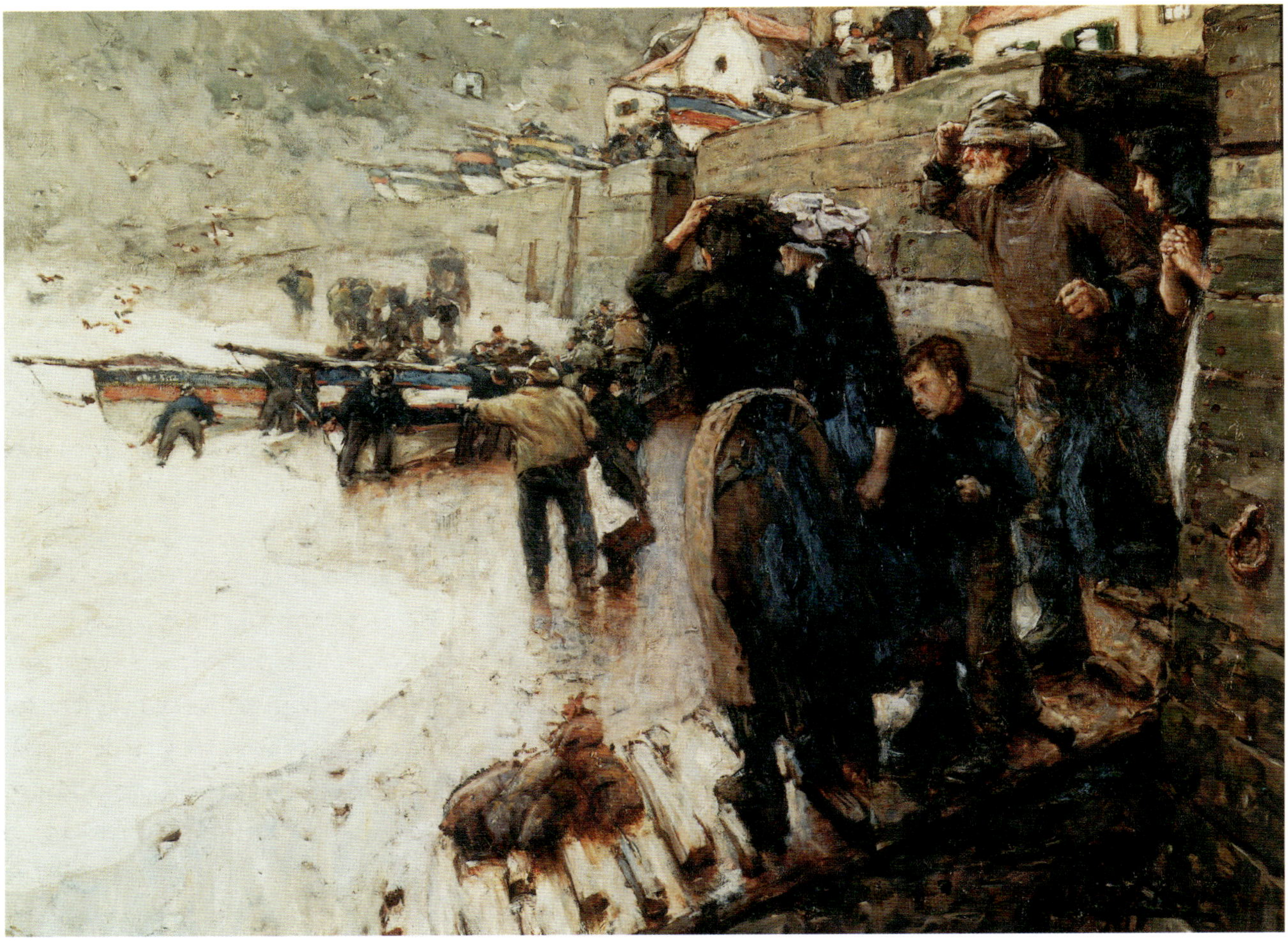

An early success, *Industry*, was bought by the Chantrey Bequest from the Royal Academy in 1894 (fig.61).[27] This touching interior suggests a debt to Hague School artists such as Josef Israels, with its combination of still-life elements and gentle narrative. Later pictures, including *Bethankit* (RA 1901), use the same female model.[28] Margaret Calvert, who also appears in Mark Senior's works, *Firelight* (c.1907) and *Peggy* (1902), lived at the White Cottage in Runswick.[29]

Like Jackson, Hopwood travelled a great deal, often holding London exhibitions to sell pictures from particular sketching trips. These included a Fine Art Society exhibition in 1897 of works from Pont-Aven and northern France; one at Van Wisselingh's gallery in 1907 of North African and Staithes pictures; and a 1913 Fine Art Society exhibition of pictures of the Near and Far East. Other exhibited works confirm that he travelled to Montreuil, Tangiers, the Hebrides, Newlyn, Venice and Fifeshire, as well as his trip to Holland with the Knights

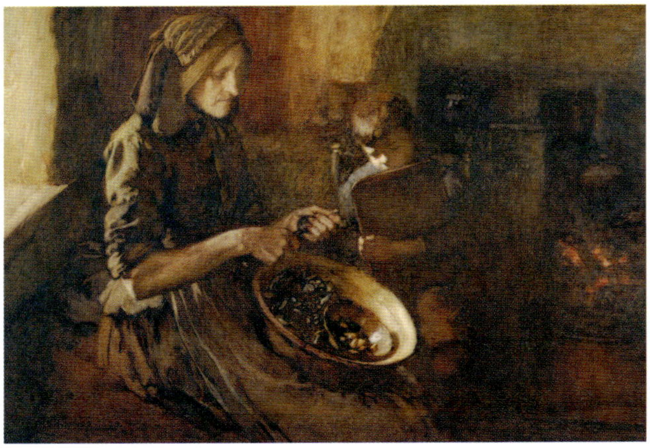

Fig.62
Isa Jobling (née Thompson), *Fisher Folk*, 1893, oil on canvas
Laing Art Gallery, Newcastle upon Tyne

F.M. Sutcliffe, *Staithes and Cowbar Beck*, photograph

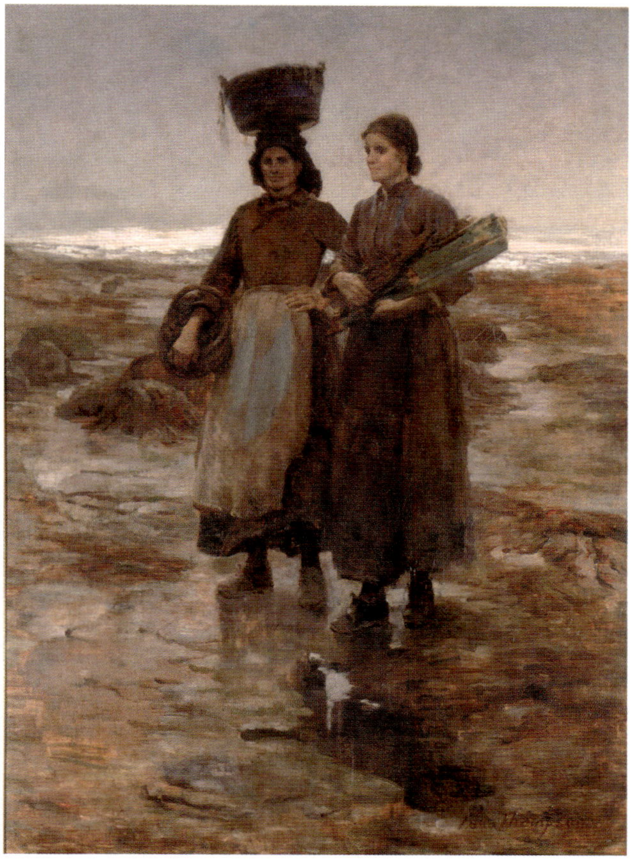

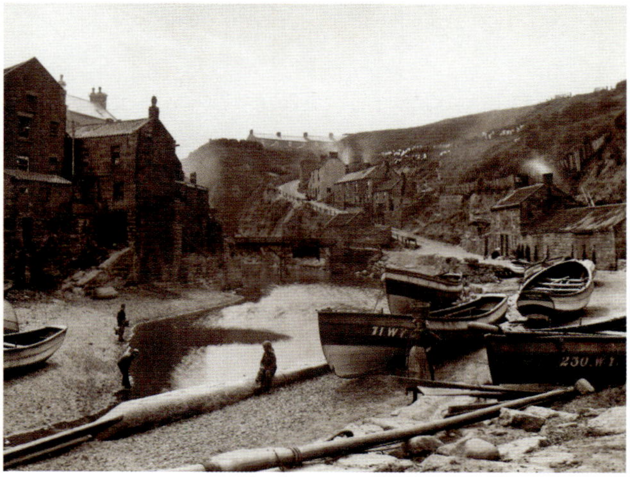

in 1904. His work was highly regarded by contemporary critics, one 1910 article reproducing his earlier picture *Bethankit*, here renamed *Grace After Meat*, to 'get some idea of the stages through which his work has progressed to its present freedom.' It goes on, 'He is now concerned with impressionism, not with subject painting. His art is now one of interpretation, and of creation only in that sense.' This critic's description of Hopwood's later work as 'in a silvery and quiet key' suggests a marked move away from the earlier earth-based palette of works such as *Industry*.[30]

However, many other Staithes artists produced often powerful works exploring the hardships of fisher life. Isa Thompson's *Fisher Folk* (RA 1893) is an uncompromising exploration of these women's struggle for survival (fig.62).[31] Their figures seem almost to illustrate Nelly Erichsen's description of the Staithes women:

> bands of sturdy girls may be seen, all through the winter, winding their way across the slippery rocks towards the town. They have been gathering limpets for bait, and have perhaps walked eight or ten miles along the coast for them. They stride heartily along, holding their heads very erect, as if the heavy baskets of limpet were of no weight at all; one or two of them with a bundle of driftwood picked up on the way adding to the burden.[32]

Laura Knight's *The Fishing Fleet* (1900, Bolton Art Gallery) is a similarly stark image, offering the tantalizing suggestion that the younger artist was at least aware of the older woman's work. By 1900 Thompson would have been a familiar figure at Staithes, and is likely to have been a founder member of the Staithes Art Club, offering a role model for younger female artists such as Knight and Hannah Hoyland. Her husband, Robert Jobling, also quickly developed a twin allegiance to the colonies at Cullercoats and Staithes, retaining a fascination with fisher life but adopting a more painterly style and brighter palette, demonstrated in his 1910 picture *Winter Fuel* (fig.63). This theme of collecting driftwood along the shoreline was common amongst all coastal colonies, perhaps because it reflected the

Fig.63
Robert Jobling, *Winter Fuel*, 1910
South Shields Museum and Art Gallery

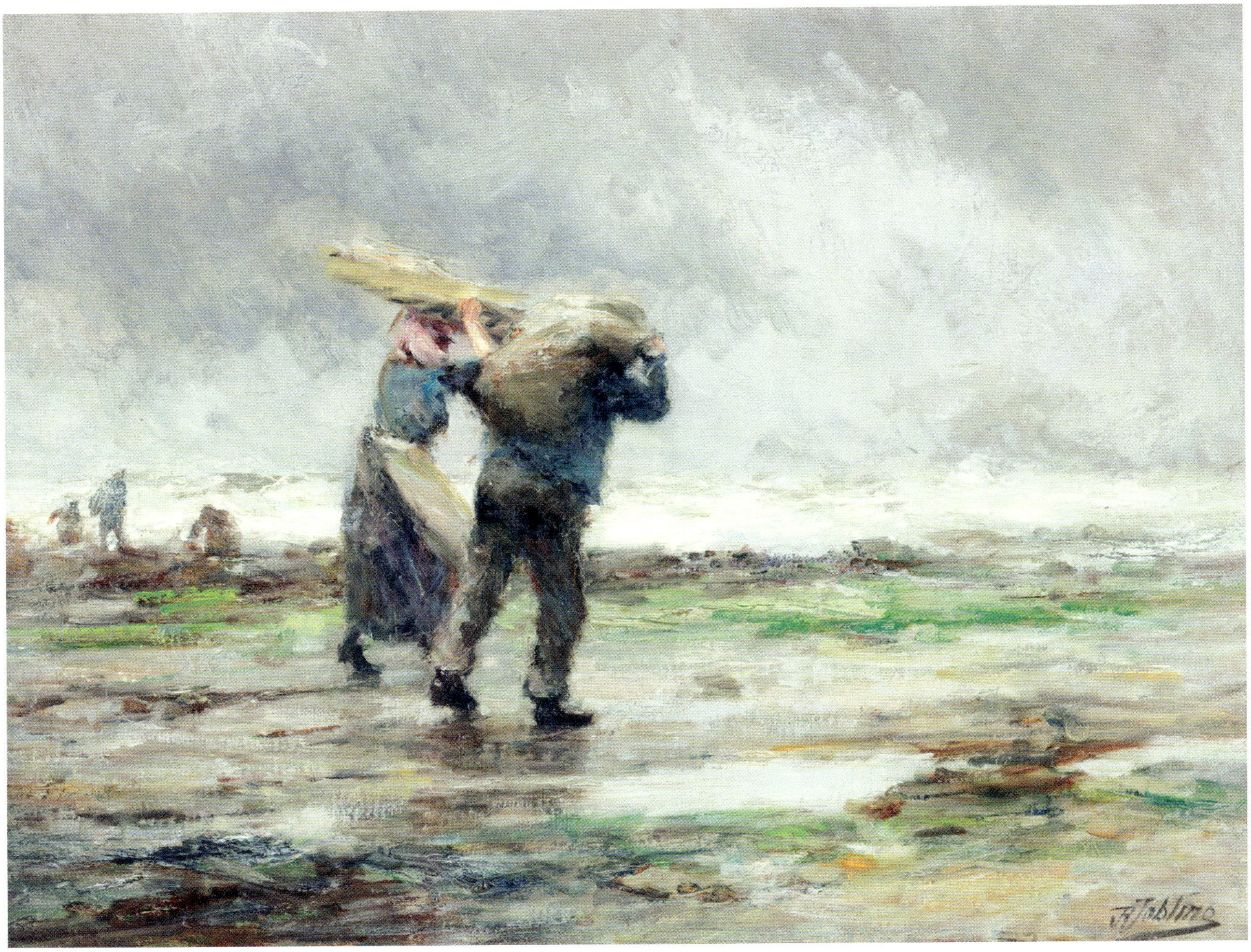

very real poverty of fisher life, but was a subject which could be treated in a more symbolic, and therefore less challenging, way.

The importance of Dutch art and of Holland as an alternative sketching ground is clearly seen in the work of many Staithes artists, perhaps most obviously in that of the Knights, following their trips between 1904 and 1906. Laura had already begun to concentrate on the mundane chores of family life, as in *Peeling Potatoes* (1900). Often featuring children because they were cheap models, her work showed increasing depths of feeling and subtlety following lessons from Mackie. The trips to Holland built on this foundation, so that pictures such as *Dressing the Children* (RA 1906), although a Staithes picture, show a debt to Neuhuys and Dutch seventeenth-century masters (fig.64). Her subtle use of diffused light, helped by a grainy impasto, in this and similar works suggests a feeling of mundane routine, dispelling any tendency the subject might have to take on a more symbolic quality.[33] Harold, however, was more influenced by Vermeer's interiors, seen on visits to the Rijksmuseum. His 1906 RA picture, *The Girl and the Letter* (fig.65), demonstrates this influence clearly, with its limited palette, its figures set again a dramatic single light source, the lack of sentimentality and a palpable, psychologically intense restraint. The figures of the young woman and child appear to be those also used by Laura in *Dressing*

Fig.64
Dame Laura Knight, *Dressing the Children*, 1906, oil on canvas
Ferens Art Gallery, Hull Museums and Art Gallery

Fig.65
Harold Knight, *The Girl and the Letter*, 1906, oil on canvas
Harris Museum and Art Gallery, Preston

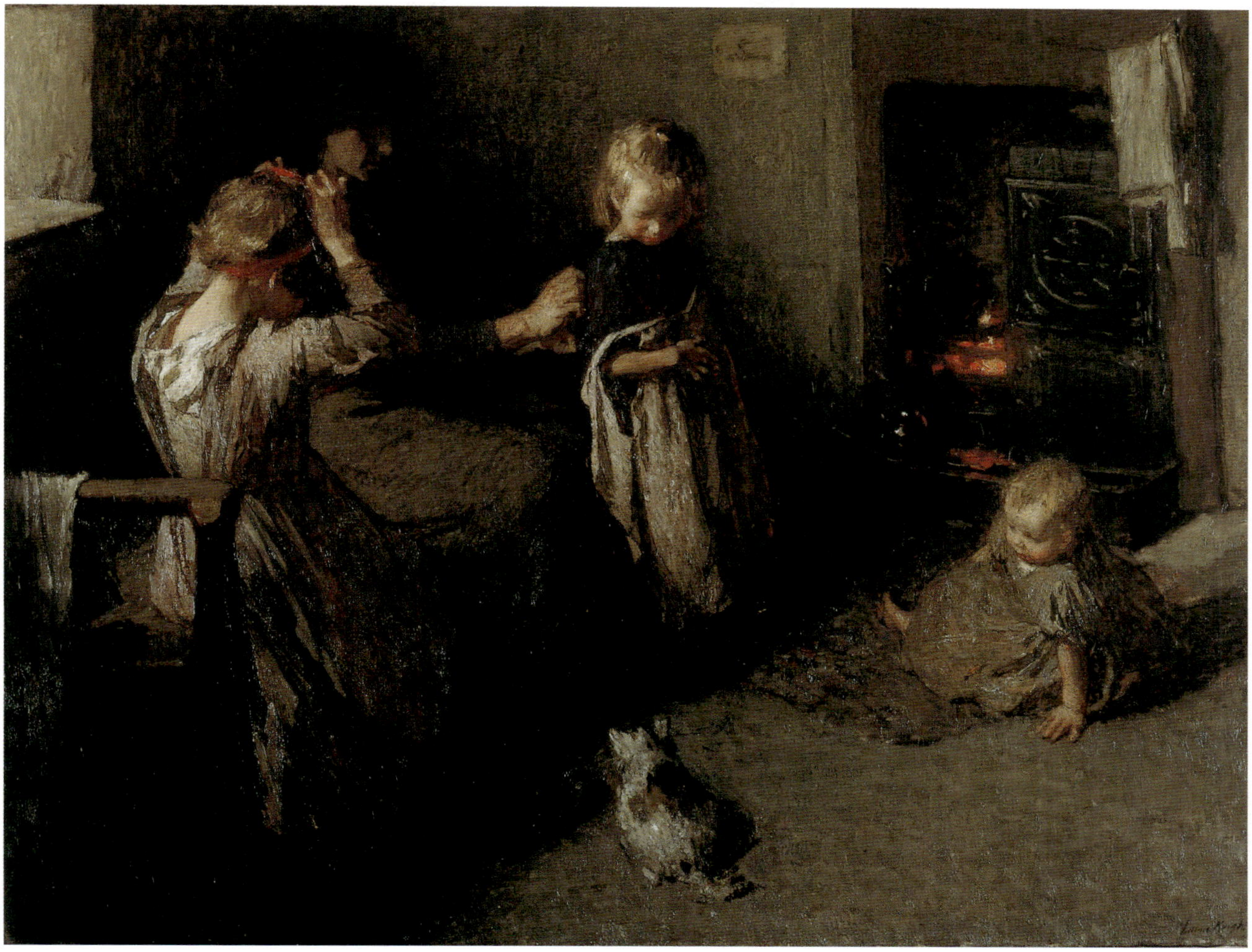

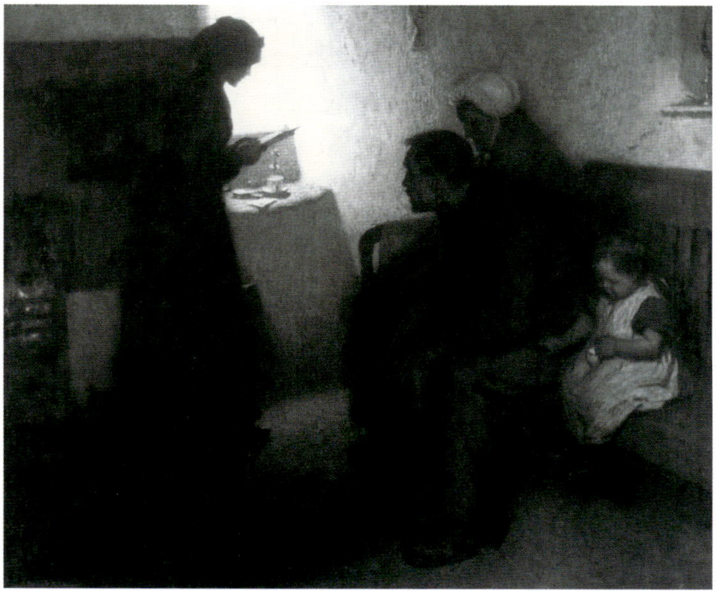

the Children, whilst the theme of letter-reading was one which reappeared in a number of Harold's paintings throughout this period, and again can be traced to the influence of Dutch seventeenth-century subjects.[34]

1906 was a particularly important year for the Knights; as well as successful Royal Academy pictures, they secured their first exhibition of Dutch pictures at the Leicester Galleries in London and showed for the first and last time at the Yorkshire Union of Artists. Following a second Leicester Galleries exhibition in 1907 the Knights decided to decamp to Newlyn. They must have felt the need for a clean break since

Fig.66
Mark Senior, *The Flemish Washhouse*, c.1908, oil on canvas
Leeds City Art Gallery

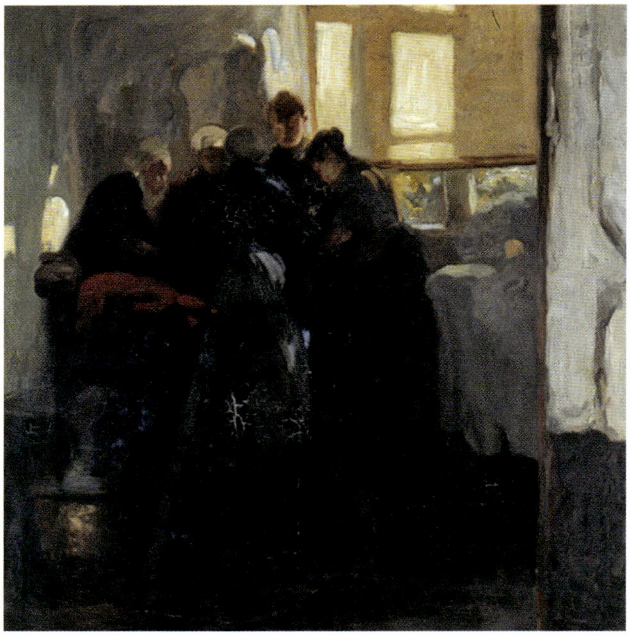

neither did they return to Holland, a decision which Laura explained was taken because 'The ready-made picturesque palled – it had all been used before'.[35] Nevertheless, the importance of their Staithes period cannot be overestimated, and it is telling that an article on Harold in 1911 used paintings of c.1905-8 to demonstrate his 'unusual sincerity of conviction and freshness of style … sureness and breadth of handling, his flexibility of draughtsmanship, and his clever management of subtleties of colour-gradation'.[36] Similarly, Laura maintained that many of her Newlyn paintings of children 'were derived from Staithes'.[37]

Born near Dewsbury, Mark Senior must be regarded as a crucial figure in the art world of Yorkshire throughout the period. After early successes, he settled at Ossett, spending Easter to October at Runswick, a pattern he maintained throughout the rest of his life.[38] He maintained his early friendships with Steer, Tonks and Brown through the Chelsea Arts Club and sketching trips abroad. Whilst his earliest work shows a debt to the Naturalism of George Clausen, Senior was always quick to try new techniques married to a variety of subject matter. Following a trip to Walberswick with Steer and Georg Sauter in 1906, Steer's influence can be clearly seen in works such as *By the Sea* and *Away to the Sea*. A series of annual visits to Bruges with Frank Brangwyn and Alfred Gilbert between 1907 and 1910 resulted in a number of paintings which experiment with the decorative qualities of flat areas of colour and arabesque outlines, very like Brangwyn's pictures of this period and perhaps also suggesting a knowledge of Serusier via Mackie.[39] *The Flemish Washhouse* (c.1908, fig.66) brought Senior to national attention, forming part of Britain's section at the Venice Biennale in 1910, where it was bought by the Leeds collector Sam Wilson. In an article on Wilson's collection in 1916 a critic noted that *The Flemish Washhouse* is 'broadly treated and rich in impasto' affiliating him to 'the best colourists of the Flemish School. Unlike Orpen he does not introduce any literary intention into his pictures. … And like Clausen he possesses a very poetic feeling for nature, whose essential beauties he interprets independently of any theory.' The critic goes on to applaud Senior for 'the frank sincerity of the artist, a true painter in the best sense of the word.'[40] Certainly this washhouse scene has none of the sexually-charged voyeurism often associated with Degas' treatment of similar themes, but is instead a bravura exploration of dramatic light effects.

The development of a more decorative, painterly style amongst the Staithes artists from the late 1890s was perhaps in response to the growing anti-Naturalism of the metropolitan British Impressionist group.[41] Up to the First World War they adopted a variety of differing approaches and techniques. Like Senior, Charles Mackie's work, for example, varied widely.[42] Having 'burst upon the public gaze in the Scottish Academy of 1888' with naturalist landscapes 'pregnant with the emotion of time and place',[43] Mackie's contact with the Nabis led to a more sinuous, Serusier-like Symbolism, most

Fig.67
Charles Hodge Mackie, *The Windmill*, 1900, oil on canvas
Leeds City Art Gallery

Fig.68
Arthur Friedenson, *October Sunshine*, 1905, oil on canvas
Leeds City Art Gallery

obviously seen in the mural and design work executed for Patrick Geddes in Edinburgh in the early 1890s.[44] Although slightly scathing of Mackie's new 'decorative and half-scientific' style, James Caw admired his 'interest in true values, a desire for dignified composition, and a curiosity in effects of lighting, natural and artificial, which show him thoroughly alive to many modern art problems'.[45] When the decorative schemes for Geddes dried up in 1895–6, Mackie returned to easel painting, although he clearly carried on experimenting: 'an original landscapist constantly researching new techniques; he has talent, much talent perhaps. In any case he is not banal.'[46] But whilst he evidently experimented, he did maintain some key colour theory principles learnt from Serusier, the central tenet of which was the importance of grey in establishing the keynote for the palette. This could partly explain his attraction to Staithes, with its particularly grey light. Some of his Staithes landscapes, such as *The Windmill* (RSA 1900, fig.67) have an encrusted, granular effect more akin to Matthew Maris or Monticelli (see page 147).[47] This more painterly, yet still decorative, style supports Caw's estimation that 'he has shown an increased tendency to rely on his instincts, and a disposition to express his personal and immediate impressions of reality'.[48]

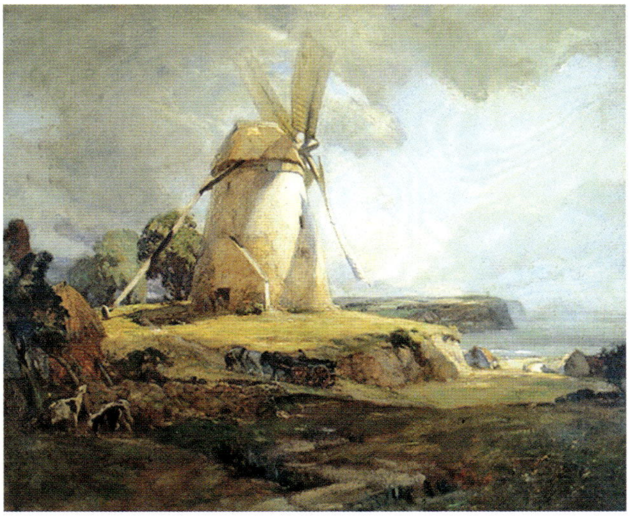

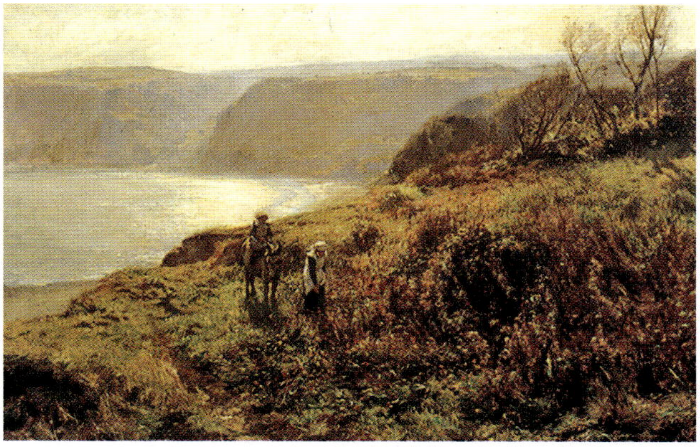

A similar technique was also adopted by Arthur Friedenson for his landscapes of this period, such as *October Sunshine* (RA 1905, fig.68). His Royal Academy picture of 1907, *Runswick Bay*, was bought by the Chantrey Bequest, whilst *Blackberry-Time* (RA 1911) reveals that he stuck to the winning formula even after his move to Dorset in 1909; not only is the coastline uncannily like that of *October Sunshine*, but the figure of the girl, complete with Staithes bonnet, is almost identical.[49]

This decorative treatment of the landscape is also found in the work of Roland Henry Hill, a younger artist who had been encouraged to train by Ralph Hedley whom he had met on a sketching trip to Runswick. Having studied with Herkomer at Bushey, Hill exhibited at the Royal Academy, Yorkshire Union of Artists, Paris Salon and the International Exhibition in Venice in 1899, as well as with the Staithes Art Club.[50] *Runswick Cottages* (fig.69) is a fairly typical example of Hill's sunny palette and loose watercolour technique, whilst oils such as *The Primrose Walk* (1921) suggest a great debt to Senior, not only in terms of the subject but in the working of the paint surface.[51] Senior's own landscapes became more abstract towards the beginning of the War, as his interest in genre subjects diminished and colour became increasingly rich. Possibly through the influence of Sauter, his brilliant colour schemes were sometimes laid down as flat areas of colour, a Symbolist-inspired vehicle for the expression of emotion. More often colour is used with

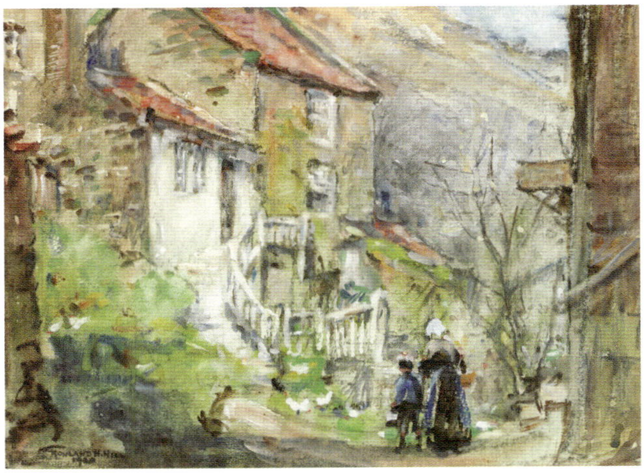

Fig.69
Roland Henry Hill, *Runswick Cottages*, watercolour
South Shields Museum and Art Gallery

heavy impasto, as in *Apple Blossoms* (fig.70), where the encrusted surface combines with touches of Senior's famously vivid blue, of which S.C. Kaines Smith noted, 'That blue of yours is wonderful; it sings'.[52]

Although more usually associated with subjects of labour, Hedley too indulged in more decorative, brighter painting at Runswick. His *Pleasant Memories*, probably dating from the mid-1880s, is a relatively early example of the influence of the British Impressionists on the artists at Staithes and Runswick. His influence on the Tyneside artists working at Cullercoats is difficult to gauge,

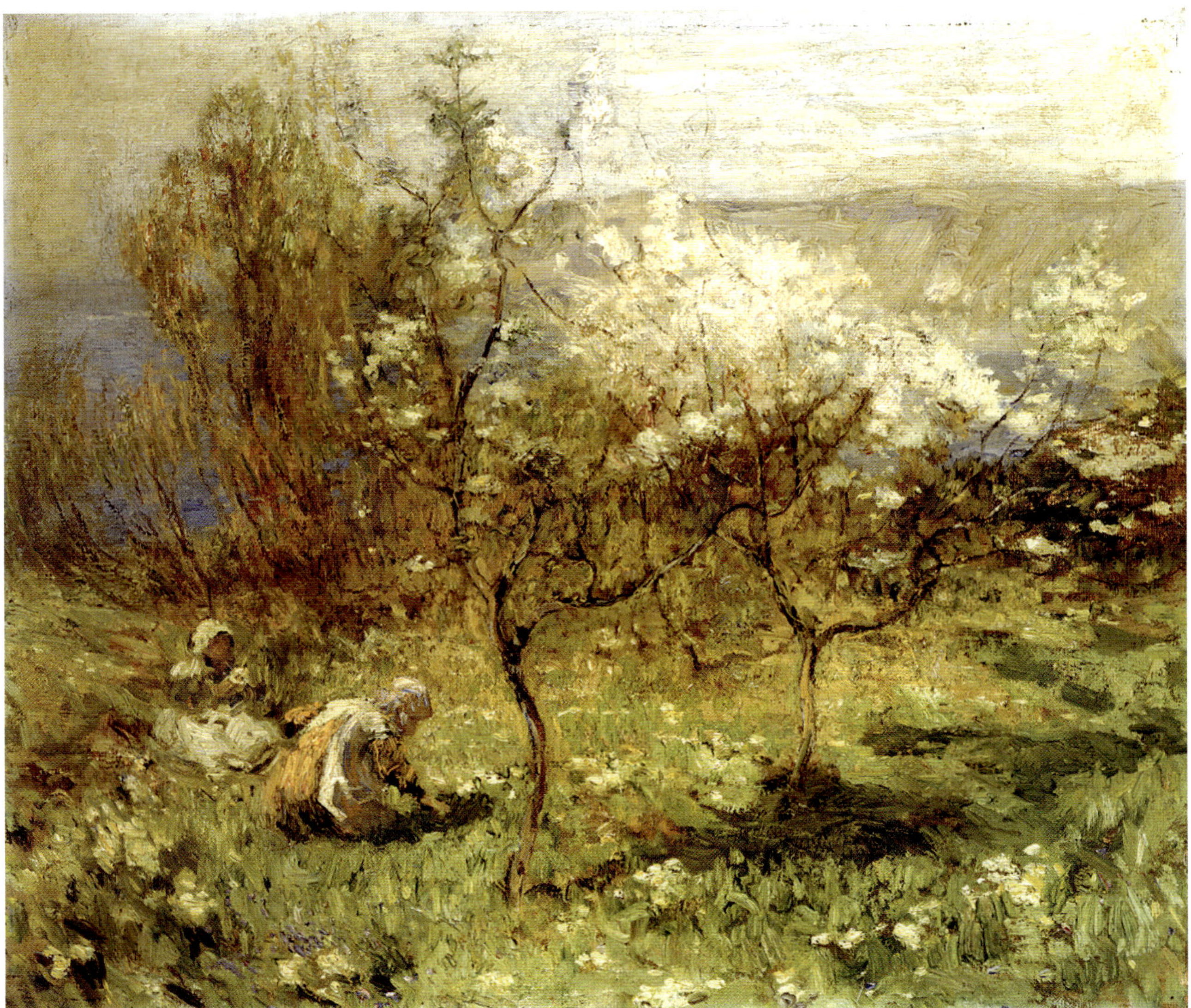

Fig.70
Mark Senior, *Apple Blossoms*, oil on canvas
Leeds City Art Gallery

Fig.71
Isa Jobling (née Thompson), *Haymaking*, post-1900, oil on canvas
Shipley Art Gallery, Gateshead

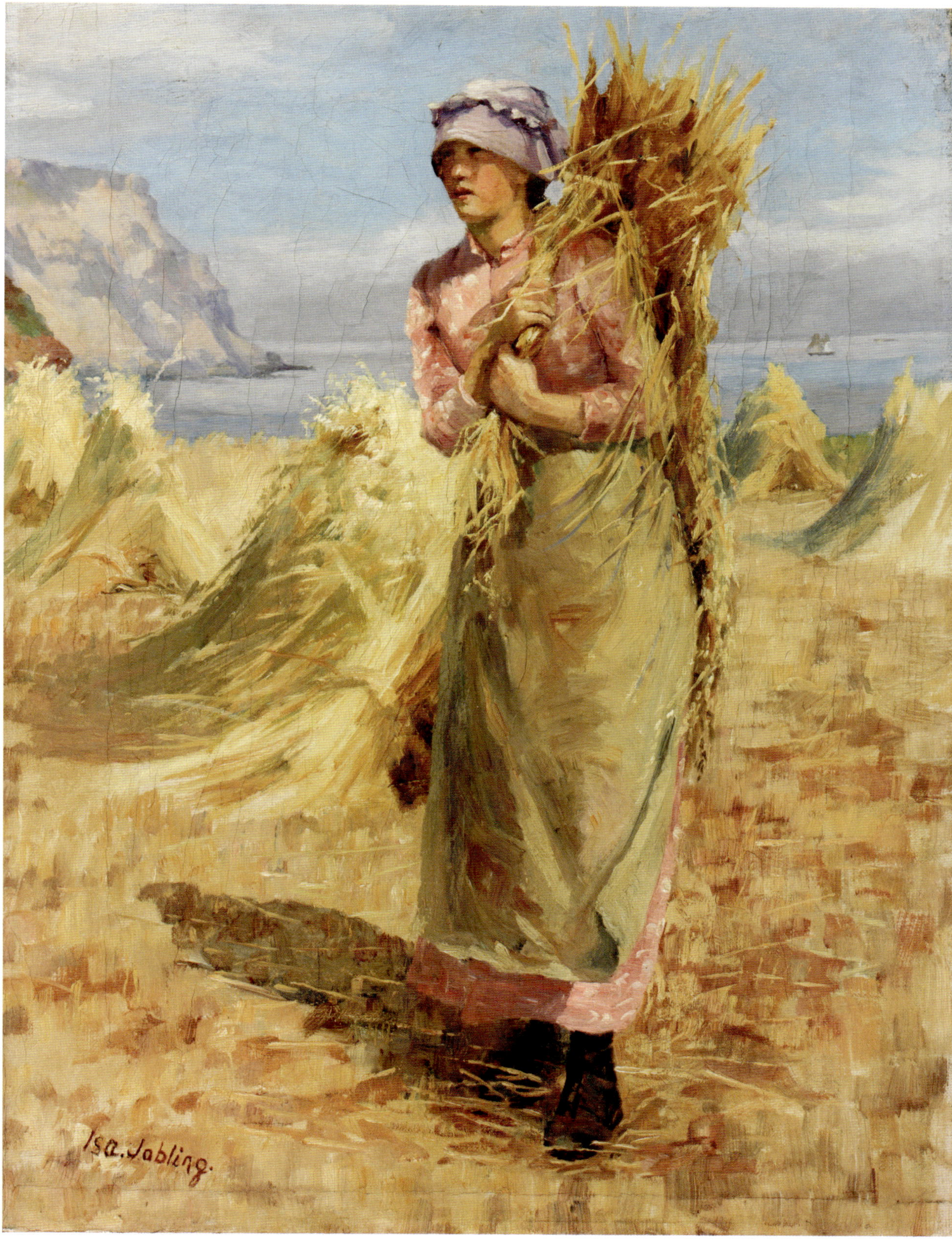

Fig.72
Harrington Mann, *Low Tide on the Beck*, 1895, oil on panel
Pannett Gallery, Whitby

yet his example must surely have persuaded the young Isa Thompson to try her luck at Staithes from the early 1890s.[53] In *Haymaking* (fig.71) Thompson combines the rural labour subject with a decorative treatment; the areas of square-brush technique and vivid palette recall her first Royal Academy picture *Blossom* (1892, see page 126), yet the theme – a young woman working in a hostile environment – is more closely allied to *Fisher Folk* (fig.62). There are also compositional similarities with the latter painting, including the closeness of the figure to the picture plane giving a high horizon which anchors her in the landscape; the backdrop of sea and sky; and the daydream-like distant gaze of the girl. But the uncompromising qualities of *Fisher Folk* are negated here by the small scale of this painting which denies any monumentalization of the figure, and with the bright clothes of the girl complementing the vivid blues of sea and sky, distracts from the harsh realities of this back-breaking work.

Like Mackie's, the extent of Harrington Mann's involvement with the Staithes colony is unclear. Although affiliated to the Glasgow Boys until about 1892, it is evident from works sent to the Glasgow Institute in 1886 and 1887 that Mann was already spending time at Staithes; indeed, according to Caw, it was these works which 'first attracted attention'.[54] He must have continued to visit regularly during the 1890s as Laura Knight mentions see-

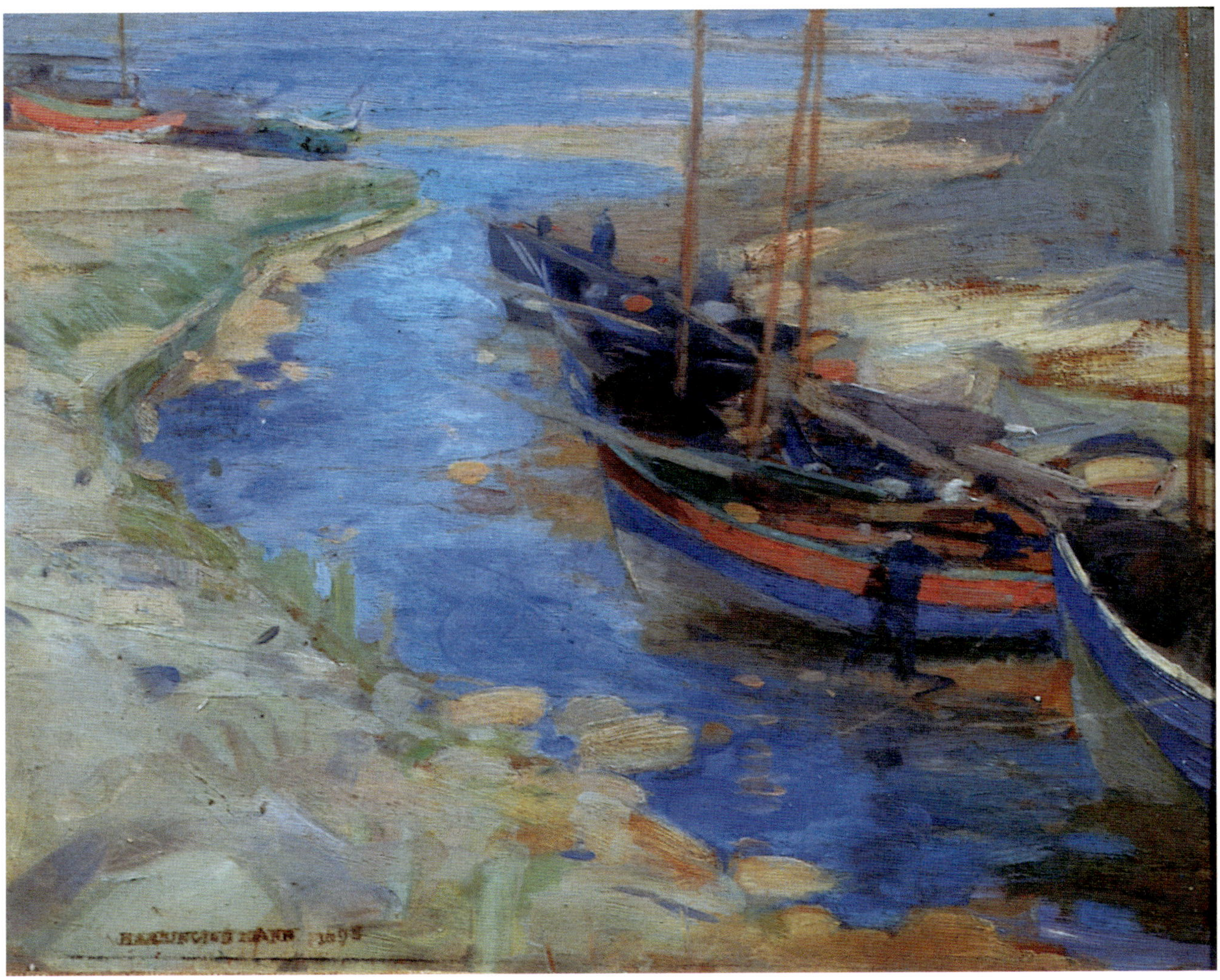

ing him on her first trip, which was not until 1897.[55] From the mid 1890s he showed only portraits at major exhibitions, although pictures such as *Low Tide on the Beck* 1895 suggest that he continued to paint subject pictures, perhaps for private clients or his own pleasure (fig.72). This delightful oil sketch uses a limited palette and bold brushwork, reminiscent of the early Walberswick paintings of Steer before his experimentation with pointillism. Mann was known for painting 'with considerable bravura and dash in bold and slashing … brush strokes', a style to which he obviously adhered in this painting.[56] Other Staithes pictures, such as *Girl in a Lilac Hat*, combine this bold handling with his growing interest in portraiture.[57] It is unknown when Mann's association with Staithes ceased, and although he became a member of the Society of Eight in Edinburgh in 1912, more of his professional life was spent in New York, where he eventually died.[58]

Although Laura Knight later dismissed the Staithes Art Club exhibitions, saying that they 'did not cover us with glory', their importance as a sales outlet and advertisement for the colony members must be considered.[59] By enlisting important local industrialists W.D. Turnbull and J. Bruce as vice-presidents of the Club (perhaps aided by Joseph Bagshawe's marriage into the Turnbull family in 1901), it provided a crucial link between the artists and potential local patrons. The pictures shown at the Fishermen's Institute in Staithes were small in number (around 40), generally of small size and selling for a few pounds.[60] But by 1904 larger premises were necessary, so the annual exhibition moved to Whitby, where it was hoped they would also benefit from the busier tourist industry. From 1905 the Club became affiliated to the Yorkshire Union of Artists, ceasing to exist as a separate club after 1907. Many of the Staithes artists had already been associated with the YUA from its inception in 1888, and because of its multi-centred exhibitions it was arguably a much more useful shop window. Certainly Leeds and Bradford, the main centres of the YUA, had reputations for more 'avant-garde' collectors, thereby attracting many professional artists to the YUA exhibitions and helping to keep standards high.[61]

1907 is usually regarded as the watershed for the Staithes colony because of the removal of the Knights to Newlyn, the Mayors to London and Friedenson to Dorset. However, arguably the most crucial figures of the colony, Jackson and Senior, remained, both continuing to develop a vital and energetic artistic practice in step with the developments elsewhere in Britain. Their influence is clearly visible in the work of the other colonists and regular summer visitors and, as we have seen, the colony continued to attract other artists.[62]

Writers on the Staithes colony are always indebted to Laura Knight's unique accounts of her time there, as they paint such a vivid picture of this important period. But her obvious biases and careful omissions should alert us to a much richer artistic milieu than she would allow. Nevertheless, it is probably through her fame that the paintings of the Staithes colonists are once again attracting attention. Unfortunately, unlike Newlyn and St. Ives, Staithes has so far failed to capitalize on its former glory. Today it boasts few attractions other than the Captain Cook and Staithes Heritage Centre, housed in the redundant Methodist Chapel – its contents and building a forlorn reminder of a past way of life and a past colony. To understand the lure of Staithes, it seems we must abandon ourselves to the mythology:

> The life and place were what I had yearned for – the freedom, the austerity, the savagery, the wildness. I loved it passionately, overwhelmingly. I loved the cold and the northerly storms when no covering would protect you. I loved the strange race of people who lived there, whose stern almost forbidding exterior formed such contrast to the warmth and richness of their natures. … It bordered on the theatrical.[63]

Notes

1. *Whitby Gazette*, August 1901, quoted in P Phillips, *The Staithes Group*, Phillips & Son, 1993, p.17. The title quotation is also from this source.
2. A deeper harbour capable of taking steam vessels was not constructed until 1924, long after the fishing industry ceased to be the main employment.
3. See for example J Black, *Black's Guide to Scarborough, Whitby and Vicinity*, 1883; J Leyland, *The Yorkshire Coast*, 1892; G.S. Forman, *A Holiday Tour in and Around Whitby*, 1896; and G Home, *Yorkshire Coast and Moorland*, 1904.
4. Du Maurier's novel *The Martian* (1897) describes the fisherfolk of Staithes.
5. 'Round and About Whitby', *The Graphic*, 6 September 1884, p.246.
6. 'Runswick Bay', *Newcastle Weekly Chronicle*, 23 June 1900, p.7.
7. *Whitby Gazette*, August 1901.
8. For example, Aumonier's *Autumn Landscape near Runswick* was shown at the RBA in 1874, whilst Knight's *Rough Weather – Runswick Bay* was seen there in 1877.
9. For example, Senior, Mackie, Crawshaw, Jackson, Jelley, Brymner and Tollemache worked mainly at Runswick.
10. Laura Knight, *Oil Paint and Grease Paint*, Nicholson & Watson, 1936, pp.87-8.
11. Hopwood held an exhibition of his French watercolours at the Fine Art Society in 1897, selling 31 of 63 pictures, making £600.
12. Georg Sauter also accompanied Senior to Walberswick. In Bruges, Senior met the sculptor Alfred Gilbert, securing a commission for him for a decorative fireplace (now in Leeds City Art Gallery) from his patron Sam Wilson. He also met George Clausen there. Brangwyn had worked at Walberswick in 1890.
13. Hornel's involvement with the Staithes colony remains unknown, but it is intriguing to consider that he was elected to the council of the Yorkshire Union of Artists in 1908 (as was Mackie) and made their vice-president in 1912. This suggests that it was something more than just another commercial outlet for his paintings.
14. This picture is illustrated in P Haworth, *Paintings by Members of the Staithes Group*, exhibition catalogue, 2002, p.13.
15. The works included Mason's *Katwyk Sands*; Jobling's *A Dutch Maiden* and *Volendam Harbour*; Wright's *Canal at Sluys*.
16. *Whitby Gazette*, 14 August 1903.
17. 'Staithes Art Club', *Whitby Gazette*, 18 August 1905, p.7.
18. Frederick Jackson, *Staithes Art Club Catalogue*, 1905.
19. See, for example the accounts of R.H. Hill, 'A Seaside Colony of Painters', *Yorkshire Evening Post,* 30 August 1939; or Knight, *Oil Paint*, p.133. Similar stories are told by painters from other colonies; see L. Newton, 'The Cullercoats Artists' Colony c.1870–1914', unpub. PhD thesis, Northumbria University, 2001, pp.113–4.
20. Hill, ibid.
21. Laura Knight, *The Magic of a Line*, William Kimber, 1965, pp.111–2.
22. In 1884 his Salon pictures were *Au Bord de la Mer* and *Pecherie Anglais*: in 1885, *Sous Bois* and *La Seine a Bois le Roi.*
23. He was a council member of YUA in 1908 and 1912, and vice-president in 1891, 1895, 1898 and 1915.
24. He went to Russia with one of his patrons, Walter Butterworth, who also owned works by Oppenheimer, Crawshaw and Kerr-Lawson.
25. Brymner letter to his father, McCord Museum, McGill University, Montreal. Jackson had taken Brymner to see Barlow's collection in 1884.
26. Manchester Academy of Fine Arts exhibition, *The Studio*, v.47, 1909, pp.59-60. In this exhibition he and Hopwood also exhibited watercolours from North Africa.
27. The picture was reproduced in an article in *The Studio*, v.40, 1907, p.236.
28. This watercolour was illustrated in *Royal Academy Pictures* for 1901. He showed a picture called *Be Thanket* at the YUA exhibition in 1898, but it is unclear if this was the same picture.
29. Both are now at Leeds City Art Gallery and illustrated in the new catalogue of oil paintings.
30. T. Martin Wood, 'H.S. Hopwood', *The Studio*, v.49, 1910, pp.27–33. Confusingly, Hopwood's 1902 RA picture was called *Grace After Meat*, but this was presumably a different painting. This article also contained several other reproductions of his work. For other critiques of his work see *The Studio* v.27, 1902, p.295; *The Studio* v.40, 1907, p.234; *The Studio* v.41, 1907, p.61; *The Studio* v.47, 1909, p.59.
31. For more discussion of this picture see L Newton, *Cullercoats: A North-East Colony of Artists*, Sansom & Company, 2003, pp.102-4. The older woman was Lizzie Ann Sanders of Staithes.
32. Nelly Erichsen, 'A North Country Fishing Town', *English Illustrated Magazine*, v.31, 1886, pp.462-69. For a similar description see Knight, *Oil Paint,* p.80.

33. See Knight, *Oil Paint*, pp.145-47 for an account of this painting.

34. These include *The Letter* and *Portrait of Laura Knight* c.1905–6. Fox and Greenacre point to similarities with the work of Stanhope Forbes c.1900; see *Painting in Newlyn 1880–1930*, Barbican, 1985, p.150.

35. Knight, *The Magic*, p.128.

36. *The Studio*, v.54, 1911, p.60. The article illustrated *The Letter, The Reader* and *Grace before Meat* – a Dutch subject.

37. Knight, *Oil Paint*, p.103.

38. Senior exhibited at the RA regularly from 1892 until 1924, and at the YUA 1894-1908.

39. These elements can be seen in Senior's *Flemish Fishmarket* (RA 1907) or *A Bit of Bruges*, reproduced in *Mark Senior 1862-1927*, exhibition catalogue, Elizabethan Exhibition Gallery, Wakefield, 1983. It is possible that R.H. Hill also accompanied Senior since his YUA pictures in 1909 were Bruges subjects.

40. 'Modern Art in Leeds: The Collection of Mr Sam Wilson', *The Studio*, v.69, Dec 1916, pp.109-16. Senior's crucial involvement in building up the Wilson collection is well-known, leading to the purchase of works by Gilbert, Sauter, Clausen, Brangwyn, Priestman, Orpen and Steer, amongst others.

41. The work of Bastien-Lepage and the photographic qualities of Naturalist painting were increasingly criticised; see, for example Walter Sickert, 'Art and literature', *Whirlwind*, 28 June 1890; G. Moore, 'The Grosvenor Gallery', *Hawk*, 13 May 1890; D.S MacColl, 'Royal Academy', *The Spectator*, 9 May 1891, p.660.

42. Mackie's whereabouts are notoriously difficult to chart. He seems to have maintained a base in Edinburgh, but travelled extensively. He showed at the 2nd Staithes Art Club exhibition, and at the YUA 1906-9, including being vice-president in 1907.

43. J.L. Caw, *Scottish Painting 1620-1908* [1908], Kingsmead Publishing, Bath, 1975, p.423.

44. See F Fowle and B Thomson eds., *Patrick Geddes: The French Connection*, White Cockade Publishing, Oxford, 2004, for more on Mackie's decorative work.

45. Caw, *Scottish Painting*, p.424.

46. Letter, Augustin Hamon to Lucien Pissarro, 3 February 1895, Pissarro Archive, Ashmolean Museum, Oxford, quoted in B Thomson, 'Patrick Geddes's "Clan d'Artistes": Some Elusive French Connections' in Fowle and Thomson, *Geddes*, p.61.

47. Another work, *Whitby Market*, also dates from 1899, so we can be sure that Mackie was already in the area by that date. Monticelli was an important influence on the Glasgow Boys and on Mackie's later work especially.

48. Caw, *Scottish Painting*, p.424.

49. This is illustrated in *Royal Academy Pictures*, 1911. Friedenson continued to show at YUA until 1915 and at the RA until 1938.

50. He exhibited at the RA from 1896; the YUA from 1898, becoming vice-president in 1912, 1915 and 1920; the Salon in 1899; and SAC from 1901.

51. *The Primrose Walk* is illustrated in Haworth, *Paintings*, p.32.

52. Quoted in *Mark Senior 1864-1927*, exhibition catalogue, Michael Parkin Fine Art Ltd, 1974, p.6.

53. Thompson exhibited at the SAC from 1902 onwards and at the YUA in 1906, as well as at the usual national exhibitions. See Newton, *Cullercoats*, for more details of her career.

54. Caw, *Scottish Painting*, p.431. He showed *Breeze and Sunshine – Yorkshire Fishing Station* in 1886 and *The Beck* and *Packing Fish – Yorkshire Coast* in 1887.

55. See Knight, *Oil Paint*, p.74.

56. Caw, *Scottish Painting*, p.431.

57. This picture, the same size as *Low Tide on the Beck*, can be seen on the Fine Art Society website.

58. Interestingly, Mann was initially listed as amongst the missing from the *Titanic* disaster in 1912; see *New York Times*, 19 April 1912 on www.encyclopedia-titanica.org

59. Knight, *Oil Paint*, p.91.

60. An exception to this was Mackie's 1902 exhibit, *Moonlight on the Bay*, for sale at £60. The *Whitby Gazette* (21 August 1903) noted that Jackson's relatively expensive picture, *Off to the Rescue* (£25) was sold on the opening day of the exhibition.

61. For a history of the YUA see D Child, *The Yorkshire Union of Artists 1888-1922*, Leeds Philosophical and Literary Society Ltd, Leeds, 2001.

62. Regular colonists such as Bagshawe, Booth, Hill, Ingall, the Joblings, Stevens, Richardson, Dade, Atkinson, Hedley, James Watson, Joseph Terry, Teasdale, Florence Hess and Owen Bowen continued to work at Staithes and Runswick.

63. Knight, *Oil Paint*, p.75.

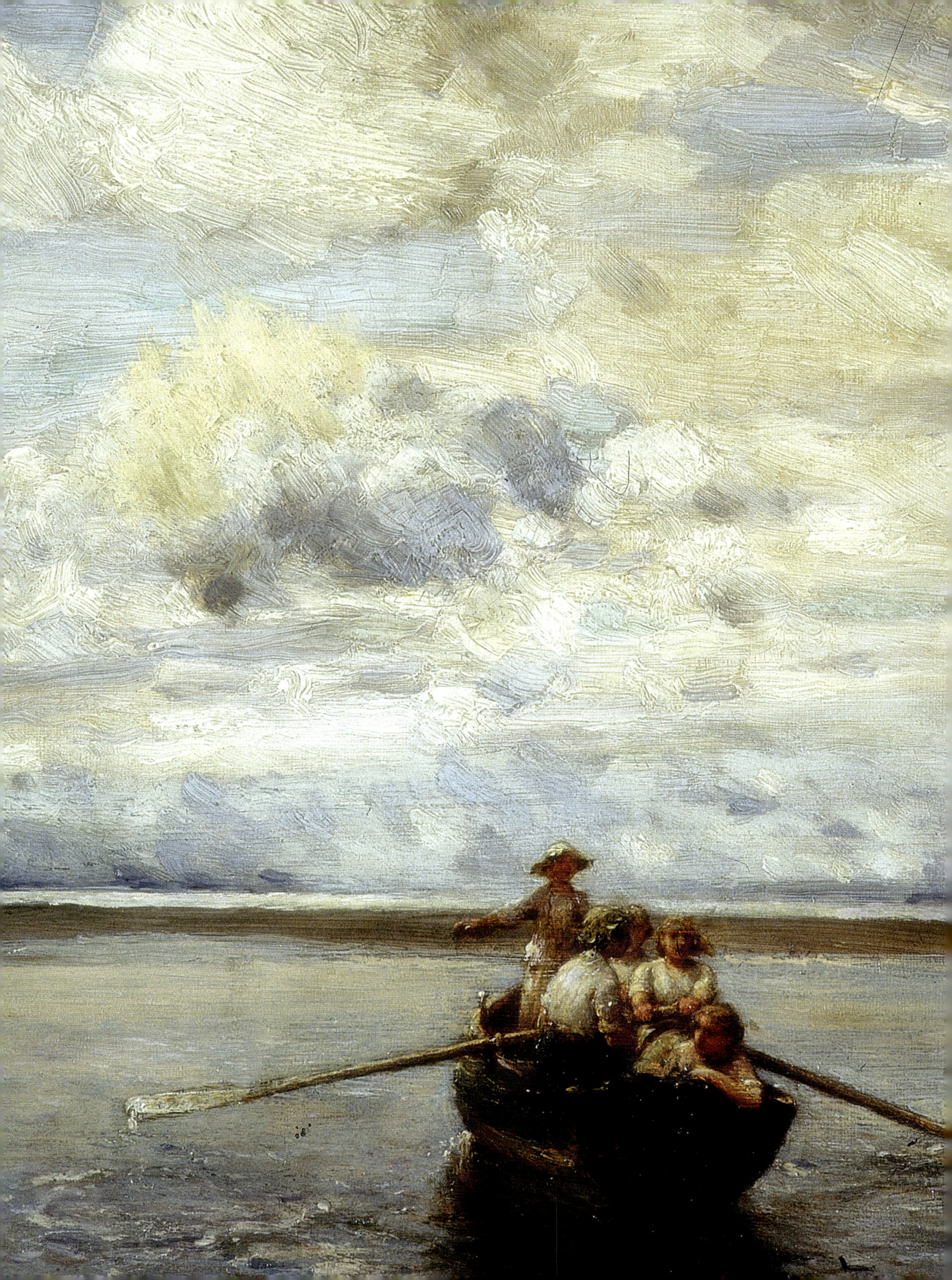

CHAPTER 7

Cullercoats
'The Region of Poetry'

LAURA NEWTON

Like other coastal villages that later became artists' colonies, Cullercoats on the Northumberland coast had a long history as a sketching ground. During the first half of the nineteenth century the area was particularly popular with marine artists, many of national repute, such as John Wilson Carmichael, Thomas Miles Richardson and Henry Perlee Parker. Whilst the majority of them concentrated on the coastline and picturesque ruins of Tynemouth Priory and Castle just to the south of Cullercoats, Parker took a closer interest in Cullercoats and its inhabitants. He often used the local people as the subjects of his paintings, depicting them in anecdotal scenes about fisherfolk and smugglers. However, when these artists tried and failed to establish a succession of exhibiting societies in the north-east region, the more successful artists moved away to try their luck elsewhere.[1] The mantle of continuity was shouldered by a small number of local artists such as James Shotton, Robert Watson and Isabella Errington, who worked along this coastline throughout the mid-nineteenth century.

Arguably the more important development for art on Tyneside was the presence of William Bell Scott as head of the Newcastle School of Art between 1842 and 1862. This Pre-Raphaelite artist not only encouraged the collecting of important contemporary British art by new northern collectors (especially paintings by his Pre-Raphaelite brethren), but was responsible for training the first wave of artists on Tyneside. Hence the early work of future Cullercoats artists such as Henry Hetherington Emmerson, Robert Jobling and Ralph Hedley reveals the influence of the Pre-Raphaelite principle of working directly from nature. Indeed, this was later translated into the concern to paint the minutiae of fisherfolk and rural life, and by younger artists to capture the fleeting effects of nature as it was experienced.

Having studied with Bell Scott, Emmerson trained briefly in Paris, developing a lifelong admiration for the work of Jean-Francois Millet. Returning to London, he attended Heatherleys Academy, where he met amongst others Phil Morris, Fred Walker, Edward Poynter and Henry Moore. During this period Emmerson's first Royal Academy picture, *A Village Tailor*, was hung 'on the line' in 1851 and he was already gaining a reputation for portraiture. Amongst his earliest patrons was the north-east industrialist and collector James Leathart. However, perhaps still influenced by his Ruskinian roots, or with the example of Millet and the Barbizon school in mind, Emmerson gave up his flourishing metropolitan portrait career and returned to the North East. Although he continued to paint portraits and anecdotal scenes, they were increasingly based on the rural workers and fisherfolk of the region, especially after he gained the patronage of Sir William Armstrong in the mid-1860s. Armstrong proved to be a valuable lifelong patron to Emmerson, regularly buying works to hang in his rebuilt rural retreat, Cragside.[2] In 1866 Emmerson bought a house in Cullercoats, unwittingly establishing himself as the patriarch of the fledgling Cullercoats colony.

Emmerson's ability to survive as a professional artist in the North East was indicative of a renewed interest in art collecting in the region at this period. A series of loan exhibitions in Newcastle demonstrated that many industrialists, businessmen and gentry were buying contemporary British and European art. The realist art of Emmerson, Jobling and others was of sufficient standard to be readily accepted by collectors as part of this reinvigorated contemporary art market.[3] In 1869 the Tynemouth businessman and art collector, Alexander Shannan Stevenson, invited a number of London-based artists (whom he had met through their mutual friend Myles Birket Foster), to stay at his home. William Quiller Orchardson, John Dawson Watson and Arthur Hardwick Marsh were amongst those who enjoyed Stevenson's hospitality and the use of Emmerson's Cullercoats studio during that summer. The fruits of this visit included Orchardson's *Toilers of the Sea* (RA 1870, Aberdeen Art Gallery) Watson's *The Lifebrigade Man* (illustrated in *The Graphic* 1870) and Marsh's *Baiting the Lines* (RA 1870).

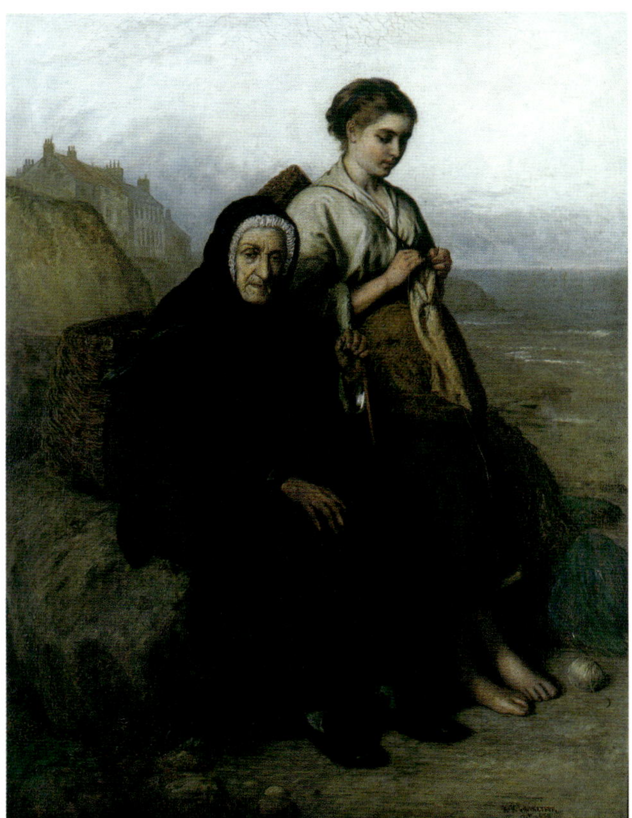

Fig.73
Henry Hetherington Emmerson, *Waiting for the Boats*, 1870
oil on canvas, Private collection, photograph courtesy Anderson & Garland Auctioneers

Fig.74
Frank Holl, *No Tidings from the Sea*, 1871, oil on canvas
The Royal Collection © 2005, Her Majesty Queen Elizabeth II

The visit also seemed to inspire Emmerson to produce his first clutch of truly Cullercoats works, including *Waiting for the Boats*, which was exhibited in Newcastle in 1870 (fig.73).[4] Juxtaposing youth and age – the young wife and old mother – awaiting the return of their loved one, this painting establishes one of the key themes of coastal colony art. The superb characterization of these women displays Emmerson's formidable portrait technique. The older woman, Betty Donkin, a favourite model, sits bowed by age, seemingly gazing across the years; yet the creel on her back indicates that she still awaits the catch. The knitting figure of Meggie Arthur is a serene, classical beauty, monumentalized against the pearly sky. Emmerson's technique betrays his academic training informed by Pre-Raphaelite principles, yet there is no hint of the anecdote which sometimes dogged his work. The specificity of place is not yet an important factor – he has not painted the tell-tale local 'tucked' skirts – although local audiences would have readily identified the place as Cullercoats. Despite this, *Waiting for the Boats* marks a crucial moment in the development of a colony aesthetic.

Perhaps through his friendship with Orchardson, the social-realist artist Frank Holl also came to Cullercoats in 1870, fulfilling a commission from Queen Victoria with *No Tidings from the Sea* (RA 1871), based on an incident which he witnessed during his stay (fig.74). This tragic twist on the 'youth and age waiting' theme was met with polite praise by many London critics. The critic of *The Graphic* noted that 'the execution is somewhat gaunt and crude', although went on to add that 'There is no more touching picture in the collection than this.'[5] Holl successfully conveys the loneliness of grief by isolating the young wife in the centre of the picture; and the child clinging to the old woman's skirt in startled incomprehension is a convincing passage. However, there is something 'staged' about the poses and, as a later critic noted, the central figure is 'grotesquely out of proportion'.[6] Even so, this iconography inspired a number of other colony artists in the coming years, including Frank Bramley, Walter Langley and Emmerson.

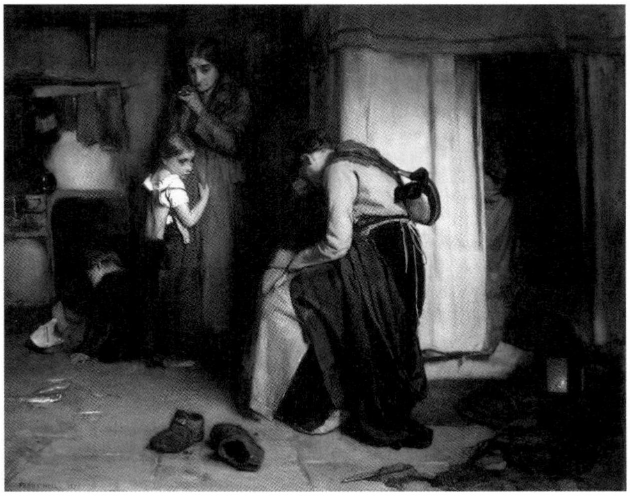

Watson and Marsh were so enthralled by Cullercoats that they repeatedly visited the area throughout the 1870s, with Marsh eventually settling here permanently in the early 1880s. The importance of this early interest by visiting artists in the nascent colony can only be surmised, but the fact that the village and its people featured in numerous paintings in the annual rounds of exhibitions in London and the provinces, as well as in the pages of mass-circulation newspapers such as *The Graphic*, did not go unnoticed.[7] But, perhaps more importantly, it crystallized local artists' determination to resist the lure of a metropolitan career and focus instead on the artistic possibilities offered by Cullercoats and its environs. Using the typologies established by this small group of artists in the 1870s – the heroic fishermen and lifebrigade men, the stoic women as workers, helpmates and watchers, the distinctive topography of the village and its working life – the local artists developed a naturalistic style to capture the pre-industrial way of life of the Cullercoats inhabitants, seemingly threatened on all sides by industry and urbanization.

Fisher Folk, c.1900, photograph
Newcastle Libraries and Information Service

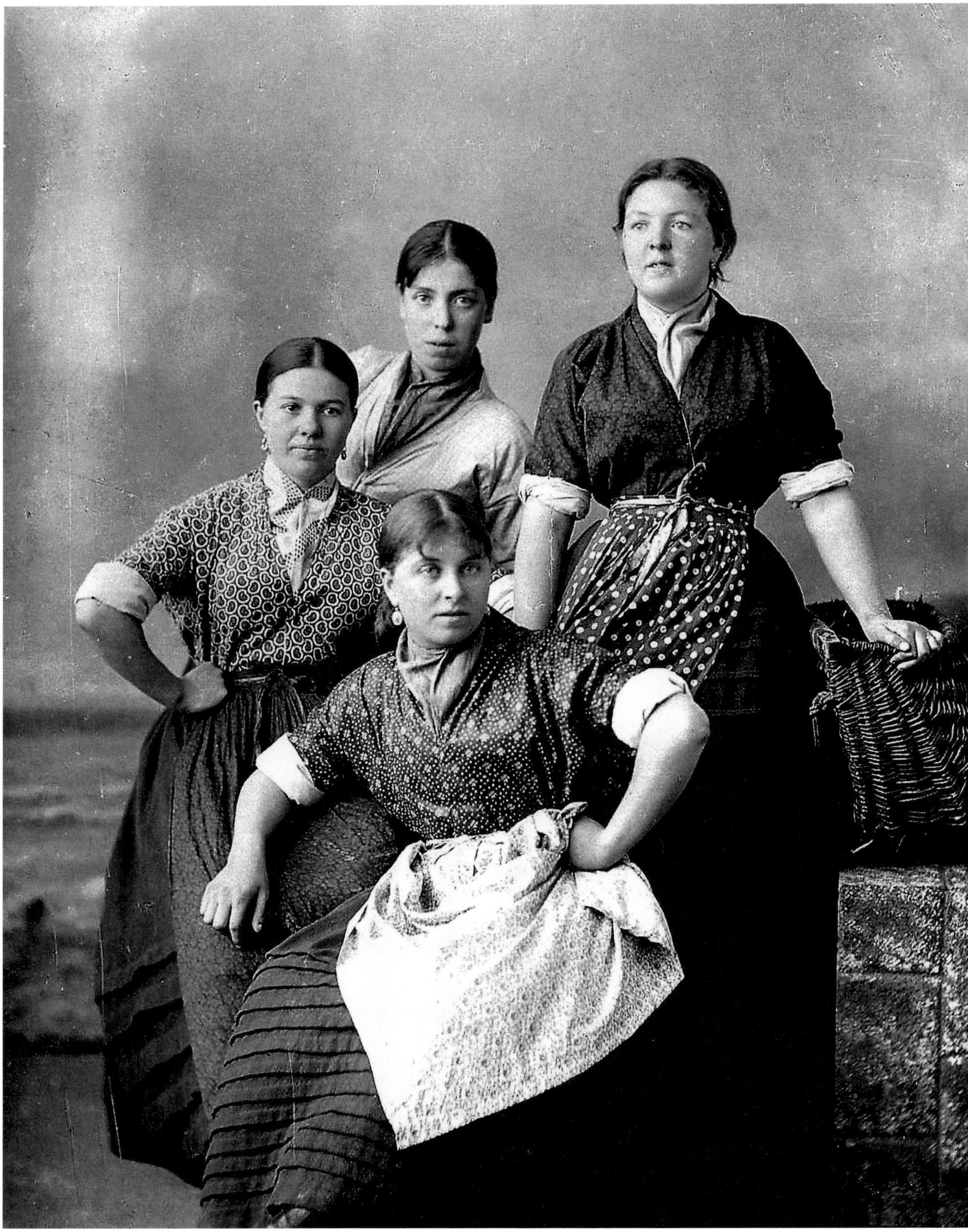

Cullercoats, c.1890, photograph
Newcastle Libraries and Information Service

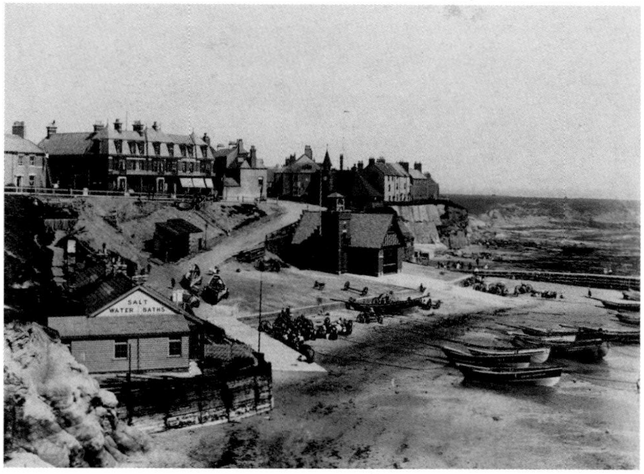

The embryonic colony was also sustained by the inauguration of the Newcastle Arts Association in 1878. This exhibiting society, run by many of the most significant patrons and collectors in the region, provided both an opportunity to see major pictures by contemporary British and Continental artists and a crucial exhibition forum for the growing numbers of north-east artists. As a result, many younger artists began to settle and/or work at Cullercoats during the late 1870s and early 1880s, including Robert Jobling, Isa Thompson, Stephen Brownlow, John Hodgson Campbell, the Sticks family, the Hemy brothers, Thomas Eyre Macklin, George Horton, the Ogilvie brothers and William Cosens Way. Throughout the 1880s they were joined by others: Marsh, John Falconer Slater, Thomas Swift Hutton, James Watson and Charles George. Even John Charlton and John Surtees, local artists who had found fame and fortune in London, kept houses at Cullercoats in order to sketch there during the summer months. This group became the backbone of the Bewick Club, which took over the exhibiting function of the Newcastle Arts Association in 1884.[8]

The most famous visitor to the Cullercoats colony during this period was the American artist Winslow Homer, whose watercolour drawing of two Cullercoats fishergirls received a surprising amount of critical attention when it was shown at the Arts Association exhibition in the autumn of 1881.[9] Homer's output during his Cullercoats sojourn has been hailed as marking a turning point in his career, the beginning of his mature phase as an artist. These works were clearly both an invaluable consolidation of his watercolour technique and the basis for several major oils after his return to America in 1882.[10] [Homer's work is illustrated in the author's *Cullercoats: A North-East Colony of Artists.*]

The influence of Homer on the indigenous artists is a matter of much debate, since his visit coincided with a key period of development during which artists such as Jobling, Thompson and Emmerson were abandoning the remaining vestiges of an anecdotal style in favour of a more naturalistic technique. Poetic titles were replaced by descriptive ones; overt story-telling replaced by seemingly factual reportage; the emphasis shifted from the fisherfolk as compositional devices to the main subject. Cullercoats' distinctive local features were brought to the fore: the traditional dress of the fisher women, especially their 'tucked' skirts; the landmark of the newly-built Look-Out House on the clifftop or the warren of lanes and fisher-cottages including the centuries-old 'Sparrow Hall'; the depiction of specific tasks and tools related to fishing, including the particular shape of the north-east coble; the proliferation of blond-haired, blue-eyed models suggesting their Nordic ancestry. These elements, in various permutations, are found in the majority of Cullercoats paintings from this period.

If Homer can be said to have influenced the other artists at all it is more likely through a small number of compositional devices which seem to recur in the work of a number of artists over the following years. Of these, perhaps the most important is the monumentalization of the fisher women, which is achieved by separating them from the sphere of male activity, placing them close to the picture plane and set against an uncluttered background, preferably a storm-laden sky, as for example in *Inside the Bar* (1883, Metropolitan

Fig.75
Arthur Hardwick Marsh, *Lighting the Beacon*, 1887
watercolour, bodycolour and pencil, Laing Art Gallery, Newcastle upon Tyne

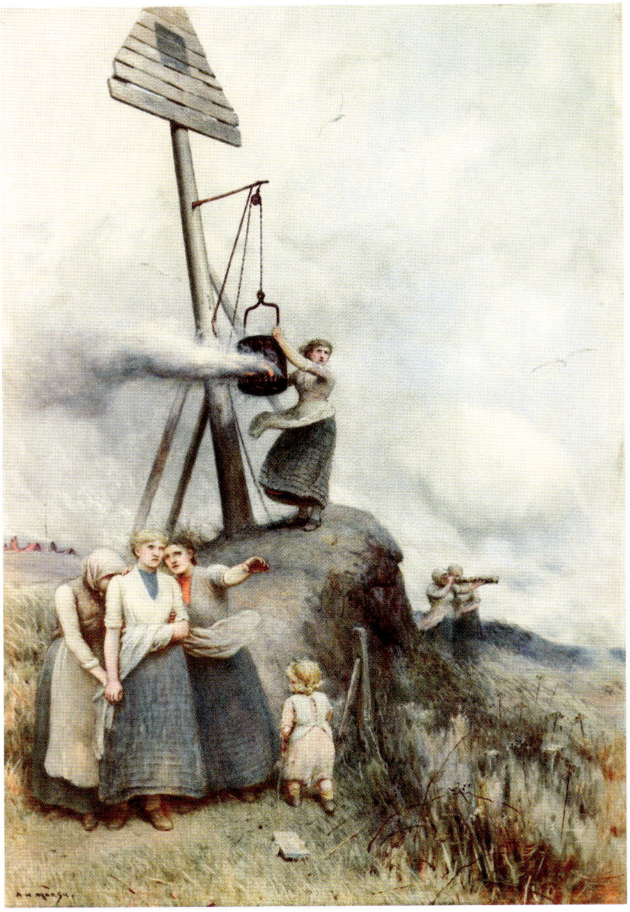

Fig.76
Robert Jobling, *Anxious Times*, 1889, oil on canvas
Laing Art Gallery, Newcastle upon Tyne

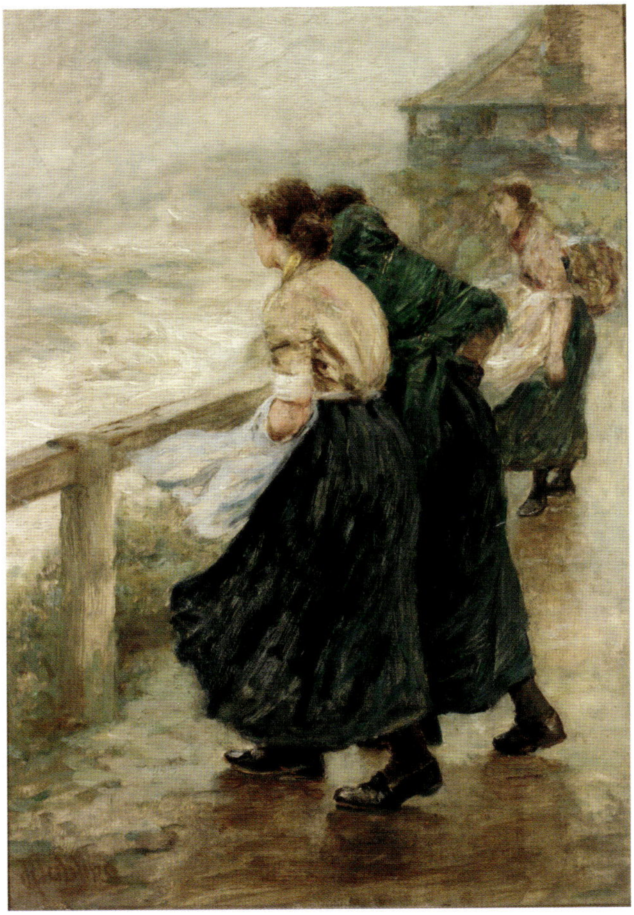

Museum of Art, New York). Thus, even in the smallest watercolours, the women have a heroic quality rarely found in the depictions of their male counterparts. In the numerous paintings of women waiting or grieving this heroism takes on a stoic quality; they are rarely depicted as abject and there is often a strong sense of female solidarity, with the women offering mutual support and comfort. The particularities of the Cullercoats costume included elements such as bare arms and heads, short skirts showing the ankle, and a tight-fitting blouse and scarf tucked into the waist, which under normal circumstances would have lent a highly sexualized charge to these working women. However, this is mostly dissipated precisely by that heroic air.

In the work of Homer, and to a lesser extent Marsh, the figures have a classical quality which heightens idealization, placing the women even further out of reach of the appropriating gaze, and suggesting perhaps a shared debt to artists such as Millet and Jules Breton, whose paintings were well known on both sides of the Atlantic.[11] Nevertheless, Marsh's *Lighting the Beacon* (1887) certainly recalls Homer's pictures in the use of the three-women grouping and the classicism of figures, faces and poses (fig.75). Originally exhibited at the Royal Society of Painters in Watercolour in 1887 as *Men must Work and Women must Weep*, this is a far less emotive rendition of Kingsley's poem than, for example, Langley's painting of 1882.[12] Perhaps Marsh's change of title was aimed at downplaying the melodrama of the poem in favour of a more restrained exploration of the theme. So grief hides its face whilst we explore the feelings of fear, anxiety, fascination, hope and even excitement that the young

Fig.77
Henry Hetherington Emmerson, *Bereaved*, 1888, oil on canvas
Private collection

women are experiencing as they are 'stung by salt spray and pelted by sand and shingle until the blood comes'.[13] Widely praised in the north-east press when shown at the Bewick Club in 1891, Marsh's picture used an earth-based palette to provide compositional unity and maximize the brooding sense of the coming storm.[14] The vast expanse of sky suggests the smallness and futility of human endeavour in the face of Nature's power. The lone girl standing on the rock lacks the monumentality of Homer's girls, and is instead dwarfed by both the beacon and the enormity of her task to warn 'those in peril on the sea'.

Jobling's *Anxious Times* (1889, fig.76) also explores the 'waiting women' theme, but without the obvious narrative of Marsh's picture. Here the women are not dwarfed by nature but instead dominate the picture, encouraging us to share their seaward, searching gaze. The sea is a seething, violent force, whipped by the wind that snaps around the women, blowing their skirts. The Lookout House in the background loses its distinctiveness and Jobling makes no attempt at characterization in the figures. Instead, this painting signals Jobling's shifting concerns, away from Naturalism to a more experimental use of paint and subject. The turned-away figures favour emotional exploration over narrative, and the artist's looser paint handling, directional brush strokes and sketchier draughtsmanship imply a desire to develop his picture-making practices whilst retaining his fascination with the Cullercoats subject.

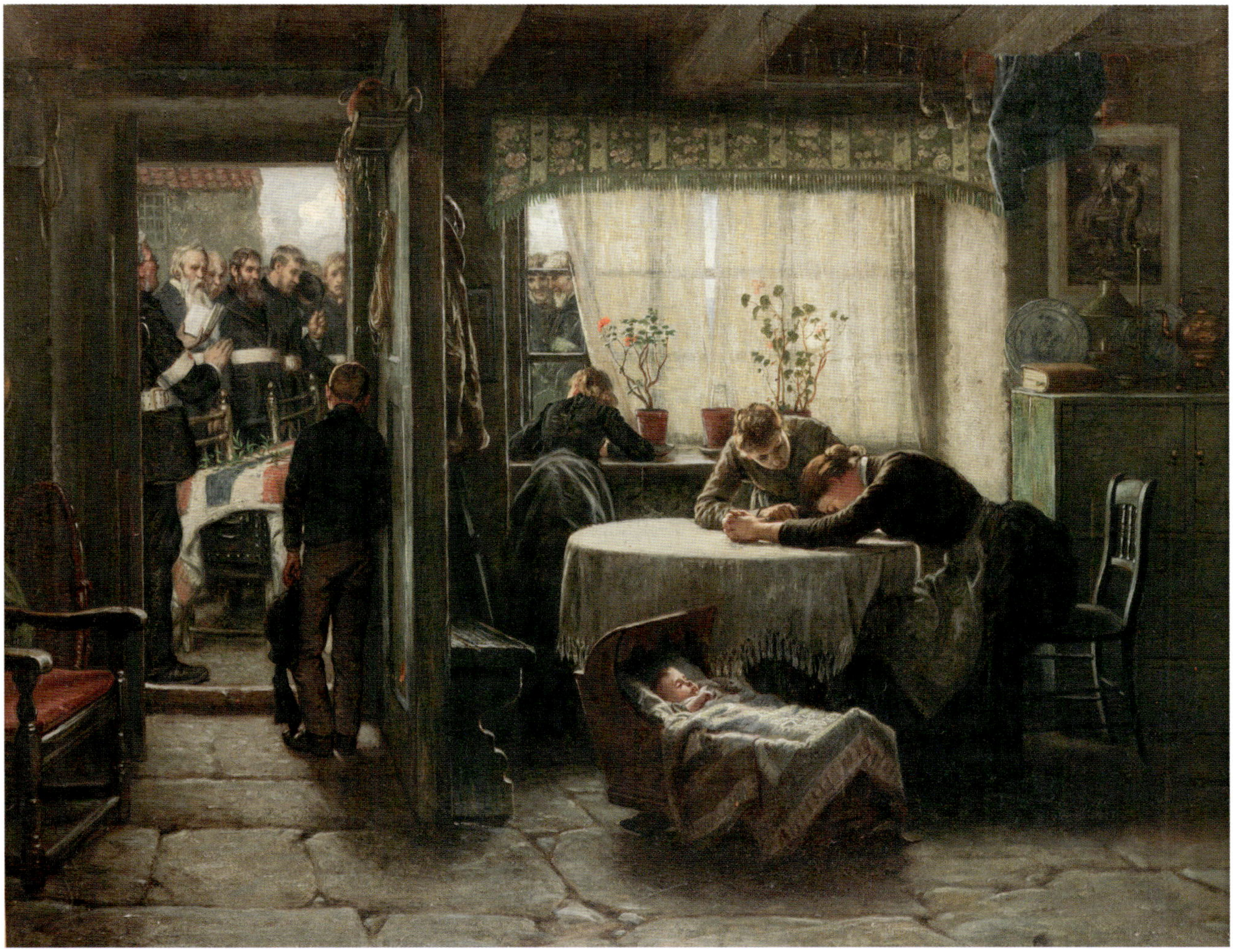

Fig.78
Robert Jobling, *The Day is Done and Darkness Falls from the Wings of Night*, 1885, oil on canvas, Laing Art Gallery, Newcastle upon Tyne

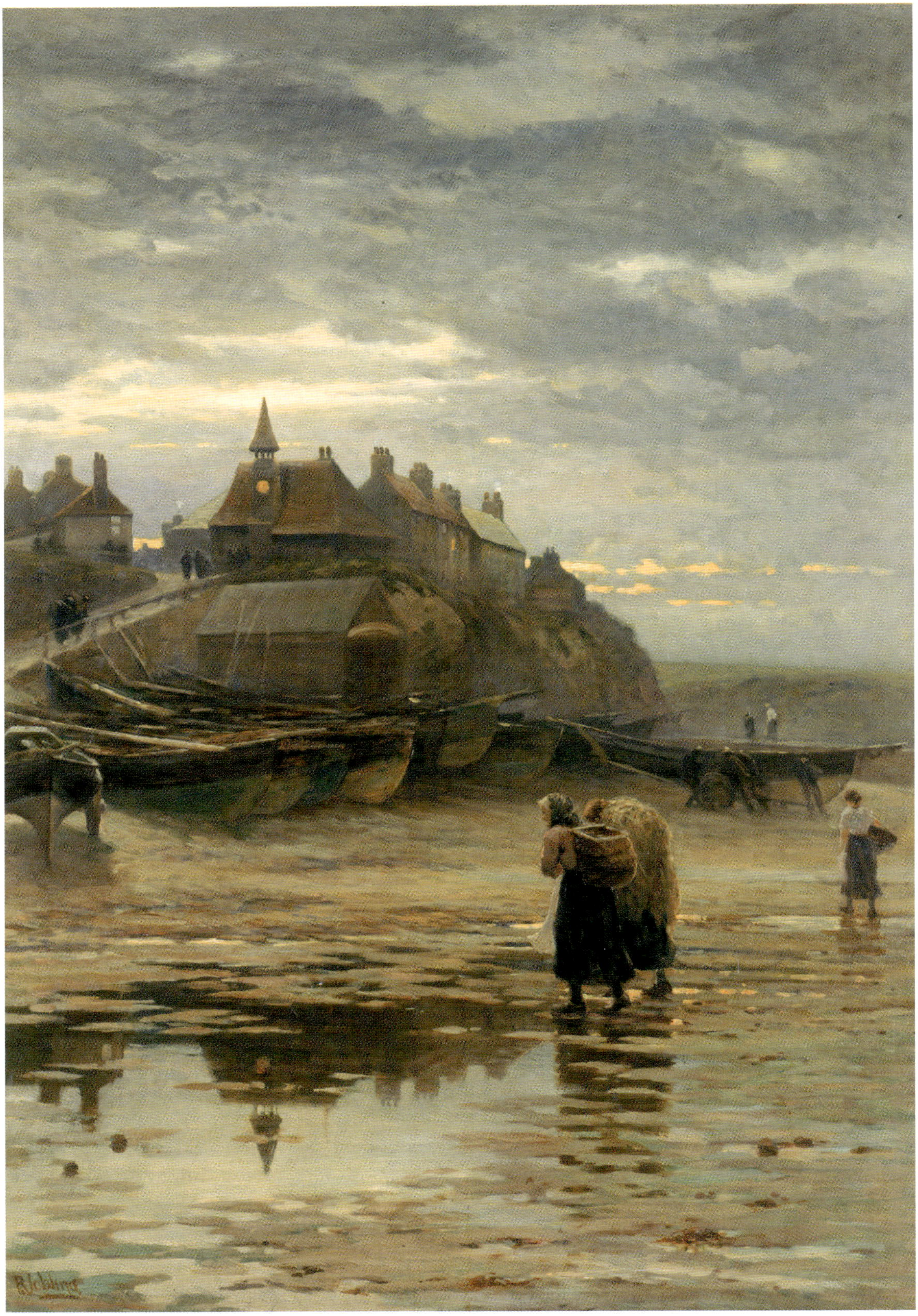

Fig.79
Robert Jobling, *Hauling up the Boats*, 1890, oil on canvas
Laing Art Gallery, Newcastle upon Tyne

In *Bereaved* (1888) Emmerson takes the theme to its sorry conclusion, the funeral of a drowned fisherman (fig.77). Compositionally, there are strong affinities with both Holl's *No Tidings from the Sea* and with Bramley's *Hopeless Dawn* (see page 32), which was shown at the RA in 1888, although it is unclear if Emmerson saw either before painting his own picture. However, the similarities with Bramley's work are striking, in particular the 'haloed' grieving young women with heads cradled in out-flung arms. The strong religious connotations attached to both paintings – in the Bramley, the title taken from a pious line in Ruskin, together with the imagery of a bible and Raphael's cartoon of *Christ giving the Keys to St Peter*, and in the Emmerson a bible plus an illustration of J.D. Watson's *Saved* (an allusion to Christ as the fisher of men) – suggest a debt to Renaissance imagery of the pietà. The stoic suffering of the women as an adjunct to the bravery of their menfolk also resonates with the neo-classical imagery of Jacques-Louis David, underscoring the importance of classical role models in the construction of late-nineteenth-century ideals of Britishness, in this case providing a code of behaviour (and of depiction) appropriate for the demonstration of loss and hope.[15]

Every element of *Bereaved* seems painstakingly worked-out and rendered, from the meticulous still-life elements of the cottage interior and the individual portraits of the funeral gathering, to the symbolism of the empty plant pot (the missing man) and the Christ-like infant lit by the sun (hope), to the gendered reactions to death as embodied in the use of pictorial space. This is Emmerson at the height of his powers; a photographic Naturalism tempered by the allusory capacities of the artist.

All of these paintings demonstrate the importance of this theme as a subject of coastal colony art, perhaps because it provided opportunities to explore or affirm certain notions and anxieties about women's place in relation to men, society and the nation. However, during the 1880s the theme of work was equally popular amongst colonists. Paintings such as Jobling's *The Day is Done and Darkness falls from the Wings of Night* (1885, fig.78), *Hauling Up the Boats* (1890, fig.79), Marsh's *Cockle Gatherers* (1885, fig.80) or Homer's *Mending the Nets* (1882, National Gallery of Art, Washington) reveal very different treatments provoked by this subject.

The growth of the colony during the 1880s, aided by the strengthening regional patronage base and annual round of local and national exhibitions, frequently came to the attention of the art press.[16] This ranged from critiques of the Newcastle exhibitions to more general articles about Cullercoats as a popular colony.[17] In common with similar literature on art colonies, these articles followed a certain formula – a description of the village and its fisherfolk, pointing out particularly picturesque subjects or views, the Viking ancestry of the people, and reference to the pre-industrial way of life which meant that old costumes, work practices and superstitions had been maintained. Local people were inevitably portrayed as deeply pious, hardworking, heroic in the face of constant danger and as being 'at one' with nature as a result of their daily travails. Accounts would

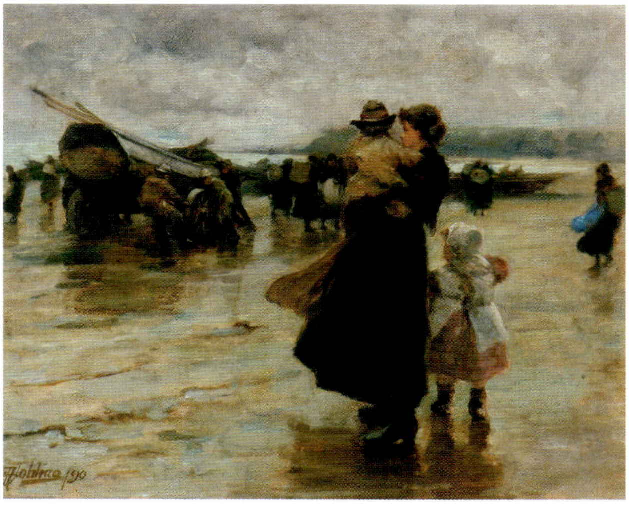

Fig.80
Arthur Hardwick Marsh, *Cockle Gatherers*, 1885, oil on canvas
Laing Art Gallery, Newcastle upon Tyne

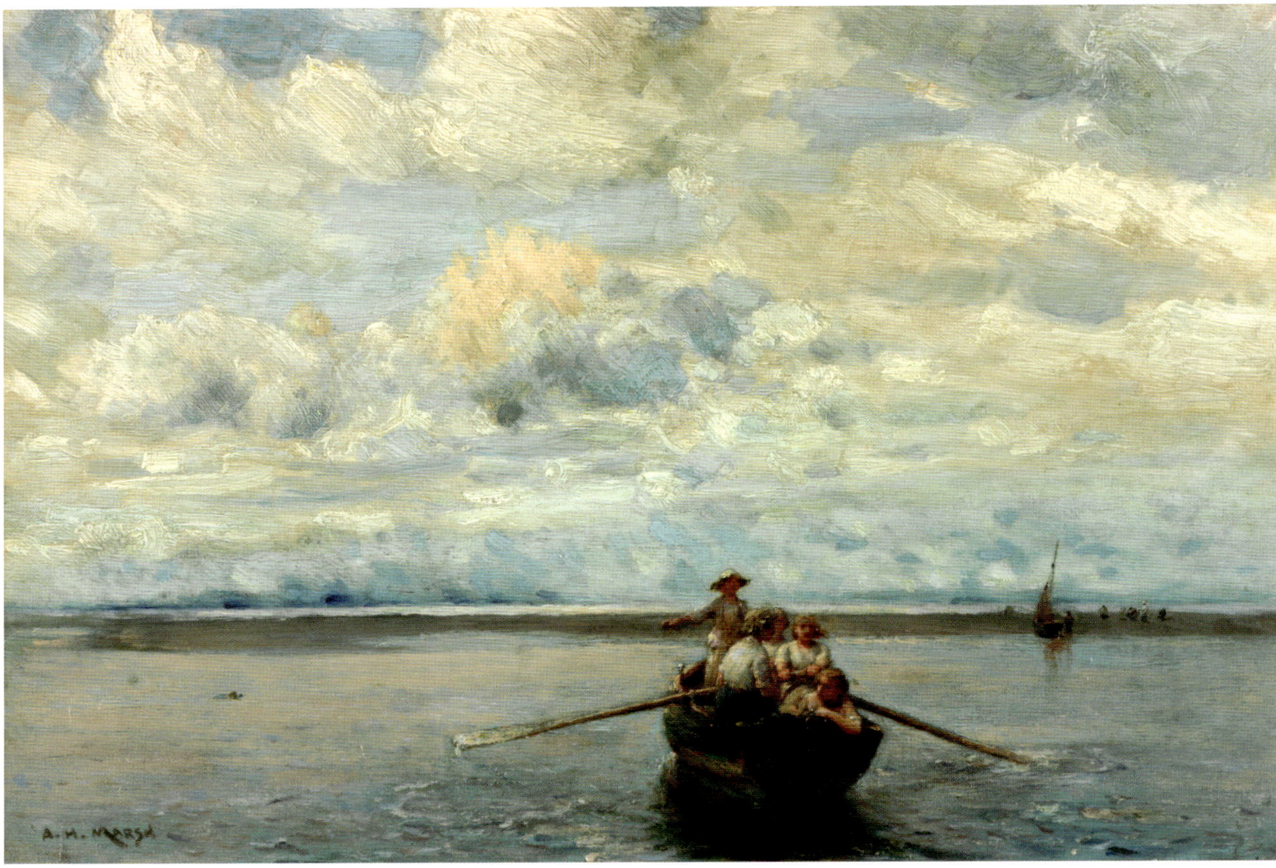

then move to a discussion of the venue as a colony or sketching ground, mentioning key artists and paintings, and pointing out its particular attractions in painterly terms – the quality of light, the climate, the availability of models, etc.

Such types of articles were generally designed to alert artists to suitable sketching grounds.[18] The succession of articles on Cullercoats throughout the 1880s and 90s must have contributed to the increasing profile of the colony's artists. As mentioned earlier, the colonists played a major part in the organization of the exhibitions and classes of the Bewick Club in Newcastle, which, as the period progressed, attracted ever greater numbers of paintings by artists from other coastal colonies around Britain. This mutual support helped to legitimize the working-class fisherfolk as a valid subject for 'high' art, whilst also aiding the dissemination of new ideas such as the use of the 'square-brush' technique during the mid-1880s. Some of this cross-fertilization came about through personal contacts and friendships; for example Northumberland-born Joseph Crawhall's involvement with the Glasgow Boys saw their early works being tested on the Newcastle art scene from the early 1880s.[19] Similarly, during the 1890s many of the Staithes artists sent work to the Newcastle exhibitions after contact with Isa Thompson, Jobling, Hedley and John Atkinson, all of whom regularly worked at Staithes during this period.[20] Indeed Jobling, and probably Thompson also, were founder members of the Staithes Art Club when it formed in 1901. Other Naturalist artists also regularly sent to Newcastle, including George Clausen, Walter Osborne, Blandford Fletcher and members of the Newlyn colony such as Walter Langley, Norman Garstin, Thomas Cooper Gotch and Fred Hall.[21]

If the 1880s can be understood as the period of consolidation for the Cullercoats colony, the 1890s was one of diversification. As suggested, a number of artists started to work at other colonies and sketching grounds, visiting not just Staithes but Newlyn, St. Ives, Walberswick and Holland. This led to the swifter dissemination of newer techniques and a wider variety of subjects. The photographic quality of Naturalism gave way in many instances to a broader, more painterly style in which the presence of the artist was re-asserted. For the older artists such as Jobling change was manifest in the adoption of a brighter palette, the occasional swapping of the usual fisherfolk subject for that of rural workers, river scenes or even leisure subjects. Hedley, never a permanent member at Cullercoats, embarked on what now appears to have been a deliberate project to record the diversity of rural work practices in Northumberland and North Yorkshire, with exhibition canvases depicting weaving, threshing, winnowing, brickmaking, harvesting and potato-picking.[22]

After her marriage to Jobling in 1893, Isa Thompson seems to have all but abandoned large-scale works in favour of paintings more suited to a domestic setting, probably because she gave up her studio and so no longer had the space for such work. She also relinquished the fisherfolk subject, turning her attention to rural scenes, landscapes and flower pictures, and it is tempting to speculate on whether this was because her former subjects had provided too much competition for her new husband. Whatever the cause of her change of direction, she thrived on it, escaping the tyranny of Naturalism's demands and finding, perhaps for the first time, her true voice as an artist. She began to visit Staithes at least as early as 1891, since her first Royal Academy picture, *Blossom*, was painted there (fig.81). The following year she painted one of her final and most powerful large-scale fisherfolk pictures, *Fisher Folk* (RA 1893, see page 103), but again taking a Staithes subject rather than a Cullercoats one.

Of course some of the older artists did not change direction or technique. Before his death in 1895 Emmerson became increasingly preoccupied with large-scale works on religious themes, whilst Marsh continued in his realist manner of the 1870s. Ironically, Marsh's Milletesque qualities – the unsentimental, unidealized working figures going about their daily tasks with an air of quiet resignation – take on a more symbolic quality during the 1890s, very much in keeping with the demands for something more than just a photographic Naturalism.

However, it was also during this period that a group of younger artists started to make their mark, artists without the same loyalties to the Cullercoats fisherfolk. This enabled them to embrace a wider variety of subjects much more readily. Artists such as George Horton, John F Slater, John Atkinson and James Watson turned their attention to new leisure and urban subjects, as well as pure seascapes and busy river scenes. In addition to the artistic impulse to experiment, develop and mature, there were obvious practical reasons for casting the net wider. Cullercoats' heyday as a fishing village was over, its coble fleet in steep decline, and its inhabitants ever more reliant on the income from trippers and holidaymakers. As early as 1887 an article on Cullercoats in the *Art Journal* complained of the effects that the arrival of the railway in 1882 had had on the village; its 'primitive and picturesque' look threatened by the 'avalanche of bricks and mortar' that 'has blotted out the old features of the place with startling rapidity.'[23] Although Cullercoats' history as a genteel watering place reached back to the eighteenth century, the attention turned on it by artistic representations and by the Victorian quest for unspoilt holiday destinations inevitably resulted in an influx of summer visitors. One Newcastle paper went so far as to declare that 'Mr Jobling has made Cullercoats famous by his canvases, and by-and-by he will be the

Fig.81
Isa Jobling (née Thompson), *Blossom*, 1892, oil on canvas
Private collection

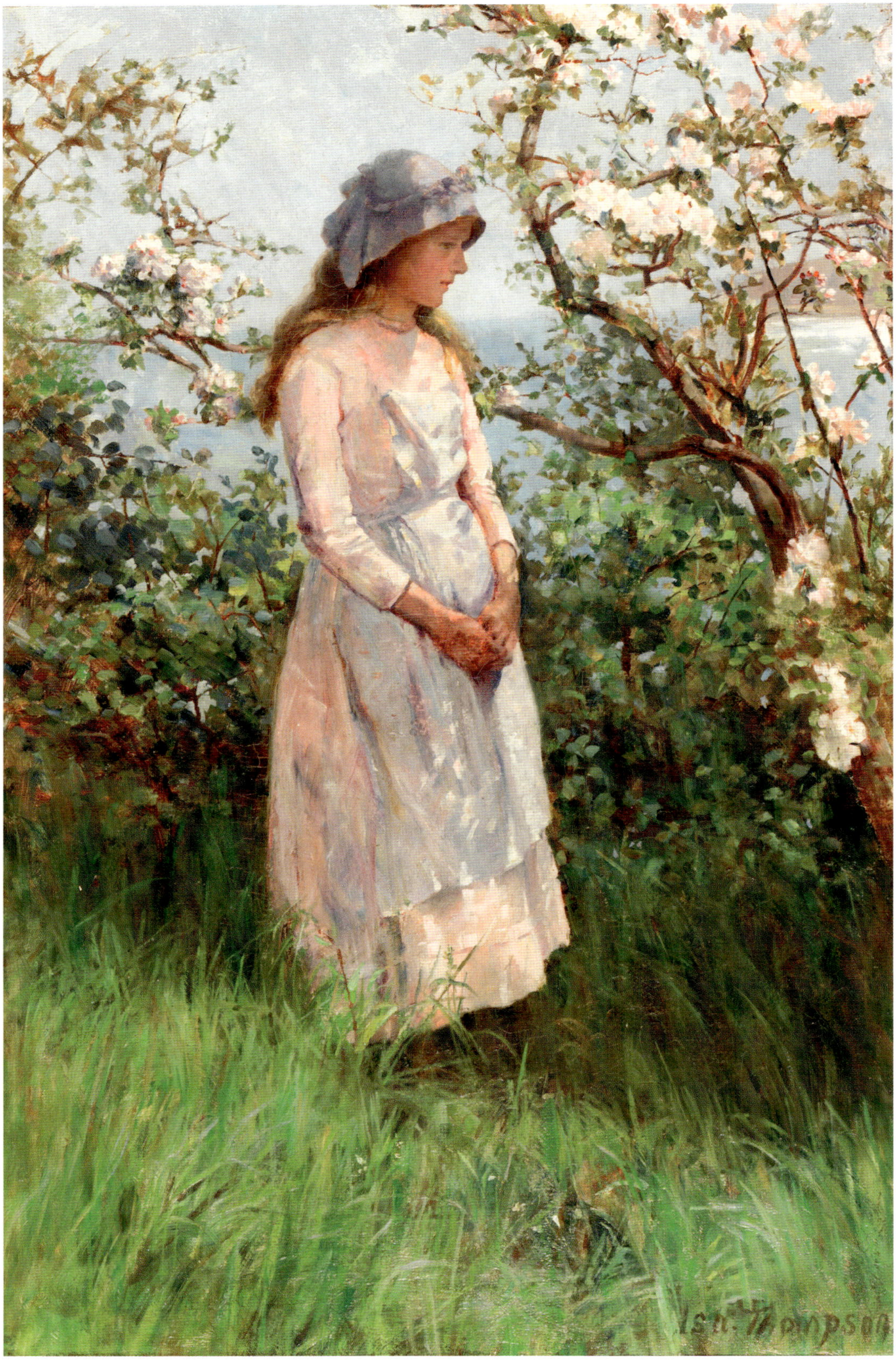

Fig.82
John Falconer Slater, *At the Seaside*, 1922, oil on canvas
Private collection

means of over-running the village with tourists'.[24]

But it was not Jobling who depicted the new 'industry' at Cullercoats; this was left to the younger artists who could more readily embrace the long-resisted signs of modernity – a seaside inhabited by mothers with children, middle-class promenaders, bathing tents, donkey rides and pleasure craft. These elements are clearly seen in the paintings and watercolours by Atkinson (*Tynemouth Sands* 1907 and *On the Beach, Whitley Bay*), Slater and Horton from the 1890s through to (in Horton's case) the Second World War. Slater's *At the Seaside* (1922, fig.82) shows the artist at the height of his Impressionistic phase, the jewel-like primary colours conveying the innocent exuberance of the theme. The empty deckchair in the foreground recalls Monet's similarly empty chair in *The Beach at Trouville* (1870), whilst the luminous blue of the sea suggests a debt to Steer's Walberswick paintings of the late 1880s and early 1890s. Horton's *On Tynemouth Sands* is one of a series of watercolours and pencil drawings of a subject he returned to throughout his career, few of them dated and therefore possibly from as late as the 1930s (fig.83). The view is from the Cullercoats end of the beach, looking towards Tynemouth village with the grandiose Aquarium on the right. This unpeopled beach with its vast crystalline sky shows Horton's lack of concern for the seaside-leisure aspect of the subject. As his writings make clear, he was more concerned with the formal issues of picture making – the light effects, tonal and colour relationships and compositional harmony – than with any socio-political message.[25] The beach huts and other paraphernalia merely add interest to his design.

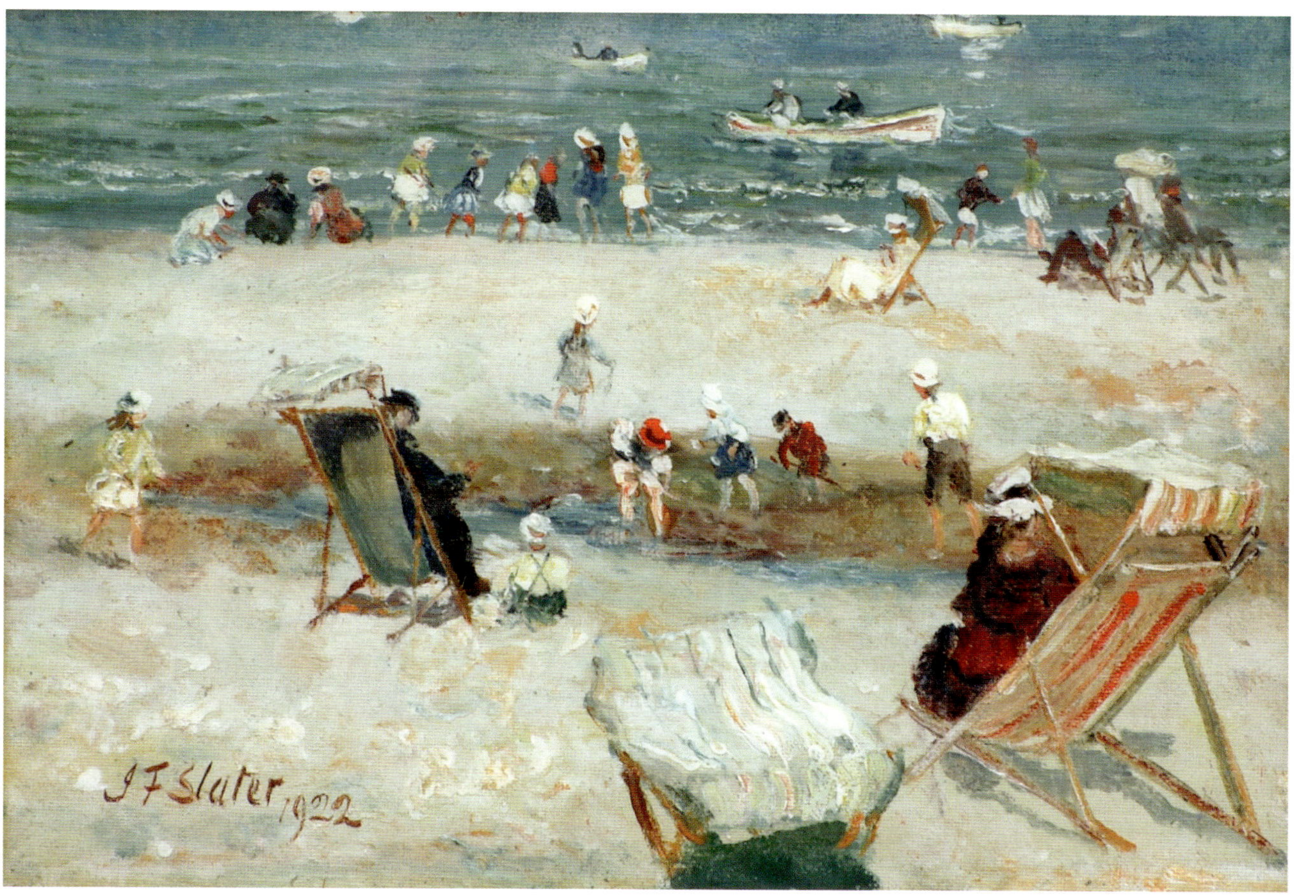

Fig.83
George Edward Horton, *On Tynemouth Sands*
watercolour, charcoal and pencil, Laing Art Gallery, Newcastle upon Tyne

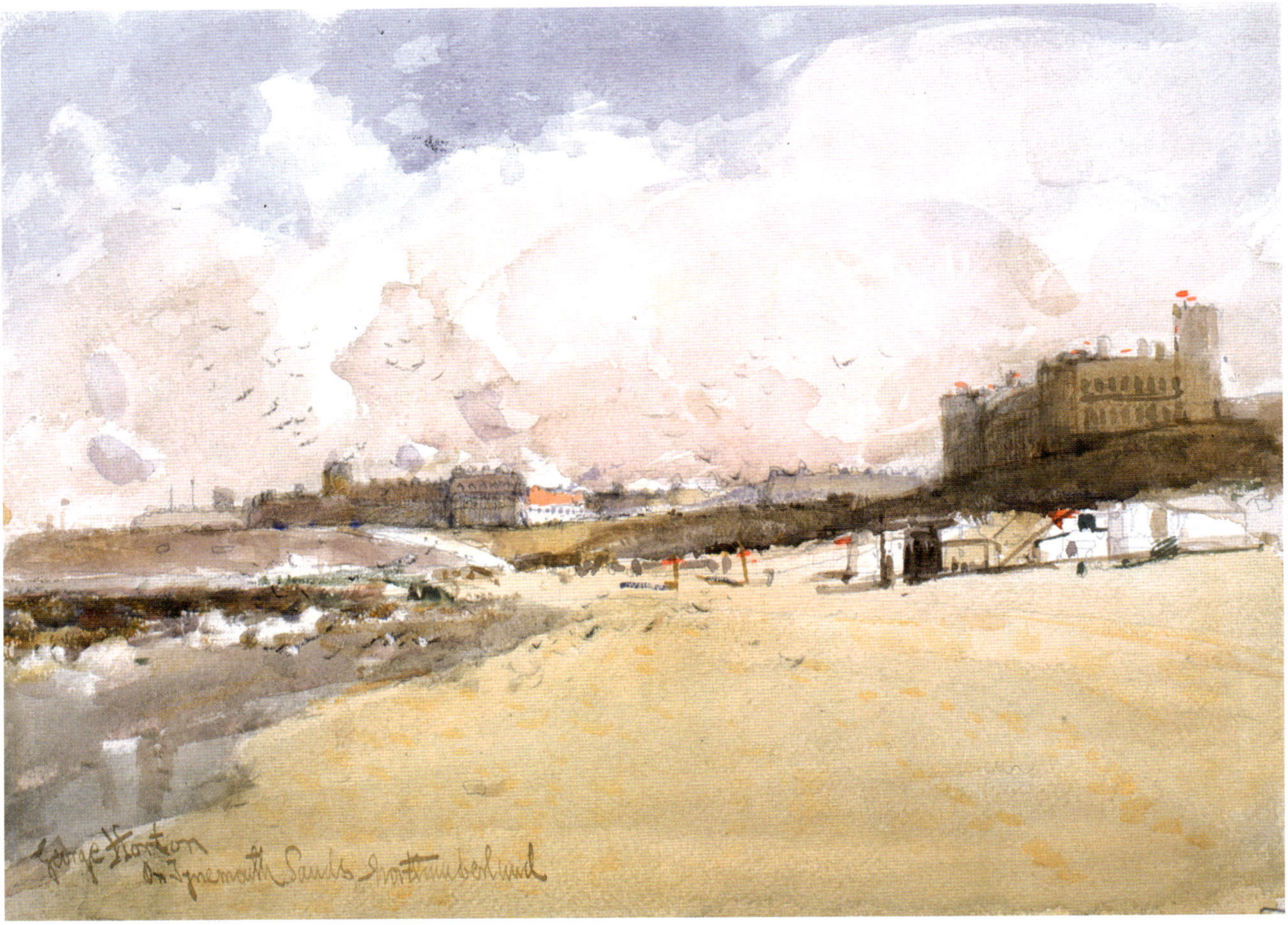

Of course, leisure scenes were not unknown before this date at Cullercoats, but they had usually been associated more with fisher children at play or fisher-folk resting. George W Brownlow, Emmerson, Homer and Jobling had all produced pictures of this kind, but because they were still of the fisherfolk there was inevitably a sense of time snatched between bouts of labour, rather than true leisure time. The pictures of fisher children playing rarely escaped the symbolic overtones so easily attached to such pictures – God's innocents dwarfed by Nature, or indulging in the role-play which foretold their inescapable destiny in life. Jobling only really overcame such pitfalls after he adopted a much brighter palette and looser style on coming into contact with the Staithes artists. So pictures such as *Minding the Bairn* (1915) or *Sunshine – Children sitting on a wall* do achieve a more modern aesthetic, and in this he was undoubtedly influenced by the developments of his wife's style such as in *Girl on a Quay at Staithes*.[26] It is telling, however, that Jobling did not chose to transfer this new technique to his Cullercoats subjects, perhaps because they were so deeply associated with his Naturalist style and to have connected them with modern life in any way would have seemed like a betrayal.

Unable to bring himself to adapt to the changing nature of Cullercoats, Jobling explored instead the busy port at nearby North Shields with its steam trawlers and bustling, more cosmopolitan quayside. In some ways this was a return to the river subject of his early career, before he discovered Cullercoats, but now the Turneresque moonlit scenes are gone. Instead, the watercolours Jobling produced here around 1910 are amongst his most successful and are about as close as he ever came to depicting elements of modern life. Of course the river had remained a popular subject throughout the period, especially with maritime artists such as John Chambers, the Hemy brothers, T. S. Hutton, Stephen Brownlow and others. But towards the end of the nineteenth century North Shields fish quay also became a popular venue amongst the younger artists, searching for modern-life subjects.

Horton's first Royal Academy picture, a small oil *Fish Quay, North Shields* (1896), was hung on the line and described by one critic as a 'daring impressionistic sketch', presumably because of the loosely-painted, ethereal quality of its figures.[27] The fish quay and its environs continued to stimulate Horton throughout his career, even after he moved to London in around 1918, where he worked from memory on street and river scenes such as *Wooden Bridge Bank* or *Comical Corner* (see fig.84). Like Horton, Slater's river scenes concentrated on the formal qualities of the ramshackle warehouses and jetties, or the plumes of steam and smoke from the tugs and trawlers moving on the river. These pictures share many of the same impressionistic qualities as his huge seascapes that regularly appeared at the Royal Academy before the War. John Atkinson and Victor Noble Rainbird, on the other hand, were always more interested in the quayside hustle and bustle, the dynamic possibilities of masts, funnels, scurrying figures and horse-drawn wagons (see fig.85).

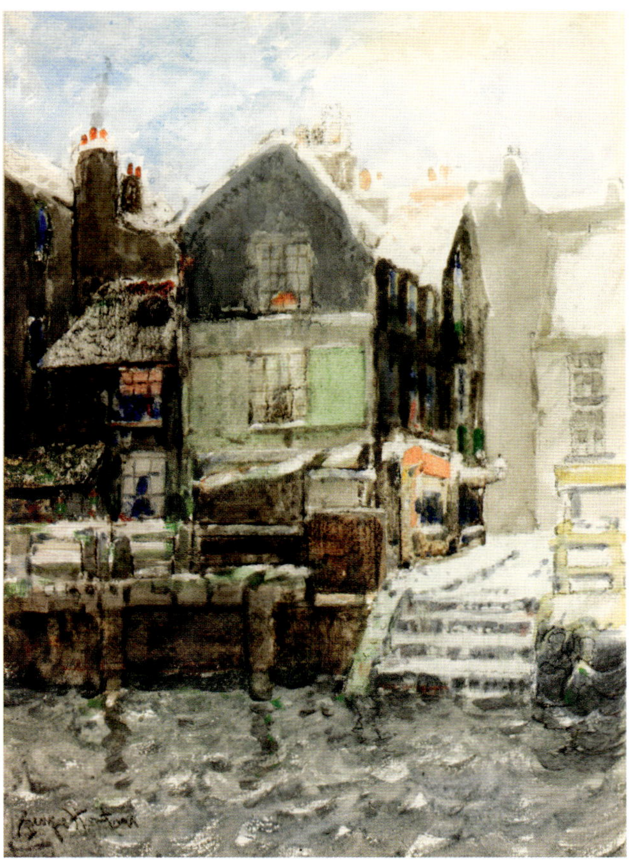

Fig.84
George Edward Horton, *Comical Corner, South Shields*
1935, watercolour and charcoal, South Shields Museum and Art Gallery

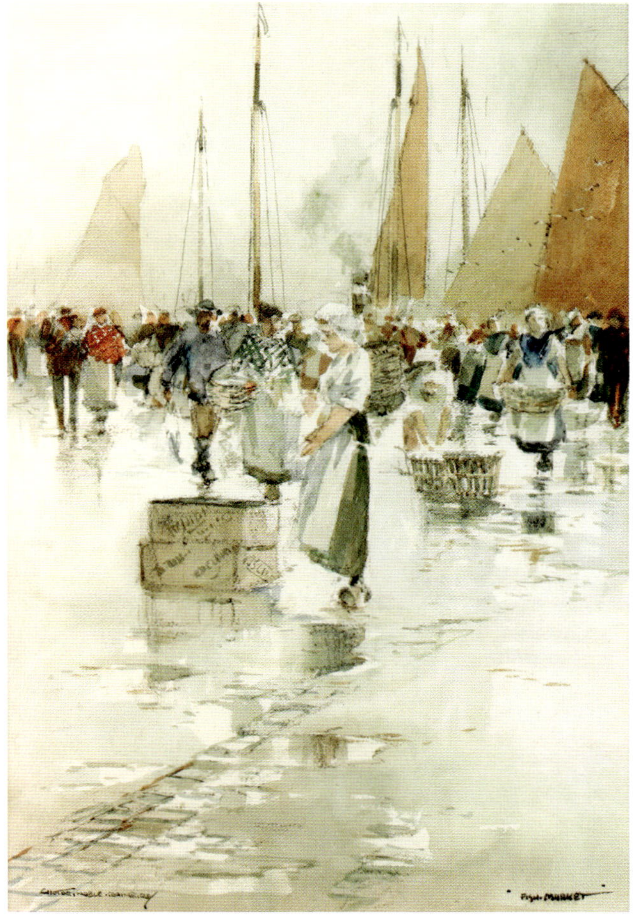

Fig.85
Victor Noble Rainbird, *Fish Market*, watercolour and charcoal
Laing Art Gallery, Newcastle upon Tyne

Fig.86
John Charlton, *The Women*, 1910, oil on canvas
Laing Art Gallery, Newcastle upon Tyne

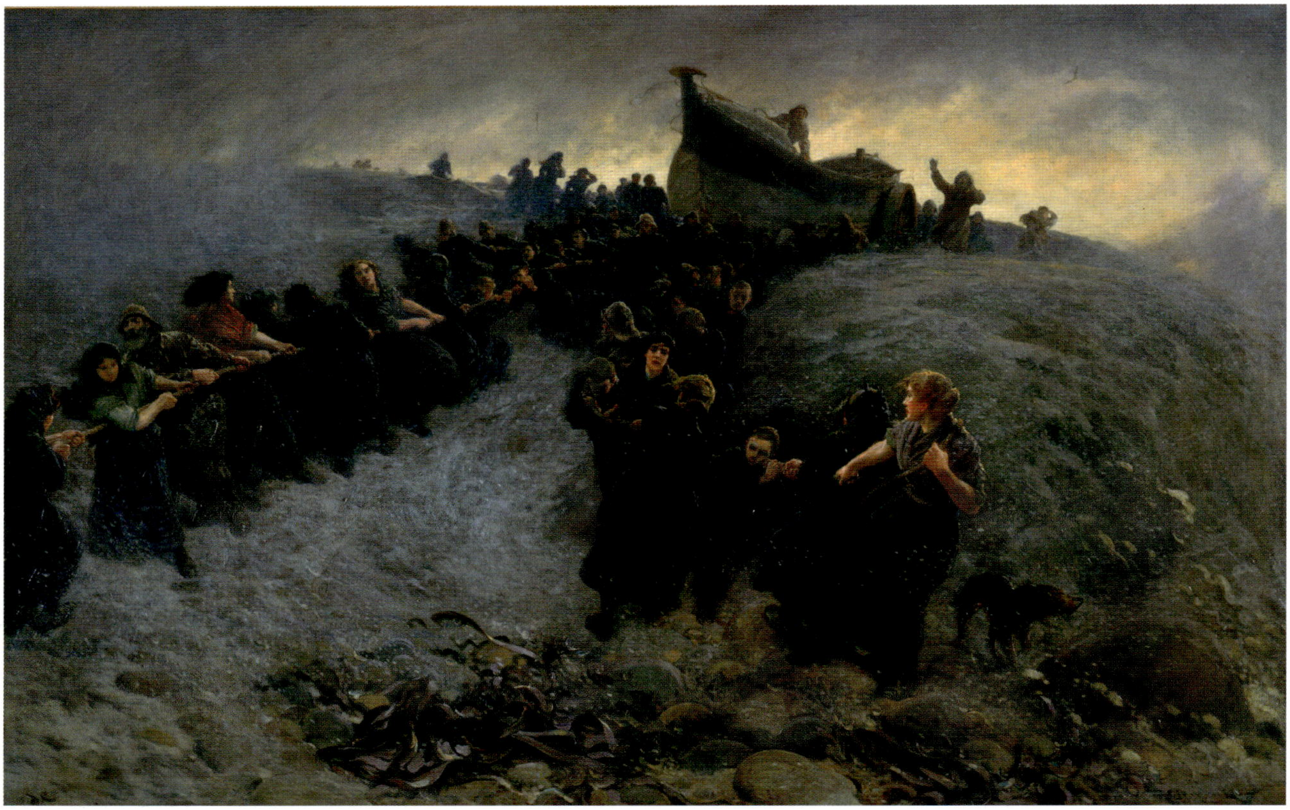

But into this more experimental phase of the Cullercoats colony must be inserted a stunning throw-back to the concerns of the early 1880s, John Charlton's *The Women* (Royal Academy 1910, fig.86). This anachronistic painting, based on an episode from Cullercoats' recent history, seems to confirm Stephen Daniels' notion of a national identity constructed on 'legends and landscapes'.[28] Yet these Amazonian women, bare-armed and bare-headed, seem to have adopted all the heroic attributes normally reserved for men in colony art. Is Charlton suggesting an affinity with notions of the *fin-de-siècle* 'New Woman', with its rejection of Victorian ideals of propriety and the woman's 'place' in favour of new political and social freedoms, and an emphasis on healthy bodies and practical clothing? Contemporary audiences did not seem to make this connection, probably because of the obvious historicity of the image, both in subject and treatment.[29] Furthermore, Charlton arguably encouraged a more traditional reading of the image by fetishizing the female figures (bare flesh and wet, clinging clothing) that allows the (male) spectator to maintain a dominant viewing position. Any potentially threatening implications which the imagery of contemporary working women often provoked at this period are further negated by more embedded notions evoked by this subject, of women's position in the defence and maintenance of the community and the country.

This later period in the colony's life was also marked by a wider diversity of exhibition venues and art clubs. This was undoubtedly because many of the artists were now involved in other colonies or visiting other sketching grounds – Staithes being an obvious example. However, even in Newcastle the supremacy of the Bewick Club was challenged by other exhibitions and outlets. Organisations such as the Art Circle, set up in unapologetic imitation of London's New Gallery in 1897, attempted to lay claim to the best, most cutting-edge or successful artists, 'to cultivate the aesthetic side of art' in the hope of creaming off the best patrons.[30] The number of privately-run galleries specializing in one-man shows and seasonal exhibitions also increased, adding to the diversity. One of the most important of these one-off shows was undoubtedly that of the New English Art Club artists in July/August 1893 of which, as one critic noted, 'Such opportunity of witnessing a representative collection of the work of an important school has rarely, if ever, been offered on Tyneside.'[31] And of course, the major London and provincial annual exhibitions continued to draw the region's artists, with some large works by artists such as Jobling or Hedley being shown at a number of venues around the country before reaching a north-east audience. This fragmentation or specialization of the market was a national phenomenon, symptomatic of a changing art-collecting public. Artists could no longer rely on the continued patronage of the big-spending Northern industrialists and businessmen (who had fuelled the rejuvenation of British art in the middle of the nineteenth century) because of the downturn in British industry due to foreign competition. Similarly, the agricultural depression of the 1880s and 1890s had turned the traditionally abundant patronage by the landed gentry into fallow ground. Artists had to identify and adapt their work to a different marketplace, one that accommodated the professional classes, the avant-garde speculator and the lower-class enthusiast.[32]

The diversification of the Cullercoats colonists to other subjects and sketching grounds, prompted by the changing nature of the village itself and by the need to adapt to new markets, continued apace in the years immediately before the First World War. The camaraderie and self-help ethos of the original colony was ironically undermined by the opening of the Laing Art Gallery in Newcastle in 1904.[33] The achievement of what had always been a long-term goal removed one of the key motivations of the colonists' mutual support. And the forum for that support, the educational, exhibiting and recreational activities of the Bewick Club, was dealt a serious blow, firstly by the inauguration of the 'Artists of the Northern Counties' exhibitions at the Laing in 1905, and then by the interruption necessitated by the war, from which it never really recovered.

By now, of course, many of the old guard had died: Emmerson in 1895, Marsh in 1909, Hedley in 1913, Charlton in 1917, Jobling in 1923 and Thompson in 1926. However, others remained, still working at Cullercoats and along the coast, and involved with the annual exhibitions at the Laing and with new exhibiting societies such as the North East Coast Club, the Benwell Art Club and the Northern Society of Artists. The latter society, in particular, did much to maintain a professional standard amongst its members. The nature of the colony at Cullercoats, like that of other coastal colonies, inevitably changed with the withdrawal of its original members and the influx of mainly amateur artists.

Even today Cullercoats retains its art club. Yet, except for the forlorn presence of a handful of small cobles resting on the green outside the Queen's Head pub, there are few other signs of Cullercoats' artistic or fishing past. The fishermen's cottages and Sparrow Hall were swept away during the slum clearances of the 1960s and 1970s. The Look-Out House remains, its vigilance rendered useless by boarded-up windows to deter vandals. Yet, standing on the small beach in the grey light of a winter's day, it is not impossible to imagine why so many artists agreed with the writer who declared that 'There are few things so impressive as our gigantic panoramas of cloud, or so beautiful as our wind-swept seas, with their innumerable hues, fleeting and returning as the lights and shadows come and go.'[34]

Notes

1. See Paul Usherwood, *Art for Newcastle. T.M. Richardson and the Newcastle exhibitions 1822-43*, exhibition catalogue, Tyne & Wear Museums, 1984. The quotation in the chapter title is from R.J. Charleton, 'Cullercoats', *Magazine of Art*, 1886, p.456.
2. Cragside near Rothbury was substantially rebuilt by Norman Shaw in the Gothic Revival style. Now owned by the National Trust, much of Armstrong's original art collection has been recovered for the house, including a number of important works by Emmerson.
3. For more on the art market and patronage in the North East see Laura Newton, *Cullercoats: A North East Colony of Artists*, Sansom & Company, 2003, chapter 2: and Laura Newton, 'The Cullercoats Artists' Colony c.1870-1914', unpubl. PhD thesis, University of Northumbria, 2001, chapters 1 and 2.
4. It was bought by Hugh Taylor of Chipchase Castle for £10; see W.W. Tomlinson, *Historical Notes on Cullercoats, Whitley and Monkseaton* [1893], republ. F. Graham, 1980, p.103.
5. *The Graphic*, 17 June, 1871.
6. G.E. Campbell, 'Frank Holl and His Works', *Art Journal*, 1889, p.53.
7. For more on these pictures see Newton, 'Cullercoats Artists' Colony', pp.147, 150-2, 210 fn.4.
8. For the role of the Cullercoats artists in the formation and running of the Bewick Club see Laura Newton, 'The Bewick Club and the Cullercoats connection', in D Gardner-Medwin ed., *Bewick Studies*, British Library, 2003.
9. See for example *Newcastle Daily Chronicle*, 25 August 1881; *Newcastle Courant*, 26 August 1881; and *Tyneside Daily Echo*, 31 August 1881.
10. For a reasoned account of Homer's visit to Cullercoats see A Booth-Gerdts, 'The Winslow Homer Connection', in Newton, *Cullercoats*.
11. For example, Homer's 'fisher girls' picture at the 1881 Arts Association exhibition was likened by one critic to the work of Breton; and Marsh's pictures were frequently compared to those of Millet, perhaps because of the similarities of modelling figure subjects.
12. This poem was also the inspiration for paintings by Jobling, Isa Thompson and Laura Knight.
13. 'Notes by Altona', *Newcastle Daily Journal*, 17 February 1891.
14. See ibid. and *Newcastle Daily Journal*, 14 February 1891 for critiques.
15. For a fuller discussion of this issue see Newton, *Cullercoats*, pp.87-9, 93-4. Examples of David's work include *Oath of the Horatii* (1785) and *Brutus* (1789).
16. For a full discussion of the contemporary literature on Cullercoats and other colonies see Newton, 'The Cullercoats Artists' Colony', chapter 4.
17. Charleton, 'Cullercoats'. See also Aaron Watson, 'After the Herring', *Magazine of Art*, 1882; 'The Lifebrigade Man', *The Graphic*, Feb. 1870; Lillias Wasserman, 'Where the North Wind Blows', *Newcastle Weekly Leader*, Dec. 1886 – Jan 1887; W.G. Larkins, 'Reminiscences of Artistic Cullercoats', *Tyneside*, vol.1 no.1, 1894; Rudolf Dircks, 'Northumberland and Some Artists', *Art Journal*, 1904.
18. The exception to this is probably Alice Meynell's article on Newlyn (*Art Journal*, 1889, p.97), which was clearly intended more as a celebration of those artists.
19. James Guthrie, Joseph Crawhall, Arthur Melville and Edward Walton sent pictures to the 1880 Arts Association exhibition. Guthrie and Walton also sent works the following year.
20. Fred Jackson, Arthur Friedenson, Gilbert Foster, Bernard Sickert, Henry S Hopwood and later Laura and Harold Knight, sent work to Newcastle during the late 1880s and 1890s.
21. See Newton, *Cullercoats*, pp.54-5.
22. For example *Sharpening the Scythe* (1897), *The Winnowing Sheet* (1898) and *The Threshing Floor* (1898).
23. Lillias Wasserman, 'Some Fisher Folk', *Art Journal*, 1887, p.37.
24. *Newcastle Daily Journal*, 7 May 1890, p.5.
25. See Horton archive material at Tyne & Wear Archive, Newcastle.
26. These pictures are all in private collections but are reproduced in Newton, *Cullercoats*, 2003.
27. Royal Academy critique, *Newcastle Daily Leader*, 2 May 1896. For a fuller discussion see Newton, *Cullercoats*, p.118.
28. See S Daniels, *Fields of Vision. Landscape Imagery and National Identity in England and the US*, Polity Press, 1993. The painting refers to the incident when the women of Cullercoats dragged the lifeboat across the fields to rescue the crew of the *Lovely Nellie* in 1861. A similar incident was reported involving the Runswick Bay women in *The Graphic* 1901.
29. A more avant-garde technique might have suggested more challenging readings for contemporary viewers, but as this picture was hung at the entrance to the RA exhibition, one can assume that it was accepted as a more traditional

history painting, similar to the rest of Charlton's oeuvre. For contemporary critiques see *Newcastle Daily Chronicle* 30 April 1910 and *Art Journal* 1910.

30. Art Circle critique, *Newcastle Daily Chronicle*, 6 January 1897.

31. *Newcastle Daily Journal*, 27 July 1893, p.8. See also *Newcastle Daily Chronicle*, 21 and 29 July 1893; *Newcastle Courant,* 29 July 1893, p.5. This exhibition at the Central Exchange Gallery was billed as 'Conventionalism in Art; A Protest' and included artists such as Steer, Roger Fry, Anning Bell and Bernard Sickert, yet also contained works by artists more familiar to north-east audiences such as Fred Brown, Olsson, Mark Fisher and J.W.B. Knight.

32. For a fuller discussion see Newton, *Cullercoats*, p.57 and Julie Codell, 'Artists' Professional Societies: Production, Consumption and Aesthetics', in B Allen ed., *Towards a Modern Art World*, Yale University Press, 1995.

33. For a discussion of the events leading up to the opening of the Laing Art Gallery see Newton, 'The Cullercoats Artists' Colony', chapter 2, pp.78-85.

34. Wasserman, 'Some Fisher Folk', p.37.

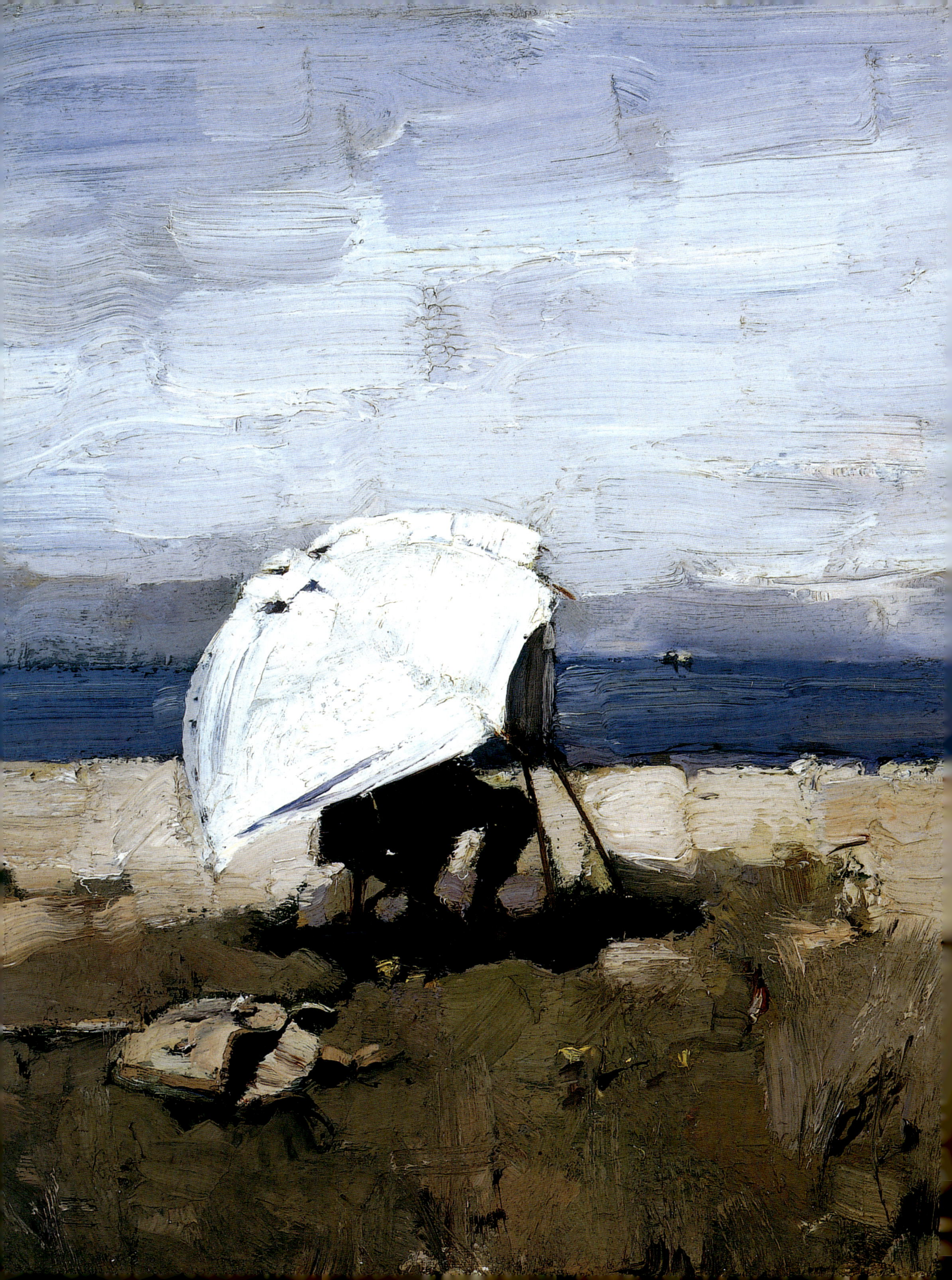

CHAPTER 8

Cockburnspath to Kirkcudbright
Travelling East to West

YSANNE HOLT

Reflecting on 'Art in the West of Scotland' in 1888, the critic of *The Scottish Art Review* described a great change in the aims of a body of artists mainly identified with Glasgow. Many of these, in pursuit of the serious study of form, had 'been impelled to a temporary expatriation and to the discovery that there were greater things in art than were dreamt of in the local philosophy'.[1] Several of the artists considered in this chapter had shared, from the late 1870s, distaste for the apparently arrogant insularity of Edinburgh's Royal Scottish Academy and the predominance of what was perceived to be the over-sentimentality of the subject – pictures identified with the so-called 'Glue Pot School'.[2] Some opted instead for formal training in private ateliers in Antwerp or Paris, encountering exhibitions like Durand Ruel's large Barbizon collection in 1878. Others witnessed the growing presence in Edinburgh and Glasgow public exhibitions and private dealers' galleries of painters from Constable to Corot to Millet to the Hague School. As a result, many of the Scottish painters commonly referred to as the 'Glasgow Boys' had arrived, as the *Art Review* critic put it, 'at much the same conclusions as to what qualities in art they most value and must most ardently strive to attain ... perfect tonality, the intelligent sacrifice of small things in nature [for] the great truths of structure, atmosphere, and dignity of presentation'.[3]

For these Glasgow-based artists – including James Guthrie and Edward Arthur Walton – there was also, initially, a commitment to a particular type of rustic subject matter derived to varying degrees from Dutch and French artists but also from native predecessors like John Robertson Reid and W.D Mackay.[4] From the early 1880s these examples encouraged their departure to specific locations in the Scottish countryside in search of simple landscapes and scenes of rural life and labour. For the most part sending the fruits of their own artistic labour to annual exhibitions at the Glasgow Institute, or further afield to London venues like the New English Art Club or Grosvenor Gallery, these painters participated in the colony movement with its, to us, now familiar rejection of academicism and narrative, and its pursuit of authenticity in a staged retreat from the city, whether London, Edinburgh or Glasgow. The concern here is with the development of two colonies in the Scottish borders, Cockburnspath on the east coast and Kirkcudbright on the west, in the period from the 1880s to the early years of the Great War.

For painters like Arthur Melville, who visited both, the impetus towards remote rural locations had already begun in France in the late 1870s, in extended stays at the ancient and tranquil village of Grez-sur-Loing.[5] In the early 1880s members of the Glasgow group rapidly established their own pattern of *plein air* summer painting trips. Joseph Crawhall and Guthrie both painted in the flat, open pastures at Crowland in Lincolnshire in 1882, although increasingly their focus was on ideal locations in Scotland. Crawhall, Guthrie and Walton had first painted together at Rosneath on the Gare Loch in 1879 and, with George Henry, made an extended visit to Brig o' Turk on the Trossachs trail north west of Stirling in 1881.[6] As Roger Billcliffe points out, Brig o' Turk had earlier drawn Scottish landscape painters like Horatio McCulloch and Sam Bough for its panoramic scenes of mountains and lochs, whereas the younger group, following the example of Dutch and Barbizon painters, favoured more intimate views of rural life and activity.[7] The extraordinary impact in London and Glasgow exhibitions of the early 1880s of Jules Bastien-Lepage's direct observations of everyday life in his native village of Damvillers like, for example, *Pauvre Fauvette* (1881, fig.87) certainly confirmed their convictions.[8]

Guthrie's biographer, James Caw, later asserted that at Brig o' Turk he and Walton were already striving for a simple and emphatic manner in their painting technique and favoured a 'less-glamoured light'.[9] But failing to find ideal conditions there the artists crossed the Forth into

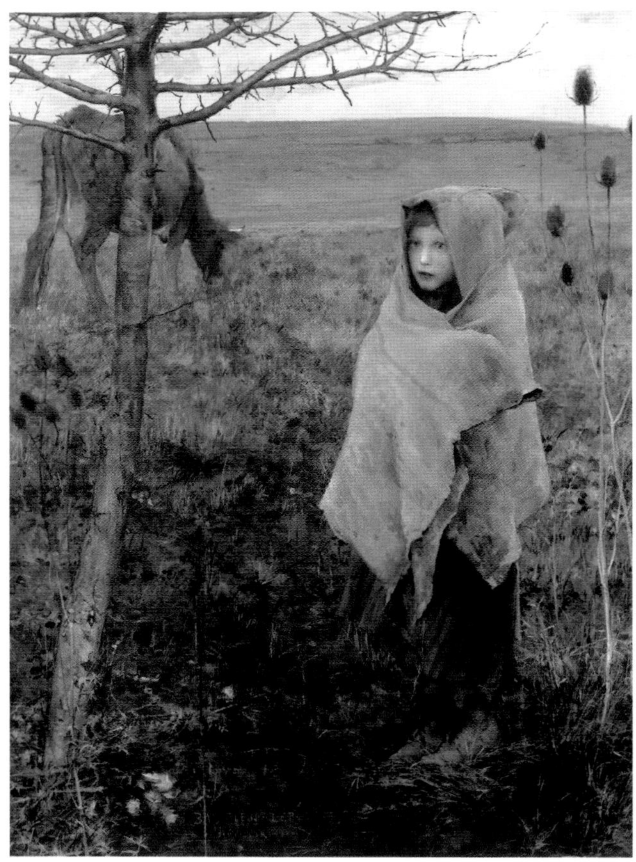

Fig.87
Jules Bastien-Lepage, *Pauvre Fauvette*, 1881, oil on canvas
Glasgow City Council (Museums)

Berwickshire where, at Cockburnspath, Guthrie found the 'simple country life with virginal settings' he sought for his figure-in-landscape pictures. The sense of distance from Glasgow, both culturally and geographically, was crucial and Caw's account of Guthrie's sojourn is a fascinating example of the symbolic mapping of specific location and artistic practice that so often emerges in accounts of artists' colonies. Caw sets the scene: the village, on the edge of East Lothian only eight miles from Dunbar, is sited in 'the narrowing belt of cultivated country between the higher pastoral uplands of the Lammermoors and the bold rocky coast along the North Sea'.[10] The general terrain, far from picturesque is 'windswept and somewhat austere in aspect', it 'has spaciousness and dignity and a character quite its own' – qualities of place which the critic will also discern in the artist's formal handling and compositions. The reader is directed off the post-road from Edinburgh to London which,

> after running parallel with the shore from Dunbar, skirts Bilsdean, with its cottages and tinkling waterfall, and then a mile and more farther on, after crossing the high bridge over the romantic wooded Dean at Dunglass, swings inland and uphill. Here on a slope, with a white-washed verandahed Inn on the highway, the village lies.

Secluded and off the beaten track and a hundred yards or so from the sea, the village, once gained, still presented itself in the early 1930s as a peaceful and antiquated idyll:

> Approached by a few yards of side road, with a clump of ash and plane trees at the entrance, the red-tiled and occasionally blue-slated cottages cluster round an oblong square, with an old Market Cross towards the lower end. Pends lead to other cottages in gardens behind, where, on a green knowe to the east, a Pre-Reformation church with squat and round tower stands above a hollow in which a bush-fringed pond twinkles. As a rule quiet pervades the square, for it is off the main road and there are few visitors.

Co'path, originally Kolbrand's Path, was indeed an ancient community with nearby archaeological remains and burial cists dating back to the Bronze Age and before. The market (mercat) cross with its thistle and rose commemorates the marriage of James IV to Margaret Tudor in 1503, the Pre-Reformation St Helen's Church was originally built in the 1500s and nearby Fast Castle provided the setting for Edgar Ravenswood's solitary tower in Sir Walter Scott's novel *The Bride of Lammermoor* of 1819.[11] And while these ancient monuments and historic houses rarely figure in paintings of the early 1880s, the village and its surroundings would, nonetheless, have appeared to the artists as steeped in history and with that marked regional and cultural distinction that often manifests itself most strongly in border areas – at edges and margins.

Caw's account echoes many of those of French colonies and, in England, of Newlyn especially. Frequently difficult to reach, once found they appear enchantingly timeless and untainted by modern conditions.[12] But modern conditions had certainly affected the lives of those native to this particular region, as elsewhere, by the early 1880s.[13] For one commentator in 1912, by the 1880s rural Scotland had lost its 'pride, its security, its traditions'.[14] Processes of modernization in counties like Berwickshire had pronounced effects on the families of agricultural labourers, and the subject of one of Guthrie's first and most important Co'path paintings, *A Hind's Daughter* (1883), is of interest here (see fig.88).[15] Traditionally the hind, a skilled ploughman, had provided female 'bondaged' labour to the farm in the form of his wife or daughters, although by the time of Guthrie's painting the hind's daughter was more likely to

Fig.88
Sir James Guthrie, *A Hind's Daughter*, 1883, oil on canvas
The National Gallery of Scotland

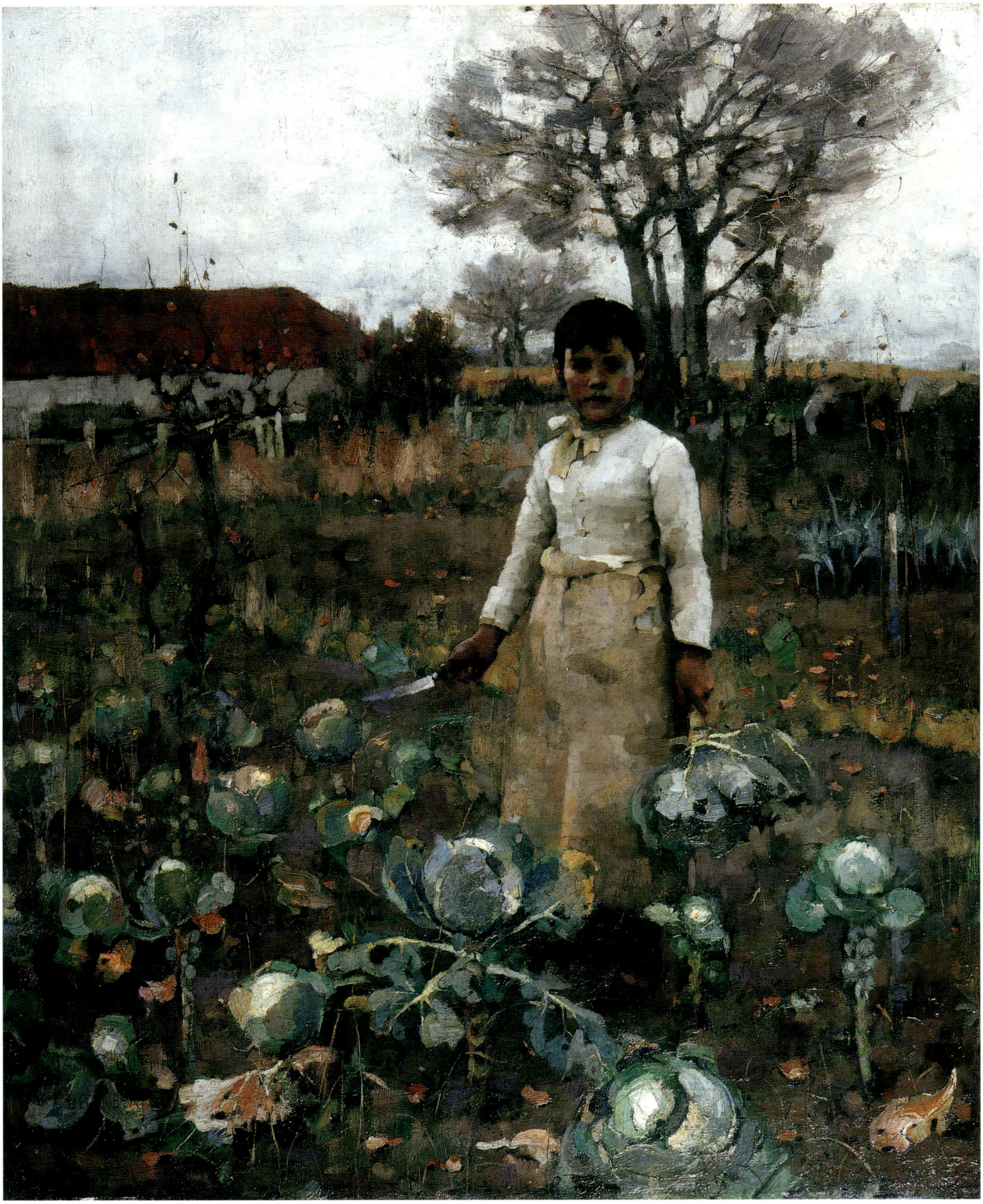

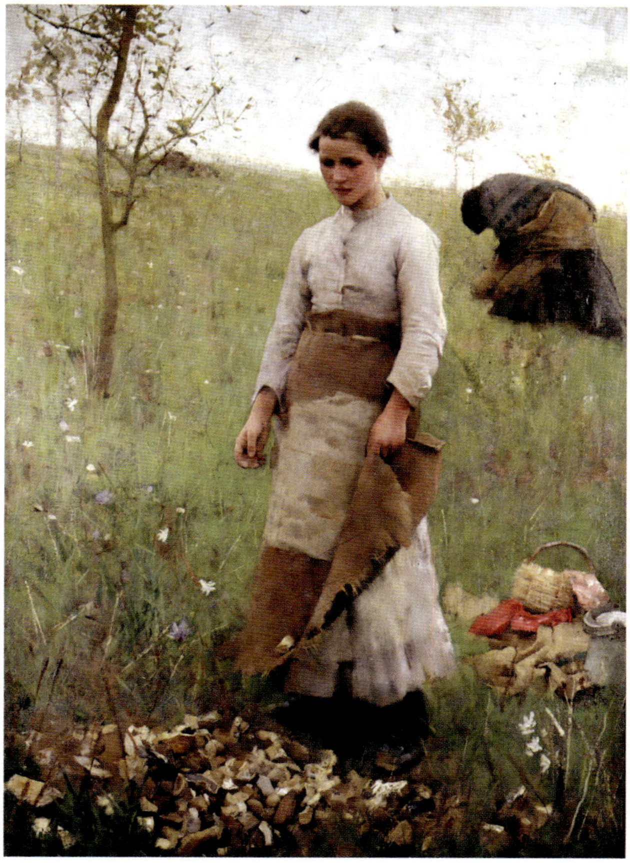

Fig.89
George Clausen, *The Stone Pickers*, 1887
Laing Art Gallery, Newcastle upon Tyne

leave home to find employment in service elsewhere. So Guthrie's painting depicts a young girl cutting cabbages at a precise moment of transition in the traditional rural economy. The subject matter as well as the handling is characteristic of several contemporary painters in England, of Henry Herbert La Thangue, Edward Stott and George Clausen.[16]

Characteristically, the square-brush technique of painting across forms and the direct frontal composition of Guthrie's painting recalls the Rustic Naturalism of Bastien-Lepage but here, as Iain Gale points out, filtered through the particular influence of Arthur Melville's own *A Cabbage Garden*, painted in 1877.[17] Although it lacks obvious narrative there is perhaps, as in Clausen's later *The Stone Pickers* of 1887 (fig.89), conventional symbolism in the rendering of a young girl in nature and a sense of the inevitable passage of time that belie the direct representation of fact – associations which become increasingly more significant by the 1890s.

A degree of nostalgia already underlies these images, a melancholic quality provoked by an awareness of the speed of change. In the case of the hind's daughter, the advent of compulsory education from the 1870s perhaps exacerbated the desire of artists like Guthrie to 'fix' an image that was becoming increasingly less typical.[18] The same impulse led artists to record scenes of curious local custom or exotic costume as, for example, in the local women field-workers' bonnets, commonly known as 'uglies' and depicted by Walton in his *A Berwickshire Fieldworker* in 1884 (fig.90). Walton presents a rural 'type' in what becomes a familiar figure and field relationship, set against a steeply rising background derived

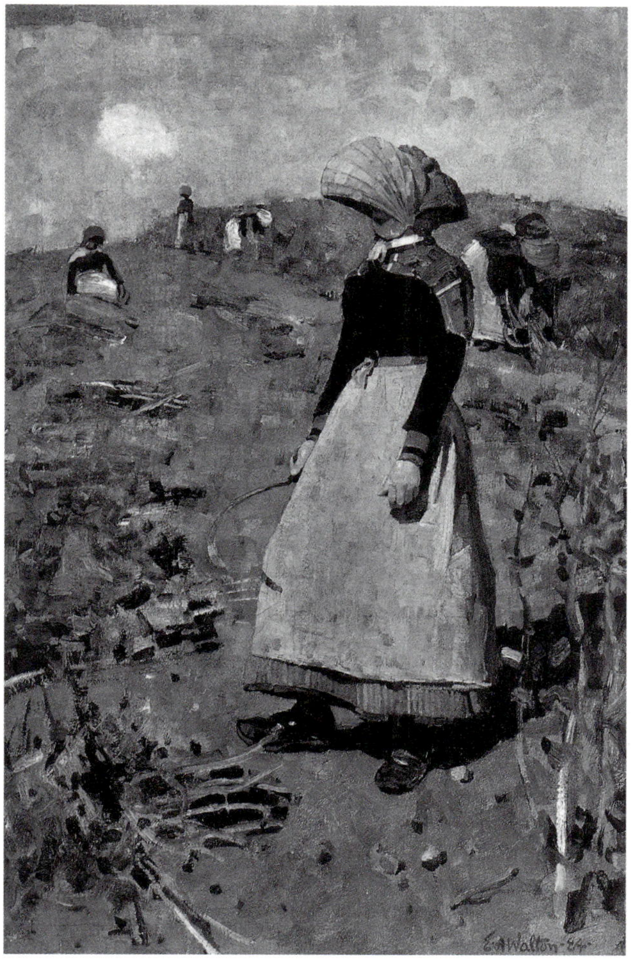

Fig.90
Edward Arthur Walton, *A Berwickshire Fieldworker*, 1884
oil on canvas, © Tate, London 2005

Fig.91
Sir James Guthrie, *Hard at It*, 1883, oil on canvas
Glasgow City Council (Museums)

Fig.92
Edward Arthur Walton, *The Fishing Village*, 1883, watercolour
Private collection

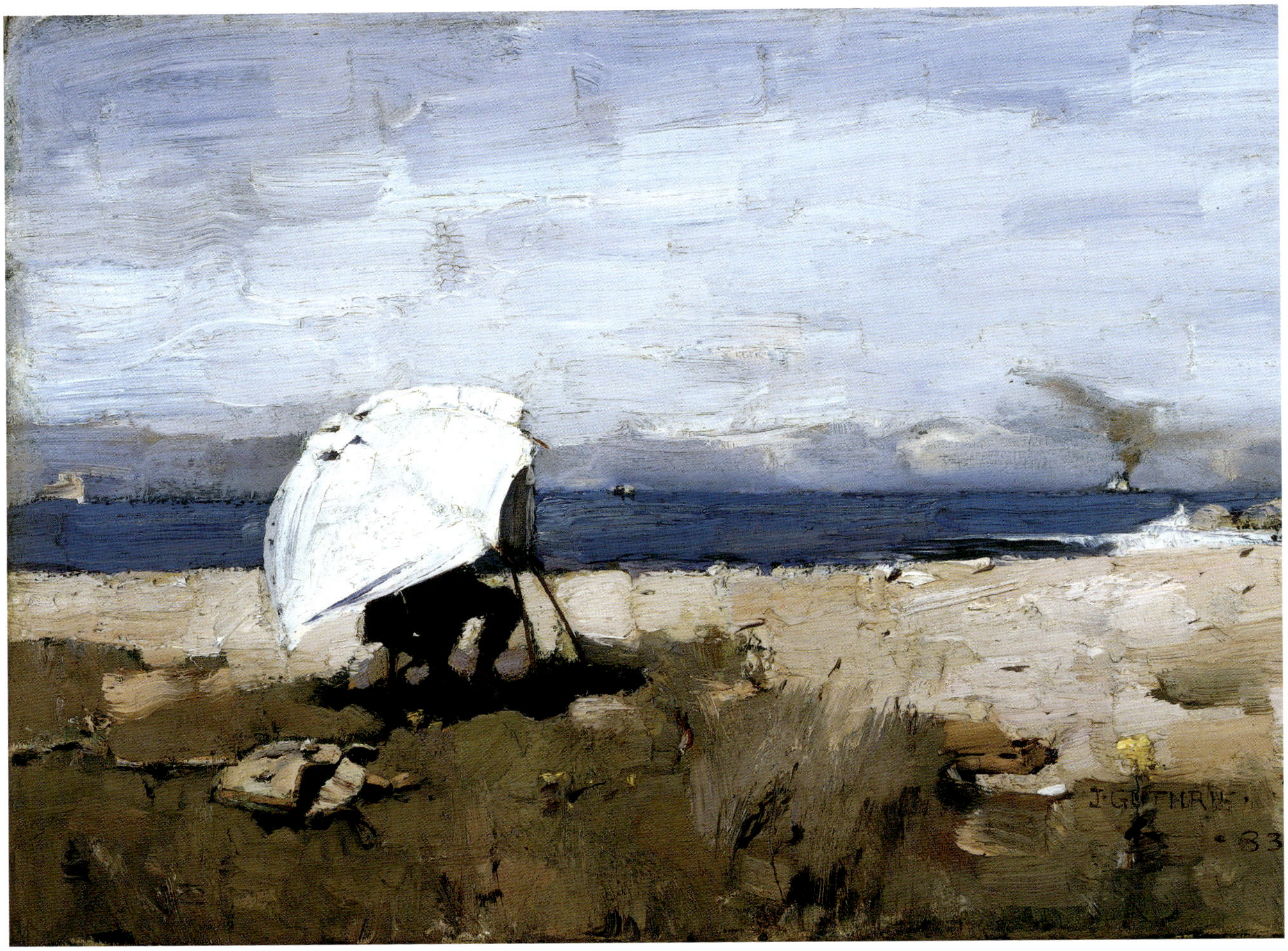

from Bastien-Lepage and evoked not just by other rustic naturalist painters in Britain but by the naturalist photographer Peter Henry Emerson. In these we have a sense of the individual observing the distinct peculiarities of others, a motivation which, to some extent, underpinned the spread of artists' colonies in the later nineteenth century.[19]

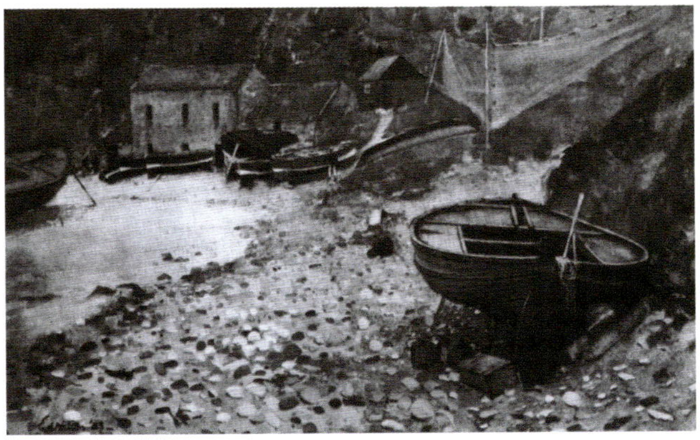

The common purpose and camaraderie amongst artists that was so much a feature of the movement in general was a particular feature of experience at Co'path where, for Caw, 'For a few summers in the early eighties nearly every cottage had an artist lodger and easels were to be seen pitched in the gardens or the square, in the fields close by, or near the little harbour in the rocks below the cluster of white cottages at the Cove, perhaps half a mile away'.[20] In other words, wherever the daily lives of the local population could be depicted, *en plein air*, as demonstrated by Guthrie himself in *Hard at It* of 1883 (fig.91), showing one of the group at his easel beneath the familiar white sketching umbrella. The picture is interesting in that the easel is turned towards the

Fig.93
Sir James Guthrie, *Schoolmates*, 1884–85, oil on canvas
Musée des Beaux-Arts, Ghent

sea whereas, apart from some paintings of fishing boats in the harbour as in Walton's watercolour *The Fishing Village* (1883, fig.92), artists here concentrated on scenes of fieldwork, gardens and village activities, suggesting again the importance at this period of Bastien-Lepage.

Guthrie was the first to establish himself in the village and the only artist (with his mother as housekeeper) to remain after the annual summer painting season had ended. From 1883 to the end of 1885 he rented the factor's house at Dunglass and used a barn in the village as a studio. Guthrie and then Walton were followed at varying times by Crawhall, Whitelaw Hamilton, George Henry (then painting at the nearby fishing village of Eyemouth), Henry's old school friend T. Corsan Morton and by Arthur Melville.[21] For the following three years 'this East coast village remained the country centre of the nascent artistic movement in the West of Scotland'.[22] Community clearly fostered identity – a Co'path 'look' – which went beyond recognizable motifs and locations as in Crawhall's and Morton's views of 'The Duckpond', but extended more typically to a particular handling and to an identification of this east coast village as 'the Boys' Barbizon'.

Roger Billcliffe maintained that Guthrie's decision to render in full sunlight such subjects as *Schoolmates* (1884–5, fig.93), where the village children file solemnly schoolwards with their satchels, and *In the Orchard* (1885–6), where they gather windfalls into their basket, soon distinguished his work from that of Bastien and his followers. Caw also felt he possessed a 'more sensitive feeling for beauty of colour and atmosphere' than did Bastien, who was 'not enough in love with beauty'.[23] Similar distinctions were made between French and British artistic sensibilities by critics of the later 1880s and 1890s. In the midst of these, national artistic differences were established, in which French Naturalism emerges as excessively objective, even scientific and British art as innately romantic and poetic. These distinctions are yet more complex in the context of the defining and refining of characteristic traits within England and Scotland at a moment in which cultural nationalism becomes increasingly dominant. So by 1897 Francis Newbery, director of Glasgow School of Art, was asserting that 'beyond any possible fructifying it might have had, by the study of work other than its own, the Glasgow men owe nothing … to continental teaching … nor were their early efforts – as is commonly supposed – a second hand reflection of the work of some continental artists'.[24] This critical tendency appeared later in writers like William Hardie, who maintained that *A Hind's Daughter* and *Schoolmates* derived rather from Scots artists like Robert McGregor who painted rural subjects such as *Gathering Stones* (1877), although he himself is believed to have worked for a time in Brittany.[25] But we also find assertions of 'Scottishness' in accounts that argue for a more intensely decorative quality in the work of native artists, assertions borne out by Arthur Melville's depiction of a scene from Shakespeare (and so a departure from

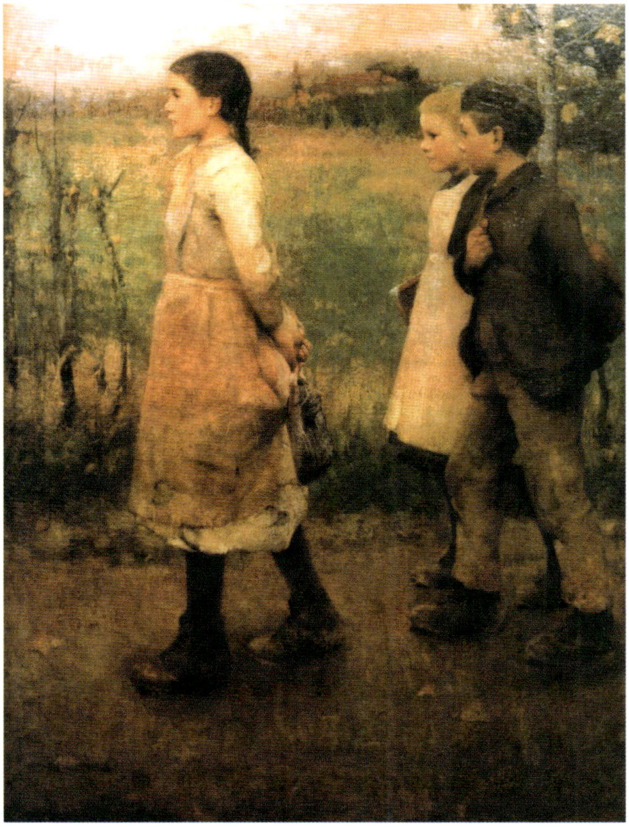

Fig.94
Arthur Melville, *Audrey and her Goats*, 1884–90, oil on canvas

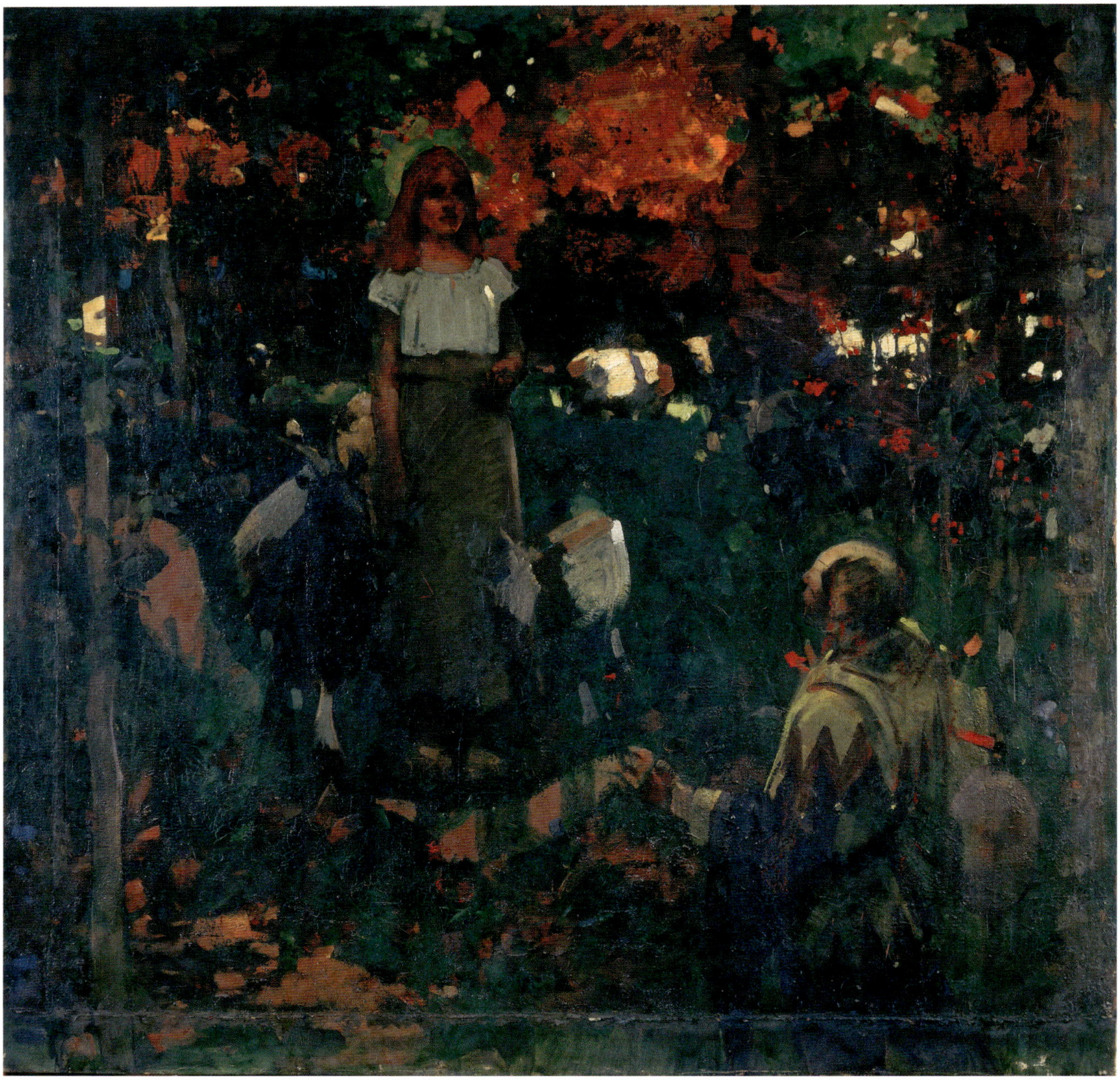

strictly local subjects), *Audrey and her Goats*, begun at Co'path in 1884 and re-worked over six years (fig.94). Iain Gale describes Melville's painting as a synthesis of Naturalism with a decorative Symbolism relating to the circle of Patrick Geddes, although his reference to Bastien's rather untypical *Joan of Arc listening to the Voices* seems equally feasible. Certainly the painting, composed (finally) in golden-red with a thick, unmixed pigment, was a clear departure from the conventional grey tonalities and prosaic subjects of Rustic Naturalism.[26]

A move to a more decorative aesthetic in the later 1880s coincides with the rise to prominence of the second borders' colony, the small town of Kirkcudbright in the Galloway countryside on the west coast. Links between these two locations were established most closely per-

Fig.95
George Henry, *A Cottar's Garden*, 1885, watercolour The National Trust for Scotland Photographic Library / Broughton House Collection, Kirkcudbright

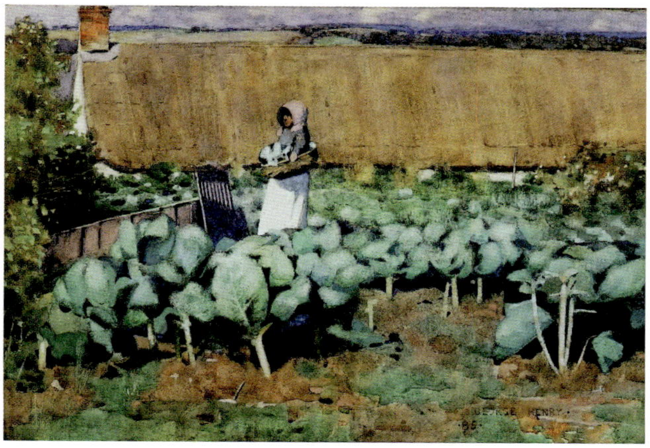

haps by George Henry, whose Co'path watercolour *A Cottar's Garden* of 1885 (fig.95) repeated the subject of Guthrie's *A Hind's Daughter*. But in Henry's work the young girl in her sun-bonnet stands further back in the composition, almost submerged in a tall clump of cabbages, and perhaps a closer connection might be drawn with Edward Stott's *A French Kitchen Garden* shown at the Royal Academy in 1883.[27] With Henry's entire scene flooded by sunlight, that impression of a childhood at one with nature is still more intense and presages the symbolist tendency that emerges most strongly in the Kirkcudbright paintings of Henry and his new acquaintance, the painter Edward Atkinson Hornel. Similarly, in Henry's *Noon* (1885, fig.96), likely to have been painted in Kirkcudbright, the girl supposedly tending cattle gazes abstractly into the distance and the artist reveals what David Martin described as 'more of a decorative spirit than a liberal interpretation.'[28] Depicted in profile, the handling of the model in particular implies Rustic Naturalism, but the brighter colour and more conscious quality of design suggest the artist's future direction.

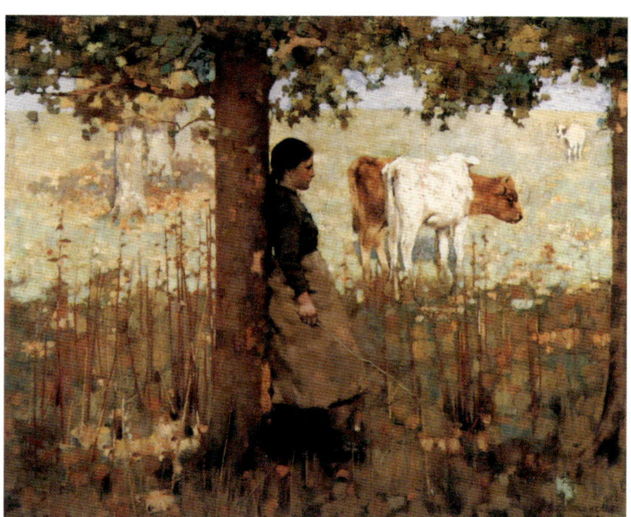

Fig.96
George Henry, *Noon*, 1885, oil on canvas
Private collection

The theme of the rural labourer and the working community gradually declines and the year 1886 is perhaps transitional in this respect. At this date Guthrie gives up his cottage and studio in Co'path essentially to return to Glasgow, but makes the first of several visits to Kirkcudbright, where he completes *In the Orchard*, paints an exemplary head and shoulders naturalistic portrait of the local Kirkcudbright character, Auld Wullie – later entitled *A Village Worthy* – and another key work, *The Stone Breaker* (fig.97). The latter began as a scene of the stonebreaker at rest from his labours, in conversation with a passing farm hand on a white horse. Cut down by the artist himself in 1923, original narrative interest is lost and the work becomes a much simpler single figure composition. By 1887, Guthrie was being praised in the pages of the journal *Quiz* for 'unforced spontaneity and power' and for 'representing the deep truths of NATURE without that sense of labour in the doing'.[29] From here the sense emerges amongst the Glasgow Boys, and more widely amidst the European colony movement, that there were fundamental universal truths to be expressed in art that went beyond the simple observation of actual facts. Such a departure from strict Naturalism coincides essentially with the artists' departure from Cockburnspath – the Boys' Barbizon – to, in Henry's case especially, Kirkcudbright where, for a time up to the mid 1890s, certain identifications with the art of another French artists' colony – Pont-Aven – might be perceived.[30]

Whilst Co'path's importance to painters was intense but short-lived, Kirkcudbright had already established a reputation as a centre for artists, and it remains so today.

Fig.97
Sir James Guthrie, *The Stone Breaker*, 1886, oil on canvas
Renfrew District Museum and Art Gallery, Paisley

Fig.98
David Gauld, *Kirkcudbright Harbour*, oil on canvas
Dick Institute, Kilmarnock

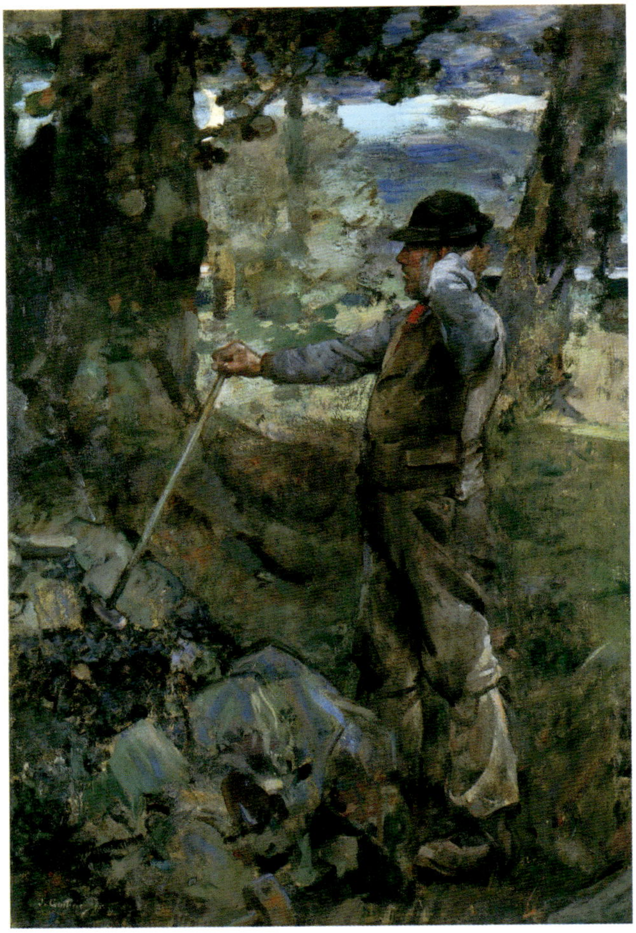

Also positioned on the coast – in a sheltered harbour on the estuary of the River Dee on the north Solway shore, the town was established as a Royal Burgh in 1455 and so permitted to trade with ports outside of Scotland. As Dorothy L. Sayers, whose novel *Five Red Herrings* of 1931 was based there, recorded, 'In Kirkcudbright one either fishes or paints'.[31] Noticeable amongst most of the artists associated with the town, however, is the relative absence of scenes associated with the fishing trade. Attention focuses inland from the harbour; on the eighteenth-century houses, the town gaol, the Tolbooth – described in Walter Scott's *Guy Mannering* (1815), or the striking silhouette of the ruined MacLellan's castle – as depicted in Bertram Priestman's atmospheric *Topsail Schooner at the Harbour at Night* and David Gauld's *Kirkcudbright Harbour* (fig.98).[32] But most particularly, both local and visiting artists concentrated on the surrounding green wooded valleys, streams and moorlands.

The earliest artistic connections were established by the Faed family from nearby Gatehouse-of-Fleet, as recorded by Mary McKerrow.[33] John, James and Thomas Faed – sons of a local millwright – all achieved success at Royal Academy and Royal Scottish Academy exhibitions in the later 1800s. The eldest brother John trained in Edinburgh, graduating to portraiture and to illustrations of Scott and Robert Burns, whilst Thomas painted popular renderings of rustic cottagers or their bonny bairns set in picturesque Scottish scenery. Both with successful careers, they maintained strong local connections. John, in particular, served in his later years as President of the Kirkcudbrightshire Fine Arts Association from its founding in 1886 and continued to paint local landscapes. But he also painted scenes like *The Little Seamstress* (1890, fig.99) which, while a fairly conventional Victorian genre scene of quiet domestic virtue, also reflects more contemporary artistic fashions with its background depiction of a Japanese fan. The third Faed brother, James, an accomplished engraver, also produced landscapes, five of which appeared as illustrations for the first edition of Malcolm McL Harper's *Rambles in Galloway* in 1876.[34] The success and reputation of the Faed family perhaps

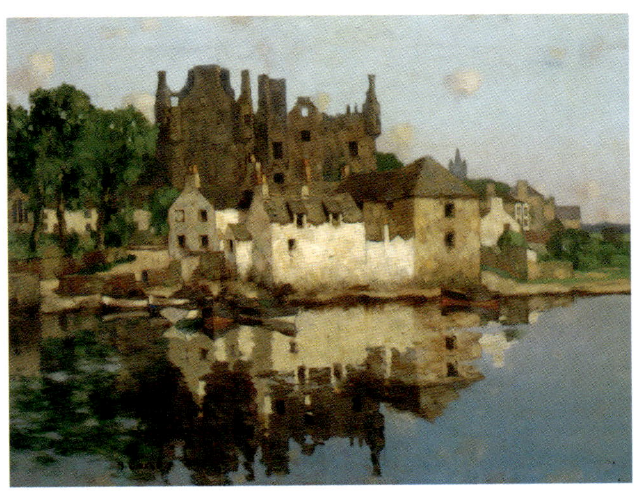

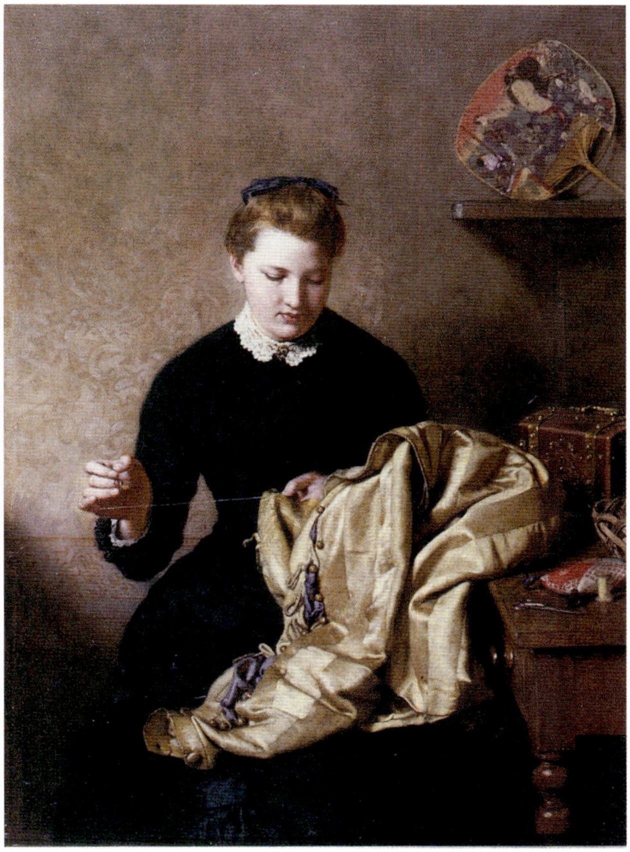

Fig.99
John Faed, *The Little Seamstress*, 1890, oil on canvas
The Stewartry Museum, Kirkcudbright
© Dumfries and Galloway Council

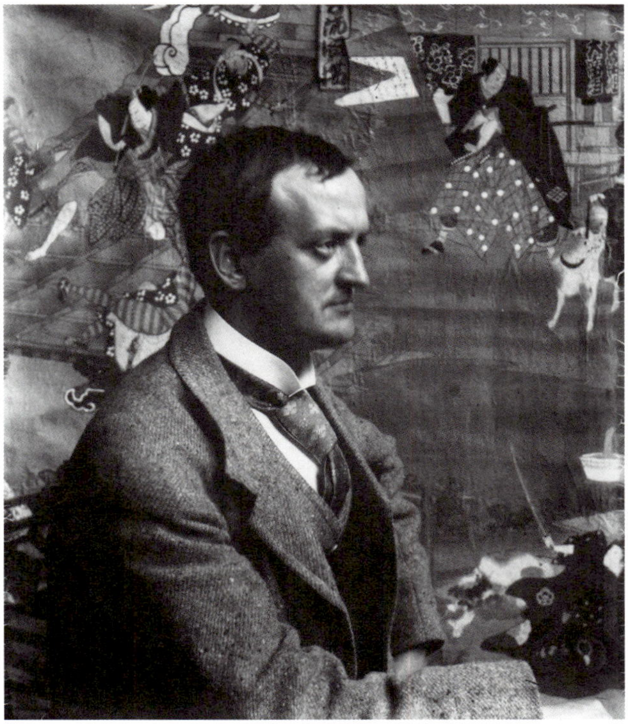

E A Hornel, photographer Robert McConchie, 1900, photograph
The Stewartry Museum, Kirkcudbright, © Dumfries and Galloway Council

encouraged the families of three local boys – of Hornel himself, Thomas Bromley Blacklock and William Stewart MacGeorge – to allow their sons to leave Kirkcudbright (or in MacGeorge's case, nearby Castle Douglas) for art training in Edinburgh.[35]

But the key figure in the emerging identity of this 'artists' town' is certainly Hornel.[36] After study in Edinburgh and then Antwerp, Hornel's earliest paintings in Kirkcudbright in 1885 follow the formulae of Bastien-Lepage: in the familiar low-tones and square brush-strokes of the 1886 *Potato Planting* (fig.100), an elderly man shovels soil while his young assistant stands by, her sack slung over her shoulder. This is one of only a few Hornels to depict scenes of field-work or allotment gardening after his painting of the previous year, *In the Crofts, Kirkcudbright*, with its inevitable allotment cabbage patch in a broader composition with stooping figures that allude to Millet's *Angelus*. But here, the late afternoon sunlight reflecting against the distant walls of the town's Tolbooth presents a scene of pleasant tranquility without the air of fatalism and timeless toil characteristic of Millet.

From 1885 Henry and Hornel began what was to be a close working relationship for the next eight or nine years, at times sharing a studio whilst Henry was in the town, or corresponding regularly from Glasgow. Both artists from this point were working away from Naturalism – as revealed in a letter from Henry late that October on seeing three paintings by Thomas Millie Dow at the Glasgow Institute. These he believed 'the most beautiful things I have ever seen. I don't know of any other fellow who has managed to make one feel on seeing those pictures so much of the spirituality of nature. They are intense in this way. One especially seems to make you creep with the strong quietness and mystery of nature'.[37] Henry perhaps referred to Dow's *The Hudson River* which, to David Martin, gave a 'dream-like impression of the great river', 'delicate

Fig.100
Edward Atkinson Hornel, *Potato Planting*, 1886, oil on canvas
Private collection

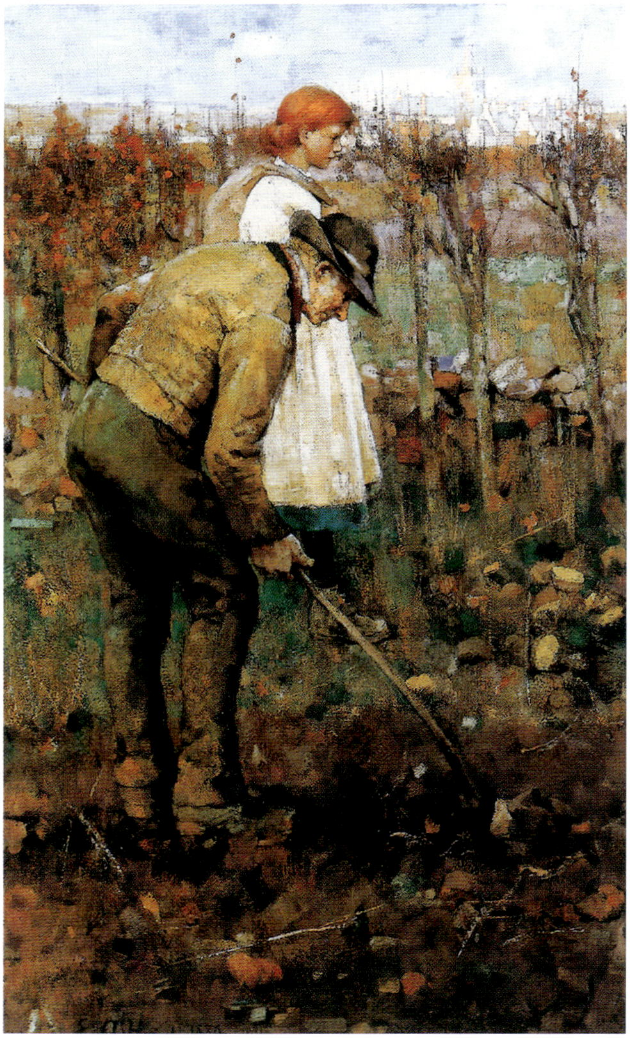

and suave' in colour.[38] Later Henry described his own ambitions; 'I want to paint this summer about eight feet of a canvas. It is time now I was trying to paint something. I feel I have just been living a useless stupid kind of life, all these years, as if no fine thoughts existed in this world.'[39] At that same exhibition Henry had shown his own *A Hedge Cutter,* which essentially brought to a close his depictions of rustic types in characteristic poses. With the flattening, frieze-like depiction of the hedgerow, the work compares with La Thangue's own later version of that subject, *The Hedger* (1888), but the mood of concentration and rhythmic gesture in the La Thangue is relieved in Henry's painting, again by the effect of full sunlight.[40]

Mention of sunlight and the warmth supplied by the gulf stream often appear in literary accounts of Kirkcudbright by the end of the decade as, for example, in *Quiz* in 1887; 'rumour has it that the sunny South of Scotland – that garden of our land – is made sunnier to artists' eyes by the smile of beauty.'[41] All of this encouraged scenes of the symbolic beauty of nature rather than sober rural industry, and it seems Henry was more attuned to the atmosphere there than elsewhere. Confusion at this time over his own artistic purpose is clear, and in another letter to Hornel he complains of his current lot, then in Arbroath painting portraits of 'flax kings and jute gods [who know] how to spin out their money as well as other commodities while we the apostles of virtue and sincerity, the pioneers of culture, starve for a few crumbs from the millionaires' table'. Over-stated and suggestive of too long spent in the rain (another complaint), Henry's conviction is typical of those who frequented the artists' colonies – the artists themselves, their chosen subjects and the sites in which paint all embody integrity and authenticity. Henry ends with an enquiry after any 'cheap and good' digs at the 'Kirk'.[42]

But the sociability of sunny Kirkcudbright was important too, the like-mindedness and the anticipation of mingling again with those permanent residents like Hornel and his brother-in-law William Mouncey (the latter had no formal training and rarely left the area), or others who moved more freely from one painting location to another, like Henry himself, Whitelaw Hamilton, Guthrie and Morton. The visiting artists arranged landladies and often models in advance, and Henry on occasions hired the studio of a local photographer which, 'having one end nearly all glass has the same effect as open air'.[43] On their extended stays, these visitors might fancy that they merged into the local community, but it was still nec-

Fig.101
Aldolphe Joseph Thomas Monticelli, *A Woodland Fête*
The National Gallery of Scotland

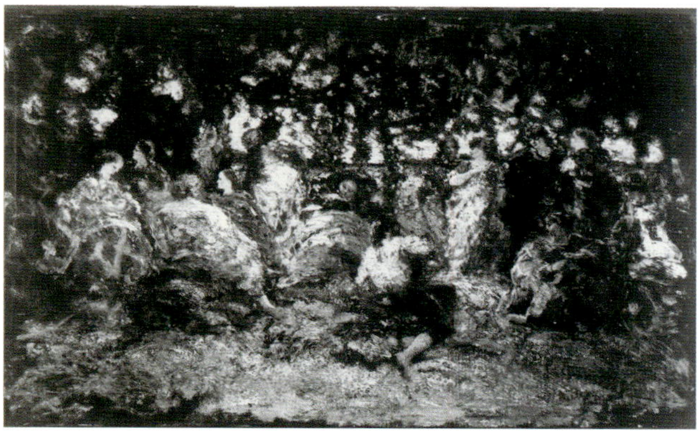

essary to retain connections with the urban centres. So in the summer of 1887 Henry urges Hornel to send to the Glasgow Art Club: 'you must do something to keep yourself before people here – one is apt to forget.' A balance was to be maintained between relative isolation and immersion in nature, and crucial contacts with metropolitan markets and critical opinion.

To a considerable degree, a certain primitivism amongst artists was fostered by those very markets in the cities. Henry and Hornel's work, for example, was much affected by relations with the Glasgow dealer Alexander Reid from the later 1880s. Through exhibitions at Reid's La Société des Beaux Arts gallery they were exposed to new visual sources and, most importantly for their immediate development, to the French Provençal painter Adolphe Monticelli and to Japanese

Fig.102
George Henry, *A Galloway Landscape*, 1889, oil on canvas
Glasgow City Council (Museums)

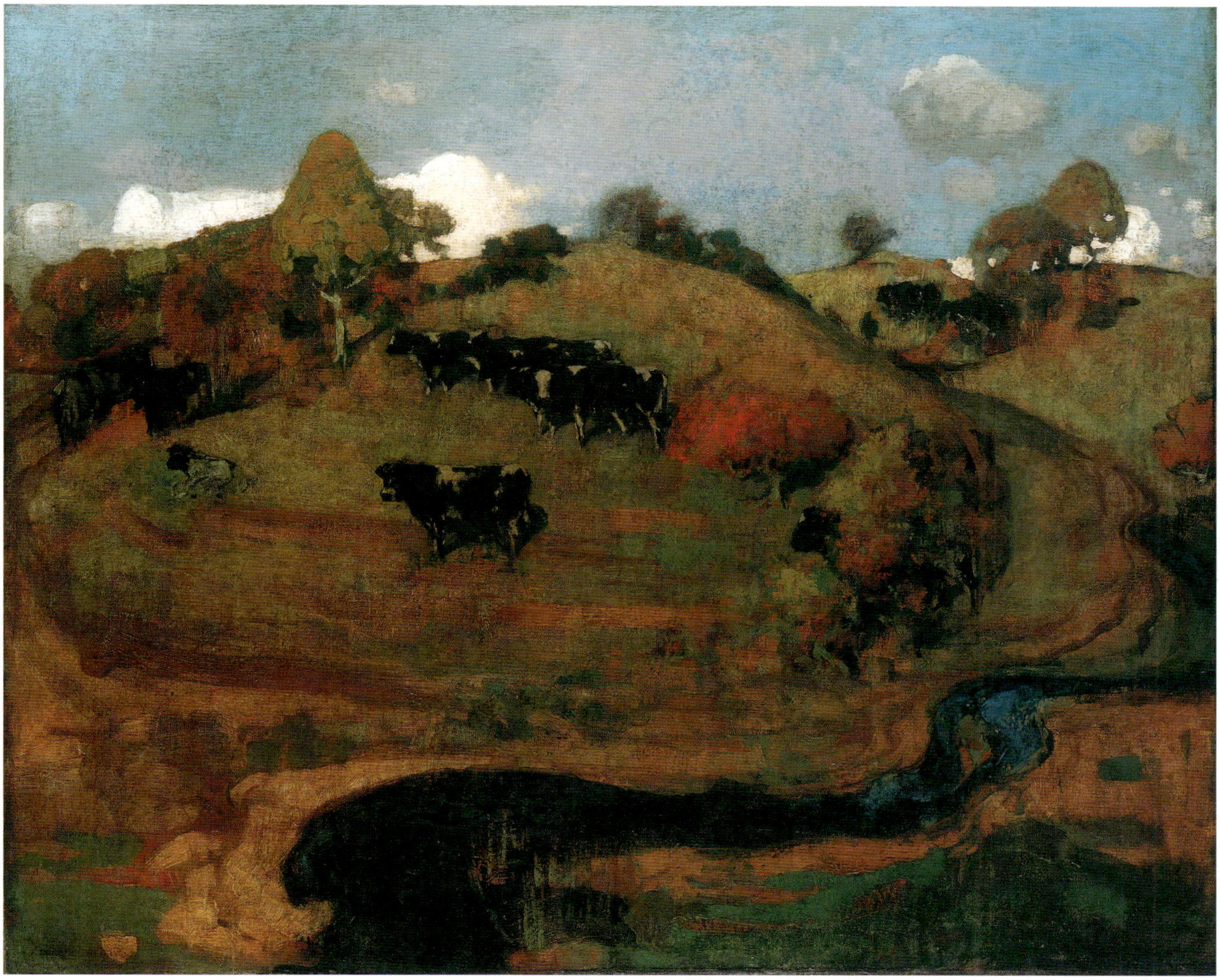

woodblock prints.[44] In a developing tendency towards Aestheticism and Symbolism, both artists responded to the Monticellis on view at the International Exhibition in Edinburgh in 1886 (see fig.101). With his mosaic-like brushwork and impenetrable surfaces, the French artist proposed an enchanted and exotic world, remote from everyday experience. But to attain this ideal it was now necessary to quite abandon the conventions of Naturalism, and by 1889-90 these Scots artists were drawn to visionary evocations of a universal timelessness that went far beyond the portrayal of cabbage plots.

Henry's *A Galloway Landscape* (1889, fig.102) was a crucial indication of this shift. As David Martin described it, the artist's intention was to 'express by means of colour the sentiment of the fulness [sic] and fecundity of nature; form being kept subservient, and the methods and treatment as simple and primitive in character as possible'.[45] Regardless of topography, Henry produced a poetic conception of place (a particular location at Lochfergus, near Kirkcudbright), with a rhythmic and decorative patterning, an absence of perspective and a flattened asymmetrical composition derived in part from the Japanese print – features too of Hornel's *A Galloway Idyll* of 1890 (fig.103). Henry's were 'sumptuous dreams of landscapes of beauty', 'imaginative subjects of deep import and sombre power'.[46]

Increasingly, both artists were to celebrate a Galloway of ancient mysteries and magic, and in this their work shared in the growing interest in the region's folklore. In 1889 Hornel produced illustrations for Malcolm Mc L Harper's *Bards of Galloway,* a collection of the legends and poetry of the region deemed well-fitted to the 'poet's eye and heart', with its 'poetic superstitions', 'picturesque glens' and the 'venerable relics of antiquity with which its villages are studded'.[47] Harper's closing lament is familiar; 'cheap literature, railways, telegraphs, the bustle and hurry of commerce, a refinement of life and manners, all mean that the old customs ... of the country are fast disappearing'. Fairies are no longer believed in and 'the romance has disappeared' in all but a few of the most secluded districts removed from railways and modern customs. As revealed in that impulse to record the past – old skills, customs and costumes at Co'path, old legends and fairy-tales in Kirkcudbright – the real character or 'essence' of place always lies far away or in the past, in a time, for Harper, of 'national simplicity'.

Hornel and Henry's *The Druids bringing in the Mistletoe* (1890, fig.104) responded to Harper with an expression of the mystery and primitive simplicity of the county, and with evident interest in the remnants of the Celtic past and its sacred customs.[48] The compressed picture space in *The Druids,* the symbolic motifs, gold leaf and decorative ceremonial robes all demonstrate a knowledge of Celtic artistic practice and reveal, for John Morrison, that Henry and Hornel were in the vanguard of the Celtic Revival movement that sought to 'trace the true origins of Scots and Scottish culture and to develop a language, both formal and iconographic that would serve as an archetype for Scottish art'.[49] But that flattened perspective and asymmetrical composition also witness the Japanese print. So both painters (like Harper) dismissed material reality for evocations of an ancient local culture, but drew on certain formal qualities of the Japanese print to emphasize those distinctions. And these allusions to an ancient Scottish past via characteristics of both Monticelli and Japonisme, all signified fantasy and a world of enchantment.[50]

The supposedly unique characteristics of Celtic culture and temperament continued to inform their practice, but more obliquely. Hence Hornel's interest, and more particularly that of his friend Charles Mackie, was in the decorative *synthetisme* and rhythmic design of Nabis painters like Paul Serusier for whom the 'celticity' of Brittany was crucial. Mackie, along with

Fig.103
Edward Atkinson Hornel, *A Galloway Idyll*, 1890, oil on canvas
The Robertson Collection

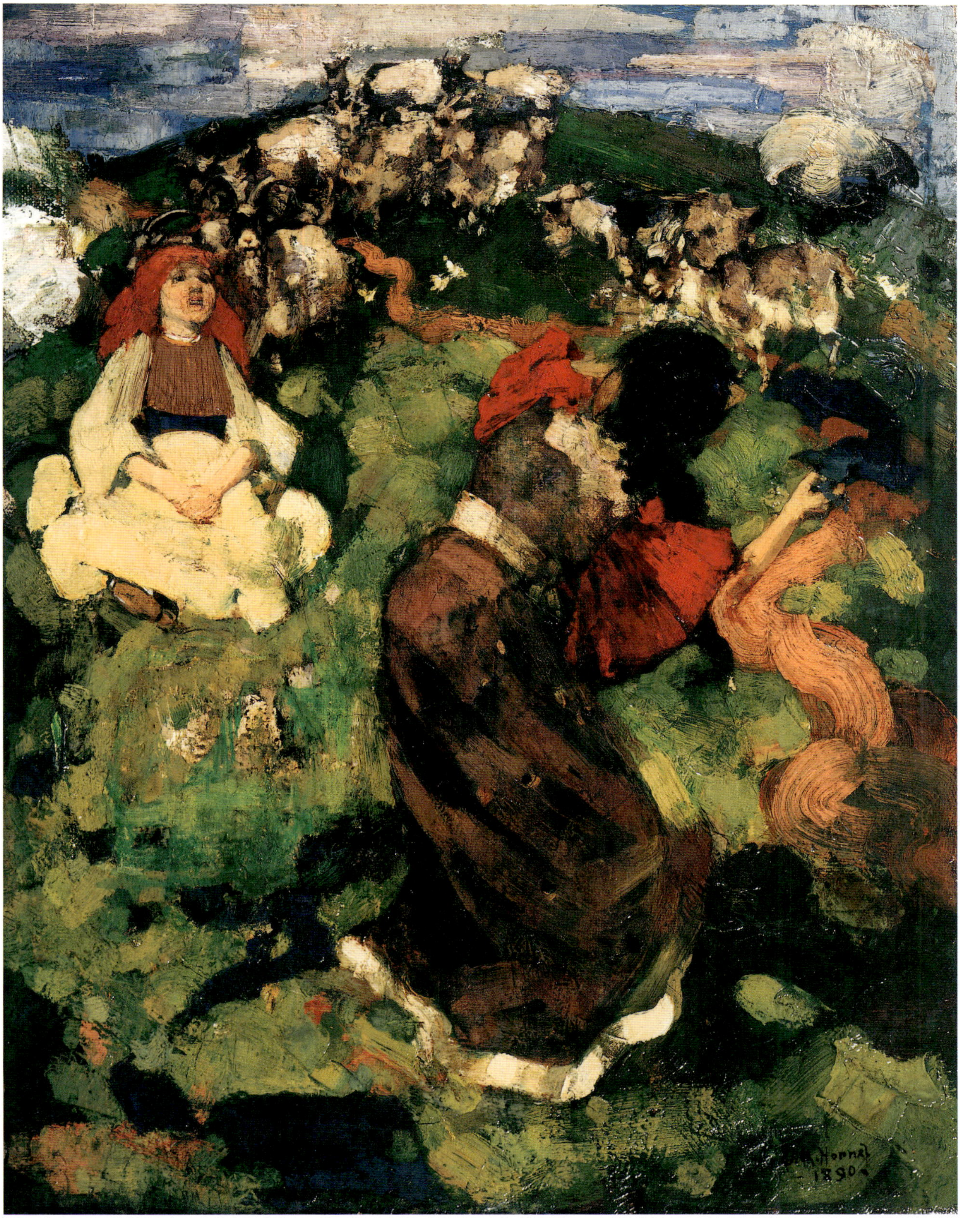

Fig.104
George Henry and Edward Atkinson Hornel,
The Druids Bringing In the Mistletoe, 1890, oil on canvas
Glasgow City Council (Museums)

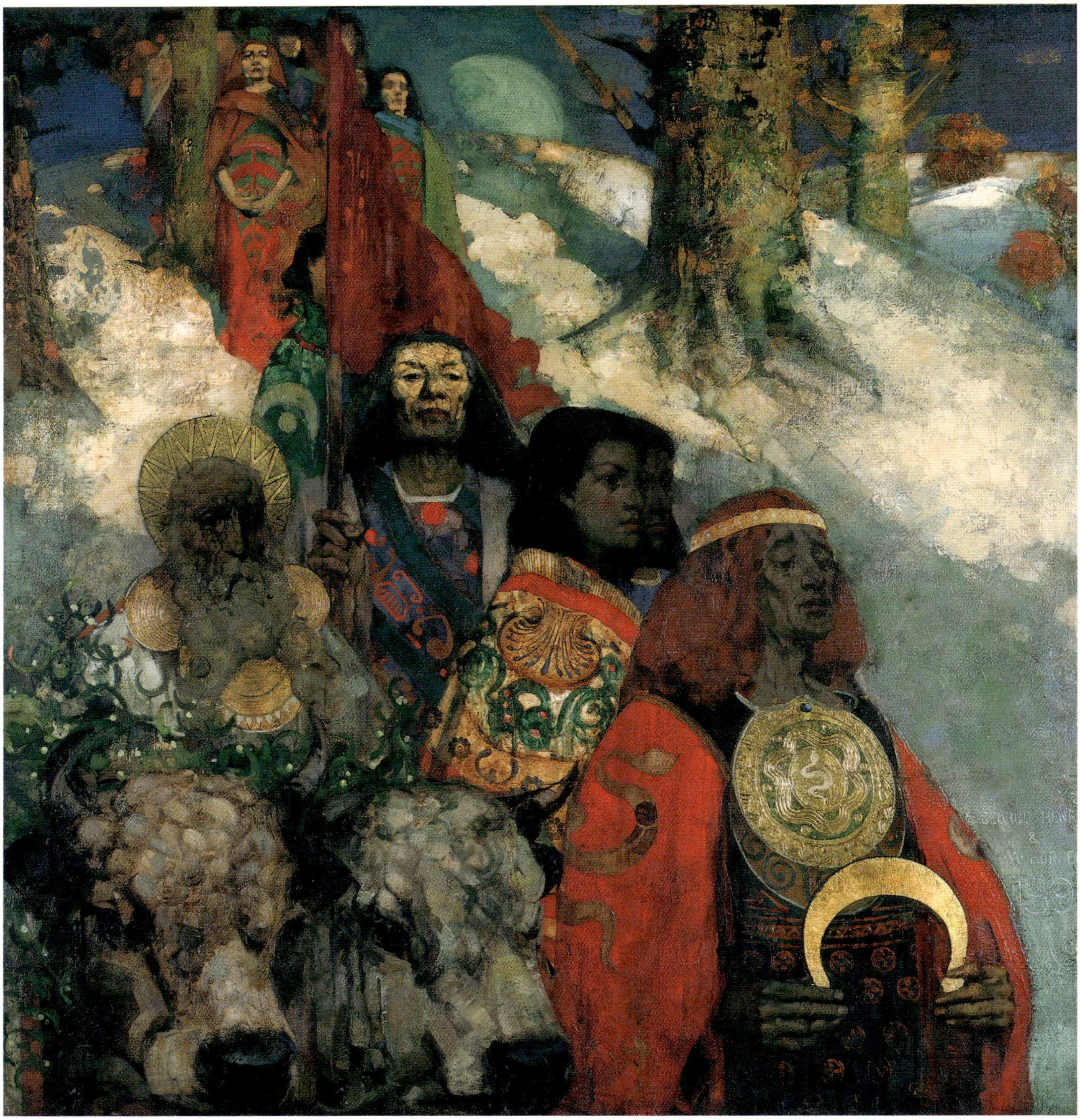

the painter and writer A.S. Hartrick (an early visitor to Co'path who later visited Gauguin in 1886), were important connections between colonies, both in Britain and France.[51] An influential figure for Laura Knight at Staithes around 1900, Mackie had himself painted a view of *The Crofts, Kirkcudbright* (fig.105) from an almost identical position as Hornel, but in late autumn rather than summer and with a richer, more impasted surface. In 1891–92 Mackie travelled in Brittany, where he encountered painters of the Pont-Aven group, Vuillard and Paul Serusier, and later also visited Gauguin in Paris, newly returned from Tahiti.[52] As Harper por-

Fig.105
Charles Hodge Mackie, *The Crofts, Kirkcudbright*, c.1890
oil on canvas, Private collection

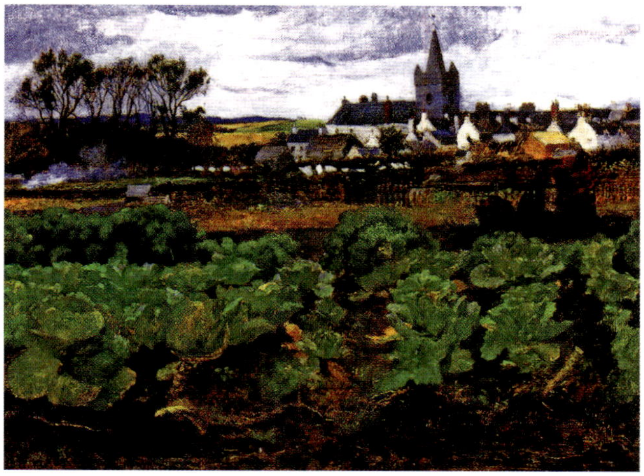

trayed Galloway so, typically, was Brittany described in both travel guides and artists' notes.[53] Pan-Celtic connections were frequently emphasized. Across Europe since the mid-nineteenth century the Celts were 'variously constructed as a figure of otherness ... irrational, magical, non-scientific, emotional' and often 'regarded as a healthy alternative to western rationality'.[54] Another element, then, in the rejection of Naturalism. Writing in the 1940s, Ian Finlay maintained this assertion of Scottishness – emphasis on colour and design and 'exclusion of representation in the obvious sense' was a enduring feature of northern and most especially Celtic people.[55] A degree of national and racial identity was to be inferred from formal handling as much as from subject matter.

In Hornel's painting a new formal language of high horizons, steep foregrounds and snaking arabesques was claimed for this re-discovered cultural identity in works like *Summer* (see page 21) which, to the reviewer D.S. MacColl, demonstrated an ability to 'make an image out of [nature] and ... bring in the element of strangeness ... Messrs Henry and Hornel give us pastorals from Ayrshire, but they are also pastorals from Wonderland'.[56] *Summer*, like *In the Orchard*, exemplifies what was to be a continual theme for Hornel, the depiction of Galloway girls entwined in magical, self-sufficient, natural idylls – blossoming orchards, gardens and woodlands, or in bright sunlight on the seashore at nearby Brighouse Bay. With intense colour and animated surfaces, the paintings seem to merge in and out of focus and possess a densely claustrophobic quality. For William Buchanan, Hornel transformed the pictures of little girls, as in Guthrie's *Schoolmates*, with their 'original, cool, static, tonal East coast setting and imbued them with a Gallovidian headiness to rush and turn through mellow landscapes'.[57] The eye now has difficulty in deciphering what is intended to be a world quite unlike our own. Particular formal influences continue over following years to be derived from Monticelli and from the Japanese print. In 1893 he and Henry, at Reid's expense, travelled to Japan, a country Hornel idealized as 'a lotus land', believing its people to possess (like the Celts) a special reverence for nature; 'Nature to them is symbolism itself'.[58] And to a degree the decorative, unworldly quality of Hornel's work allies him with the pan-Celticism of the circle around Geddes, Scots artists like John Duncan, Robert Brough and Mackie, in their fusion of French Symbolism, Art Nouveau and Celtic imagery.[59] Hornel's imagery also coincided with the literary representations of Galloway in Harper's 1889 anthology, with its inclusion of Cromek's eulogy of the local peasantry who have 'none of that vulgar broadness so disgusting in those sea coast towns which commerce has corrupted'. In Galloway's rustic pastoral, 'Imagery, drawn from the select resources of nature, will clothe itself in chaste and becoming language; the summer mind – the gloaming dew-fall among the loose locks of the lovely maiden – the flower tops bent with dew – the balmy smell of the woods ... afford fine poetic images'. Both artists and writers contributed to what might be perceived as the 'place myth' of Galloway.[60] The effects of repeated emphasis on a special sense of place emerges perhaps in the marked shift in subjects

Fig.106
William Stewart MacGeorge, *A Galloway Peat Moss*, 1888
The National Gallery of Scotland

Fig.107
William Mouncey, *In a Galloway Wood*, oil on canvas
The Stewartry Museum, Kirkcudbright
© Dumfries & Galloway Council

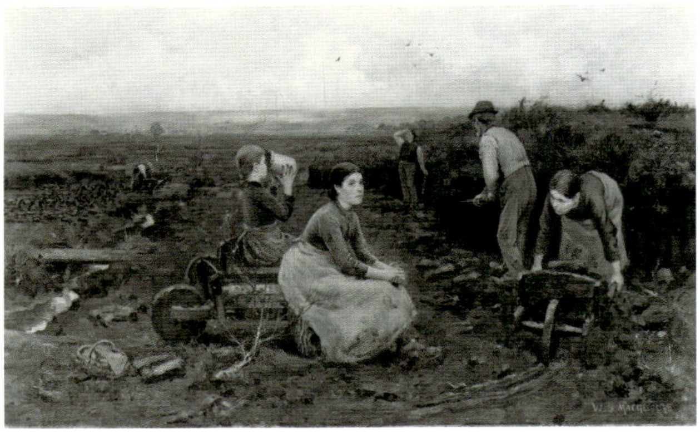

and handling between William MacGeorge's *A Galloway Peat Moss* of 1888 (see fig.106), with its stoical hard-labouring women in a flat and dreich landscape, to the frolicking children in his *A Host of Golden Daffodils*. In a similar vein, Mouncey's view of children *In a Galloway Wood* of the later 1890s (fig.107) shares something of the impasted quality of Monticelli and a similar sense of fusion in deep nature. After his death Harper eulogized his friend Mouncey as a true landscape painter, one who was 'cradled and brought up' in the scenery in which he delighted, 'the wooded hills of the Barrhill, the quaint old orchards of the Buckland Burn and the Millhouse, a strange old world aspect, surrounded by appropriate sylvan accessories'.[61] Along with these painterly and literary examples, local photographers like Robert McConchie and those compa-

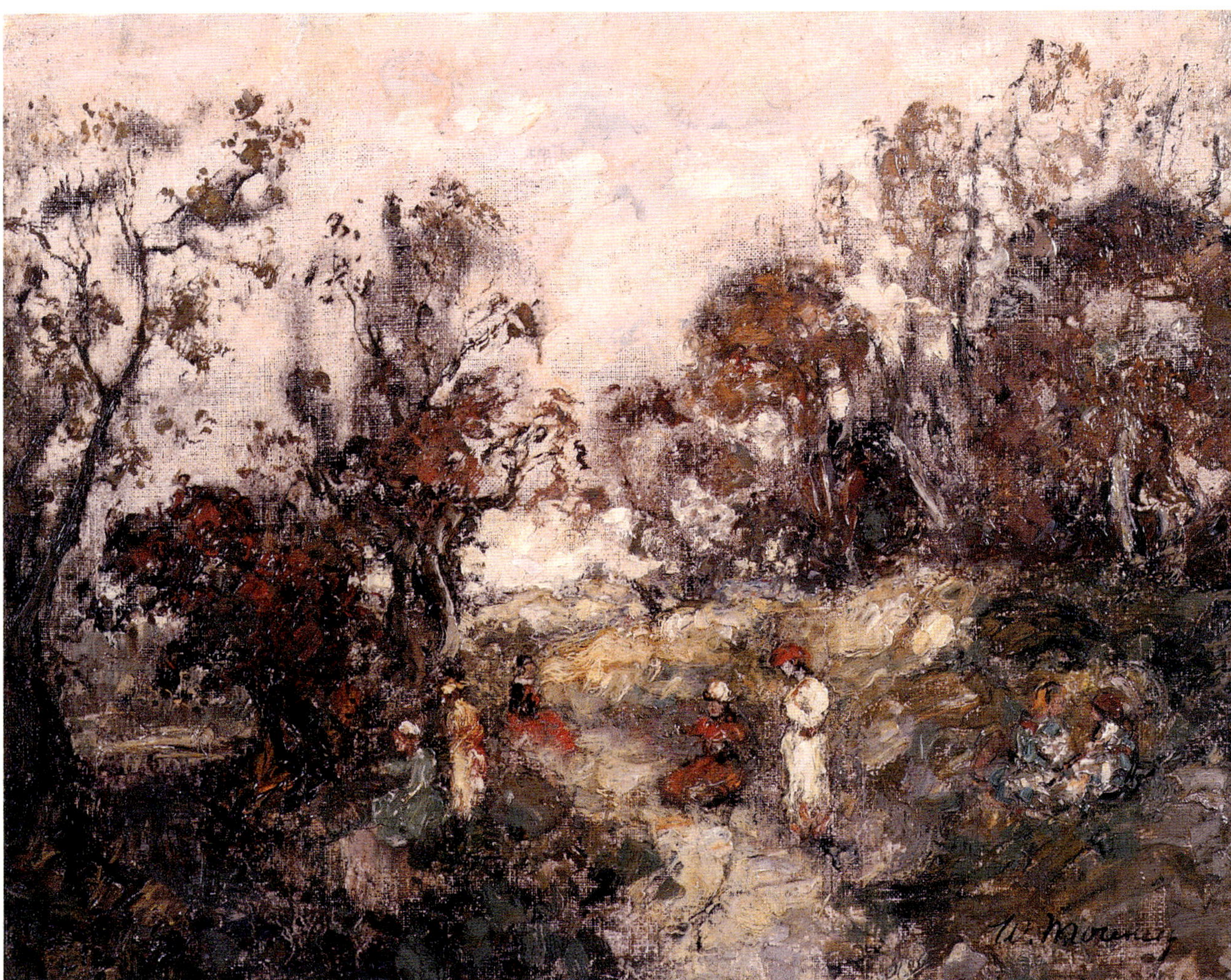

nies producing albums, postcards and mounted prints of local scenery all helped to perpetuate the place myth of Galloway.[62]

In the 1896 edition of his *Rambles in Galloway*, Harper acknowledged that the old superstitions of the region had now passed away, that 'Amulets have lost their influence'. But the region was saved from too great an onslaught of modernity by the absence of industry; lacking coal or limestone it was 'free from the noise and bustle of engines and the smoke furnace'. With the advent of coach and railway, Harper's hope was that potential visitors in 'search of health, the picturesque, or agreeable summer retirement' will delight in the 'hoary antiquity' of the Kirkcudbright from whence William Wallace set sail for France. But the ancient is mingled with the modern and Harper cut to the present day locality with its 'handsome and commodious railway station', its 'many handsome villas and cottages of recent erection, with flower pots in front'. He moved finally to his main focus, the cultivation of Kirkcudbright as a centre for artists, focusing on the 'studio of Mr E.A. Hornel' situated in the High Street, which:

> is well known in art circles. For some years there have emanated from it works of art so original in their conception and treatment as to colour, tones and values that Kirkcudbright, like Newlyn, was looked upon as having founded a new school of art. It was for long known as 'the Kirkcudbright School' but now it is alluded to and working in harmony with the Glasgow School … As an artists' haunt Kirkcudbright has now become a favourite resort, and Mr Hornel's studio is the general 'howff' of artists, local and cosmopolitan, visiting the district.[63]

Following the success of the 1895 exhibition of his and Henry's Japanese pictures at Reid's gallery and the continued market and appeal of his idyllic but increasingly sentimental scenes of local children cavorting in the woods, Hornel settled with his sister Tizzie to the cultivation of his antiquarian library, his collection of local history and to design of his garden, from 1901, at his newly-acquired Broughton House – a fine Georgian building situated on the High Street.[64] From that point Hornel played an important role in local activities and committees, but by degrees the focus of artistic life in the town shifted towards a newer generation, fostered essentially by the presence of illustrator Jessie Marion King and her husband the painter and designer, Ernest Archibald Taylor.

Both of these artists had studied under Francis Newbury at the Glasgow School of Art, and the linear and decorative 'Glasgow Style' is clearly evident in King's *Castle Gardens, Kirkcudbright* (fig.108). King had first visited Kirkcudbright in 1903 and, with Hornel's encouragement, the couple took 'Green Gate' off the High Street on their marriage in 1908, although they stayed in Paris until 1915, where King absorbed the exotic influences of the designer for the Russian Ballet, Leon Bakst.[65] On settling finally in Kirkcudbright, 'the most artistic town in the United Kingdom', King developed her skills in applied and decorative arts, in watercolour and in book illustration, resulting in her 1934 collection of drawings with the letterpress – *Kirkcudbright: A Royal Burgh* – of

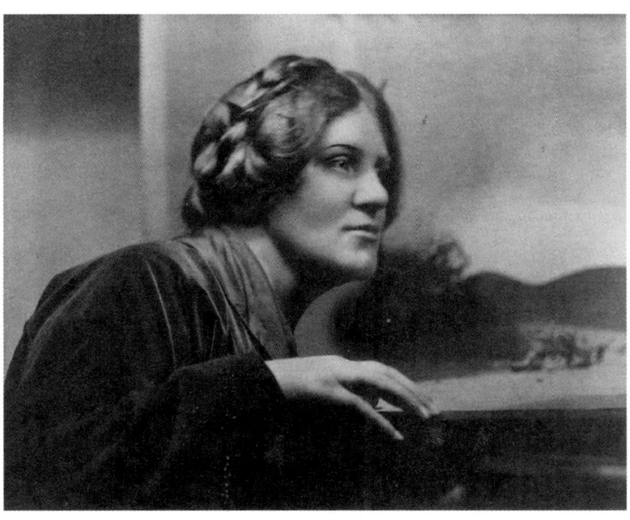

Jessie M King, c.1919, photograph
The Stewartry Museum, Kirkcudbright
© Dumfries & Galloway Council

Fig.108
Jessie Marion King, *Castle Gardens, Kirkcudbright*, watercolour
The Stewartry Museum, Kirkcudbright

Fig.109
Ernest Archibald Taylor, *Banks o' Dee*, oil on canvas,
The Stewartry Museum, Kirkcudbright

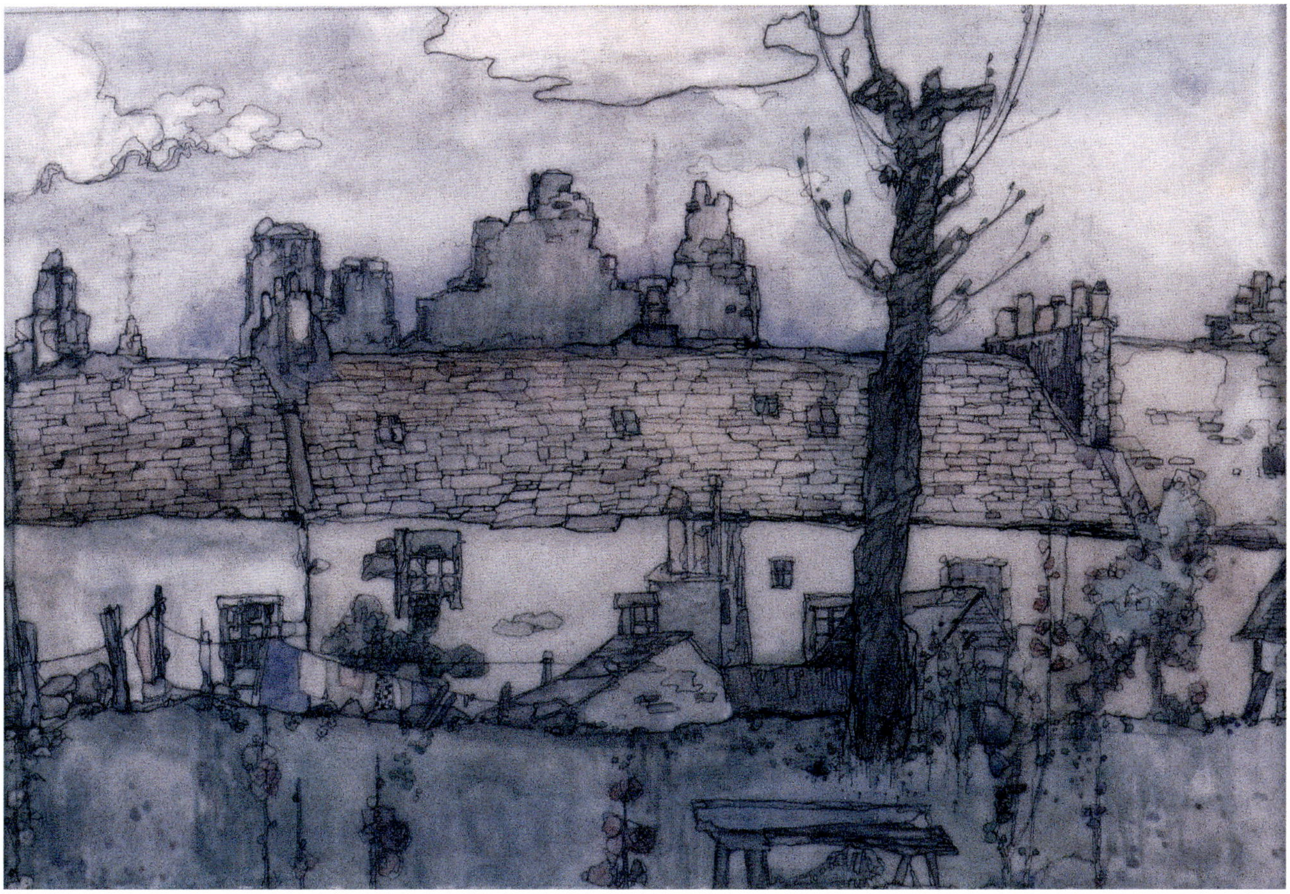

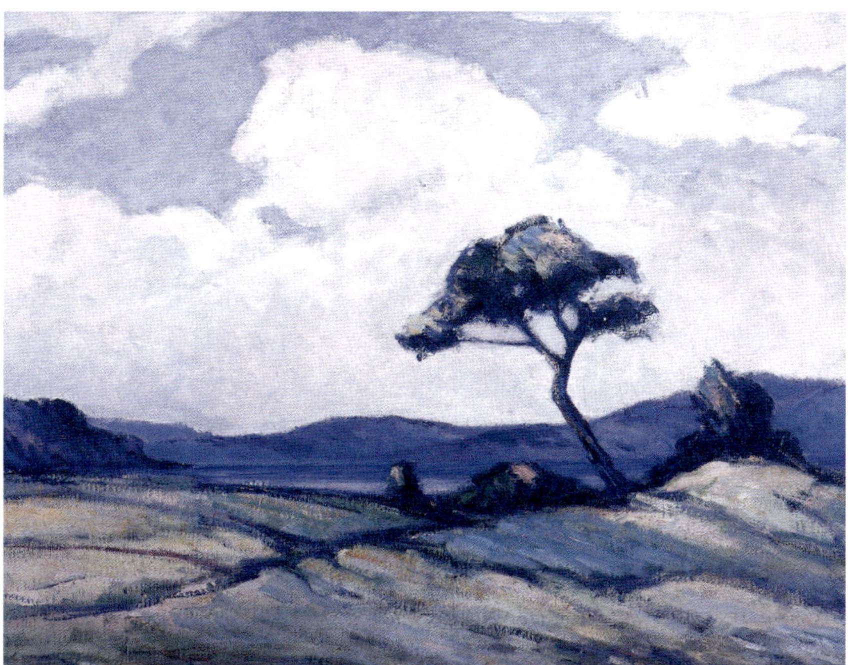

the picturesque old scenery of the town, its crosses, cobbled lanes and closes. Taylor, by contrast, increasingly revealed an engagement with rather more modernist forms of representation in paintings like *Banks o' Dee* (fig.109), where unnecessary detail is eliminated in favour of the underlying formal relations in the landscape.

The Kirkcudbright style increasingly shifts from the scenes of childhood revelry in the woodland and gardens of Hornel and Mouncey. As with *Spring Landscape, Galloway* (fig.110) by the

Fig.110
Charles Oppenheimer, *Spring Landscape, Galloway,* oil on canvas
The Stewartry Museum, Kirkcudbright © Dumfries & Galloway Council

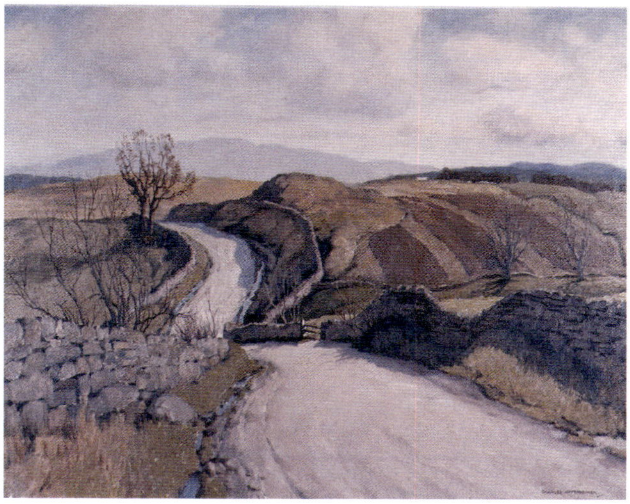

Charles Oppenheimer, photograph

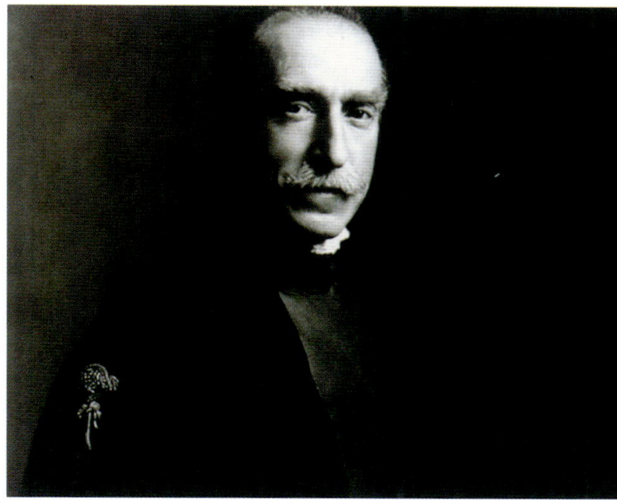

Manchester-born painter Charles Oppenheimer who settled in Kirkcudbright around 1912, the emphasis is on a more elemental and essential apprehension of form.[66] And this direction was confirmed from 1915 by the visits to the town of King and Taylor's friend, the painter Samuel Peploe. In yet another connection with French painting, Peploe brought his experience of painting in the Midi between 1910 and 1913 and his understanding of the rhythmic patterning and intense unmodulated colour of Fauvism to his depictions of the ancient Tolbooth (see fig.111).[67] In Peploe's vision, the surrounding woodlands – now free from the encumbrance of fairies and 'gleesome bairns' – equate rather to the elemental and harmonious Mediterranean landscapes of Cézanne, André Derain and Orthon Friesz and so suppress local, and even national, differences. To some extent then, the representation of Kirkcudbright had, by the inter-war years, already charted the aesthetic geographies of modern French art, from naturalist scenes of rural labour in the north, to the pleasurable, decorative and rhythmic universality of the south. This direction was confirmed in the work of later artist settlers in the town – of David Sassoon in particular and, to a degree, in that of E.A. Walton's daughter, Cecile.[68] And in the midst of these processes, the particular place myth of Kirkcudbright that had evolved amongst painters, writers and photographers from the mid 1880s, with its special emphasis on the idealized character of its native inhabitants, its unique folklore and its distinctive regional culture, all begin to lose their significance – a situation which that earlier generation had, perhaps, always envisaged.

Fig.111
Samuel J Peploe, *The Tolbooth, Kirkcudbright*, c.1915, oil on canvas
The Stewartry Museum, Kirkcudbright
© Dumfries & Galloway Council / Artist's Estate

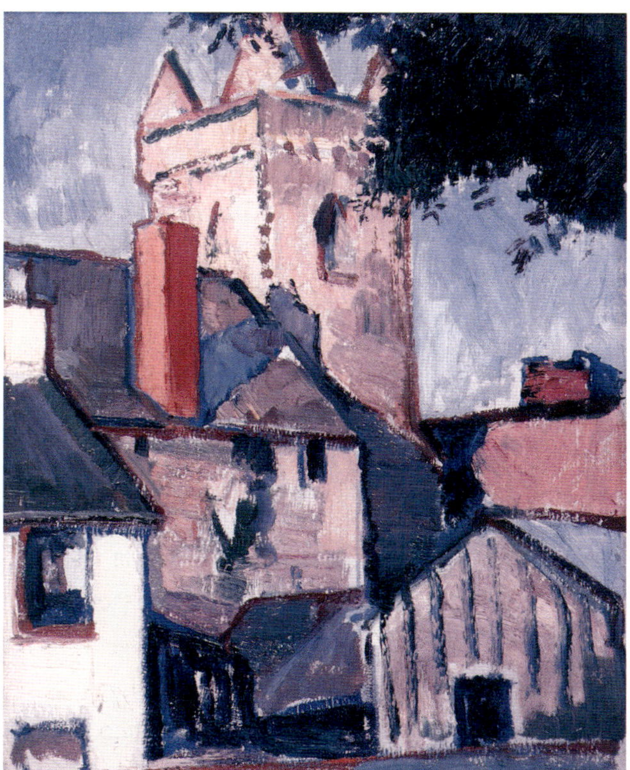

1. 'Art in the West Coast of Scotland', *The Scottish Art Review*, November 1888, pp.146-149.

2. The Glue Pot (or Pat) School included Glasgow painters like Alexander Davidson and Duncan McKellar who covered their paintings with brown megilp varnish which effectively gave them the patina of age.

3. The label 'The Glasgow Boys' refers to a larger group of artists than I discuss here and includes at various times, W.Y. McGregor, John Lavery, Alexander Roche, James Paterson and William Kennedy. I only discuss here those artists who painted at Cockburnspath and (briefly) at Kirkcudbright. For an excellent, authoritative study of the wider group see Roger Billcliffe, *The Glasgow Boys: The Glasgow School of Painting, 1875-1895*, John Murray, 1985.

4. Like John Pettie and W.Q. Orchardson, Reid worked in London. The first two artists produced costume pieces but Reid concentrated on rural subjects like *The Old Gardener*, 1878, reproduced in Billcliffe, ibid., p.114. Mackay, an artist born at Gifford in East Lothian in 1860, trained in Edinburgh and later painted simple rustic subjects in his native county, which may also have acted as an initial attraction to the area for Guthrie. Thanks to Laura Newton for discussion on this point.

5. Arthur Melville studied first in Edinburgh and then at the Académie Julian in Paris from 1878 alongside Robert Weir Allan, being joined by Thomas Millie Dow and Alexander Mann. As well as extended visits to Grez, Melville also travelled to Brittany and Normandy. He returned briefly to Edinburgh in 1880, before moving on to Egypt and then to Baghdad in 1882. Works from these visits were shown at the RA and RSA in 1883. For detailed study of the artist see Iain Gale, *Arthur Melville*, Atelier Books, 1996; see also Agnes Ethel Mackay, *Arthur Melville, Scottish Impressionist, 1855-1904*, F. Lewis, 1951.

6. For Crawhall see Adrian Bury, *Joseph Crawhall: The Man and the Artist*, Charles Skilton Ltd 1958. Crawhall was born in Morpeth, near Newcastle upon Tyne in 1861 and displayed early skill in sketching animals, a continually favourite subject. After Crowland, Crawhall studied briefly in Paris in the studio of Aimé Morot. Edward Arthur Walton was born in Renfrewshire in 1860. He attended Glasgow School of Art under Francis Newbery and the Dusseldorf Academy. Throughout the 1880s his work demonstrates a shift from the influence of the Barbizon painters to a more decorative, Whistlerian handling by the end of the decade. Born in Ayrshire in 1860, George Henry moved from his original career drawing wood-blocks for engravers and producing poster designs, to studies of figures (and/or cattle) in landscapes usually produced *en plein air* – as at Brig O'Turk, then studied for a period at Glasgow School of Art. See Percy Bate, 'The Work of George Henry, R.S.A: A Review and an Appreciation', *The Studio*, vol.31, February 1904, pp.3-12.

7. See Roger Billcliffe, *Guthrie and the Scottish Realists*, exhibition catalogue, Fine Art Society, 1981, np.

8. James Guthrie was born in Greenock in 1859 and received little formal art training. His earliest important work, *A Highland Funeral* (1882) bears comparison with Courbet's *Burial at Ornans* (1849-50). At the Glasgow Institute exhibition in 1883, Guthrie's painting, which was begun at Brig O'Turk, was hung alongside Bastien-Lepage's *The Beggar* and Millet's *Going to Work*.

9. Sir James L. Caw, *Sir James Guthrie, P.R.S.A, H.R.A, R.S.W, LLD*, Macmillan & Co., 1932, pp.21-2.

10. Ibid.

11. On the village and parish see www.cockburnspath.net: see also Eric Rankin, *Cockburnspath: A Documentary Social History of a Border Parish*, Edinburgh, 1981 and Sally Smith, *Cockburnspath; A History of a People and a Place*, Dunglass Mill Press, 1999.

12. For excellent discussion of common characteristics and impulses in the colony movement, see Nina Lübbren, *Rural Artists' Colonies in Europe, 1870-1910*, Manchester University Press, 2001. Newlyn is the only colony in the United Kingdom referred to by Lübbren both here and in her essay, '"Toilers of the Sea": Fisherfolk and the Geographies of Tourism in England, 1880-1900', in David Peters Corbett, Ysanne Holt and Fiona Russell, eds, *The Geographies of Englishness: Landscape and the National Past, 1880-1940*, Yale University Press, 2002.

13. The local population declined from 1191 in 1861 to 1112 in 1891 – see Co'path web-site, note 11.

14. A.G. Bradley, 'The Gateway of Scotland', London, 1912, p.276, quoted in John Shaw, 'Farming and Rural Life in East Lothian, 1850-1914', in *Pastoral Art in East Lothian*, exhibition catalogue, City Art Centre, Edinburgh, 1995-6.

15. *The Hind's Daughter* was shown at the Glasgow Institute in 1884 and acquired by the watercolour painter William Carlaw.

16. On these artists see especially Kenneth McConkey, *British Impressionism*, Phaidon, 1989.

17. See Gale, *Melville*.

18. I discuss these characteristics of Clausen and La Thangue's paintings of rural workers and the culture of ruralism in

'The Poetry of the Peasant' in *British Artists and the Modernist Landscape*, Ashgate Publishing, 2003.

19. For a discussion of Emerson's photography in this regard, see chapter 3 in John Taylor, *A Dream of England: Landscape, Photography and the Tourists' Imagination*, Manchester University Press, 1994.

20. Caw, *Guthrie*, p.22.

21. James Whitelaw Hamilton was the son of a successful Glasgow manufacturer living in Helensburgh. He painted with Crawhall, Guthrie and Walton in 1883 and was at Co'path with his sister Maggie, also a painter, in 1884. T. Corsan Morton, according to David Martin, was typically drawn to scenes of solitude and 'the quiet repose of nature': David Martin, *The Glasgow School of Painting*, George Bell & Son, 1897, p.49. He showed regularly at annual exhibitions in Munich.

22. Caw, *Guthrie*, p.24

23. Ibid.

24. Francis Newbery, Introduction to Martin, *The Glasgow School*, p.xxiii.

25. See William Hardie, *Scottish Painting, 1837 to the Present*, Studio Vista, 1976, p.83. McGregor, who showed at the RA and RSA from the late 1870s, visited Guthrie, Walton and Crawhall at Brig O'Turk in 1881. On McGregor, see Kenneth McConkey, *Peasantries: Nineteenth Century French and British Pictures of Peasants and Field Workers*, exhibition catalogue, Newcastle upon Tyne, 1981.

26. See *The Glasgow Boys*, exhibition catalogue, Scottish Arts Council, 1968, p.60.

27. Stott's painting from Sheffield City Art Gallery is reproduced in McConkey, *Peasantries*, p.57.

28. See Martin, *The Glasgow School*, pp.24-5.

29. *Quiz*, 2 December 1887, p.121.

30. For an interesting investigation of the connections between the French and Scottish colonies see *Kirkcudbright Pont-Aven: Artists in search of Inspiration*, exhibition catalogue, Tolbooth Art Centre, Kirkcudbright, June 2004.

31. See local website's account of this 'artists' town', www.kirkcudbright.co.uk

32. Priestman's painting and another version of the Gauld painting are held at the Stewartry Museum, Kirkcudbright.

33. I am indebted here to McKerrow's essay in Patrick Bourne ed., *Kirkcudbright, 100 Years of an Artists' Colony*, Atelier Books, 2000.

34. The artist lived in London but visited and finally retired to New Galloway after the Great War. As McKerrow also records, in 1886 five Faed artists, including James' son, James jnr., exhibited at the local Fine Arts Association and James jnr. went on to exhibit scenes of the Galloway countryside, of which 20 were reproduced in A&C Black's *Galloway Watercolours* in 1908.

35. I am grateful to David Devereux for discussion of the importance of the Faed brothers in establishing Kirkcudbright as a centre for artists. MacGeorge studied at Edinburgh School of Art in 1880 and, with Hornel, at Antwerp under Charles Verlat in 1883. On his return MacGeorge painted in the summer at Kirkcudbright and worked in Edinburgh in the winter. Blacklock also trained and then lived in Edinburgh but spent the last eight years of his life until 1903 living in Kirkcudbright. For more discussion see Vivian Macmillan's essay 'MacGeorge, Mouncey and Blacklock' in Bourne, *Kirkcudbright*.

36. The family emigrated briefly to Australia, returning to Kirkcudbright when Hornel was still a small child. For the best, detailed study of Hornel see Bill Smith, *Hornel: The Life & Work of Edward Atkinson Hornel*, Atelier Books, 1997.

37. The letters from Henry to Hornel cited here are held in the Hornel collection at Broughton House, Kirkcudbright.

38. *The Hudson River* is in Glasgow Art Gallery. The two other pictures shown in 1885 were *Twilight at Rye* and *Chrysanthemums*. For reference see Martin, *The Glasgow School*, pp.10-11. Dow was born in Fifeshire, trained in Gérôme's atelier in Paris in the late 1870s and exhibited consistently throughout his career at Munich exhibitions and at the Glasgow Institute. His *Spring*, exhibited there the following year, depicting a young girl and a lamb surrounded by blossoms would have appealed to Hornel still more, given the development of his own art.

39. Letter from Henry to Hornel, early 1886: Hornel collection, no.1.4.

40. *The Hedge-Cutter* is untraced, but a black and white illustration appears in Billcliffe, *The Glasgow Boys*, p.156. It was also illustrated in Bate, 'George Henry'.

41. *Quiz*, 23 September 1887.

42. Henry wrote to Hornel after a painting trip to Stirling with William Kennedy, a place he didn't 'quite tumble to' – of feeling 'clean off the boil', of 'changing methods and mode of expression' and of the problems of eternally 'getting a picture a cross between decoration and pictorial expression of an artistic motive'. Hornel collection, no.1.15.

43. In his letter Henry gives the photographer's name as Monyson.

44. On Reid see Frances Fowle, 'Alexander Reid in Context: Collecting and Dealing in Scotland in the Late 19th and Early 20th Centuries', unpublished PhD thesis, University of Edinburgh, 1993.

45. Martin, *The Glasgow School*, p.26.

46. Bate, 'George Henry', p.12

47. Malcolm McL Harper ed. and intro., *The Bards of Galloway; A Collection of the Poems, Songs, Ballads etc by Natives of Galloway*, Thomas Fraser, 1889, p.vi.

48. Hornel in fact was a member of both the local Field Naturalists and Antiquarian Society and a fellow of the Society of Antiquaries of Scotland.

49. John Morrison, 'Nationalism and Nationhood: Late Nineteenth Century Painting in Scotland', in M. Faco and S.L. Hirsch eds., *Art, Culture and National Identity in Fin de Siècle Europe*, Cambridge University Press, 2003, pp.195-8.

50. For informed discussion of *The Druids*, see also Lindsay Errington, 'Celtic elements in Scottish art at the turn of the century', in John Christian, ed., *The Last Romantics, the Romantic Tradition in British Art from Burne Jones to Stanley Spencer*, Barbican Art Gallery and Lund Humphries, 1989.

51. William Hardie points out that Hartrick, who had painted a picture of Gauguin's house at Pont-Aven in 1886, commented also on Henry's *A Galloway Landscape*: 'I have seen the spot where it was painted, a very ordinary field with a hill in it; but Henry introduced a blue burn, painted with a palette knife, around it; then put a stain over all and it became an object of derision for the man in the street as well as for the Glue Pot School'; (*Scottish Painting*, p.98). See also A.S. Hartrick, *A Painter's Pilgrimage through Fifty Years*, Cambridge University Press, 1939. Hartrick notes a visit to Cockburnspath with his stepfather and being introduced to Guthrie. The Stewartry Museum possesses an interesting, undated Hartrick painting, *Kirkin' of the Incorporated Trades of Kirkcudbright*, which depicts Hornel, Mouncey and MacGeorge.

52. See also essays by Frances Fowle and Belinda Thompson in Fowle and Thompson eds., *Patrick Geddes: The French Connection*, White Cockade Publishing, 2004.

53. For instance, in *The Studio* magazine's 1895 account of 'Concarneau as a Sketching Ground' – a place where 'Druidical remains abound and help to keep alive the old fables and traditions so dear to this poetic race', vol.24, 1895, p.180.

54. Malcolm Chapman, *The Celts: The Construction of a Myth*, Macmillan Press, 1992, p.228.

55. Ian Finlay, *Art in Scotland*, Oxford University Press, 1948, p.132.

56. D.S. MacColl, *The Spectator*, 22 October 1892.

57. See Buchanan's essay in Scottish Arts Council, *Glasgow Boys*, p.50.

58. See Hornel's lecture, 'Japan', delivered at the Corporation Art Galleries, Glasgow, 9 February 1895. Transcript in collection at Broughton House.

59. Hornel produced a line drawing *Madame Chrysanthème* for the second issue of Geddes' short-lived journal, *The Evergreen* in 1895. On the visual characteristics of pan-Celticism see Fowle and Thompson, *Patrick Geddes*.

60. For discussion of place myths, see Rob Shields, *Places on the Margin: Alternative Geographies of Modernity*, Routledge, 1991.

61. An obituary to Mouncey written by Harper which appeared in *The Gallovidian* in 1904. Reprinted at www.old-kirkcudbright.co.uk

62. An exhibition of their collection of these photographs was held at the Stewartry Museum in late 2004.

63. Malcolm Mc L.Harper, *Rambles in Galloway* [1876], Thomas Fraser, 2nd ed. 1896, pp.80-103.

64. I consider aspects of Hornel's art and the design of his garden in an article '"The Veriest Poem of Art in Nature": E.A. Hornel's Japanese Garden in the Scottish Borders', *Tate Papers* online at www.tate.org.uk/research/tateresearch/tatepapers/

65. For a fuller account of their work at Kirkcudbright, see Patrick Bourne's own essay in *Kirkcudbright*. The quotation here is from an undated press clipping cited in Judy Burkhauser, ed., *Glasgow Girls: Women in Art and Design 1880-1920*, Canongate, 1990, p.135. As Burkhauser comments, Green Gate Close became an important centre for women artists with King as the central inspiration.

66. Oppenheimer studied under Walter Crane at Manchester School of Art and then worked for a time in Italy.

67. Peploe trained in the 1890s in Edinburgh and for a brief period at the Académie Julian. With his friend J.D. Fergusson, the artist painted in France on the Channel coast between 1904 and 1906 and again in Paris. In this period his style shifts from a Whistlerian to a more rhythmic, intensely coloured and thickly applied handling by the time the artist arrived in the Midi at Cassis in 1913 – two years before his first visit to Kirkcudbright. For a detailed study see Guy Peploe, *S.J. Peploe 1871-1935*, Edinburgh, 2000.

68. Cecile Walton stayed in Kirkcudbright for much of the Great War and settled there again in 1948. David Sassoon had studied at the Slade and lived for period in Berlin and Paris. He settled in Kirkcudbright in 1926.

A Selected List of Artists working at the Colonies

Newlyn

Artist	**Dates**	**Date at colony**
BATEMAN Benjamin Arthur	1847–1894	1885–94
BODILLY Francis (Frank)	1860–1926	1884
BOURDILLON Frank Wright	1851–1924	1885, 1887–92
BRAMLEY Frank	1857–1915	1884, 1885–95
BROWN Frederick	1851–1941	1886
BRUFORD Marjorie ('Midge')	1902–1958	??
CRAFT Percy Robert	1856–1934	1884, 1885–?
DA COSTA John	1866–1931	late 1880s
DETMOLD Henry Edward	1854–1924	1885
DOBSON Frank	1886–1963	1904–6, 1913–15, 1919–20
EVANS Frederick James McNamara	1859–1929	late 1880s
FLETCHER William Teulon Blandford	1858–1936	1884–85
FORBES Elizabeth Adela (née Armstrong)	1859–1912	1885–1912
FORBES Stanhope Alexander	1857–1947	1884–1947
FORTESCUE William Banks	1850–1924	1885
GARSTIN Alethea	1894–1978	lifetime
GARSTIN Norman	1847–1926	1886–1926
GOTCH Caroline (née Yates)	1854–1945	1879, 81, 84, 86, 87–91
GOTCH Thomas Cooper	1854–1931	1879, 81, 84, 86, 87–91, visiting
HALL Frederick	1860–1948	1884, 1886–1897
HARRIS Edwin	1855–1906	1881, 1882, 1883–95
HARVEY Harold Charles	1874–1941	lifetime
HARVEY Gertrude (née Bodinar)	1886–1966	lifetime
HAINES Arthur Lett	1894–1978	1919–20, visits in 1920s
HEATH Frank Gascoigne	1873–1936	1908–1910
HUGHES Eleanor (née Waymouth)	1882–1959	1907–10
HUGHES Robert Morson	1873–1953	1909–10
HYNES Gladys	1888–1958	1906–19
KNIGHT Harold	1874–1961	1907
KNIGHT Laura (née Johnson)	1877–1972	1907
LANGLEY Walter	1852–1922	1880, 81, 82–86, 1887–22
MACKENZIE John Drew	1861–1918	1888–?
MILLARD Frederick	1857–1937	1884

MORRIS Cedric	1889–1982	1919–20, visits in 1920s
MUNNINGS Alfred James	1878–1959	visits c.1908–1916
PROCTER Doris ('Dod', née Shaw)	1892–1972	1907–10, 1911–72
PROCTER Ernest	1886–1935	1906–10, 1911–12, 1919–1935
RHEAM Henry Meynell	1859–1920	late 1880s
RICHARDS Frank	1863–1935	late 1880s
SIMPSON Charles	1885–1971	1905–10, 1911–c.1916
SIMPSON Ruth (née Alison)	1889–1964	1911/12–c.16
SUTHERS Leghe (John Lees)	1855–1924	1883, 1886–7
SYKES Dorcie	1908–1998	??
TAYLER Albert Chevallier	1862–1925	1884–85, 86–87, 88–95
TODD Ralph	1856–1932	1883–early 1890s
TUKE Henry Scott	1858–1929	1879, 1883, 1884, visiting
WAINWRIGHT William John	1855–1931	1884
WELLS John	1907–2000	1928, 1945–2000

Lamorna

Artist	**Dates**	**Date at colony**
BARLOW John Noble	1861–1917	1890s–1917
BIRCH Samuel John Lamorna	1869–1955	1892–1955
BRUFORD Marjorie Frances [Midge]	1902–1958	1930s–1950
COLQUHOUN Ithell	1906–1988	visits from 1940
COX Garstin	1892–1933	pre–1919
FAWKES Madeline [Madge]	c1885–c1935	1909–1919
FORBES Elizabeth Adela	1859–1912	1907–1910
FORBES Stanhope Alexander	1857–1947	visits to 1940
GARDINER Stanley Horace	1888–1952	1923–52
GILLICK Ernest George	1874–1951	visits from 1910
GLUCKSTEIN Hannah [Gluck]	1895–1978	1915–1937, visits to 1975
GOTCH Thomas Cooper	1854–1931	visits to c1914
HARVEY Harold	1874–1941	visits to 1930s
HEATH Frank Gascoigne	1873–1936	1910–1936
HUGHES Eleanor Hughes	1882–1959	1910–59
HUGHES Robert Morson	1873–1953	1910–53
KERR Elizabeth Lamorna [Mornie]	1904–1990	1920s–1990
KNIGHT Harold	1874–1961	resident 1907–1918, visits from 1920s
KNIGHT Laura	1877–1970	resident 1907–1918, visits from 1920s
LEADER Benjamin Eastlake	1889–1916	from 1911
MUNNINGS Alfred James	1879–1959	1912–1916
NAPER Charles	1882–1968	1910–1968

NAPER Ella	1886–1972	1910–1968
NEWTON Algernon	1880–1968	1908–1920
NIXON Job	1891–1938	1931–1933
PROCTER Doris [Dod]	1892–1972	1908–1910
RHEAM Henry Meynell	1859–1920	1900–1914
ROBINSON Frederick Cayley	1906–1920	??
SIMPSON Charles Walter	1889–1964	1916
SYKES John Gutteridge	1866–1941	1900–1915
TANNER Arthur Jacob	1857–1916	1902–1915
THOMPSON Charles		1903–1916
THOMPSON Heather		1903–1916
TUKE Henry Scott	1858–1929	visits 1890s–1908
WEATHERBY Richard Copeland	1881–1953	1912–1948
WESTRUP Ethel Kate	1885–c1940	from 1910
WOLSELEY Garnet Ruskin	1884–1967	1909–1914

St. Ives

Artist	**Dates**	**Date at colony**
ARMSTRONG Elizabeth	1859–1912	1887
BRADSHAW George Fagan	1887–1961	c.1921
BLOMEFIELD Eardley W	exh.1880–1900	1889
BROMLEY John Mallard	1858–1939	??
BROWN John Alfred Arnesby	1866–1955	1891
CARR Emily	1871–1945	Studied under Olsson
CHADWICK Frank	1850–1943	1894
DAY William Cave	1862–1924	1919–1924
DEACON Allan	exh.1895–1914	by 1889–c.1921
DETMOLD Henry E	1854–1924	??
DOW Thomas Millie	1848–1919	1895–1919
DYER Lowell	1856–1939	1889–1939
EADIE William	exh 1880–1894	1885
FOWERAKER A Moulton	1873–1942	1901–1918
FROST Terry	1915–2003	1946, 1957–2003
FULLER Leonard	1891–1973	1938–1973
GRIER Louis	1864–1920	1884–1920
GOTCH Thomas Cooper	1854–1931	visiting 1880s
HARRISON Alexander	1853–1930	1889
HARTLEY Alfred	1855–1933	1923–33
HAYWARD Arthur	1889–c.1950	by 1924–?
HEPWORTH Barbara	1903–1975	1939–75

HIND Charles Lewis	1862–1927	??
HODGKINS Frances	1870–1947	1914–c.1919
KORTRIGHT Guy	b.1877, exh.1901–1939	??
LANYON W Herbert	1865–1937	??
LANYON Peter	1918–1964	lifetime
LEACH Bernard	1887–1979	1920–79
LINDNER Moffatt	1852–1949	c.1905; 1918–23; 1930–?
MARRIOTT Charles	1869–1957	1901–1910
MOTTRAM Charles	exh.1880–1919	??
NICHOLSON Ben	1894–1982	??
NIXON Job	1891–1938	1934–35
OLSSON Julius	1864–1942	c.1889–1912
PARK John Anthony	1878–1962	1902–1957
ROBINSON Henry Harewood	exh 1884–1904	1885–1904
SCHJERFBECK Helene	1862–1946	1887
SICKERT Bernard	1863–1932	??
SIMMONS Edward E	1852–1931	1885–1891
SIMPSON Charles W	1889–1964	1916–24, 1931–64
SMART Robert Borlase	1881–1947	1913; 1918–47
STOKES Adrian	1854–1935	c.1886–?
STOKES Marianne	1855–1927	c.1886–?
STOKES Alan Gardner Folliott	1875–1939	by 1889
TALMAGE Algernon	1871–1939	1893–1907
TITCOMB John Henry	1862–1952	??
TITCOMB William H.Y.	1858–1930	1887–1930
WALLIS Alfred	1855–1942	fl.1925–42
WILK Maria	1853–1928	1887
ZORN Anders	1860–1920	1887–8

Walberswick

Artist	**Dates**	**Date at colony**
ARMSTRONG Elizabeth	1859–1912	mid–late 1880s
AUMONIER James	1832–1911	mid 1870s –80s
BENHAM Thomas	1856–1922	late 1880s
BLACKLOCK William Kay	1872–1922	1908–17
BONE Muirhead	1876–1953	early 1900s
BRANGWYN Frank	1867–1956	1890
BROWN Frederick	1851–1941	mid 1880s
BURKE Augustus	1838–1891	1883
CRANE Walter	1845–1915	late 1880s

CRITALL W F	1887–1956	lifetime
DALGLIESH Theodore	1855–1941	c.1880
DAVIDSON Thomas	1842–1919	early 1900s
DAVIDSON Allan	1873–1932	mid 1920s on
EMMANUEL Frank	1865–1948	c.1890
EVERSHED Arthur	1836–1919	c.1880
FLETCHER William Blandford	1858–1936	1884–85
GRACE James	1851–1908	mid 1870s
GREIFFENHAGEN Maurice	1862–1931	c.1905
GWYNNE–JONES Allen	1892–1983	1912–14
HALL Frederick	1860–1948	1884–5
HALL Mildred	1881–1955	early 1900s–1930s
HILL Nathaniel	1861–1934	1884–85
HOEBER Arthur	1854–1915	mid 1880s
HOPKINS Arthur	1848–1930	early 1880s
HORSLEY Charles	1848–1921	1907–16
KENNINGTON Eric	1888–1960	visiting
KINSLEY Alfred	1852–1945	1890s
KIRKPATRICK Ida	1866–1950	late 1890s–c.1920
KIRKPATRICK Ethel	1869–1966	late 1890s–c.1920
LANGLEY Walter	1852–1922	c.1891–2
LLEWELLYN William	1858–1941	1886 +
LUDBY Max	1858–1943	1884–85
MACKINTOSH Charles Rennie	1868–1928	1897, 1911, 1914–15
MACKINTOSH Margaret Mcdonald	1865–1933	1914–15
MANN Alexander	1853–1908	1890, 1902, 1903
MELVILLE Arthur	1855–1904	1890
METCALF Willard	1853–1925	1885
MOORE Henry	1831–1895	1881, 1884
MOORE John	1821–1902	early 1880s
NEWBERY Francis	1855–1946	1880s; late 1890s–1915
NEWBERY Jessie	1864–1948	1880s; late 1890s–1915
OSBORNE Walter	1859–1903	1884–85
OSS Tom van	1901–1941	??
PRIESTMAN Bertram	1868–1951	1914 on
RENDALL Arthur	1861–1936	1891 on
ROWE Tom Trythall	1856–1940	mid 1880s
SAUTER Georg	1866–1937	1906
SEAGO Edward	1910–1974	??
SENIOR Mark	1864–1927	1906
SHORT Frank	1857–1945	1890
SICKERT Walter	1860–1942	early 1890s

SOUTHALL Joseph	1861–1944	c.1907–27
SPENLOVE Frank Spenlove	1868–1933	??
STANNARD Henry J Sylvester	1870–1951	after 1900
STANNARD Lilian	1877–1944	after 1900
STARR Sidney	1857–1925	1890
STEER Philip Wilson	1860–1942	1884–89; 1906
STOTT Edward	1859–1918	1884
SWINSTEAD George Hillyard	1860–1926	1890s
TURNER John Doman	1873–1938	??
WALTON Edward Arthur	1860–1922	early 1900s
YGLESIAS Vincent	1845–1911	late 1880s

Staithes

Artist	Dates	Date at colony
ATKINSON John	1863–1924	1900–1914
AUMONIER James	1832–1911	1870–80s
BAGSHAWE Joseph R	1870–1909	1890s–1909
BOOTH James W	1867–1953	c.1900–?
BOWEN Owen	1873–1967	1898–1908
BRYMNER William	1855–1925	1883–84
CARMICHAEL John Wilson	1799–1868	1850s
CRAWSHAW Lionel	1864–1949	c.1903–c.1930
DADE Ernest	1864–1935	late 1880s–1913
ERICHSEN Nelly	fl.1883–1900	c.1885–86
FLETCHER William T Blandford	1858–1936	1894–95
FOSTER William Gilbert	1855–1906	1890–1906
FRIEDENSON Arthur	1872–1955	c.1896–1909
HEDLEY Ralph	1848–1913	mid 1880s–c.1900
HEMY Thomas M	1852–1937	c.1884–86
HILL Roland Henry	1873–1952	late 1890s–1952
HOPWOOD Henry Silkstone	1860–1914	c.1893–1914
HOYLAND Hannah (née Mayor)	1871–1947	late 1890s–1902
INGALL John Spence	1850–1936	c.1900–1936
JACKSON Frederick William	1859–1918	c.1883–1918
JELLEY J V	fl.1878–1942	1884
JOBLING Robert	1841–1923	c.1893–1920s
KNIGHT J W B	1843–1908	1870s–80s
KNIGHT Laura (née Johnson)	1877–1970	1897, 1899–1907
KNIGHT Harold	1874–1961	1897, 1898–1907
LLEWELLYN William	1858–1941	late 1880s

MACKIE Charles Hodge	1862–1920	c.1899–1900s
MANN Harrington	1864–1937	mid 1880s–c.1900
MASON Frank H.A.	1875–1965	c.1900–?
MAYOR William Frederick	1866–1916	1897–1902
OPPENHEIMER Charles	1875–1961	after 1900–1909
REID John Robertson	1851–1925	c.1912–13
RICHARDSON Frederick S	1855–1934	1890s on
RIGG Ernest	1868–1947	1896, 1904, 1907
SENIOR Mark	1862–1927	early 1880s–1927
SHORT Frank	1857–1945	late 1880s
STEVENS Albert George	1863–1925	c.1903–1925
TAYLOR Ernest Archibald	1874–1952	1906–08, visiting until 1915/16
TEASDALE Percy Morton	1870–1961	c.1905
TERRY Joseph Alfred	1872–1939	c.1906–1939
THOMPSON Isa (Jobling)	1851–1926	c.1890–1920s
TOLLMACHE Duff Randolph	1859–1936	1883–84
WATSON James	1851–1936	c.1885–1930s
WILLIAMS John Terrick	1860–1937	1889–90
WRIGHT John	1857–1933	c.1904
YGLESIAS Vincent	1845–1911	late 1880s–1911

Cullercoats

Artist	Dates	Date at colony
ATKINSON John	1863–1924	after 1900
BOYCE W T N	1857–1911	1890s
BROWNLOW Stephen	1828–1896	1866–1896
CAMPBELL John Hodgson	1855–1927	1880s–90s
CHAMBERS John	1852–1928	1880s–90s
CHARLTON John	1849–1917	visiting 1880s–1917
ELLIOTT Robinson	1814–1894	1850s–70s
EMMERSON Henry Hetherington	1831–1895	1866–1895
ERRINGTON Isabella	1806–1890	1840s–70s
GEORGE Charles	1872–1937	c.1890–1937
GILROY John William	1868–1944	1890s–1940
HEDLEY Ralph	1850–1913	visiting from 1880s
HEMY Bernard B	1845–1913	1880s–90s
HEMY Thomas M	1852–1937	early 1880s
HOLL Frank	1845–1888	1870
HOMER Winslow	1836–1910	1881–82
HORTON George Edward	1859–1950	early 1880s–c.1920

HUTTON Thomas Swift	fl1965–1935	late 1880s–90s
JOBLING Isa (née Thompson)	1851–1926	by 1884–mid 1920s
JOBLING Robert	1841–1923	c.1880–1923
MACKLIN Thomas Eyre	1963–1943	early 1880s, 1890s–1940s
MARSH Arthur Hardwick	1842–1909	1869–1909
MITCHELL J Edgar	1871–1922	1908–?
ORCHARDSON William Quiller	1831–1910	1869–70
OGILVIE Frank S	1856–1936	1880s–90s
OGILVIE Fred D	1851–1921	early 1880s
RAINBIRD Victor Noble	1889–1936	c.1910–1936
SLATER John Falconer	1857–1937	c.1882–1937
SPENCE Charles J	1848–1905	1870s–1905
STICKS Andrew James	b.1855	late 1880s on
SURTEES John	1819–1915	1850s on
WASSERMAN John Conrad	1846–1884	mid 1870s–early 80s
WATSON James	1851–1936	1880s
WATSON John Dawson	1832–1892	1869, through 1870s
WATSON Robert	1815–1885	1830s–40s, 1860s
WATSON Thomas J	1847–1912	1869–early 1870s
WAY William Cosens	1833–1905	1870s–90s
WOOD Stanley A	1902–1934	1920s–30s

Cockburnspath

Artist	**Dates**	**Date at colony**
CRAWHALL Joseph	1861–1913	1883–85
GUTHRIE James	1859–1930	1883–86
HAMILTON James Whitelaw	1860–1932	1884–85
HARTRICK A S	1864–1950	1883?
HENRY George	1858–1943	1883–86
MACKAY William Darling	1844–1923	1870s–80s
MELVILLE Arthur	1855–1904	1884
MORTON T Corsan	1859–1928	1884–85
NAIRN James	1859–1904	1884
WALTON Edward Arthur	1860–1922	1883–85

Kirkcudbright

Artist	Dates	Date at colony
BLACKLOCK Thomas Bromley	1863–1903	1886, 1895–1903
CLARKE William Hanna	1882–1924	1916–24
DOW Thomas Millie	1848–1919	c.1886
FAED John	1819–1902	lifelong
FAED James	1822–1912	lifelong, intermittently
FAED Thomas	1826–1900	lifelong, intermittently
GAULD David	1865–1936	1920s
GUTHRIE James	1859–1930	1885, 86, 87
HAMILTON James Whitelaw	1860–1932	late 1880s–1911
HARTRICK A S	1864–1950	visiting 1890s
HENRY George	1858–1943	visiting 1885–mid 1890s
HORNEL Edward Atkinson	1864–1933	1885–1933
JOHNSTONE Helen S	1888–1931	1917–31
KING Jessie Marion	1875–1949	1903, 1915–49
MACGEORGE William Stewart	1861–1931	c.1885
MACKIE Charles Hodge	1862–1920	late 1880s–early 1890s
MACNICOL Bessie	1869–1904	1896, 1897
MORTON T Corsan	1859–1928	1885, 86
MOUNCEY William	1852–1901	lifelong
OPPENHEIMER Charles	1875–1961	1908–1961
PEPLOE Samuel	1871–1935	c.1914, 1917, 1919–1930s
PRIESTMAN Bertram	1868–1951	??
ROBSON William	1868–1952	1904–14, 1924–52
SASSOON David	1888–1978	c.1925
SPENCE Harry	1860–1928	c.1895–1900
STEVENSON R A M	1854–1952	c.1886, 1932–51
TAYLOR Ernest Archibald	1874–1951	1915–51
WALTON Cecile	1891–1956	1817–18, 1948–56

Suggested further reading

ADAMS, S. *The Barbizon School and the Origins of Impressionism*, Phaidon, 1994

ANON, *F. W. Jackson 1859–1918*, exhibition catalogue, Rochdale Art Gallery, 1978

ANON, *Kirkcudbright Pont-Aven: Artists in Search of Inspiration*, exhibition catalogue, Tolbooth Art Centre, Kirkcudbright, 2004

ANON, *Mark Senior, 1862–1927*, exhibition catalogue, Elizabethan Exhibition Gallery, Wakefield, 1983

BEDNAR, G. *Every Corner was a Picture*, Truran Books, 2nd ed., 2004

BERLIN, S *Alfred Wallis*, Poetry London/Nicholson & Watson, 1949; new edition, Sansom & Company, 2000

BILLCLIFFE, R. *Guthrie and the Scottish Realists*, exhibition catalogue, Fine Art Society, 1981

BILLCLIFFE, R. *The Glasgow Boys*, John Murray, 1985

BIRCH, Mrs Lionel *Stanhope Forbes and Elizabeth Forbes*, Cassell & Co Ltd 1906, Reprinted Truran Books 2005

BOURNE, P. *Kirkcudbright: 100 Years of an Artists' Colony*, Atelier Books, 2000

BRANFIELD, J. *Ella and Charles Naper: Art and Life at Lamorna*, Sansom & Company, 2003

BURY, A. *Joseph Crawhall: The Man and the Artist*, Charles Skilton Ltd, 1958

CAW, J.L. *Sir James Guthrie, P.R.S.A., H.R.A., R.S.W., LLD*, Macmillan & Co, 1932

CAW, J.L. *Scottish Painting 1620–1908* [1908], Kingsmead Reprint, 1975

CIKOVSKY, N. and Kelly, F. *Winslow Homer*, exhibition catalogue, National Gallery of Art, Washington, 1995

COOK, J., Hardie, M. and Payne, C. *Singing from the Walls: The Life and Art of Elizabeth Forbes*, Sansom & Company, 2000

FOX, C. *Stanhope Forbes and the Newlyn School*, David & Charles, 1993

FOX, C. and Greenacre, F. *Painting in Newlyn, 1880–1930*, exhibition catalogue, Barbican Art Gallery, 1985

GALE, I. *Arthur Melville*, Atelier Books, 1996

GREEN, N. *The Spectacle of Nature: Landscape and Bourgeois Culture in Nineteenth century France*, Manchester University Press, 1990

GREG, A. *Charles Napier Hemy, RA, 1841–1917*, exhibition catalogue, Tyne & Wear Museums, 1984

HARDIE, M. ed. *100 Years in Newlyn: Diary of a Gallery*, Patten Press, 1995

HAWORTH, P. *Paintings by Members of the Staithes Group*, exhibition catalogue, 2002

HERBERT, R.L. *Barbizon Revisited*, exhibition catalogue, California Palace of the Legion of Honour, 1962

JACOBS, M. *The Good and Simple Life: Artist Colonies in Europe and America*, Phaidon Press, 1985

JENKINS, Adrian *Painters and Peasants: Henry La Thangue and British Rural Naturalism 1880–1905*, Bolton Museum & Art Gallery 2000

KNIGHT, L. *Oil Paint and Grease Paint*, Nicholson and Watson, 1936

KNIGHT, L. *The Magic of a Line*, William Kimber, 1965

LANGLEY, R. *Walter Langley: Pioneer of the Newlyn Art Colony*, Sansom & Company, 1997

LAUGHTON, B. *Philip Wilson Steer*, Clarendon Press, 1971

LOMAX, P. *A Golden Dream: Thomas Cooper Gotch*, Sansom & Company, 2004

LÜBBREN, N. *Rural Artists' Colonies in Europe*, Manchester University Press, 2001

McCONKEY, Risdon & Sheppard *Harold Harvey: Painter of Cornwall*, Sansom & Company, 2001

MILLARD, J. *A Romance with the North East: Robert and Isa Jobling*, exhibition catalogue, Tyne & Wear Museums, 1992

NEWTON, L. *Cullercoats: A North-East Colony of Artists*, Sansom & Company, 2003

PHILLIPS, P, *The Staithes Group*, Phillips & Son, 1993

SCOTT, R. *Artists at Walberswick: East Anglian Interludes, 1880–2000*, Art Dictionaries Ltd, 2002

SMITH, B. *Hornel: The Life and Work of Edward Atkinson Hornel*, Atelier Books, 1997

TOVEY, D. *Creating a Splash: The St. Ives Society of Artists. The first 25 years (1927–1952)*, exhibition catalogue, Wilson Books, 2003

TOVEY, D. *WHY Titcomb: A Newlyner in St Ives* Wilson Books 2003

VAL BAKER, D. *Britain's Art Colony by the Sea*, George Ronald, 1959; new edition, Sansom & Company, 2000

WALLACE, K. *Under the Open Sky,* Truran 2003

WEISBERG, G.P. *Beyond Impressionism: The Naturalist Impulse in European Art 1860–1905*, Thames & Hudson, 1992

WHYBROW, M. *St. Ives 1883-1993: Portrait of an Art Colony*, Antique Collectors' Club, 1994

WHYBROW, M. *The Leach Legacy: The St. Ives Pottery and its Legacy*, Sansom & Company, 1996

WORMLEIGHTON, A. *A Painter Laureate: Lamorna Birch and his Circle*, Sansom & Company, 1995

WORMLEIGHTON, A. *Morning Tide: John Anthony Park and the Painters of Light: St. Ives 1900–1950*, Stockbridge Books, 1998

Acknowledgments

ALISON BEVAN

Sincere thanks to George Bednar, Vince Bevan, Iris Green, Melissa Hardie (West Cornwall Art Archive) and David Tovey for their comments on this chapter; to Katie Herbert and the Penlee House team for their invaluable contributions to the project, and to Caroline Fox and all those who have made the Newlyners known. I am also indebted to John Sansom, publisher, and Laura Newton, editor, for embracing the dream of putting the Newlyn colony in context.

DAVID WILKINSON

Countless thanks are due to David Tovey for advice after reading through this chapter in draft form and for his spontaneous and very generous help with the choice of paintings.

RICHARD SCOTT

Much of the research for this short account of a vital part of Walberswick's artistic history has been an organic process spanning many years. Warm thanks are due to more than 100 individuals who have contributed fragments of information, but the following provided particularly useful access to archive material or hard-won research: Maria Beston, Richard Boyle, David Buckman, George Bumstead, William Buncombe, Pamela Carr, Pat Carter, Mary Clayton, John and Doreen Cragie, Ian Collins, Elizabeth Crittall, Janet Croston, John Day, Timothy Easton, Hugh Ferguson, Adam Gordon, Carola Haigh, Nigel Hensman, John Hill, Peter Hopkins, Libby Horner, Philip Kett, Hanns Lange, Roger Langley, Marie-Louise Legg, Judith Legrove, Ros McDermott, Dorothy Meade, Geoffrey Munn, Colin Nicholls, Michael Parkin, Adrian Parry, Marjorie Riley, Keith and Nicky Roberts, Pamela Robertson, Toby Robinson, David Routledge, Frank and June Scoble, Mary Stratton-Ryan, Adrian Thomas, Margaret Thomas, Carol Tooke, Camilla Uytman, Richard Van Oss, Chlo Veale, Neil Walker, Rebecca Weaver and Michael Wickins.

LAURA NEWTON

I am grateful to Alexander Robertson at Leeds City Art Gallery, Mike Shaw of the Sutcliffe Gallery, Dilys Harding at Newcastle City Library, staff of the Laing Art Gallery and the anonymous private collectors for their help and generosity in locating and loaning suitable pictures. I would also like to thank Ysanne Holt for her helpful comments on early versions of these chapters.

YSANNE HOLT

For discussion on various aspects of this essay and for help in tracing particular pictures I would like to thank Jim Allan, Roger Billcliffe, Patrick Bourne, Laura Newton, David Devereux and Bill Smith.

Index

References to the British art colonies, appearing as they do throughout the book, are not indexed; neither are the lists of artists to be found on page 159 *et seq*. End-notes are not indexed. Illustrations appear in **bold**.